TWENTIETH CENTURY AMERICAN NICKNAMES

TWENTIETH CENTURY AMERICAN NICKNAMES

EDITED BY LAURENCE URDANG

COMPILED BY
WALTER C. KIDNEY AND GEORGE C. KOHN

WITH A FOREWORD BY
LESLIE ALAN DUNKLING

THE
H. W. WILSON COMPANY
NEW YORK
1979

PRINTED IN THE UNITED STATES OF AMERICA

Library of Congress Cataloging in Publication Data

Main entry under title:

Twentieth century American nicknames.

   1. Nicknames—United States. I. Urdang, Laurence. II. Kidney, Walter C. III. Kohn, George C.
CT108.T83   929.4'0973   79-23390
ISBN 0-8242-0642-8

FOREWORD

THE NICKNAMES that fill the following pages are of great interest from many different points of view. The linguist studies them because he is concerned with all kinds of word creation. The dictionary-maker collects them and defines them because they have a legitimate referential meaning. The sociologist is concerned with reasons for nicknaming; the psychologist with personal reactions to them. As for the journalist, he finds nicknames interesting because of the anecdotes that are often associated with them.

Unfortunately, perhaps, it is not a display of wit or imagination in itself that justifies an entry in a dictionary of nicknames. A particular nickname only comes to have the referential meaning I mentioned above when it is widely enough used. The vast majority of nicknames are known and used in highly restricted contexts. Pupils at most schools, for instance, can refer to classmates and teachers among themselves by using nicknames that would be meaningless to an outsider. Any social group that meets regularly may have its own internal naming system; indeed, knowledge of that system may become a sign of inclusion in the group, a kind of verbal membership badge. Nicknames, along with certain slang expressions, often help to create a private language that excludes strangers.

The most extreme example of such a private language is that used between lovers. The partners are likely to have nicknames for each other that are uttered only in moments of intimacy, and that otherwise remain a closely guarded secret. In recent years we have

v

8402916

been able to get some hints as to the form these nicknames take from the Valentine's Day messages published in various newspapers. On February 14, 1979, for instance, the British newspaper *The Guardian* carried announcements to the effect that **Crunchy Body** loved **Smokey Bear, Wimbo** loved **Widget,** and so forth. Several hundred such coded nicknames, or love names, appeared on the same page, all of them testifying to the importance of a shared language as an indication of a special relationship.

What is also revealed by the nicknaming that occurs between lovers is an insistence that possession carries with it the right to bestow a name. At this level, naming is a God-like act, demonstrating dominance over the person being named. As the social group widens, so the significance of a nickname and the reason for it become less intense. The nickname may merely be a shared joke, or a reflection of what H. L. Mencken once called "linguistic exuberance, an excess of word-making energy." As it happens, Mencken was referring to slang, not nicknames, but by the time we come to expressions like **Big Apple** for New York City, or **Blue Flu,** for the police strike that occurred there in 1960, we are in any case on the borderline between slang and nicknames. "Slangnames" would be a highly appropriate description of such terms.

There is certainly a need to break up the general concept of "nickname" into various subdivisions. From an etymologist's point of view, a nickname is merely any kind of unofficial, additional name. In Middle English it was still written as "an eke name," later "a neke name." in which *eke* meant, simply, "also." The term fails to comment on either the extent of usage a name enjoys, or the underlying attitude that caused it to come into being. Nicknames can be friendly, of course, but they can also be decidedly hostile. A careful writer might want to refer to the latter as sobriquets. "Sobriquet," or "soubriquet" as it sometimes appears, has been used in English since the seventeenth century. In modern French it still suggests a contemptuous nickname rather than a friendly one.

There also exists a special kind of nickname that is a genuinely needed substitute name. This is because the real name of the person concerned is unknown. A typical example occurs when a criminal's deeds attract the attention of the public although his identity remains hidden. Some criminals, like London's **Jack the Ripper,** retain the nickname as their only certain identification. Others may later be known by their real names, yet the nickname may well remain better known. There are many people, for instance, to whom the name Albert DeSalvo would mean nothing, though they would know of his activities as **The Boston Strangler.**

Nicknames, then, can be friendly, hostile or neutral. They can also be classed as individual or generic. When Elvis Presley became **The Pelvis,** the nickname was apt in a highly individual way, blending elements of his real name in a way that drew attention to a characteristic bodily movement. The nickname was the very best kind of verbal caricature. Such a name almost justifies the comment made by a nineteenth century writer, Harry Long, that a nickname is "a biography crowded into a word." But countless nicknames are far less personal, being inherited by certain categories of people. A man with red hair automatically becomes **Red;** someone from Indiana is a **Hoosier;** someone who is bald—by the common process of naming after opposites—is **Curly.** The passing on of these traditional nicknames—"inseparables" as Eric Partridge called them—is clearly not a recognition of uniqueness, but the conferring of such names is usually a friendly act, a sign of social acceptance.

That fact is generally recognized, of course, and people such as politicians who depend on public support often encourage the media to use nicknames when referring to them, always provided that those nicknames are friendly or flattering. The wrong nickname could easily ruin a public reputation, just as it can cause great problems in private life. Those interested in such aspects of the subject could usefully turn to Nicknames: Their Origins and Social Consequences (1979), by Morgan, O'Neill and Harré. The message relayed by all such psychological and sociological studies is fairly consistent—that nicknames given with friendly intentions, even when they appear to be unflattering in themselves, show that the person concerned is thoroughly in harmony with the social group.

Acceptance of a nickname by an individual shows personal stability and adjustment. In that respect, nicknames are no different from more formal personal names, since psychiatrists have long interpreted a patient's dislike of his own name as a distinct danger signal.

Such, then, is the way a psychologist or sociologist might look at nicknames. A lexicographer naturally has a different viewpoint, and his criteria for including or excluding an entry in a dictionary of nicknames has nothing to do with the views of those who bear the names or with the reasons for their choice. He must, in any case, interpret "nickname" in its widest sense and include the additional, less formal, names of places, sports teams, companies, newspapers, railways, vehicles, events and even abstract ideas (such as **Me-Too-ism**) as well as those of people, if it can be shown that such names are or have been widely used in contemporary speech and literature. He must be convinced that a significant number of speakers and writers would, at one period or another in this century, have referred to the **It Girl,** say, or to the **Lucky Seventh,** without feeling it necessary to explain that Clara Bow and the Seventh Armored Division were meant. Whenever usage of a nickname becomes that widespread, for however short a period, it must be recorded for future reference. Like slang expressions, nicknames are especially vulnerable to the passing of time, and something that is totally familiar to one generation may be almost unknown to the next.

A dictionary of nicknames, therefore, justifies its existence in the way that all good dictionaries justify themselves. *Twentieth Century American Nicknames* will certainly claim its rightful place among the reference works that record the progress of the American language and culture. Those who make use of it will surely find no disadvantage in the fact that its pages are a good deal more entertaining than those of most linguistic reference works. Nicknames, like slang terms, enliven the language: they also manage to make many a pithy comment on the society in which we live.

LESLIE ALAN DUNKLING
Thames Ditton, Surrey
August 1979

EDITOR'S FOREWORD

AMERICANS like nicknames. They apply them to people, places, and things; they apply them descriptively, fondly, humorously, sarcastically, or abusively. *Twentieth Century American Nicknames* lists thousands of important and widely recognized nicknames. Since nicknames (as well as their bearers) are often evanescent, the editors have selected those that are better known from the enormous number that could have been documented.

Although it is true that *Larry* is a nickname for *Laurence* (or *Lawrence*) and *Molly* a nickname for *Mary*, we have omitted those, confining ourselves to the nicknames of well-known people—politicians, businessmen, military figures, socialites, entertainers, gangsters—in effect, of noted and notorious American men and women from all walks of life. By "American" we mean "active in American life": thus **Lucky** Luciano is in, even though he never became an American citizen.

In the world of professional athletics, names like *Aztecs, Bears, Flyers,* and so on are the official names of those teams, hence do not qualify as nicknames. However, in nonprofessional sports, many names of college teams are nicknames—**Boilermakers, Badgers, Buckeyes,** and so forth—and these have been listed. In addition to their official names, many teams have acquired nicknames, so entries like **Bosox** (Boston Red Sox) and **Maramen** (New York Giants) do appear. Professional names like *Red* Skelton, *Babe* Ruth, *Doc* Severinsen, and *Duke* Ellington, have not been considered for inclusion as nicknames; however, where a professional name is also an unusual nickname, it has been included: **Bobo** Olson, **Stumpy** Brady, **Zoot** Sims, **Monk** Hazel. This decision was a matter of editorial choice.

A category that has been covered includes nicknames of miscellaneous items like horses (**Big Red** for Man o' War), places (**The Big Apple** for New York City), roads (**Alligator Alley** for the Everglades Parkway), restaurants (**Ho-Jo** for Howard Johnson's, now adopted as a trade name), government agencies (**Fannie Mae** for FNMA, the Federal National Mortgage Association), companies (**Thundering Herd** for Merrill Lynch, Pierce, Fenner & Smith), and military units, organizations, equipment, weapons, and more. The huge number of place nicknames precludes the coverage of all of them, because they have proliferated to such an extent over the years that an exhaustive list would have doubled the size of this book. Many official nicknames—**Empire State, City of Brotherly Love,** etc.—are listed.

By its very nature, a work like *Twentieth Century American Nicknames* cannot be exhaustive, for the kinds of information it contains must be sifted and evaluated to create uniformity of treatment. For instance, insofar as possible, the editors have attempted to avoid duplication of nicknames appearing in George Earlie Shankle's *American Nicknames* (H. W. Wilson, second edition, 1955). Also, the present work, unlike Shankle's, lists people, places, and things that are sufficiently contemporary to admit of research in newspaper files, chronologies, and other sources that are easily accessible in libraries. Thus, the emphasis has been on the accuracy of the information rather than on the presentation of details that can be readily found elsewhere. The editors apologize for any glaring omissions, which we should appreciate having called to our attention.

It is hoped that those referring to *Twentieth Century American Nicknames* will find it helpful, informative, and easy to use.

LAURENCE URDANG
Essex, Connecticut
September 1979

THE ARRANGEMENT
OF INFORMATION

ALL NICKNAMES are listed in two places: alphabetically by
the nickname itself and, in the same listing, alphabetically
by surname. For example:

Cherokee Kid. Rogers, Will.

Rogers, Will (1879–1935). Humorist and actor: **Ambassador of
Good Will, Cherokee Kid, Cowboy Philosopher, Man Who Can
Say Anything and Make Everybody Like It, Prince of Wit and
Wisdom.** Legal name: William Penn Adair Rogers.

In other words, in addition to **Cherokee Kid,** all of Will Rogers'
other nicknames are given in their proper alphabetical places. Also,
as can be seen, the basic information is given at each main entry:
birth (and death) dates or, in some cases, the period of activity or
prominence, a brief identification of the entry, and, where appropriate, the legal name or name at birth of anyone whose professional
name may differ.

We have included a number of entries that have no name other
than what we have taken as an informal appellation. Thus, **Armory
Show, Ashcan School,** and similar names are listed without formal
equivalents, because they have none.

Every effort has been made to present the information in
Twentieth Century American Nicknames in a clear and straightfor-
ward manner, and the editors hope that its arrangement will serve
the user efficiently and effectively.

TWENTIETH CENTURY
AMERICAN NICKNAMES

A

Aaron, Hank (born 1934). Baseball outfielder and manager: **Atlanta Slugger, New Sultan of Swat.** Legal name: Henry Louis Aaron.

Ab. Jenkins, David Abbot, Jr.; Walker, Albert Bailey.

Abbadabba. Biederman, Otto.

Abbey, Edwin Austin (1852–1911). Painter and illustrator: **The Chestnut.**

Abbitt, Jim (born 1916). Football halfback: **Jackrabbit.**

Abbott, Burton W. (1928–57). Convicted murderer executed for the 1955 kidnap-slaying of Stephanie Bryan: **Bud.**

ABC's of the New Deal. U.S. government agencies under the New Deal.

Abe the Newsboy. Hollandersky, Abraham.

Abplanalp, Robert H. (born 1922). Inventor and industrialist: **Aerosol King, President's [Nixon's] Other Friend.**

Abrams, Creighton William (1914–74). U.S. Army General: **Patton's Peer.**

Abzug, Bella S[avitsky] (born 1920). U.S. Representative from New York: **Battling Bella, Bellicose Bella, Hurricane Bella, Mother Courage.**

Accardo, Anthony Joseph (born 1906). Gangster: **Big Tuna, Joe Batty, Mr. Big in Crime.** Born: Antonio Leonardo Accardo.

Accidental President, The. Johnson, Lyndon Baines.

Accounts. Warren, Lindsay Carter.

Ace. Bailey, Garnet Edward; Pancoast, Asa; Parker, Clarence; Sorrell, Vic[tor Garland].

Ace Drummer Man. Krupa, [Eu]gene [Bertram].

Ace of Aces. Rickenbacker, Eddie.

Ack-Ack. Aluminum Company of America.

Acorn Division. Eighty-Seventh Division.

Acropolis of America. Morningside Heights, New York City.

Actor, The. Sutton, William Francis.

Actors Studio. New York institution for training actors: **The Temple.**

Acuff, Roy [Claxton] (born 1903). Country and Western fiddler, singer, and bandleader: **King of Country Music, King of the Hillbillies, Smoky Mountain Boy.**

Adams, Albert (1871–1907). Gambler: **Policy King.**

Adams, Ansel (born 1902). Photographer: **Photographic Purist.**

Adams, Charles Benjamin (1883–1968). Baseball pitcher: **Babe.**

Adams, Charles Francis (1835–1915). Economist, historian, and lawyer: **Irascible Patrician.**

Adams, Charles Francis (1866–1954). Banker and U.S. Secretary of the Navy: **Uncle Charlie.**

Adams, Franklin Pierce (1881–1960). Newspaper columnist and author: **FPA.**

Adams, John W. (1921–69). Football back: **Tree.**

Adams, Park (born 1930). Jazz saxophonist: **Pepper.**

Adams, Rose (1910–71). Gypsy leader: **Queen of the Gypsies.**

Adamson, Gary (born c. 1940). Murderer: **Cotton.**

Adaptable State. New Jersey.

Addams, Charles [Samuel] (born 1912). Cartoonist: **Cartoonist of the Macabre.**

Adderley, Julian Edwin (1928–75). Jazz saxophonist: **Cannonball.**

Administration's Marco Polo, The. Kissinger, Henry A[lfred].

Adonis. Terry, William H.

Advertiser, The. Barton, Bruce.

Advertising King, The. Barton, Bruce.

Advertising Wizard. Lasker, Albert Davis.

Adviser of Presidents. Baruch, Bernard M[annes].

Advocate of Hatchetation. Nation, Carry or Carrie [Amelia Moore Gloyd].

Advocate of the Five Cent Cigar. Marshall, Thomas Riley.

Aerosol King. Abplanalp, Robert H.

Afflis, Richard (born 1943). Wrestler: **Dick the Bruiser, Richard the Ruffian.**

Agajanian, Ben[jamin] (born 1919). Football kicker: **Automatic.**

Aged Eagle. Eliot, T[homas] S[tearns].

Aggies. Athletic teams of New Mexico State University, Las Cruces; Texas A & M, College Station; and Utah State University, Logan.

Agnew, Spiro [Theodore] (born 1918). U.S. Vice President: **Spiro T. Eggplant, Nixon's Nixon, White Knight.**

Agricultural Jones. Jones, [John] Marvin.

Agricultural Moses. Tillman, Benjamin Ryan.

Ahbez, Eden (born c. 1912). Song writer: **Nature Boy from Brooklyn.**

Ahola, Sylvester (born 1902). Jazz musician: **Hooley.**

Aiken, Gus (born c. 1904). Jazz trumpeter: **Rice.**

Aiken, South Carolina. U.S. city: **City in the Land of the Pines.**

Airacobra. Bell P-39 fighter plane, World War II.

Air Capital. Wichita, Kansas.

Air Capital of America. Wichita, Kansas.

Air Capital of the West. San Diego, California.

Air Capital of the World. Montreal, Quebec.

Air-conditioned City. Duluth, Minnesota.

Air Crossroads of the World. Anchorage, Alaska.

Airplane Ears. Anderson, John Z.

Akeman, David (1916–73). Country Singer: **Stringbean.**

Akron, Ohio. U.S. city: **Rubber Capital of the United States, Rubber City, Soap Box Derby Center, Summit City, Tire City of the United States.**

Akron, University of, athletic teams of: **Zips.**

Alabama. Pitts, Edwin Collins.

Alabama. Twenty-second U.S. state: **Alligator State, 'Bama, Cotton Plantation State, Cotton State, Cornucopia of the South, Heart of Dixie, Heart of the New Industrial South, Land of Flowers, Lizard State, Star of the South.**

Alabama, University of, athletic teams of: **Crimson Tide.**

Alabama's Only Port. Mobile, Alabama.

Alameda County, California. U.S. county: **Gold Medal County.**

Alamo City. San Antonio, Texas.

Alaska. Forty-ninth U.S. state: **America's Icebox, America's Last Frontier, Arctic Treasureland, Big State, Frozen Wilderness, Great Land, Land of the Midnight Sun, Last Frontier, Seward's Folly, Seward's Icebox, State of Contrasts, Uncle Sam's Icebox.**

Alaska Highway. Highway between Fairbanks, Alaska, and Dawson Creek, British Columbia; World War II military road: **Alcan Highway.**

Alaska's Scenic Capital. Juneau, Alaska.

Albany, New York. U.S. city: **Cradle of the American Union, Edinburgh of America.**

Albee, Mrs. P. F. E. (1836–1914). Saleswoman: **First Avon Lady.**

Albemarle County, Virginia. U.S. county: **Jefferson's Country.**

Alberta. Canadian province: **Oil Province, Sunshine Province, Western Prairie Province.**

Albin, David (active 1920–30). Racketeer: **Cockeye Mulligan.**

Albuquerque, New Mexico. U.S. city: **Duke City.**

Alcan Highway. Alaska Highway.

Alcatraz Federal Prison. Former U.S. maximum-security prison in San Francisco Bay, California: **America's Devil's Island, The Rock.**

Alcorn State University, Lorman, Mississippi, athletic teams: **Braves.**

Alderisio, Felix Anthony (1922–71). Gangster: **Milwaukee Phil.**

Aldrin, Edwin Eugene, Jr. (born 1930). Astronaut: **Buzz, Second Man on the Moon.**

Aleichem, Shalom (or Sholom) (1859–1916). Yiddish short story writer and journalist: **Yiddish Mark Twain.** Born: Solomon J. Rabinowitz (Rabinovitz).

Alex. Alexander, William Anderson.

Alexander, Grover Cleveland (1887–1950). Baseball pitcher: **Old Pete, Pete.**

Alexander, William Anderson (1899–1950). Football coach: **Alex, Old Alex, Old Man.**

Alexandria, Virginia. U.S. city: **Heart of the Nation's Heritage.**

Alfalfa Bill. Murray, William Henry.

Algonquin Round Table. Group of writers and critics that met regularly for lunch at the Algonquin Hotel, New York, c. 1930: **Vicious Circle.**

Ali, Muhammad (born 1942). Heavyweight boxer: **Cassius the Brashest, Gaseous Cassius, The Greatest, Louisville Lip.** Born: Cassius [Marcellus] Clay, Jr.

Ali Baba. Babartsky, Al[bert] J.

Alice. Allis-Chalmers Manufacturing Company.

All-American Division. Eighty-second Airborne Division; Eighty-second Division.

All-American Mirror. Sinclair, Upton.

All-American Mustang. Walker, [Ewell] Doak, [Jr.].

All-American Town. Dallas, Texas.

Allen, Dick (born 1942). Baseball first baseman: **Crash.** Born: Richard Anthony Allen.

Allen, Forrest Claire (1886–1974). Physician, basketball coach, and baseball coach: **Phog, Dr. Foghorn, Foghorn.**

Allen, Fred (1894–1956). Comedian: **King of the Quick Quip.** Born: John Florence Sullivan. Also known as Paul Huckle, Freddy James.

Allen, Mel (born 1913). Sports announcer: **Mr. How-About-That.** Born: Melvin Allen Israel.

Allen, Steve. (born 1921). Musician and comedian: **Steverino.** Born: Stephen Valentine Patrick William Allen.

Allen, William Franklin (1883–1946). U.S. Representative from Delaware: **Lovebird.**

Allentown, Pennsylvania. U.S. city: **Cement City, Queen City of the Lehigh Valley, Scrapple City.**

Allgood, Miles Clayton (born 1878). U.S. Representative from Alabama: **Simon.**

Alligator Alley. Everglades Parkway; Tamiami Trail.

Alligator Bait. Miller, William Mosley.

Alligator State. Alabama; Florida; Louisiana; Mississippi; Texas.

Allis-Chalmers Manufacturing Company. U.S. company: **Alice.**

Allison, Leonard B. (active 1920–44). Football coach: **Stub.**

Alma College, athletic teams of: **Scots.**

Almond Capital of the World. Sacramento, California.

Aloha State. Hawaii.

Alpert, Herman S. (born 1913). Jazz musician: **Trigger.**

Alphabet Soup. U.S. government agencies, esp. under Franklin D. Roosevelt's New Deal, when called by their initials.

Alston, Walt[er Emmons] (born 1911). Baseball manager: **Smokey.**

Alterie, Louis (1892–1935). Bootlegger: **Two-Gun Alterie.**

Altoona, Pennsylvania. U.S. city: **Horseshoe Curve, Mineral Springs City, Mountain City, Railroad City.**

Aluminum Company of America. U.S. corporation: **Ack-Ack.**

Alvarez, Al[fred] (born 1920). Jazz trumpeter: **Chico.**

Alworth, Lance D. (born 1940). Football end: **Bambi.**

Amarillo, Texas. U.S. city: **Metropolis of the Panhandle, Plains Empire City.**

Amarillo Slim. Preston, Thomas Austin, Jr.

Amazing Mays. Mays, Willie [Howard].

Ambassador of Basketball. Taylor, Chuck.

Ambassador of Good Will. Lindbergh, Charles A[ugustus]; Rogers, Will.

Ambassador of the Air. Lindbergh, Charles A[ugustus].

Ambers, Lou (born 1913). Lightweight boxer: **Herkimer Hurricane.** Born: Louis D'Ambrosio.

Ambridge. American Bridge Company.

Ameche, Alan (born 1933). Football back: **The Horse.**

America Firster. Member of the America First Committee, 1940.

American Athens. Boston, Massachusetts.

American Balzac. Faulkner, William.

American Bernhardt. Carter, Mrs. Leslie.

American Bridge Company. U.S. company: **Ambridge.**

American Broadcasting Company. Television and radio organization: **Hard Rock.**

American Cossacks. Mounted constabulary used against strikers, 1900s.

American Dreyfus. Ballinger, Richard Achilles.

American Express Company. U.S. company: **Amex, Amexco.**

American Florence Nightingale. Maxwell, Anna Caroline.

American Gauguin. Leeteg, Edgar.

American Hogarth. Shahn, Ben[jamin].

American Kipling. London, Jack.

American League of Professional Baseball Clubs. Organization of major-league teams: **Junior Circuit.**

American Lyons. Paterson, New Jersey.

American Maupassant. Henry, O.

American Motors Corporation. U.S. company: **Ammo.**

American Music-Master, The. Herbert, Victor.

American Nationalist. Beveridge, Albert Jeremiah.

American Nile. Saint Johns River, Florida.

American Renoir. Peirce, Waldo.

American Samoa. U.S. Pacific territory: **Heart of Polynesia.**

American Shakespeare. Griffith, D[avid Lewelyn] W[ark].

American Stock Exchange. Securities market: **Amex.**

American Troubadour. Scott, Tom.

American Venice. Rhode Island.

American Veterans of World War II. U.S. war veterans' organization: **Amvets.**

American Volunteer Group. Group of air force volunteers serving China in World War II: **Flying Tigers.**

America's All-Year Playground. Lake Tahoe, California-Nevada.

America's Answer to Brigitte Bardot. Remick, Lee.

America's Bermuda. Block Island, Rhode Island.

America's Boyfriend. Rogers, Charles.

America's City of History. Newport, Rhode Island.

America's Dairyland. Wisconsin.

America's Desert Resort. Palm Springs, California.

America's Devil's Island. Alcatraz Federal Prison, San Francisco Bay, California.

America's Favorite Cowboy. Mix, Tom.

America's First Citizen. Eliot, Charles William.

America's First Negro Big Leaguer. Robinson, Jackie.

America's First World War II Hero. Kelly, Colin P.

America's Foremost Architect. White, Stanford.

America's Foremost Expatriate. Stearns, Harold Edmund.

America's Foremost Historian. Turner, Frederick Jackson.

America's Foremost Speculative Philosopher. Weiss, Paul.

America's Good Will Music Ambassador. Ellington, Duke.

America's Greatest Architect. Wright, Frank Lloyd.

America's Greatest Showman. Todd, Michael.

America's Great Winter Garden. Imperial Valley, California.

America's Home Town. Plymouth, Massachusetts.

America's Icebox. Alaska.

America's Last Frontier. Alaska.

America's Legendary Speed King. Oldfield, Barney.

America's Master Gardener. Baker, Jerry.

America's Most Decorated Soldier. Murphy, Audie.

America's Most Historic City. Charleston, South Carolina; Fredericksburg, Virginia.

America's Most Mysterious Man. Cayce, Edgar.

America's Most Perfectly Developed Man. Atlas, Charles.

America's No. 1. Hostess. Maxwell, Elsa.

America's Number One Boatbuilder. Higgins, Andrew Jackson.

America's Oldest City. St. Augustine, Florida.

America's One-Man Newspaper. Winchell, Walter.

America's Own Spa. Hot Springs, Arkansas.

America's Own Violinist. Spalding, Albert.

America's Premier Air Woman. Earhart, Amelia [Mary].

America's Red Leader. Browder, Earl [Russell].

America's Riviera. Biloxi, Mississippi.

America's Singapore. Key West, Florida.

America's Society Capital. Newport, Rhode Island.

America's Sunrise Gateway. Portland, Maine.

America's Sweetheart. Pickford, Mary.

America's Sweetheart Emeritus. Pickford, Mary.

America's Switzerland. Lake Placid, New York.

Ames, Knowlton L. (1868–1931). Football player and coach: **Snake.**

Ames, Leon Kessling (1882–1936). Baseball pitcher: **Red.**

Amex. American Express Company; American Stock Exchange.

Amexco. American Express Company.

Amherst College. 1. Athletic teams of: **Lord Jeffs, The Sabrinas.** 2. Athletic teams of, with teams of Wesleyan University and Williams College: **Little Three.**

Amiable Swindler. Weinberg, Stephen Jacob.

Ammo. American Motors Corporation.

Ammons, Eugene (1925–74). Jazz saxophonist: **Jug.**

Amvets. American Veterans of World War II.

Anaheim, California. U.S. city: **City of Beautiful Parks, Family City, Home of Disneyland, Recreation Center.**

Ananias Club. Theodore Roosevelt's name for a group of newspaper reporters who published information given to them in confidence.

Ananias of Jazz. Mesirow, Milton.

Anastasia, Albert (1903?–57). Gangster: **The Boss, Lord High Executioner.**

Anastasio, Anthony (1905?–63). Leader of International Longshoremen's Association: **Tough Tony.**

Anchorage, Alaska. U.S. city: **Air Crossroads of the World, Hub City, Largest City in the Largest State, Nerve Center of Alaska.**

Ancient and Honorable Pueblo. Tucson, Arizona.

Ancient City. Annapolis, Maryland.

Ancient Dominion. Virginia.

Anderson, Dorothy May Stevens (1929–74). Woman who was frozen: **Deep-Freeze Woman.**

9

Anderson, Edward N. (born 1900). Football end and coach: **Football Doctor.**

Anderson, George Lee (born 1934). Baseball second baseman and manager: **Captain Hook, Sparky.**

Anderson, Gilbert (1882–1971). Motion-picture actor: **Bronco Billy** (Broncho Billy). Born: Max Aronson.

Anderson, Heartley (1899–1978). Football coach: **Hunk.**

Anderson, Jack[son Northman] (born 1922). Newspaper columnist: **Modern Muckraker, Muckraker with a Mission, Square Scourge of Washington, Voice of the Voiceless.**

Anderson, John Z. (born 1904). Politician: **Airplane Ears.**

Anderson, Marian (born 1902). Singer: **Lady from Philadelphia, Voice of the Century.**

Anderson, William [Alonzo] (born 1916). Jazz trumpeter and composer: **Cat.**

Andrews, Ivy Paul (1907–1970). Baseball pitcher: **Poison Ivy.**

Angela the Red. Davis, Angela [Yvonne].

Angel City. Los Angeles, California.

Angeleno. Native or resident of Los Angeles.

Angels. Eleventh Airborne Division.

Anglo. In the U.S. Southwest, a Caucasian person not of Latin-American descent.

Angry Eagle of Aviation. Mitchell, William.

Angry Man of the Press. Pegler, [James] Westbrook.

Animal. Butkus, Dick.

Annapolis, Maryland. U.S. city: **Ancient City, Crabtown, Home of the U.S. Naval Academy, Venice of America.**

Annapolis of the Air. Pensacola, Florida.

Ann Arbor, Michigan, U.S. city: **Research Center of the Midwest.**

Annie Oakley. Free ticket.

Annixter, Julius (active 1920–30). Gambler: **Lovin' Putty.**

Anselm, Felix (born 1909). Poet and librarian: **Master of Words and Guardian of Magazines.** Born: Felix Pollack.

Anson, Adrian Constantine (1852–1922). Baseball first baseman and manager: **Cap.**

Antelope State. Nebraska.

Antheil, George (1900–59). Composer: **Bad Boy of Music, Exponent of Futurism.**

Anthracite City. Scranton, Pennsylvania.

Anti-Chain-Store Patman. Patman, Wright.

Anti-McFarlane. McFarlane, William Dodridge.

Anti-war Knutson. Knutson, Harold.

Antoinette Perry Award. Award for excellence in the theater: **Tony.**

Apache State. Arizona.

A-pill. Pill causing abortion.

Apostle of Light and Power. Lieb, John William.

Apostle of Sunshine. Taylor, Robert Love.

Apostle of Temperance. Hill, Walter Barnard.

Apostle of the Grand Manner. Whalen, Grover Aloysius.

Appalachian State. West Virginia.

Appalachian State University, athletic teams of: **Mountaineers.**

Apple, The. New York City.

Appling, Luke (born 1909). Baseball player: **Old Aches and Pains.** Legal name: Lucius Benjamin Appling.

April. Fourth month in the year: **Battle Month.**

Aqueduct City. Rochester, New York.

Aqueduct Race Track. Horse racing track, New York City: **Big A.**

Arbuckle, Roscoe (1887–1932). Motion-picture comedian: **Fatty.**

Arcaro, Eddie (born 1916). Jockey: **Banana Nose, Big A, King of Little Men, King of the Stakes Riders, The Master.** Legal name: George Edward Arcaro.

Archbishop, The. McCormack, John W[illiam].

Archbishop of Fundamentalism. Ironside, Henry Allan.

Arch City. St. Louis, Missouri.

Archer-Gillian, Amy (active c. 1910). Nurse and poisoner: **Sister Amy, Twentieth-Century Borgia.**

Archibald, Nate (born 1948). Basketball player: **Little Big Man, Tiny.**

Archie. Belany, George Stansfield.

Archie the Manager. Gardner, Ed.

Architect of the "Containing Communism" Policy. Dulles, John Foster.

Arctic Treasureland. Alaska.

Argentine Firecracker. Foxe, F.

Argyrol King. Barnes, Albert C.

Aristocrat of Swing. Ellington, Duke.

Arizona. Forty-eighth state: **Apache State, Aztec State, Baby State, Copper State, Grand Canyon State, Italy of America, Sand Hill State, Solar Energy State, Sunset Land, Sunset State.**

Arizona, University of. 1. Athletic teams of: **Wildcats.** 2. Athletic teams of, with other teams in regional conference: **Pacific Ten.**

Arizona Slim. Preston, Thomas Austin, Jr.

Arizona State University. 1. Athletic teams of: **Sun Devils.** 2. Athletic teams of, with other teams in regional conference: **Pacific Ten.**

Arkansas. Twenty-fifth U.S. state: **Bear State; Bowie State; Diamond State; Guinea Pig State; Home of the Peach, Strawberry, and Vine; Hot Water State; Land of Opportunity; Toothpick State; Wonder State.**

Arkansas, University of, athletic teams of: **Razorbacks.**

Arkansas Hummingbird. Warnecke, Lonnie.

Arkansas Hunkerer, The. Mills, Wilbur [Daigh].

Arkansas State University, athletic teams of: **Indians.**

Arkansas Traveler. Burns, Bob.

Arkansawyer. Native or resident of Arkansas.

Arkie. 1. Migrant farm laborer, esp. from Arkansas. 2. Native or citizen of Arkansas.

Arkopolis. Little Rock, Arkansas.

Arky. Vaughan, Joseph Floyd.

Arlington, Virginia. U.S. city: **Bedroom of Washington.**

Arlington National Cemetery. Military cemetery in Arlington, Virginia: **City of the Slain.**

Armadillo Man. Franklin, James.

Armes, Monroe (active 1933). Gangster: **Blackie.**

Armory Show. Exhibition of American and European avant-garde art, 69th Regiment Armory, New York City, February 1913.

12

Armour Institute of Technology, athletic teams of: **Packers, Tech Hawks.**

Armstrong, Anne [Legendre] (born 1927). U.S. ambassador: **Auntie Sam, London's Rose of Texas.**

Armstrong, [Daniel] Louis (1900–71). Jazz trumpeter and singer: **Gatemouth, King, Satch, Satchmo, Pops.**

Armstrong, Gerald Ralph (born 1942). Stockholder rights advocate: **Corporate Gadfly.**

Armstrong, Henry (born 1912). Welterweight and lightweight boxer: **Hurricane Henry.** Born: Henry Jackson.

Armstrong, Lucille (born c. 1915). Wife of Louis Armstrong: **Brown Sugar.**

Armstrong, Neil A. (born 1930). Astronaut: **First Man on the Moon.**

Arndstein, Jules Arnold (born c. 1879). Gambler: **Nickelplate.**

Arness, James (born 1925). Television actor: **Big Jim.** Born: James Aurness.

Arnheim, Gus (1897–1955). Jazz musician: **The Old Colonel.**

Arnie's Army. Fans of golfer Arnold Palmer.

Arnold, Eddie (born 1918). Folk singer: **The Tennessee Plowboy.** Born: Richard Edward Arnold.

Arnold, Henry Harley (1886–1950). U.S. Army Air Forces General, World War II: **Father of the U.S. Air Force, Hap.**

Aroostook County, Maine. U.S. county: **Garden of Maine.**

Aroostook Potato. Brewster, Ralph Owen.

Arsenal of Democracy. 1. Fort Worth, Texas. 2. The United States of America, as a supplier of the Allies, World War II.

Art Deco. Art Decoratif

Art Decoratif. Style of art and decoration using geometric shapes and industrial materials, 1920s and 1930s: **Art Deco.**

Artesian State. South Dakota.

A's, The. Oakland Athletics.

Ashbrook, John Milan (born 1928). U.S. Representative from Ohio: **Small Paul Revere.**

Ashcan School. Group of artists that portrayed city life realistically, c. 1910.

13

Asheville, North Carolina. U.S. city: **City in the Land of the Sky.**

Ashurst, Henry Fountain (1874–1962). U.S. Senator from Arizona: **The Cowboy Senator, The Fountain.**

Aspen, Colorado. U.S. city: **Ski Capital U.S.A.**

Assassinator of Syncopation. La Rocca, Nick.

Assassin's Assassin. Ruby, Jack.

Assemblyman from the Bowery. Smith, Alfred Emanuel.

Assunto, Jacob (born 1905). Jazz musician: **Papa Jac.**

Astoria Assassin. Berlenbach, Paul.

Astro-Bluebonnet Bowl. Football stadium in Houston, Texas.

Athens of Alabama. Tuscaloosa, Alabama.

Athens of America. Boston, Massachusetts.

Athens of Texas. Waco, Texas.

Athens of the New World. Boston, Massachusetts.

Athens of the South. Nashville, Tennessee.

Athens of the United States. Boston, Massachusetts.

Athens of the West. Berkeley, California; Lexington, Kentucky.

Athletic Phenomenon of All Time—Man or Woman. Zaharias, Babe [Didrikson].

Atkins, Chet (born 1924). Guitarist: **Mr. Guitar.** Legal name: Chester Burton Atkins.

Atkinson, Ted (active 1959). Jockey: **Slasher.**

Atlanta, Georgia. U.S. city: **Big A, Citadel of the Confederacy, Dogwood City, Gate City, Gate City of the South, Hub of the Southeast, Insurance City, Manufacturing and Industrial Metropolis of the Southeast, New York of the South, Paris of the South, Southern Crossroads City.**

Atlanta Slugger. Aaron, Hank.

Atlantic City, New Jersey. U.S. city: **City of Fun and Frolic, Number-One Host of the Jersey Coast, World's Playground.**

Atlas, Charles (1892–1972). Physical culturist and body-builder: **America's Most Perfectly Developed Man.** Born: Angelo Siciliano.

Atomic Cities. Los Alamos, New Mexico; Oak Ridge, Tennessee; Richland, Washington.

14

Atomic City. Los Alamos, New Mexico; Oak Ridge, Tennessee; Richland, Washington.

Atomic Energy City. Oak Ridge, Tennessee.

Atomic Puncher. Graziano, Rocky.

Attell, Abe (1884–1970). Featherweight boxer: **Little Hebrew.** Legal name: Abraham W. Attell.

Attell, Monte (1885–1960). Bantamweight boxer: **Nob Hill Terror.**

Attorney General of the United States. U.S. official: **First Lawyer of the Land.**

Auburn University, athletic teams of: **Tigers.**

Auctioneer Mayor. Shank, Samuel Lewis.

Augusta, Georgia. U.S. city: **Garden City of Georgia, Lowell of the South.**

Augusta, Maine. U.S. city: **City of Manifold Advantages.**

Auker, Elden Leroy (born 1910). Basketball player: **Big Six.**

Auntie Sam. Armstrong, Anne [Legendre].

Austin, Gene (1900–72). Singer: **The Whispering Tenor.**

Austin, James Philip (1879–1965). Baseball third baseman and coach: **Peppes.**

Austin, Texas. U.S. city: **Big Heart of Texas, City of the Violet Crown.**

Author of the New Deal. Burke, Edward Raymond.

Author of the Volstead Act. Wheeler, Wayne Bidwell.

Automatic. Agajanian, Ben[jamin]; Karamatic, George; Manders, Jack.

Automobile City. Detroit, Michigan.

Automobile City of the World. Detroit, Michigan.

Automobile Wizard. Ford, Henry.

Auto State. Michigan.

Autry, Gene [Orvon] (born 1908). Actor and singer: **Oklahoma's Yodeling Cowboy.**

Avenger. Grumman TBF-1 fighter plane, World War II.

Axis Sally. Sisk, Mildred Elizabeth; Zucca, Rita Louise.

Ayers, Yancey W[yatt] (1891–1968). Baseball pitcher: **Doc.**

Aylesworth, Merlin Hall (1886–1952). Lawyer and radio executive: **Deac.**

Ayres, Agnes (1890–1940). Motion-picture actress: **The O. Henry Girl.**

Aztecs. Athletic teams of San Diego State University, San Diego, California.

Aztec State. Arizona.

B

Babartsky, Al[bert J.] (active 1930s). Football player: **Ali Baba.** Also known as Al Bart. With other members of Fordham team: **Seven Blocks of Granite.**

Babbling Burglar. Morrison, Richard C.

Babe. Adams, Charles Benjamin; Brown, John H., Jr.; Dahlgren, Ellsworth Tenney; Herman, Floyd Caves; Leopold, Nathan F., Jr.; Patt, Maurice; Phelps, Ernest Gordon; Pratt, Walter; Risko, Eddie; Rusin, Irving.

Babe Ruth of Hockey. Morenz, Howie; Richard, Maurice [Joseph Henri].

Babe Ruth of Polo. Hitchcock, Thomas, Jr.

Babe Ruth of the New Deal. Johnson, Hugh Samuel.

Babes. Chicago Cubs.

Baby. Dodds, Warren; Laine, Albert; Langdon, Harry; Murphy, Audie.

Baby Bonds. Twenty-five cent savings stamps and five-dollar savings certificates issued during World War I by the United States Treasury Department.

Baby Bull. Cepeda, Orlando.

Baby Doll. Cowan, Sarah; Sorrell, Vic:[tor Garland].

Baby Face. McLarnin, James.

Baby-Faced Assassin. Corbus, William.

Baby Face Nelson. Gillis, Lester M.

Babylon on the Bluff. Memphis, Tennessee.

Baby Margaret. Picon, Molly.

Baby Peggy. Montgomery, Peggy.

Baby Star. Waters, Ethel.

Baby Traps. Rich, Bernard.

Baby Vamp. West, Mae.

Bach. Bachrach, William.

Bacharach, Isaac (1870–1956). U.S. Representative from New Jersey: **Boardwalk Ike.**

Bachrach, William (1879–1959). Swimming coach. **Bach.**

Backbone of North America. Rocky Mountains.

Backbone of the Continent. Rocky Mountains.

Bad Bill. Dahlen, William Frederick.

Bad Birmingham. Birmingham, Alabama.

Bad Body. Munson, Thurman [Lee].

Bad Boy Colson. Colson, Charles W[endell].

Bad Boy of Music. Antheil, George.

Bad Boy of Publishing. Stuart, Lyle.

Baden-Baden of America. Hot Springs, Arkansas.

Badger. Native or resident of Wisconsin.

Badgers. Athletic teams of the University of Wisconsin, Madison.

Badger State. Wisconsin.

Badlands. Arid region in southwestern South Dakota.

Bad News. Barnes, Jim; Cafego, George; Hale, Arvel Odell.

Baer, Arthur (1886–1969). Newspaper columnist: **Bugs.**

Baer, Max[imilian Adelbert] (1909–59). Heavyweight boxer: **Clouting Clown, Fistic Harlequin, Larruping Lothario of Pugilism, Livermore Butcher Boy, Livermore Larruper, Madcap Maxie, Magnificent Screwball, Playboy of Pugilism, Pugilistic Poseur.**

Baez, Joan (born 1941). Folk singer: **Non-violent Singer.**

Bagby, James Charles Jacob, Sr. (1889–1954). Baseball pitcher: **Sarge.**

Baghdad by the Bay. San Francisco, California.

Baghdad on the Hudson. New York City.

Baghdad on the Subway. New York City.

Bags. Jackson, Milt[on].

Bag Town. San Diego, California.

Bailey, Donald Orlando (born 1934). Jazz drummer: **Donald Duck.**

Bailey, Ernest Harold (born 1925). Jazz trumpeter: **Benny.**

Bailey, F[rancis] Lee (born 1933). Lawyer: **Head Hunter, Heff Lee.**

Bailey, Garnet Edward (born 1948). Hockey forward: **Ace.**

Bailey, Harvey (1894–1963). Bank robber: **Old Harve.**

Bailey, Howard Henry (born 1913). Football tackle: **Screeno.**

Bailey, Mildred (1906–51). Jazz musician and singer: **Rocking Chair Lady.** Born: Mildred Bailey Norville.

Bailey, Pearl (born 1918). Singer: **Pearlie Mae.**

Baked Bean. Native or resident of Boston.

Baked Bean State. Massachusetts.

Baker, Anderson Yancey (1876–1930). Politician: **The Millionaire Sheriff.**

Baker, Bobby (born 1927). U.S. government official: **Fast Talker from Pickens, Operations Man, Washington's Profumo.** Legal name: Robert Gene Baker.

Baker, Erwin George (1881–1960). Automobile racing driver: **Cannonball.**

Baker, George Pierce (1866–1935). Teacher of dramatic composition: **Father of the 47 Workshop.**

Baker, Gloria (Mrs. Edward Alexander) (active 1937). Society glamour girl: **Mimi.**

Baker, Harlan F. (active 1922). Football player: **Pink.**

Baker, Hobart Amory Hare (1892–1918). Hockey player and aviator: **Hobey.**

Baker, Jerry (active c. 1970). Authority on gardening: **America's Master Gardener, Mr. Grow-it-all.**

Baker, [John] Frank[lin] (1886–1963). Baseball third baseman: **Home Run.**

Baker, Ralph (active mid-1920s). Football back: **Moon.**

Baker, Richard E. (born 1916). Jazz musician: **Two Ton Baker.**

Baker, Roy (active 1926–31). Football quarterback: **Bullet.**

Balanced City. Berkeley, California.

Bald Eagle. Tittle, Y[elberton] A[braham].

19

Baldelli, Ecola (active 1920–30). Gangster: **The Eagle.**

Baldy. Rudolph, Richard.

Ballard, Francis Drake (1899–1960). Composer and author: **Pat.**

Ballinger, Richard Achilles (1858–1922). Lawyer and U.S. Secretary of the Interior: **American Dreyfus.**

Balloon Buster. Luke, Frank, Jr.

Ball State University, athletic teams of: **Cardinals.**

Balti. Baltimore.

Baltimore, Maryland. U.S. city: **Balti, City of Monuments, Monumental City, Monument City, National Anthem City.**

Baltimore, University of, athletic teams of: **Bees.**

Baltimore and Ohio Railroad. U.S. railroad: **The B and O.**

'Bama. Alabama.

Bama. Rowell, Carvel William.

Bambi. Alworth, Lance D.; Rentzel, [Thomas] Lance.

Bambino. Ruth, Babe.

Ban. Johnson, Byron Bancroft.

Banana Nose. Arcaro, Eddie.

Bancroft, David James (1892–1972). Baseball shortstop: **Beauty.**

Band City. Elkhart, Indiana.

B and O, The. Baltimore and Ohio Railroad.

Banghart, Basil (active 1920–1930). Gangster: **Larry the Aviator, The Owl.**

Bangor, Maine. U.S. city: **Lumber City, Metropolis of the Northeast, Penobscot River City, Queen City of the East.**

Baniszewski, Gertrude Wright (born 1929). Murderer; **Torture Murderess.**

Banjo. Robinson, Ikey L.; Santley, Joseph H.

Banjo Eyes. Cantor, Eddie.

Bankhead, John H[ollis] (1872–1946). U.S. Senator from Alabama: **Parity John.**

Bankhead, Tallulah [Brockman] (1903–68). Actress: **Darling of the Gods, Tallu.**

Bankhead, William Brockman (1874–1940). U.S. Representative from Alabama: **Tallulah's Papa.**

Banking's Technocrat. Rockwell, George E.

Banks, David (1901–52). Basketball player: **Pretzel.**

Banner State. Texas.

Bantam Ben. Hogan, [William] Ben[jamin].

Banty. Hancock, Clarence Eugene.

Bara, Theda (1890–1955). U.S. film actress: **Original Glamour Girl, Queen of the Vampires.** Born: Theodosia Goodman.

Barbary Coast. Formerly boisterous waterfront area in San Francisco.

Barber, Red (born 1908). Sports commentator: **The Ol' Redhead.** Born: Walter Lanier Barber.

Barber, The. Como, Perry; Maglie, Salvatore Anthony.

Barbour, William Warren (1888–1943). Politician and industrialist: **Champ.**

Barefoot Boy of the Blue Muskingum. Christy, Howard Chandler.

Barefoot Boy of Wall Street. Willkie, Wendell [Lewis].

Barend, John (born 1945). Wrestler: **Handsome Johnny, Handsome One, Prince of Darkness, The Psycho.**

Barker, Arthur (1899–1939). Gangster: **Dock.**

Barker, George (active 1920–30). Racketeer: **Red.**

Barker, Kate Clark (1879–1935). Gangster: **Ma.**

Barkley, Alben William (1877–1956). U.S. Vice President: **Dear Alben, Little Alby, The Veep.**

Barley King. Buerger, John.

Barnacle Bill. Sutphin, William Halstead.

Barnacle Bill the Sailor. Soubier, Cliff.

Barnard College. Educational institution; with six other women's colleges: **Seven Sisters.**

Barnes, Albert (1873–1951). Art collector and manufacturer: **Argyrol King.**

Barnes, Florence Lowe (1909–75). Resort owner and stunt pilot: **Pancho.**

Barnes, James M. (1887–1966). Golfer: **Long Jim.**

Barnes, Jim (born 1941). Basketball player: **Bad News.**

Barnes, Leroy (born 1932). Convicted leader of major narcotics ring in New York City: **Mr. Untouchable, Nicky.**

Barnes, Marvin (born 1952). Basketball center and forward: **The Eraser, Good News, The Magnificent.**

Barnes, Paul D. (born 1901). Jazz clarinetist and saxophonist: **Polo.**

Barnes, Virgil Jennings (1897–1958). Baseball pitcher: **Zeke.**

Barney. Bertche, Christian; Johnson, Walter Perry; Rose Marie, Baby; Shotton, Burton Edwin.

Barney, Lemuel J. (born 1945). Football back and kicker: **Stroll.**

Barnhill, John (born 1938). Basketball player: **Rabbit.**

Barnum of Basketball. Saperstein, Abraham.

Barnum of Broadway Producers. Merrick, David.

Baron of Bluegrass Country. Rupp, Adolph Frederick.

Barr, Jim (born 1948). Baseball pitcher: **JB.** Legal name: James Leland Barr.

Barre, Vermont. U.S. city: **Granite Center.**

Barrett, Emma (born 1905). Jazz pianist and singer: **Sweet Emma the Bell Gal.**

Barris, Charles (born c. 1929). Television producer: **King of Television Gamesmanship.**

Barry, John C. (1876–1936). Baseball outfielder: **Shad.**

Barry, Wesley (born 1907). Motion-picture actor: **Freckles.**

Barrymore, John [Blythe] (1882–1942). Actor: **The Great Profile.** Born: John Blythe.

Barrymore, Lionel (1878–1954). Actor: **Hollywood's Grand Old Man.** Born: Lionel Blythe.

Barrymore of the Brain Trust. Tugwell, Rexford Guy.

Bartell, Richard William (born 1907). Baseball shortstop: **Pepper Box, Rowdy Dick, Rowdy Richard.**

Bartlett, Edward Lewis (1904–68). U.S. Senator from Alaska: **Bob.**

Barton, Bruce (1886–1967). Advertising executive: **The Advertiser, The Advertising King, The Great Repealer.**

Baruch, Bernard M[annes] (1870–1965). Financier: **Adviser of Presidents, Financial Wizard of Hobcaw Barony.**

Baseball Eddy. Kelly, Edward Austin.

Basement Barnum. Rose, Billy.

Bash Boulevard. Three blocks on Franklin Street in Oakland, California, where the boxing crowd gathered, 1920s.

Basie, Count (born 1904). Jazz composer and bandleader: **The Count.** Born William Basie.

Basilio, Carmen (born 1927). Welterweight and middleweight boxer: **Canastota Onion Farmer, Uncrowned Champion.**

Bassett, Arthur (born 1903). Jazz musician: **Rip.**

Bassey, Hogan (born 1932). Featherweight boxer: **Kid.** Born: Okon Bassey Asuque.

Bataan Death March. Forced march in 1942 of American and Philippine prisoners of war.

Bath, The. Coughlan, John Joseph.

Bathhouse John. Coughlan, John Joseph.

Batman. Greenberg, David; Ortega, Tony.

Batman and Robin. Greenberg, David and Hantz, Robert.

Battalino, Bat (1908–77). Featherweight boxer: **Battling Battalino.** Legal name: Christopher Battalino.

Battle, Edgar W. (born 1907). Jazz musician: **Puddinghead.**

Battle Axe Division. Sixty-fifth Infantry Division.

Battle Born State. Nevada.

Battle Creek, Michigan. U.S. city: **Breakfast Food City, Cereal City, Health City.**

Battlefield City. Gettysburg, Pennsylvania.

Battleground of Freedom. Kansas.

Battle Month. April.

Battle of Berlin. Struggle between the United States, Great Britain, and France, and the U.S.S.R. for control of Berlin, 1948–49.

Battle of the Philippine Sea. U.S.-Japanese naval battle, June 1944: **Marianas Turkey Shoot.**

Battler, The. Nelson, Oscar Matthew.

Battleship. Kelly, Bob.

Battling Barkeep. Galento, Tony.

Battling Battalino. Battalino, Bat.

Battling Bella. Abzug, Bella S[avitsky].

Battling Bishops. Athletic teams of Ohio Wesleyan University, Delaware, Ohio.

Battling Bob. La Follette, Robert [Marion, Sr.].

Battling Levinsky. Williams, Barney.

Battling Nelson. Nelson, Oscar.

Baugh, Samuel Adrian (born 1915). Baseball and football player: **Slinging Sammy.**

Baum, Harry (born 1882). Basketball coach: **Father of Basketball Tactics.**

Baxter, Raymond H. (active 1913). Football player: **Slats.**

Bay, The. Hudson's Bay Company, The.

Bay Dancer. War Admiral.

Bay Horse. Boston, Massachusetts.

Baylor University, athletic teams of: **Bears.**

Bayonne, New Jersey. U.S. city: **Oil City.**

Bayou City. Houston, Texas.

Bayou State. Mississippi.

Bay State. Massachusetts.

Bay Stater. 1. Native or resident of Massachusetts. 2. Sharkey, Jack.

Bazooka Bob. Burns, Bob.

BB. Berenson, Bernard.

Beadle. Native or resident of Virginia.

Beagle. Native or resident of Virginia.

Bean. Hawkins, Coleman.

Beansie. Rosenfeld, Sigmund.

Bean State. Massachusetts.

Beantown. Boston, Massachusetts.

Bear. Bryant, Paul; Gladding, Fred Earl.

Bearcats. Athletic teams of the University of Cincinnati, Cincinnati, Ohio.

Beard, Daniel Carter (1850–1941). Naturalist, illustrator, and co-founder of the Boy Scouts of America: **Uncle Dan.**

Beard, Dita [Davis] (born 1918). Lobbyist: **I.T.T.'s Memo Writer.**

Beard, The. Miller, Mitchell William.

Bearded Iceberg, The. Hughes, Charles Evans.

Bears. Athletic teams of Baylor University, Waco, Texas.

Bear State. Arkansas.

Beast. Foxx, James Emory.

Beast, The. Capone, Al[phonse].

Beat Generation. Members of a generation after World War II, especially in the late 1950s, that wanted a relaxation of authority and social responsibility; writers, artists, and intellectuals who sought mystical detachment and fulfillment through the use of alcohol and other drugs.

Beatty, Zelmo (born 1941). Basketball player: **Big Z.**

Beau Brummel of Broadway. Fay, Larry.

Beau Brummel of the Army. MacArthur, Douglas.

Beau Brummel of the Brooklyn Underworld. Yale, Frankie.

Beau Brummel of the Senate. Lewis, James Hamilton.

Beau Brummel of Vagrants. Schepps, Samuel.

Beau Jack. Walker, Sidney.

Beau James. Walker, James J[ohn].

Beaumont, Clarence Howeth (1876–1956). Baseball outfielder: **Ginger.**

Beaumont, Texas. U.S. city: **Port City, Queen of the Neches.**

Beautiful Bob. Taylor, Robert.

Beautiful City. Cincinnati, Ohio.

Beautiful City by the Sea. Portland, Maine.

Beautiful People, The. The moneyed, chic, and creative people, coined by fashion journalist Diana [Dalziel] Vreeland.

Beauty. Bancroft, David James.

Beaver. 1. Bevan, Richard. 2. Native or resident of Oregon.

Beavers. Athletic teams of the City College of New York and Oregon State University, Corvallis.

Beaver State. Oregon.

Bebe. Rebozo, Charles Gregory.

Bebop. Carroll, Joe.

Beck, Walter William (born 1906). Baseball pitcher: **Boom Boom, Elmer the Great.**

Becker, Charles (1870–1915). Corrupt police lieutenant and murderer: **Czar of the White Light District, Handsome Charley, King of Graft, Master of the Tenderloin, Murdering Policeman.**

Beckley, Jake (1867–1918). Baseball first baseman: **Eagle Eye.** Legal name: Jacob P. Beckley.

Beckoning Country. Vermont.

Beckoning Land. Virginia.

Bedford, William (active 1921). Football player: **Blink.**

Bedford-Stuyvesant. Section of Brooklyn: **Bed-Stuy.**

Bedroom of New York. Brooklyn.

Bedroom of Washington. Arlington, Virginia.

Bed-Stuy. Bedford-Stuyvesant.

Beebe, Lucius [Morris] (1902–66). Journalist and photographer: **Luscious Lucius, Social Historian of Cafe Society.**

Beedle. Smith, Walter Bedell.

Beef Barons. Major U.S. meat packers.

Beef Head. Native or resident of Texas.

Beef State. Nebraska; Texas.

Beef Trust. Combination of meat packers, 1900s, to maintain high prices; National Packing Company.

Beehive of Industry. Providence, Rhode Island.

Beehive State. Utah.

Beelzebub M. Goldwater. Goldwater, Barry [Morris].

Beer Capital of America. Milwaukee, Wisconsin.

Beer City. Milwaukee, Wisconsin.

Bees. Athletic teams of the University of Baltimore, Maryland.

Beetle. 1. Smith, Walter Bedell. 2. Volkswagen automobile with the original, rounded design.

Behemoth, The. Capone, Al[phonse].

Beiderbecke, Leon [Bismarck] (1903–31). Jazz musician: **Bix.**

Belafonte, Harry (born 1927). Singer: **Restless Troubadour.** Legal name: Harold George Belafonte, Jr.

Beland, Lucy (1872–1953). Underworld figure: **Ma.**

Belaney, George Stansfield (1888–1938). Canadian Apache writer: **Archie, Devil in Deerskins.** Born: Wa-sha-quon-asin. Also known as Grey Owl.

Belasco, David (1854–1931). Playwright and producer: **Bishop of Broadway, Sage of the Make-Believe World, Wizard of the American Drama.**

Belcastro, James (active 1920–30). Gangster: **King of the Bombers.**

Belinsky, Robert (born 1936). Baseball pitcher: **Bo.**

Beliveau, Jean (born 1931). Canadian hockey forward: **Le Gros Bill, Big Jean.**

Bell, Alexander Graham (1847–1922). Inventor: **Father of the Telephone.**

Bell, Griffin B. (born 1918). U.S. Attorney General. With other members of President Carter's administration: **Georgia Mafia.**

Bell, James Thomas (born c. 1903). Baseball player: **Black Ty Cobb, Cool Papa, Papa.**

Belle City. Racine, Wisconsin.

Belle City of the Bluegrass Regions. Lexington, Kentucky.

Belle City of the Lakes. Racine, Wisconsin.

Belle of New York. Prado, Katie.

Belle Province, La. Quebec.

Bellicose Bella. Abzug, Bella S[avitsky].

Bellino, Joseph (born 1938). Football back: **Dynamite Joe, Joe the Jet, Navy's Destroyer, Player Who Is Never Caught from Behind.**

Beloved Bruin. Spaulding, William Henry.

Beloved Brute. McLaglen, Victor.

Beloved Scientist, The. Thomson, Elihu.

Ben. Turpin, Charles Murray.

Bench, Johnny (born 1947). Baseball catcher: **Swinger from Binger.** Legal name: John Lee Bench.

Bender, Charles Albert (1883–1954). Baseball pitcher: **Chief.**

Bender, Louis (born 1910). Basketball player: **Lulu.**

Benedum, Michael (1869–1961). Oil executive: **King of the Wildcatters.**

Bengals. Athletic teams of Louisiana State University, Baton Rouge.

Benge, Ray Adelphia (born 1902). Baseball pitcher: **Silent Cal.**

Bennington, Vermont. U.S. town: **Williamsburg of the North.**

Benny. Bailey, Ernest Harold; Morton, Henry Sterling.

Benton, John Cleveland (1890–1937). Baseball pitcher: **Rube.**

Bep. Guidolin, Armand.

Berenson, Bernard (1865–1959). Art expert: **BB.**

Berg, Morris (1902–72). Baseball catcher: **Moe.**

Berger, Meyer (1898–1959). Journalist: **Mike.**

Bergeron, Victor Jules (born 1902). Restaurateur: **Trader Vic.**

Bergoff, Pearl L. (1885?–1947). Strikebreaker: **King of the Strikebreakers.**

Berigan, Rowland Bernart (1908–42). Jazz trumpet player and singer: **Bunny.**

Berkeley, Busby (1895–1976). Dance director: **Buzz.** Born: William Berkeley Enos.

Berkeley, California. U.S. city: **Athens of the West, Balanced City.**

Berkowitz, David Richard (born 1953). Convicted murderer: **.44-Caliber Killer, Son of Sam.**

Berle, Milton (born 1908). Comedian: **Mr. Television, Uncle Milty.** Born: Milton Berlinger.

Berlenbach, Paul (born 1901). Wrestler and lightweight boxer: **Astoria Assassin.**

Berlin Guy. Chamberlin, Guy.

Bernie, Ben (1893–1943). Band leader: **Old Maestro.** Born: Bernard Anzelevitz.

Bernstein, Carl (born 1944). Journalist and investigator of Watergate scandal. With Bob Woodward: **Woodstein.**

Bernstein, Joseph (1877–1931). Boxer: **Pride of the Ghetto.**

Bernstein, Joseph (active early 1920s). Football guard: **Bonecrusher Bernstein.**

Berry, Leon (1910–41). Jazz saxophonist: **Chu.**

Berry, Martha McChesney (1866–1942). Educator and philanthropist: **Sunday Lady of Possum Trot.**

Bert. Pearson, Madison.

Bertche, Christian (active 1920–30). Gambler and safecracker: **Barney.**

Bertha. Big Bertha.

Bertie. McCormick, Robert Rutherford.

Bessemer, Alabama. U.S. city: **Iron City.**

Bessie. Bethlehem Steel Corporation.

Best of the Tarzans. Weissmuller, Johnny.

Best Pitcher in Baseball. Johnson, Walter Perry.

Best Player in Hockey. Howe, Gordie.

Bet-a-Million Gates. Gates, John Warne.

Bethlehem, Pennsylvania. U.S. city: **Christmas City, Steel City.**

Bethlehem Steel Corporation. U.S. company: **Bessie.**

Bethune, Mary McLeod (1875–1955). Educator and official in the administration of President Franklin D. Roosevelt: **Ma.**

Betsytown. Elizabeth, New Jersey.

Betts, Walter M. (born 1897). Baseball pitcher: **Huck, Huckleberry.**

Beulah. McDaniel, Hattie.

Beurling, George (born 1922). Canadian R.A.F. pilot: **Screwball.**

Bevan, Roland (active 1935). Football coach: **Beaver.**

Beveridge, Albert Jeremiah (1862–1927). Historian and U.S. Senator from Indiana: **American Nationalist.**

Bevo. Francis, Clarence.

Bex. Bezdek, Hugo F[rank].

Bez, Nick (1895–1969). Businessman: **Big Nick.**

Bezdek, Hugo F[rank] (1884–1952). Football coach and baseball manager: **Bex, Hugo the Victor.**

B-58. Bombing plane: **Hustler.**

B-57. Bombing plane: **Canberra.**

B-52. Bombing plane: **Stratofortress.**

B-47. Bombing plane: **Stratojet.**

BG. Goodman, Benny.

Bible, Dana Xenophon (born 1891). Football coach: **Football classicist, DX.**

Bible Belt. Area of the U.S. South characterized and influenced in laws and customs by religious fundamentalism.

Bid. McPhee, John Alexander.

Biederman, Otto (died 1935). Gangster: **Abbadabba.**

Bierce, Ambrose Gwinett (1842–1914). Author: **Bitter Bierce.**

Bierman, Bernard William (born 1894). Football coach: **Hammer of the North, Silver Fox of the Northland.**

Biff. Jones, Lawrence McCeney; McGuire, William [Joseph, Jr.]; Schneidman, Herman.

Biffo. De Lorenzo, Frank.

Biffy. Lea, Langdon.

Big A. Aqueduct Race Track; Arcaro, Eddie; Atlanta, Georgia.

Big Al. Capone, Al[phonse].

Big Apple, The. New York City.

Big Bankroll, The. Rothstein, Arnold.

Bigbee, Carson Lee (1895–1964). Baseball outfielder: **Skeeter.**

Big Ben. *Franklin,* U.S.S.

Big Bender. Native or resident of Tennessee.

Big Bend State. Tennessee.

Big Bertha. German heavy artillery piece, World War I, with a range of about 75 miles. **Bertha.**

Big Bill. Broonzy, William Lee; Duffy, William J.; Dwyer, William Vincent; Haywood, William Dudley; Hutcheson, William Levi; James, William Henry; Knudsen, William S.; Lange, William Alexander; Lingley, William; Russell, Bill; Thompson, William Hale; Tilden, William Tatem, Jr.

Big Black. Ray, Danny.

Big Board. New York Stock Exchange.

Big Boy. Capone, Al[phonse].

Big Brave from Milwaukee. Conley, Donald [Eu]gene.

Big Burg. New York City.

Big Cat. Mize, John Robert.

Big Chief. Curtis, Charles; Moore, Russell.

Big Chief, The. Taft, William Howard.

Big Country. Nebraska.

Big D. Dallas, Texas.

Big Daddy. Garlits, Donald Glenn; Lipscomb, Gene.

Big Daddy of the Underworld. Colosimo, James.

Big Dan. Tobin, Daniel Joseph.

Big Dipper. Chamberlain, Wilt[on Norman].

Big Ditch. Panama Canal.

Big Dog. Nevers, Ernest A.

Big E. *Enterprise,* U.S.S.

Big E, The. Hayes, Elvin.

Big Ed. Danowski, Edward; Konetchy, Edward Joseph; McKeever,

Edward Clark; Reilly, Edward J.; Reulbach, Edward Marvin; Walsh, Ed[ward Augustin].

Big Eddy. Skid-row area of Portland, Maine.

Big Eight. College athletic conference composed of University of Colorado, Iowa State University, University of Kansas, Kansas State University, University of Missouri, University of Nebraska, University of Oklahoma, Oklahoma State University.

Big Eye Louis. Nelson, Louis Delisle.

Big Feller. Sullivan, Timothy Daniel.

Big Fellow. Capone, Al[phonse].

Big Fish State. Michigan.

Big Five. 1. United States, Great Britain, France, U.S.S.R. and China in World War II. 2. Representatives from the United States, Great Britain, France, Italy, and Japan that met at the Paris Peace Conference on January 12, 1919. 3. Combination of meat packers for restraint of trade and other purposes, c. 1920. 4. Basketball teams of five colleges or universities in the Philadelphia area: La Salle College, University of Pennsylvania, St. Joseph's College, Temple University, and Villanova University.

Big Four. 1. Spelling, Aaron. 2. Four stars in motion-picture Westerns: Hoot Gibson, Buck Jones, Ken Maynard, and Tom Mix. 3. Representatives from the United States, Great Britain, France, and Italy that met at the Paris Peace Conference on January 12, 1919.

Big Game Hunter. Tinkham, George Holden.

Big George. Foreman, George.

Biggers, Earl Derr (1884–1933). Writer: **Father of Charlie Chan.**

Biggest Cat. Brown, James.

Biggest Hotel Man in the World. Hilton, Conrad [Nicholson].

Biggest Little City. Reno, Nevada.

Biggest Little City in the World. Reno, Nevada.

Big Green. Athletic teams of Dartmouth College, Hanover, New Hampshire.

Big Guy. Capone, Al[phonse]; DiMaggio, Joe; Williams, Ted.

Big Heart of Texas. Austin, Texas.

Big House. Gaines, Clarence.

Big Inch. Oil pipeline running about 1,300 miles from Texas to Pennsylvania, laid 1943.

Big Island. Hawaii, Hawaii.

Big J. *New Jersey,* U.S.S.

Big Jake. Kramer, Jack.

Big Jean. Beliveau, Jean.

Big Jeff. Jeffries, Jim.

Big Jess. Willard, Jess.

Big Jim. Arness, James; Colosimo, James; Farley, James Aloysius; Lewis, James Wilson; Thompson, James R[obert].

Big Joe. Turner, Joseph.

Big John. Connally, John Bowden; McKeithen, John Julian; Patton, John; Wayne, John.

Big Judge Powell. Powell, John Stephen.

Big LIE, The. Long Island Expressway.

Big Lip. Mails, Walter.

Big M. *Missouri,* U.S.S.

Big Mac. Municipal Assistance Corporation in New York City.

Big Mamie. *Massachusetts,* U.S.S.

Big Man from Little Egypt. Keller, Kent Ellsworth.

Big Maxey. Greenberg, Max.

Big Medicine. Kelly, Clinton Wayne.

Big Miller. Miller, Clarence H.

Big Miss. Mississippi River.

Big Mo. *Missouri,* U.S.S.

Big Moose. Earnshaw, George Livingston; Walsh, Ed[ward Augustin].

Big Muddy. Mississippi River; Missouri River.

Big Navy Claude. Swanson, Claude Augustus.

Big Nick. Bez, Nick.

Big-Nose Louie. Little, Lou[is Lawrence].

Big O. Robertson, Oscar Palmer.

Big Poison. Waner, Paul Glee.

Big Potato. Borah, William Edgar.

Big Red. Athletic teams of Cornell University, Ithaca, New York; Malcolm X; Man o' War.

Big Red Machine. Cincinnati Reds.

Big Shrimp of Pro Football. Sherman, Allie.

Big Sid. Catlett, Sidney.

Big Six. Auker, Elden Leroy; Mathewson, Christy.

Big Ski Country. Montana.

Big Sky Country. Montana.

Big Smoke. Pittsburgh, Pennsylvania.

Big State. Alaska.

Big Steve. Owen, Stephen Joseph.

Big Stick Policy. President Theodore Roosevelt's policy of softly spoken words backed by force, enunciated in 1901.

Big T. Teagarden, Jack.

Big Ten. 1. Heads of government and foreign secretaries of the United States, Great Britain, France, Italy, and Japan that met at the Paris Peace Conference of 1919 to draft the Treaty of Versailles. 2. College athletic conference composed of University of Illinois, Indiana University, University of Iowa, University of Michigan, Michigan State University, University of Minnesota, Northwestern University, Ohio State University, Purdue University, and University of Wisconsin.

Big Three. 1. Woodrow Wilson, David Lloyd George, and Georges Clemenceau, at the Paris Peace Conference, 1919. 2. Franklin D. Roosevelt, Winston Churchill, and Joseph Stalin, during World War II. 3. Athletic teams of Harvard, Yale, and Princeton.

Big Tim. Sullivan, Timothy Daniel.

Big Tiny Little. Little, Dudley.

Big Town. New York City; Chicago, Illinois.

Big Train. Johnson, Walter Perry; Sisk, John.

Big Tubby. Raskin, Morris.

Big Tuna. Accardo, Anthony Joseph.

Big U. *United States*, S.S.

Big Ukrainian. Nagurski, Bronislau.

Big Windy. Chicago, Illinois.

Big Z. Beatty, Zelmo.

Bikini City. Miami, Florida.

Bilbo, Theodore Gilmore (1877–1947). U.S. Senator from Mississippi: **The Man, The Two-edged Knife.**

Bill. Horr, Marquis Franklin.

Billie Boy from Pecos. Estes, Billie Sol.

Billikens. Athletic teams of Saint Louis University, St. Louis, Missouri.

Billingkoff, Morris (born 1898). Flyweight boxer: **Young Montreal.**

Billings, Montana. U.S. city: **Magic City.**

Billingsley, [John] Sherman (1900–66). Night club proprietor: **Mr. Stork Club.**

Billionaire Recluse. Hughes, Howard [R.]

Billion Dollar Broker, The. Whalen, Grover Aloysius.

Bill the Builder. McAdoo, William Gibbs.

Billy the Kid. Southworth, William Harrison.

Biloxi, Mississippi. U.S. city: **America's Riviera, Nation's Seafood Center.**

Bimstein, Morris (1897–1969). Boxer: **Whitey.**

Bing. Miller, John E.

Binga, Jesse (1865–1950). Banker: **Black Financier.**

Bingo. DeMoss, Elwood; McMahon, William.

Bird. Grich, Robert Anthony; Parker, Charlie.

Bird, The. Fidrych, Mark.

Birddog. Cessna L-19 training plane, 1950s.

Birdie. Tebbetts, George Robert.

Bird Man of Alcatraz. Stroud, Robert Franklin.

Birds, The. St. Louis Cardinals.

Birdseye, Clarence (1886–1956). Inventor and businessman: **Father of Frozen Foods.**

Birmingham, Alabama. U.S. city: **Bad Birmingham, City of Executives, Emerging Industrial Center, Football Capital of the South, Home of Vulcan, Industrial Center of the Great South, Industrial Center of Dixie, Inland Metropolis, Magic City,**

Magic City of the South, Mineral City of the South, Pittsburgh of the South.

Birmingham, Joseph Leo (1884–1946). Baseball outfielder and manager: **Dode.**

Birmingham of America. Newark, New Jersey.

Birthplace of American Freedom. Massachusetts.

Birthplace of American Liberty. Lexington, Massachusetts; Philadelphia, Pennsylvania.

Birthplace of a Nation. Pennsylvania.

Birthplace of Aviation. Dayton, Ohio.

Birthplace of Baseball. Cooperstown, New York.

Birthplace of California. San Diego, California.

Birthplace of Dixie. Montgomery, Alabama.

Birthplace of Liberty. Old State House, Philadelphia, Pennsylvania.

Birthplace of Surfing. Waikiki, Hawaii.

Birthplace of the American Cotton Industry. Pawtucket, Rhode Island.

Birthplace of the American Navy. Marblehead, Massachusetts.

Biscuit Pants. Gehrig, [Henry] Lou[is].

Bish. Bishop, Wallace Henry.

Bishop, Cecil W. (1890–1971). U.S. Representative from Illinois: **Runt.**

Bishop, Max Frederick (1899–1962). Baseball second baseman and coach: **Tilly.**

Bishop, The. De Sapio, Carmine.

Bishop, Wallace Henry (born 1906). Jazz drummer: **Bish.**

Bishop of Broadway. Belasco, David; Irvine, Harry.

Bishop of the Big Top. Waddell, Doc.

Bismarck, North Dakota. U.S. city: **City Beside the Broad Missouri.**

Bison City. Buffalo, New York.

Bisons. Athletic teams of Bucknell University, Lewisburg, Pennsylvania.

Bitter Bierce. Bierce, Ambrose Gwinett.

Bitter-ender. 1. Opponent of a negotiated peace with the Central Powers, World War I. 2. Opponent of U.S. membership in the League of Nations, c. 1920.

35

Bituminous City. Connellsville, Pennsylvania.

Bitzer, Billy (1872–1944). Motion-picture cameraman: **Eagle Eye.** Legal name: Johann Gottlieb Wilhelm Bitzer.

Bix. Beiderbecke, Leon [Bismarck].

Bjorkland, Rosemarie Diane (born 1941). Murderer: **Penny.**

Blabbermouth. Cox, Archibald.

Black, Clinton Rutherford, Jr. (1894–1963). Football player: **Cupe.**

Black Angel of the Poor. Waddles, Charleszetta.

Black Babe Ruth, The. Gibson, Joshua.

Black Bears. Athletic teams of the University of Maine, Orono.

Black Belt. Fertile cotton-growing area extending across central Alabama and Mississippi.

Blackburne, Russell (born 1886). Baseball coach: **Lena.**

Black Cat Division. Thirteenth Armored Division.

Black Dahlia. Short, Elizabeth.

Black Diamond City. Wilkes-Barre, Pennsylvania.

Black Explorer. Henson, Matthew.

Black Financier. Binga, Jesse.

Black Giant of White Spirituals. Jackson, George Pullen.

Black Hand. Italian-American criminal society, early 20th century.

Black Hawk Division. Eighty-sixth Division; Eighty-sixth Infantry Division.

Black Heart of Montana. Butte, Montana.

Black Honus Wagner. Lloyd, John Henry.

Black Horowitz. Waller, Thomas Wright.

Blackie. Armes, Monroe; Blackwell, Ewell; Dark, Al[vin Ralph]; Mancuso, August Rodney.

Black Jack. Lanza, John; Pershing, John Joseph.

Black Knight of the Border. Malone, Percy Lay.

Black Knights. Athletic teams of the United States Military Academy, West Point, New York.

Black Messiah. Washington, Booker T[aliaferro].

Black Moses. Hayes, Isaac.

Black Nationalist. Garvey, Marcus M[oziah].

Black Panther Division. Sixty-sixth Infantry Division.

Black Power. Political and economic power of blacks as a group, invoked to achieve racial equality.

Black Raiders. A Ku Klux Klan–like group in the vicinity of Atlanta, Georgia, 1940s.

Black Ralph Nader. Sims, Phil[ip].

Black Rock. CBS; CBS Building.

Black Roger. Touhy, Roger.

Black Sox. Eight baseball players of the Chicago White Sox accused of accepting bribes to throw the 1919 World Series.

Black Thursday. October 24, 1929, day on which massive, panic selling on the stock market began, culminating in Black Tuesday (October 29, 1929).

Black Tuesday. October 29, 1929; beginning of the Great Depression.

Black Ty Cobb. Bell, James Thomas.

Black Water State. Nebraska.

Black Wednesday. October 23, 1929, day on which stock prices began to fall.

Blackwell, Ewell (born 1922). Baseball pitcher: **Blackie, The Whip.**

Black Widow. Nighttime fighting plane, World War II.

Blacky. Magnum, Leo Allan.

Blaik, Earl H[enry] (born 1897). Football coach: **Red, Colonel, Earl of Hanover.**

Blake, Hector (born 1912). Hockey forward and coach: **Toe.**

Blake, John Fred (born 1889). Baseball player: **Sheriff.**

Blanchard, Doc (born 1924). Football fullback: **Mr. Inside.** Legal name: Felix Anthony Blanchard, Jr.

Bland, Schuyler Otis (1872–1950). U.S. Representative from Virginia: **Bridge Builder Bland.**

Blanton, Darrell Elijah (1909–1945). Baseball pitcher: **Cy.**

Blanton, Thomas Lindsay (1872–1957). U.S. Representative from Texas: **Czar of the District, Hold That Line, The Scourge of the District Police, Talkative Tom, Watchdog of the Treasury.**

Blassey, Frederick (born c. 1940). Wrestler: **Classy Freddy Blassey.**

Blimp. Phelps, Ernest Gordon.

Blind Publisher. Pulitzer, Joseph.

Blind Savant. Gore, Thomas Pryor.

Blink. Bedford, William.

Blizzard State. South Dakota; Texas.

Block, Herb (born 1909). Political cartoonist: **Herblock.**

Block, The. Street of bars and places of entertainment in Baltimore, Maryland.

Block Island. Island forming part of Rhode Island: **America's Bermuda, Fisherman's Paradise of the North Atlantic.**

Blonde Bombshell. Harlow, Jean.

Blond Terror from Terre Haute. Taylor, [Charles] Bud.

Blondy. Ryan, John Collins.

Blood. McNally, John.

Blood and Fire Division. Sixty-third Infantry Division.

Blood and Guts. Patton, George Smith, Jr.

Bloody Harlan. Harlan County, Kentucky.

Bloody Thursday. July 5, 1934; clash between police and picketing longshoremen, San Francisco, California.

Bloom, Phil (born 1894). Boxer: **Ring Gorilla.**

Bloom, Sol (1870–1949). U.S. Representative from New York: **George Washington Bloom, Savior of the Constitution.**

Bloomington, Illinois. U.S. city: **Prairie City.**

Blount, Francis Nelson (born 1918). Railroad executive: **Man from Steamtown.**

Blue. Mitchell, Richard Allen.

Blue, Luzerne Atwell (1897–1958). Baseball first baseman: **Lu.**

Blue and Gray Division. Twenty-ninth Infantry Division.

Blue Angels. Team of U.S. Navy precision flyers, c. 1970.

Blue Box. Mechanically controlled Link trainer, used by the U.S. Army to teach mail-carrying pilots how to "fly blind" on instruments, 1930s and 1940s.

Blue Chips. Stocks of leading industrial companies such as IBM, General Motors, and American Can.

Blue Collar Pundit. Lavelle, Mike.

Blue Devil Division. Eighty-eighth Infantry Division.

Blue Devils. Athletic teams of Duke University, Durham, North Carolina.

Blue Eagle. Symbol of the National Recovery Administration, 1933.

Blue Flu, The. New York City police strike, late 1960, now a common designation for police "sickouts."

Bluege, Otto Adam (born 1910). Baseball pinch hitter: **Squeaky.**

Bluegrass, The. Region around Lexington, Kentucky, noted for horse breeding.

Bluegrass Capital. Frankfort, Kentucky; Lexington, Kentucky.

Bluegrass State. Kentucky.

Blue Hen Chicken. Native or resident of Delaware.

Blue Hen State. Delaware.

Blue Law. Law restricting trade, esp. on Sunday.

Blue Law State. Connecticut.

Blue Monday. First day of the work week.

Blue Moon. Odom, Johnny Lee.

Blue Norther. Cold northerly wind characteristic of Kansas, Oklahoma, and Texas.

Bluenose. Native or resident of the Canadian Maritime provinces, esp. Nova Scotia.

Bluenose Province. Nova Scotia.

Bluenthal, Arthur (1891–1918). Football player: **Bluey.**

Blue Power. Political solidarity and power of the police, esp. striking policemen and policewomen.

Blue Ridge Division. Eightieth Infantry Division.

Blues Boy. King, B. B.

Blue Sky Law. Law intended to protect investors against fraud.

Blue Streak of Vaudeville. Samuels, Rae.

Blue Streaks. Athletic teams of John Carroll University, Cleveland, Ohio.

Bluey. Bluenthal, Arthur.

Bluff City. Hannibal, Missouri; Memphis, Tennessee; Natchez, Mississippi.

Bluhdorn, Charles (born 1930). Financier and businessman: **Mad Austrian.**

Bo. Belinsky, Robert; Callaway, Howard [Hollis]; McMillin, Al[vin Nugent].

Boardwalk Ike. Bacharach, Isaac.

Boating Capital of the World. Fort Lauderdale, Florida.

Boat Rocker. Sizemore, Barbara.

Bob. Bartlett, Edward Lewis.

Bobby. Wallace, Roderick John.

Bobby Joe. Conrad, Robert J.

Bobby the Robber. Robinson, Brooks [Calbert, Jr.].

Bobcats. Athletic teams of Ohio University, Athens.

Bobie. Cahn, Norman.

Bobo. Newsom, Louis Norman; Olson, Carl; Rockefeller, Barbara [Sears].

Bobo King. Keiser, Robert.

Boca Raton, Florida. U.S. city: **Golden City of the Gold Coast.**

Bodenger, Morris (born 1909). Football guard: **Bodie.**

Bodenheim, Maxwell (1895–1954). Writer: **Bogie.**

Bodie. Bodenger, Morris.

Body, The. McDonald, Marie; McFadden, Bernarr.

Bogart, Humphrey (1899–1957). Film actor: **Bogey, Bogie.**

Bogey. Bogart, Humphrey.

Boggess, Lynton (1904–68). Baseball umpire: **Dusty.**

Boggs, Corinne C[laiborne] (born 1916). U.S. Representative from Louisiana: **Lindy.**

Bogie. Bodenheim, Maxwell; Bogart, Humphrey.

Bohlen, Charles E[ustis] (1904–74). U.S. Government official: **Chip.**

Boilermaker. Jeffries, Jim.

Boilermakers. Athletic teams of Purdue University, Lafayette, Indiana.

Boileryard. Clarke, William Jones.

Boise City, Idaho. U.S. city: **City of Trees, The Woods.**

Bojangles. Robinson, Bill.

Bolber, Morris (c. 1890–c. 1938). Quack and murderer: **Philadelphia's Murdering Faith Healer.**

Bolden, Buddy (1868–1931). Jazz cornetist and trumpeter: **King.** Born: Charles Bolden.

Bonanno, Joseph (born 1905). Racketeer. **Joe Bananas.**

Bonano, Joseph (1904–72). Jazz musician. **Sharkey.**

Bonanza Land. Region around Fort Smith, Arkansas.

Bonanza State. Montana.

Bonecrusher. Bernstein, Joseph.

Bonehead. Merkle, Frederick Charles.

Bonesteele, Jessie (1872–1932). Actress and manager: **Maker of Stars.** Legal name: Laura Justine Bonesteele.

Bonham, Ernest Edward (1913–1949). Baseball pitcher: **Tiny.**

Bonus Army (also called **Bonus Marchers).** Group of World War I veterans who marched on Washington, D.C., in 1932 in a vain effort to have a promised bonus paid at once.

Boob. McNair, Donald Eric; McNutt, Paul Vories.

Boo Boo. Hoff, Max.

Boob Tube. Television.

Boog. Powell, John Wesley.

Boom Boom. Beck, Walter William; Cannon, Larry; Geoffrion, Bernie.

Boomie. Richman, Abraham Samuel.

Booming Sooner. Owens, Steve.

Boone, Pat (born 1934). Folk and religious singer: **Mr. Clean.** Legal name: Charles Boone.

Boop-Boop-a-Doop Girl. Kane, Helen.

Booth, Albie (1908–59). Football, baseball, and basketball player: **Little Boy Blue, Mighty Atom, Mighty Mite.** Legal name: Albert J. Booth.

Boots. Grantham, George Farley; Mussulli, Henry W.

Bootsie. Cassini, Austine McDonnell.

Bootstrap Kid. Vesco, Robert L[ee].

Booze Buster. Johnson, William Eugene.

Borah, William Edgar (1865–1940). U.S. Senator from Idaho: **Big Potato, Idaho Lion, The Lion of the Senate, The Lone Lion.**

Borax King. Smith, Francis Marion.
Border City. Fall River, Massachusetts.
Border Eagle State. Mississippi.
Border State. Maine.
Borgasmord Kid. Reese, Mason.
Borough of Homes. Queens, New York City.
Borough of Universities. The Bronx, New York City.
Borries, Fred, Jr. (1911–69). Football halfback: **Buzz.**
Borscht Belt. Area of Catskill Mountain resorts, New York State.
Borscht Circuit. Group of Catskill resort hotels with a mainly Jewish clientele; term used by entertainers.
Bosco. Carter, Donald James.
Bosox. Boston Red Sox.
Boss. De Sapio, Carmine; Harding, Florence Kling DeWolfe; Penrose, Boies.
Boss, The. Anastasia, Albert; Daley, Richard Joseph; Roosevelt, Franklin Delano.
Boss Crump. Crump, Edward Hull.
Boss Curley. Curley, James Michael.
Boss Hague. Hague, Frank.
Boss Kettering. Kettering, Charles Franklin.
Boss of All Bosses. Maranzano, Salvatore.
Boss of Bosses. Morello, Peter.
Boss of the Bunny Empire. Hefner, Hugh.
Boss Pendergast. Pendergast, Thomas J.
Boston, Clarence (active 1937). Football player: **Chief.**
Boston, Massachusetts. U.S. city: **American Athens, Athens of America, Athens of the New World, Athens of the United States, Bay Horse, Beantown, City of Baked Beans, City of Kind Hearts, City of Notions, Classic City, Literary Emporium, The Hub, Hub of American Culture, Hub of New England, Hub of the Solar System, Hub of the Universe, Metropolis of New England, Modern Athens, Puritan City, Trimountain City.**
Boston Blackie. Morris, [John] Chester [Brooks].
Boston College, athletic teams of: **Eagles.**

Boston Gob. Sharkey, Jack.

Boston of the West. St. Paul, Minnesota.

Boston Pops. Series of concerts of light music played by members of the Boston Symphony Orchestra.

Boston Red Sox. American League baseball team: **Bosox.**

Boston Sailor. Sharkey, Jack.

Boston's First Perpetual Motion Machine, Cowens, Dave.

Boston Strangler. DeSalvo, Albert Henry.

Boston Strong Boy. Sullivan, John Lawrence.

Boston Tar Baby. Langford, Sam.

Boston University, athletic teams of: **Terriers.**

Boswash. Urbanized region between Boston and Washington.

Botchey. Koch, Barton.

Bottles. Capone, Ralph J.

Bottomley, James Leroy (1900–59). Baseball first baseman: **Struttin' Jim, Sunny Jim.**

Boucher, George (1896–1960). Hockey defenseman: **Buck.**

Boudin, Leonard (born 1912). Lawyer: **Left's Lawyer's Lawyer.**

Boulder, Colorado. U.S. city: **Wonderland of America.**

Bourke-White, Margaret (1906–71). Photographer: **Photo Reportress.**

Bourne, Randolph Silliman (1886–1918). Essayist and musician: **Literary Radical.**

Bourque, Napoleon (1885?–1963). Racing driver: **Pit.**

Bow, Clara (1905–65). Motion-picture actress: **It Girl, Red Head.**

Bower, Maurice (born 1922). Musician: **Bugs.**

Bowes, Edward (1874–1946). Radio entertainer and real estate executive: **Major.**

Bowie State. Arkansas.

Bowling Green State Univeristy, athletic teams of: **Falcons.**

Box Office Girl. Gray, Gilda.

Boy Bandit. Johnson, James Joy.

Boyd, Roscoe Reynolds (born 1919). Businessman: **Canary.**

Boyer, Mary Ann (born 1928). Prostitute: **Roundheels.**

Boy Explorer. Siple, Paul Allman.

Boyle, Michael J. (active 1920–30). Labor union racketeer: **Umbrella Mike.**

Boy Mayor of Burnham. Patton, John.

Boy Monologuist. Jessel, Georgie.

Boy Orator. Lee, Joshua Bryan.

Boy President. Hutchins, Robert Maynard.

Boy Producer. Thalberg, Irving Grant.

Boy Robot. Fischer, Bobby.

Boy's Town. Redlight district in a Mexican town near the U.S. border.

Boys Town, Nebraska. Institution: **City of Little Men.**

Boy Who Shut Everyone Out. Bremer, Arthur Herman.

Boy Wonder. Hammer, Armand; Harris, Stanley Raymond; Hoppe, Willie; Lee, Joshua Bryan; Welles, [George] Orson.

Boy Wonder of Broadway. Harris, Jed.

Bozo. Shupe, James.

Braddock, James J. (1905–74). Heavyweight boxer: **The Cinderella Man, The Forgotten Man.**

Bradford, Perry (1895–1970). Jazz musician: **Mule.**

Bradley, Edward R. (1859–1946). Gambler and racehorse breeder: **Colonel.**

Bradley, Omar Nelson (born 1893). U.S. Army General: **Doughboy's General.**

Bradshaw, Myron (1905–1958). Jazz musician: **Tiny.**

Brady, Floyd Maurice (born 1910). Jazz trombonist: **Stumpy.**

Brady, James Buchanan (1856–1917). Financier and man of wealth: **Diamond Jim.**

Brahma. Jones, Virgil.

Brahmin Democrat. Quincy, Josiah.

Brain, The. Rickey, Branch [Wesley]; Rothstein, Arnold.

Brainard, Bertha (active 1920s). Radio personality: **First Lady of Radio.**

Brain of the Army. Gruenther, Alfred M[aximilian].

Braintree Martyrs. Sacco, Nicola and Vanzetti, Bartolomeo.

Brain Trust or **Brain Trusters.** Advisers to Franklin Delano Roosevelt.

Brand, Adolf Johannes (born 1934). Jazz pianist and composer: **Dollar.**

Brandeis, Louis Dembitz (1856–1941). Associate Justice of the U.S. Supreme Court: **People's Attorney, People's Lawyer.**

Bransfield, William Edward (1875–1947). Baseball first baseman: **Kitty.**

Brass City. Waterbury, Connecticut.

Brattleboro, Vermont. U.S. town: **Organ Town.**

Bratwurst Capital. Sheboygan, Wisconsin.

Braun, Valentine (1891–1948). Lightweight boxer: **Knockout Brown.**

Braves. Athletic teams of Alcorn State University, Lorman, Mississippi.

Bread and Butter State. Minnesota.

Breadbasket of Canada. Saskatchewan.

Breadbasket of the Nation. Kansas.

Breakfast Food City. Battle Creek, Michigan.

Breen, May Singhi (died 1970). Radio entertainer and song writer. With Peter de Rose: **Sweethearts of the Air.**

Breezy Town. Chicago, Illinois.

Bremer, Arthur Herman (born 1950). Failed assassin: **Boy Who Shut Everyone Out, The Misanthrope.**

Bremerton, Washington. U.S. City: **Fungus Corners, Home of the Pacific Fleet, String Town.**

Brennan, Peter J. (born 1919). Labor leader and Secretary of Labor: **Loyal Hard Hat, Pistol Pete.**

Brescher, Max (active 1912). Criminal: **Muttle.**

Bresnahan, Roger Philip (1880–1944). Baseball outfielder and catcher: **Duke of Tralee.**

Bressler, Raymond Bloom (1894–1966). Baseball outfielder: **Rube.**

Breuer, Marcel (born 1902). Architect: **Compleat Designer.**

Brew. Moore, William A.

Brewing City. Reading, Pennsylvania.

Brewster, Ralph Owen (born 1888). Politician: **Aroostook Potato.**

Brick. Fleagle, Jacob Roger; Morse, Clinton R.; Muller, Harold P.; Owens, Clarence B.; Wahl, Stephen Peters.

Bricker, John William (born 1893). U.S. Senator from Ohio: **Honest John.**

Bridge Builder Bland. Bland, Schuyler Otis.

Bridgeport, Connecticut. U.S. city: **Industrial Capital of Connecticut, Park City.**

Bridges, Alfred Bryant Renton (born 1900). Labor leader: **Harry.**

Bridgey. Webber (or Weber), Louis.

Briggs, Walter O., Jr. (1878–1952). Baseball manager and team president: **Spike.**

Brigham Young University, athletic teams of: Cougars.

Bright Star of the Boston Braves. Dark, Al[vin Ralph].

Brilliant Loner. Corbett, Joseph, Jr.

Brinegar, Claude Strout (born 1926). U.S. Secretary of Transportation: **Nixon's Keen Scythe.**

Bring 'Em Back Alive Buck. Buck, Frank.

Brisbane, Arthur (1864–1936). Journalist: **Old Double Dome.**

Bristol, Connecticut. U.S. city: **Clock Center of the World.**

Britain's Mr. America. Cooke, Alistair.

British Columbia. Canadian province: **Pacific Coast Province, Pacific Province.**

British Petroleum Company. Business organization; with six other oil companies: **Seven Sisters.**

Britton, Milt (1894–1948). Orchestra leader: **Clown Prince of Music.** Born: Milton Levy.

Broadbent, Harry L. (1892–1971). Hockey player: **Punch.**

Broadway. Smith, Alexander Benjamin.

Broadway. Street in New York City: **Great White Way, Gay White Way.**

Broadway Butterfly. Keenan, Dorothy.

Broadway Joe. Namath, Joseph William.

Broadway Jones. Jones, Henry.

Broadway Sam. Roth, Sam.

Brock, William Emerson (1872–1950). U.S. Senator from Tennessee: **Candy Kid.**

Brockton Blockbuster. Marciano, Rocky.

Brockton Bull. Marciano, Rocky.

Brockton Buster. Marciano, Rocky.

Broda, Walter (1914–72). Hockey player: **Turk.**

Bromberg, Gabriel (active c. 1930). Football player: **Gay.**

Bronco. North American Rockwell OV-10A reconnaissance and convoy plane.

Bronco Billy. Anderson, Gilbert.

Broncos. Athletic teams of Western Michigan University, Kalamazoo.

Bronfman, Edgar (born 1929). Distiller: **Richest Man in the World.**

Bronfman, Samuel (1891–1971). Canadian distiller: **Richest Man in Canada.**

Bronk, The. Nagurski, Bronislau.

Bronko. Nagurski, Bronislau.

Bronx, The. Borough of New York City: **Borough of Universities.**

Bronx Bombers. New York Yankees.

Bronx Bull. La Motta, Jacob.

Brooklyn. Borough of New York City; formerly an independent city: **City of Churches, City of Homes, Bedroom of New York.**

Brooklyn Bums. Brooklyn Dodgers.

Brooklyn Dodgers. National League baseball team: **Dem Bums, The Bums, Brooklyn Bums.**

Brooklyn Rabbit. Schaffel, Albert S.

Brooks, Joseph (active 1920–30). Criminal and saloon keeper: **Dynamite Brooks.** Also known as Joey Josephs.

Broonzy, William Lee (1893–1958). Jazz musician: **Big Bill.**

Brother George. Liberace, George J.

Brother Jack McDuff. McDuffy, Eugene.

Brother John Sellers. Sellers, John B.

Brother Reilly. Reilly, Edward J.

Brothers, Leo Vincent (born 1899). Gangster: **Buster.** Also known as Leo Bader.

Brougham. Any of various monoplanes built by T. Claude Ryan and the Detroit Aircraft Corporation, 1926–31.

Brow, The. DiGiovanna, Charles.

Browder, Earl [Russell] (1891–1973). Communist party leader and office seeker: **America's Red Leader.**

Brown, Aaron L. (1883–1934). Welterweight boxer: **Dixie Kid.**

Brown, Cecil (born 1907). News commentator. With seven other broadcasters: **Murrow's Boys.**

Brown, Charles Edward (1881–1914). Baseball pitcher: **Buster.**

Brown, Edmund Gerald (born 1905). Governor of California: **Pat.**

Brown, Edmund Gerald, Jr. (born 1938). Governor of California: **Jerry.**

Brown, Harold (born 1927). Physicist and U.S. Secretary of Defense: **Dr. No.**

Brown, Henry (1870?–1909). Western outlaw: **The Sundance Kid.** Legal name: Harry Longbaugh.

Brown, James (born 1934). Singer: **Biggest Cat, Cultivated Catfish, Mr. Dynamite, Explosive Mr. Brown, King of Soul.**

Brown, Joe (born 1926). Lightweight boxer: **Old Bones.**

Brown, John H., Jr. (1891–1963). Football player: **Babe.**

Brown, Margaret Tobin (1873?–1932). *Titanic* survivor: **Unsinkable Molly Brown.**

Brown, Moe (active 1912). Gambler: **Fat Moe.**

Brown, Mordecai Peter Centennial (1876–1948). Baseball pitcher: **Three-Finger Brown.**

Brown, Rhozier Theopelius (born c. 1945). Convict and playwright: **Prison Playwright.**

Brown Bomber. Louis, Joe.

Brown Bombshell. Owens, Jesse.

Brownie. McGhee, Walter.

Browning, Edward (1874–1934). Real-estate dealer and person of notoriety: **Cinderella Man, Daddy Browning.**

Brownstone State. Connecticut.

Brown Sugar. Armstrong, Lucille.

Brown University. 1. Athletic teams of: **Bruins.** 2. Athletic teams of, with seven other teams in college conference: **Ivy League.**

Bruder, Henry (1907–70). Football quarterback: **Hard Luck Bruder.**

Bruins. Athletic teams of Brown University, Providence, Rhode Island, and the University of California at Los Angeles (UCLA).

Brumbaugh, Carl L. (1907–69). Football quarterback: **Brummie.**

Brumm, George Franklin (1880–1934). U.S. Representative from Pennsylvania: **Three-Minute Brumm.**

Brummie. Brumbaugh, Carl L.

Bruno, Henry Augustine (born 1893). Public relations expert: **Public Relations Pioneer.**

Brush King. Fuller, Alfred C.

Brute. Krulak, Victor H.

Bryan, William Jennings (1860–1925). Statesman and lecturer: **Silver-tongued Orator, Great Commoner, The Commoner.**

Bryant, Paul (born 1913). Football coach: **Bear.**

Bryn Mawr College. Educational institution; with six other women's colleges: **Seven Sisters.**

B-17. World War II bomber: **Flying Fortress.**

B-66. Bombing plane: **Destroyer.**

B-29. U.S. Air Force bomber, World War II: **Superfortress.**

Bubba. Phillips, John Melvin; Smith, Charles Aaron.

Bubber. Miley, James.

Bubbles. Hargrave, Eugene Franklin; Wilson, Imogene.

Buccieri, Fiore (1904–73). Gangster: **Fifi.**

Buchalsky, Isidore (active 1920–30). Gangster: **Izzy the Rat.**

Buchalter, Louis (1897–1944). Gangster: **Lepke, Judge Louis.**

Bucher, George (died 1923). Gangster: **Sport.**

Bucher, Helen (1905–72). Singer: **Indiana Songbird.**

Buchwald, Art[hur] (born 1925). Newspaper columnist: **Washington's Resident Humorist.**

Buck. Boucher, George; Clayton, Wilbur Dorsey; Freeman, John F.; Herzog, Charles Lincoln; Newsom, Louis Norman; O'Neil, John Francis; O'Neil, Frank J.; Shaw, Lawrence Timothy; Whittemore, Arthur; Washington, Ford Lee.

49

Buck, Frank (1884–1950). Animal hunter: **Bring 'Em Back Alive Buck.**

Buckduck. Mays, Willie [Howard].

Bucketfoot. Simmons, Al[oysius Harry].

Buckeye Bullet. Owens, Jesse.

Buckeye Division. Thirty-seventh Infantry Division.

Buckeyes. Athletic teams of Ohio State University, Columbus.

Buckeye State. Ohio.

Buckley, William F[rank], Jr. (born 1925). Newspaper columnist and author: **Conservative Columnist.**

Bucknell University, athletic teams of: **Bisons.**

Buck Private's Gary Cooper. MacArthur, Douglas.

Bucks. Tampa Bay Buccaneers.

Buckshot. Wright, Forrest Glenn.

Bucky. Fuller, R[ichard] Buckminster, [Jr.]; Harris, Stanley Raymond; Jordan, Baxter Byerly; Walters, William Henry.

Bucs. Pittsburgh Pirates.

Bucyk, Johnny (born 1935). Hockey player: **Chief.** Legal name: John Paul Bucyk.

Bud. Abbott, Burton W.; Foster, Harold; Haas, Oscar P.; Krogh, Egil, Jr.; Shank, Clifford Everett, Jr.; Smith, Wallace.

Buddy. Davis, Walt[er]; Lugar, John; O'Connor, Herbert William; Westmore, George H[amilton]; Young, Claude H.

Budge, [John] Don[ald] (born 1915). Tennis player: **Oakland Redhead.**

Buerger, John (1845–1927). Grain merchant: **Barley King.**

Buffalo. 1. Brewster F2A fighter plane, 1930s. 2. Jones, Charles Jesse.

Buffalo, New York. U.S. city: **Bison City, City of Trees, City to Canada, Flour City, Queen City of the Lakes.**

Buffalo Division. Ninety-second Infantry Division.

Buffaloes. Athletic teams of the University of Colorado, Boulder, and West Texas State University, Canyon.

Buffalo Plains State. Colorado.

Bug. General-purpose vehicle, World War II and after; jeep.

Cosmopolitan City. San Francisco, California.

Costanza, Margaret (born 1928). Politician and presidential aide: **Midge.**

Costello, Frank (1891–1973). Gambler and racketeer: **Prime Minister of the Underworld, The Politician.** Born: Francesco Saveria. Legal name: Francesco Castiglia.

Cotton. Adamson, Gary; Tierney, James Arthur; Warburton, Irvine E.

Cotton Belt. Cotton-raising area in the South, especially North and South Carolina, Georgia, Alabama, Mississippi, Arkansas, Louisiana, Oklahoma, and Texas.

Cotton Bowl. Football stadium in Dallas, Texas, site of annual Cotton Bowl college football game.

Cotton Center. Memphis, Tennessee.

Cotton Ed. Smith, Ellison DuRant.

Cotton Kingdom. Mississippi.

Cotton Plantation State. Alabama.

Cotton State. Alabama.

Cottonwood City, Leavenworth, Kansas.

Cottrell Louis (born 1911). Jazz drummer: **Old Man Cottrell.**

Coty American Fashion Critics Award. Award for fashion design: **Winnie.**

Cougars. Athletic teams of Brigham Young University, Provo, Utah; the University of Houston, Houston, Texas; and Washington State University, Pullman.

Coughlan, John Joseph (1860–1938). Chicago politician: **Bathhouse John, The Bath.**

Coughlin, Charles Edward (born 1891). Roman Catholic priest and radio speaker: **Radio Priest, Silo Charlie.**

Cougs. Cogdill, Gail R.

Coulon, Johnny (born 1889). Bantamweight boxer: **Chicago Spider.**

Coulter, DeWitt (active 1946–52). Football tackle: **Tex.**

Count. Orsi, John F.

Count, The. Basie, Count.

Count Fleet (active 1943). Racehorse: **Old Zeke.**

Country. Graham, Bonnie; Slaughter, Enos Bradsher; Warnecke, Lonnie; Washburne, Joseph.

Cournoyer, Yvan [Serge] (born 1943). Canadian hockey player: **The Roadrunner.**

Courteous Capital City. Harrisburg, Pennsylvania.

Court House. Lee, John Clifford Hodges.

Court Jouster. Tilden, Bill.

Courtney, Clint[on Dawson] (1927–75). Baseball catcher: **Scrap Iron.**

Cousin Ern. Ford, Ernest Jennings.

Cousy, Bob (born 1928). Basketball player and coach: **Cooz, Houdini of the Hardwood.** Legal name: Robert Joseph Cousy.

Couzens, James (1872–1936). U.S. Senator from Michigan and businessman: **Croesus of the Senate, Poor Man's Friend.**

Couzin Dud. LeBlanc, Dudley J.

Coveleski, Harry Frank (1886–1950). Baseball pitcher: **Giant Killer.** Legal name: Harry Frank Kowalewski.

Cowan, Sarah (1904?–74). Prostitute: **Baby Doll, Queen of the Prostitutes.**

Cowan, Thomas H. (1884?–1969). Radio announcer: **Radio's First Announcer.**

Cowboy Capital. Dodge City, Kansas.

Cowboy Carl. Hatch, Carl Atwood.

Cowboy Jack. Lanza, John.

Cowboy Jess. Willard, Jess.

Cowboy Philosopher. Rogers, Will.

Cowboys. Athletic teams of McNeese State University, Lake Charles, Louisiana; Oklahoma State University, Stillwater; and the University of Wyoming, Laramie.

Cowboy Senator, The. Ashurst, Henry Fountain.

Cowboy State. Wyoming.

Cow Capital. Wichita, Kansas.

Cow Cow. Davenport, Charles.

Cowens, Dave (born 1948). Basketball center: **Boston's First Perpetual Motion Machine.**

Cowtown. Fort Worth, Texas.

Cow Town of the South. Montgomery, Alabama.

Cox, Archibald (born 1912). Lawyer and politician: **Blabbermouth, Mr. Impeccable.**

Coyotes. Athletic teams of the University of South Dakota, Vermillion.

Coyote State. South Dakota.

Cozy. Cole, William [Randolph].

Crab. Evers, John Joseph; Warhop, John Milton.

Crab Bait. Miller, William Mosley.

Crabtown. Annapolis, Maryland; Hampton, Virginia.

Crack-down Czar of the N.R.A. Johnson, Hugh Samuel.

Crack-down Johnson. Johnson, Hugh Samuel.

Cracker. 1. Rural native or resident of Georgia or Florida. 2. Schalk, Raymond William.

Cracker State. Georgia.

Cradle of American Industry. Paterson, New Jersey.

Cradle of American Liberty. Old State House, Philadelphia, Pennsylvania.

Cradle of Aviation. Dayton, Ohio.

Cradle of Georgia. Savannah, Georgia.

Cradle of Liberty. Concord, Massachusetts; Faneuil Hall (Boston); Lexington, Massachusetts; Philadelphia, Pennsylvania.

Cradle of Naval Aviation. Pensacola, Florida.

Cradle of Texas Liberty. San Antonio, Texas.

Cradle of the American Revolution. Philadelphia, Pennsylvania.

Cradle of the American Union. Albany, New York.

Cradle of the Confederacy. Montgomery, Alabama.

Cradle of the Steel Industry. Johnstown, Pennsylvania.

Cramer, Roger Maxwell (born 1906). Baseball coach: **Doc.**

Cranberry. Gifford, Charles L.

Crandall, James Otis (1887–1951). Baseball pitcher: **Doc.**

Crape Myrtle City. Jackson, Mississippi.

Crash. Allen, Dick.

Crater, Joseph Force (1889–c. 1930). Judge: **Vanished Judge.**

Cravath, Clifford Carlton (1881–1963). Baseball outfielder: **Gavvy.**

Crawfish Town. New Orleans, Louisiana.

Crawford, Benny Ross, Jr. (born 1934). Jazz musician and composer: **Hank.**

Crawford, Clifford Rankin (born 1902). Baseball first and second baseman: **Pat.**

Crawford, Holland R. (born 1924). Jazz guitarist. **Ray.**

Crawford, Samuel Earl (1880–1968). Baseball outfielder and first baseman: **Wahoo Sam.**

Crawthumper. Native or resident of Maryland.

Crazy Fatso. Casper, Billy.

Crazy Guggenheim. Fontaine, Frank.

Crazy Joe. Gallo, Joseph.

Crazylegs. Hirsch, Elroy.

Cream City. Milwaukee, Wisconsin.

Creek, The. Oil-producing region of western Pennsylvania.

CREEP. Committee for the Re-election of the President [Richard M. Nixon], 1971–72.

Crenshaw, Benjamin (born 1952). Golfer: **Gentle Ben.**

Creole Fashion Plate. Norman, Karyl.

Creole State. Louisiana.

Crescent City. New Orleans, Louisiana.

Crimson. Athletic teams of Harvard University, Cambridge, Massachusetts.

Crimson Tide. Athletic teams of the University of Alabama, University.

Criqui, Eugene (born 1893). Featherweight boxer: **Wounded Wonder.**

Crisler, Fritz (born 1899). Football coach: **Football Statesman, The Lord.** Legal name: Herbert Orrin Crisler.

Crisp, Henry (1896–1970). Football scout and athletic coach: **One-armed Scout.**

Crockett, John C. (1864–1952). U.S. Senate reading clerk: **Uncle John.**

Crocodile, The. Harriman, [William] Averell.

Croesus of the Senate. Couzens, James.

Cromwell. Tourbillon, Robert Arthur.

Cronkite, Walter [Leland, Jr.] (born 1916). News commentator: **Uncle Walter.**

Crooner, The. Vallee, Rudy.

Crooning Troubadour. Lucas, Nick.

Crosby, Bing (1904–77). Singer and motion-picture actor: **Der Bingle, The Groaner, Old Dad.** Legal name: Harry Lillis Crosby.

Crosby, William R. (1866–1939). Trapshooter: **Tobacco Bill.**

Cross, Wilbur [Lucius] (1862–1948). Governor of Connecticut: **Uncle Toby.**

Crosseyed Comedian. Turpin, Ben[jamin].

Cross of Lorraine Division. Seventy-ninth Infantry Division.

Crossroads City. El Paso, Texas.

Crossroads of America. Indiana.

Crossroads of Connecticut. Waterbury, Connecticut.

Crossroads of the Pacific. Honolulu, Hawaii.

Crossroads State. New Jersey.

Crothers, Sherman (born 1910). Jazz musician and comedian: **Scat Man.**

Crouch, Jack Albert (born 1905). Baseball player: **Roxey.**

Crow, Floyd (active 1910–60). Football player and scout: **Jim.**

Crowder, Alvin Floyd (1899–1972). Baseball pitcher: **General.**

Crowley, Francis (1911–31). Bank robber: **Game Kid, Two Gun Crowley.**

Crowley, Jim (born 1902). Football halfback, coach, and professional league official: **Sleepy Jim.** With other members of Notre Dame backfield: **Four Horsemen.** Legal name: James H. Crowley.

Crown City. Pasadena, California.

Crown Prince. McAdoo, William Gibbs.

Crown Prince of the New Deal. Roosevelt, James.

Cruising Crooner. Owens, Jack.

Crum, William J. (active c. 1970). Businessman: **Money King of Saigon.**

Crump, Edward Hull (1875–1954). Politician: **Boss Crump.**

Crusaders. Athletic teams of the College of the Holy Cross, Worcester, Massachusetts.

Crystal City. Corning, New York.

Crystal Hills. White Mountains, New Hampshire.

Csonka, Larry (born 1946). Football fullback: **Lawnmower, Zonk.** Legal name: Lawrence Richard Csonka.

Cub. Teagarden, Clois Lee.

Cubitt, Tanya (born 1917). Dancer and nudist: **Queen of the Nudists.** Born: Florence Cubitt.

Cuddles. Sakall, S. Z.

Cugat, Xavier (born 1900). Musician: **Cugie.**

Cugie. Cugat, Xavier.

Cujo. Wolfe, William.

Culbertson, Ely (1891–1955). Bridge authority: **Contract's Greatest Player.**

Cullen, Hugh Troy (born 1881). Oil entrepreneur: **King of the Texas Wildcatters.**

Cullop, Norman Andrew (1887–1961). Baseball pitcher: **Nick.**

Cultivated Catfish. Brown, James.

Cultural Center of the West. San Francisco, California.

Cultured Perelman. Shulman, Max.

Cumberland River City. Nashville, Tennessee.

cummings, e. e. (1894–1962). Poet: **Lower Case Cummings, Magic Maker.** Legal name: Edward Estlin Cummings.

Cummings, William Arthur (1848–1924). Baseball pitcher and outfielder: **Candy, Father of the Curve Ball.**

Cumpanas, Ana (1889–1947). Woman who lured John Dillinger into a police trap: **Woman in Red.** Also known as Anna Sage.

Cunningham, Billy (born 1943). Basketball forward: **Kangaroo.**

Cunningham, Claude C. (1873–1953). Showman and presidential candidate: **Doc.**

Cupe. Black, Clinton Rutherford, Jr.

Cupid. Childs, Clarence Algernon; Spears, Clarence Wiley.

Curley, James Michael (1874–1958). Boston politician and U.S. Representative from Massachusetts: **Boss Curley.**

Curly. Byrd, Harry Clifton; Lambeau, Earl L.; Russell, Dillon.

Curmudgeon. Ickes, Harold LeClaire.

Curran, Joseph E[dwin] (born 1906). Labor leader: **Fo'c'sle Joe.**

Curtis, Charles (1860–1936). U.S. Vice President: **Big Chief.**

Curtiss, Glenn Hammond (1878–1930). Developer and builder of aircraft: **Sky-storming Yankee.**

Custer Division. Eighty-fifth Infantry Division.

Cut-Rate Carpenter. Carpenter, Terry McGovern.

Cut-Rate Showman. Todd, Michael.

Cutshall, Robert [Dewees] (1911–68). Jazz trombonist: **Cutty.**

Cutten, Arthur W. (1870–1936). Speculator: **King of the Grain Dealers.**

Cutting, Bronson (1888–1935). U.S. Senator from New Mexico: **Harvard's Gift to the West.**

Cutty. Cutshall, Robert [Dewees].

Cuy. Cuyler, Hazen Shirley.

Cuyler, Hazen Shirley (1899–1950). Baseball outfielder: **Cuy, Kiki.**

Cy. Blanton, Darrell Elijah; Falkenbert, Frederick Peter; Moore, William Wilcy; Morgan, Harry Richard; Pfirman, Charles H.; Young, Denton True.

Cyclone. Haines, William C.; Thompson, John.

Cyclone Division. Thirty-eighth Infantry Division.

Cyclone Louie. Lewis, Vach.

Cyclones. Athletic teams of Iowa State University, Ames.

Cyclone State. Kansas.

Czar, The. Nixon, Richard M[ilhous].

Czar of American Baseball. Landis, Kenesaw Mountain.

Czar of Baseball. Landis, Kenesaw Mountain.

Czar of Steel. Carnegie, Andrew.

Czar of the District. Blanton, Thomas Lindsay.

Czar of the Liquor Industry. Morgan, William Forbes.

Czar of the National Pastime. Landis, Kenesaw Mountain.

Czar of the New York Underworld. Rothstein, Arnold.

Czar of the White Light District. Becker, Charles.

Czar Reed. Reed, Thomas Brackett.

Czech Bethlehem. Racine, Wisconsin.

D

Dad. Joiner, Columbus H.; Meachum, James H.; Roberts, Theodore.
Daddy. Edwards, Eddie; Grace, Charles Manuel; Woods, Frank.
Daddy Browning. Browning, Edward.
Daddy Long Arms. Conley, Donald [Eu]gene.
Daddy Longlegs. McAdoo, William Gibbs.
Daddy Wags. Wagner, Leon Lamar.
Daffy. Dean, Paul Dee.
Dagmar. Egnor, Virginia Ruth.
Dago. San Diego, California.
Dago, The. Sinatra, Frank.
Dago Frank. Cirofici, Frank.
Dago Lawrence. Mangano, Lawrence.
Dago Mike. Carozzo, Michael.
Da Grosa, John (1902–53). Football player and coach: **Ox.**
Dahl, Percival Rollo (born 1919). Football player: **Kewpie.**
Dahlen, William Frederick (1871–1950). Baseball shortstop: **Bad Bill.**
Dahlgren, Ellsworth Tenney (born 1912). Baseball first baseman:
  Babe.
Dainty Baby June, the Pocket-sized Pavlova. Havoc, June.
Dainty Dotty. Jensen, Mrs. Owen.
Dakoming. North Dakota, South Dakota, and Wyoming.
Dakotas. North and South Dakota.
Dale the Super. Carnegie, Dale.

Daley, Richard Joseph (1902–1976). Mayor of Chicago: **The Boss, Last of the Big-City Bosses, Strong-willed Mayor.**

Dallas, Texas. U.S. city: **Big D; All-American Town.**

Dallas Chapparrals. Basketball team in Dallas, Texas: **Chaps.**

Damrosch, Walter [Johannes] (1862–1950). Orchestra conductor and commentator: **Dean of American Music.**

Dancing Fool. McAdoo, William Gibbs.

Dancing Master. Corbett, James John.

Dandolos, Nicholas Andrea (1886–1966). Gambler: **Nick the Greek.**

Dandy of Country Music. Dean, Jimmy Ray.

Danish Capital of the United States. Racine, Wisconsin.

Danning, Harry (born 1911). Baseball catcher: **The Horse.**

Danny D. DiLiberto, Danny.

Danowski, Edward (active 1933). Football player: **Big Ed.**

Dapper. Tourbillon, Robert Arthur.

Dapper Dan. Flood, Daniel J.

D'Aquino, Iva Ikuko Toguri (born 1916). American-born radio propagandist for the Japanese, World War II: **Tokyo Rose.**

Daring Young Man of Wall Street. Young, Robert Ralph.

Dark, Al[vin Ralph] (born 1923). Baseball shortstop: **Blackie, Bright Star of the Boston Braves.**

Dark and Bloody Ground. Kentucky.

Dark Angel of the Violin. South, Eddie.

Dark Destroyer, Louis, Joe.

Dark Horse Candidate. Harding, Warren G[amaliel].

Dark Strangler. Wilson, Roger.

Darling, Jay N. (1876–1962). Political cartoonist: **Ding.**

Darling of the Air. Rose Marie, Baby.

Darling of the Gods. Bankhead, Tallulah [Brockman].

Darrow, Clarence [Seward] (1857–1938). Criminal lawyer, writer, and lecturer: **Defender of the People, Old Lion, Partisan of the Unpopular, Pessimist with Hope.**

D'Artagnan of the AEF. MacArthur, Douglas.

Dartmouth College. 1. Athletic teams of: **Big Green.** 2. Athletic teams of, with seven other teams in college conference: **Ivy League.**

Daugherty, Harry [Micajah] (1860–1941). Politician and U.S. Attorney General: **Foxy Harry, Handsome Harry.**

Dauss, George August (1889–1963). Baseball pitcher: **Hooks.**

Davenport, Charles (1895–1955). Jazz pianist, composer, and singer: **Cow Cow.**

Davenport, Iowa. U.S. city: **City of Beauty, Queen City.** With Moline, East Moline, and Rock Island, Illinois: **Quad Cities.**

Davidson, Jo (1883–1952). Sculptor: **Dean of American Sculptors, Plastic Historian.**

Davis, Angela [Yvonne] (born 1944). Educator and revolutionary: Angela the Red, Enigmatic Angela.

Davis, Dwight F. (1879–1945). Politician and tennis player: **Father of the Davis Cup.**

Davis, Eddie (born 1921). Jazz saxophonist: **Lockjaw.**

Davis, Evelyn Y. (born 1929). Critic of corporate officers at annual stockholder meetings: **Corporate Gadfly.**

Davis Francis W. (1887–1978). Inventor: **Father of Power Steering.**

Davis, Frank Talmadge (1890–1944). Baseball pitcher: **Dixie.**

Davis, Garry (born 1921). Reformer: **World Citizen Number One.**

Davis, George Willis (born 1902). Baseball outfielder: **Kiddo.**

Davis, Glenn W. (born 1924). Football back: **Junior, Mr. Outside.**

Davis, Harry Albert (born 1910). Baseball first baseman: **Stinky.**

Davis, Harry P[hillips] (1868–1931). Radio innovator: **Father of Radio Broadcasting.**

Davis, James John (1873–1947). U.S. Senator from Pennsylvania: **Puddler Jim, Welsh Parson.**

Davis, Joan (1912–61). Actress and comedienne: **World's Funniest Woman.** Born: Madonna Josephine Davis.

Davis, John William (1873–1955). Lawyer and politician: **Mr. Lawyer.**

Davis, Meyer (1895–1976). Orchestra leader: **Millionaire Maestro.**

Davis, Richard J. (1904–1970). Criminal lawyer. **Dixie.**

Davis, Sammy, Jr. (born 1925). Entertainer, television personality, and actor: **Candy Man, Mr. Wonderful.**

Davis, Virgil Lawrence (born 1904). Baseball catcher: **Spud.**

Davis, Walt[er] (born 1931). High jumper and basketball player: **Buddy, Sweet D.**

Davis, William Strethen (born 1918). Jazz musician: **Wild Bill.**

Davis, Willie (born 1940). Baseball outfielder: **Comet.** Legal name: William Henry Davis.

Davison, William (born 1906). Jazz cornetist: **Wild Bill.**

Dawes, Charles Gates (1865–1951). Financier, soldier, and U.S. Vice President: **Hell and Maria Dawes.**

Dawkins, Daryl (born 1954). Basketball player: **Earthquake.**

Day, Clarence Henry (born 1901). Canadian hockey defenseman and team manager: **Hap, Happy.**

Day, Doris (born 1924). Singer and motion-picture actress: **Girl We Would Like to Take a Slow Boat Back to the States With, Golden Tonsil, Prettiest Three-Million-Dollar Corporation with Freckles in America, Tomboy with the Voice.** Born: Doris von Kappelhoff.

Day, Laraine (born 1920). Actress; wife of Leo Durocher: **First Lady of Baseball.** Born: La Raine Johnson.

Day-old Chick. Wene, Elmer H.

Dayton, Ohio. U.S. city: **Birthplace of Aviation, Cash Register City, Cradle of Aviation, Gem City.**

Dayton, University of, athletic teams of: **Flyers.**

Daytona Beach, Florida. U.S. city: **Florida's Vacation Capital.**

Dazzy. Vance, Clarence Arthur.

D-Day. 1. Day set for the beginning of a planned attack. 2. June 6, 1944, day on which the Allied invasion of Normandy, France, began. Also known as The Longest Day.

Deac. Aylesworth, Merlin Hall.

Deacon. McGuire, James Thomas; Moore, Carl; Phillippe, Charles Louis; Scott, L. Everett.

Deadeye Division. Ninety-sixth Infantry Division.

Dead Man's Hill. Center of fighting at the second battle of Verdun, France, World War I, 1916.

Deadwood Dick. Clarke, Richard W.

Dean, James (1931–55). Motion-picture actor: **Father of Rock Culture.** Born: James Byron.

Dean, Jay Hanna (1911–74). Baseball pitcher and sports announcer: **Dizzy, The Great Man, Ol' Diz.** Also known as Jerome Herman Dean.

Dean, Jimmy Ray (born 1928). Singer: **Dandy of Country Music.**

Dean, John, III (born 1938). Presidential adviser and defendant in the Watergate case: **Mr. Clean, Secret-Sharer, Watergate Defendant.**

Dean, Paul Dee (born 1913). Baseball pitcher: **Daffy.**

Dean, The. Goldberg, Rube.

DeAngelis, Anthony (born 1916). Commodity speculator and pork packer: **Salad Oil King, Tino.**

Dean of American Dramatic Critics. Mantle, Robert Burns.

Dean of American Governors. Rockefeller, Nelson [Aldrich].

Dean of American Music. Damrosch, Walter Johannes.

Dean of American Poetry. Markham, Edwin.

Dean of American Popular Music. Whiteman, Paul.

Dean of American Reporters. White, Theodore H[arold].

Dean of American Sculptors. Davidson, Jo.

Dean of American Trainers. Fitzsimmons, James Edward.

Dean of America's Show Music Composers. Kern, Jerome David.

Dean of Boxing Writers. Fleischer, Nat[haniel S.].

Dean of Commentators. Kaltenborn, H[ans] V[on].

Dean of Community Advertising. Hatfield, Charles Folsom.

Dean of Petroleum Analysts. Levy, Walter James.

Dean of Petroleum Consultants. Levy, Walter James.

Dean of the American Stage. Skinner, Otis.

Dean of the American Theater. Skinner, Otis.

Dean of Theatrical Criticism. Nathan, George Jean.

Dean of the Con Men. Skyowski, Abram.

Dean of the House. Sabath, Adolph Joachim.

Dean of the Liberals. Norris, George William.

Dean of Washington Correspondents. Sullivan, Mark.

Dean of Women Authors of America. Tarbell, Ida Minerva.

Deany. O'Banion, Dion.

Dear Alben. Barkley, Alben William.

Dearborn, Michigan. U.S. city: **City of Advantages.**

Death House Reilly. Reilly, Edward J.

Death Row Jeff. Jefferson, Cliff[ord].

Death Valley Scotty. Scott, Walter Edwin, Jr.

Death Watch. Clique of influential playgoers, New York, early 20th century.

De Bakey, Michael Ellis (born 1918). Surgeon and heart specialist: **The Texas Tornado.**

Decade's Arch Villain. Fall, Albert Bacon.

DeCarlo, Angelo (1902–73). Mafia chieftain: **Gyp.**

Dede. Pierce, Joseph de Lacrois.

Dedicated Gambler, The. Rothstein, Arnold.

Dee Cee. Washington, D.C.

Dee Jays. Agents of the Department of Justice, especially of the Federal Bureau of Investigation.

Deep-Freeze Woman. Anderson, Dorothy May Stevens.

Deep South. South Carolina, Georgia, Florida, Alabama, Mississippi, Louisiana, Arkansas, and Texas.

Deep Throat. Unknown official of the Nixon administration during the Watergate affair who leaked confidential information to the press.

Deerfoot. Milan, Jesse Clyde.

Defender of the People. Darrow, Clarence [Seward].

De Forest, Lee (1873–1961). Inventor: **Father of Radio.**

De Freeze, Donald David (1944?–74). Criminal, revolutionary, and member of the Symbionese Liberation Army: **Cinque.**

Dehner, Lou[is] (born 1914). Basketball player: **Pick.**

Deke. Slayton, Donald Kent.

Delaware. First U.S. state: **Blue Hen State, Diamond State, First State, Uncle Sam's Pocket Handkerchief.** With Maryland and Virginia: **Del-Mar-Va, Delmarva.**

Delaware, University of, athletic teams of: **Fightin' Blue Hens.**

De Leath, Vaughn (1896–1943). Singer: **Original Radio Girl.**

Deliberate Pedant. Eliot, T[homas] S[tearns].

Delightful Land. Maryland.

Del-Mar-Va. Delaware, Maryland, and Virginia. Also **Delmarva.**

De Lorenzo, Frank (1914–53). Labor leader: **Biffo.**

Delta Dart. General Dynamics F-106 interceptor-fighter plane.

De Marco, Pat (born 1928). Lightweight boxer: **Paddy.**

Dem Bums. Brooklyn Dodgers.

De Mille, Cecil B[lount] (1881–1959). Motion-picture and radio producer and director: **CB.**

Democrat Albatross. Kennedy, Edward M[oore].

Demoisey, John (born 1912). Basketball player: **Frenchy.**

Demon Deacons. Athletic teams of Wake Forest University, Winston-Salem, North Carolina.

Demon of Death Valley. Manson, Charles M.

Demons. Athletic teams of Northwestern State University, Natchitoches, Louisiana.

DeMoss, Elwood (1889–1965). Baseball player: **Bingo.**

Dempsey, Jack (born 1895). Heavyweight boxer: **The Champ, Jack the Giant Killer, Kid Blackie, The Manassa Mauler, Mighty Jack, The Thor of the Ring.** Born: William Harrison Dempsey.

Denver, Colorado. U.S. city: **Convention City, City of the Plains, Gateway to the Rockies, Mile-High City.**

Denver Nightingale. Murray, William.

Denver of South Dakota. Rapid City, South Dakota.

Depew, Chauncey Mitchell (1834–1928). Railroad executive and politician: **The Peach.**

De Pow, Johnny (active 1888–1921). Chicago politician: **Prince of Boodlers.** Legal name: John Powers.

Der Bingle. Crosby, Bing.

Derby City. Louisville, Kentucky.

Derby Kid, The. Thomas, Alvin Clarence.

De Rose, Peter (1900–53). Radio entertainer and songwriter. With May Singhi Breen: **Sweethearts of the Air.**

Derrick City. Oil City, Pennsylvania.

Derringer, Samuel Paul (born 1906). Baseball pitcher: **Duke.**

Des Allemands. Fishing village near New Orleans, Louisiana: **Catfish Capital of the World.**

DeSalvo, Albert Henry (born 1932). Murderer of at least 13 women, active in Boston 1962–64: **Boston Strangler, Green Man, Measuring Man.**

De Sapio, Carmine (born c. 1908). Democratic political boss: **The Bishop, Boss, Last of the Great New York Bosses.**

Deseret State. Utah.

Desert and Prairie Painter. O'Keeffe, Georgia.

Desert Fox. Snowden, Fred.

Des Moines, Iowa. U.S. city: **City of Certainties.**

Desperate Dan. Dillinger, John Herbert.

Despoiler of Public Lands. Lane, Franklin Knight.

Destroyer. B-66 bombing plane.

Destroyer Deal. Grant of 50 destroyers to Great Britain, September 1940, in return for a lease or grant of a chain of military bases in British territories in the Western Hemisphere.

Destroyer of the League of Nations. Lodge, Henry Cabot.

Detroit, Michigan. U.S. city: **Automobile City, Automobile City of the World, City of the Straits, Fordtown, Mo City, Motor Town, Motown.**

Detroiter. Any of various Stinson airliners, 1926–29.

Detroit of the West. Oakland, California.

Detroit Red. Malcolm X.

Devastator. Douglas TBD torpedo plane, World War II.

Devil Dogs. United States Marine Corps.

Devil in Deerskins. Belany, George Stansfield.

Dewey, John (1859–1952). Philosopher: **Father of Modern Education.**

Diablos. Athletic teams of Los Angeles State University, Los Angeles, California.

Diamond, Jack (1896–1931). Racketeer: **Clay Pigeon, Legs.** Born: John Thomas Noland. Also known as John Hart and John Higgins.

Diamond Dick. Tanner, Richard J.

Diamond Horseshoe. Two lowermost tiers of boxes in the former Metropolitan Opera House, New York City.

Diamond Jim. Brady, James Buchanan.

Diamond Lil. West, Mae.

Diamond State. Arkansas; Delaware.

Diamond Street. Forty-seventh Street, New York City.

Diamond Tooth Lil. Orstein, Honora; Prado, Katie.

Dick the Bruiser. Afflis, Richard.

Dictator of Jersey City. Hague, Frank.

Dictator of Louisiana. Long, Huey [Pierce].

Diefenbaker, John George (1895–1979). Canadian Prime Minister: **Dief the Chief.**

Dief the Chief. Diefenbaker, John George.

Dieterle, Wilhelm (born 1893). Motion-picture director and producer: **Hollywood Plutarch.**

Dietz, William H. (1886?–1964). Football guard and coach: **Lone Star.**

DiGiovanna, Charles (1930–58). Baseball bat boy: **The Brow.**

DiLiberto, Danny (born 1936). Billiard and pool player: **Danny D.**

Dillinger, John [Herbert] (1902–34). Outlaw: **Desperate Dan, Kill Crazy Dillinger, Public Enemy Number One.**

Dillon, Jack (1891–1942). Lightheavyweight boxer: **Jack the Giant Killer.** Born: Earnest Cutler Price.

DiMag. DiMaggio, Joe.

DiMaggio, Joe (born 1914). Baseball outfielder: **Big Guy, DiMag, Joe D, Joltin' Joe, Yankee Clipper.** Legal name: Joseph Paul DiMaggio, Jr.

Dimple of the Universe. Nashville, Tennessee.

Ding. Darling, Jay N.

Dingbat. Oberta, John.

Dingell, John David (1894–1955). U.S. Representative from Michigan: **Owski, Witz.**

Dinger. Sanders, Homer J. II.

Dink. Rickard, Tex; Templeton, Robert L.

Dink, The. Kenna, Michael.

Dinty. Moore, James H.

Dio, Johnny. Dioguardi, John.

Dioguardi, John (1914–79). Racketeer. **Dio, Johnny.**

Dionne, Marcel Elphege (born 1951). Hockey forward: **Little Beaver.**

Dipsy Doodler. Clinton, Larry.

Dirk. Dirksen, Everett McKinley.

Dirksen, Everett McKinley (1896–1969). U.S. Senator from Illinois: **Dirk, Distillery King, Wizard of Ooze.**

Disc Jockey. Radio or television announcer who conducts program of recorded music. **DJ.**

Disco Sally. Lippman, Sally.

Dismal Swamp City. Norfolk, Virginia.

Disney, Walt[er Elias] (1901–66). Cartoonist and motion-picture producer: **Engineer of Fantasy.**

Disney, Wesley Ernest (1883–1961). U.S. Representative from Oklahoma: **Pipeline Disney.**

Disraeli of the Chiefs of Staff. MacArthur, Douglas.

Distillery King. Dirksen, Everett McKinley.

Disturber of the Peace. Mencken H[enry] L[ouis].

Ditch, The. Panama Canal.

Ditmars, Raymond Lee (1876–1942). Naturalist and author: **The Snake Man.**

Divine One, The. Vaughan, Sarah.

Dixie. 1. Davis, Frank Talmadge; Davis, Richard J.; Howell, Millard; Walker, Fred[erick E.]; Warnecke, Lonnie. 2. Southern United States, esp. east of the Mississippi River.

Dixiecrat. Southern U.S. Democrat disagreeing with national party policy in 1948 election.

Dixie Division. Thirty-first Infantry Division.

Dixie Kid. Brown, Aaron L.

Dixon, George (1870–1909). Canadian bantamweight and featherweight boxer: **Little Chocolate.**

Dizzy. Dean, Jay Hanna; Gillespie, John [Birks]; Reece, Al[phonso Son]; Trout, Raul Howard.

DJ. 1. Agent of the Federal Bureau of Investigation (U.S. Department of Justice); 2. Disc Jockey.

Doaker, The. Walker, [Ewell] Doak, [Jr.].

Dobie, Gil[mour] (1879–1948). Football player and coach: **Gloomy, Magnificent Skeptic.**

Doble, Abner (died 1961). Inventor: **Father of the Modern Steam Automobile.**

Doc. Ayers, Yancy W[yatt]; Carlson, Henry C[lifford]; Casey, Edward L.; Cramer, Roger Maxwell; Crandall, James Otis; Cunningham, Claude C.; Farrell, Edward Stephen; Hayes, E. O.; Johnston, Wheeler Rogers; Kearns, Jack; Lawson, Andrew Cowper; Meanwell, Walter E.; Phillips, Arthur Osborne; Prothro, James Thompson; Spears, Clarence Wiley; Winner, Charles.

Dock. Barker, Arthur.

Doctor Who Would Not Die. Trudeau, Edward Livingston.

Doc Townsend of Florida. Hendricks, Joseph Edward.

Documentary Photographer. Stieglitz, Alfred.

Dodds, Gilbert Lothair (born 1918). Minister, track star, and coach: **Flying Parson.**

Dodds, Warren (1898–1959). Jazz drummer: **Baby.**

Dode. Birmingham, Joseph Leo; Paskert, George Henry.

Dodge City, Kansas. U.S. town: **Cowboy Capital, Queen of the Cow Towns.**

Dodo. Marmarosa, Michael.

Dog, The. Turner, Clyde Douglas.

Doggie. Julian, Alvin F.

Dogwood City. Atlanta, Georgia.

Dole, James Drummond (1877–1958). Pineapple grower and packer: **Hawaiian Pineapple King.**

Dollar. Brand, Adolf Johannes.

Dollar Diplomacy. U.S. government policy of supporting special business interests in foreign countries.

Dollar John. Langer, John

Dolly. Gray, Sam[uel David]; Morse, Alfreda Theodora Strandberg; Sinatra, Natalie.

Dolo. Coker, Charles Mitchell.

Domino, Antoine (born 1928). Pianist and singer: **Fats.**

Don. Byas, Carlos [Wesley]; Cameron, Gregory Duncan.

Donald Duck. Barley, Donald Orlando.

Donic. Bush, Owen Joseph.

Donna. Fox. John J.

Donnelly, Theodore (1912–1958). Jazz trombonist: **Muttonleg.**

Donovan, Patrick Joseph (1865–1953). Baseball outfielder and manager: **Patsy.**

Donovan, William Joseph (1882–1959). U.S. Army Major General: **Wild Bill.**

Don Quixote. Unterberg, David.

Don Vitone. Genovese, Vito.

Dooin, Charles S[ebastian] (1879–1952). Baseball catcher and manager: **Red.**

Doorman of the Western Hemisphere. Whalen, Grover [Aloysius].

Dorais, Charles E. (1891–1954). Football quarterback and coach: **Gus.**

Dornhoefer, Gary (born 1943). Hockey player: **Dorny.**

Dorny. Dornhoefer, Gary.

Dorsey, Tommy (1905–56). Jazz musician, trombonist, and trumpet player: **The Setimental Gentleman of Swing.** Legal name: Thomas Francis Dorsey, Jr.

Dos. Dos Passos, John.

Dos Passos, John (1896–1970). Novelist and playwright: **Dos.** Born: John Rodrigo Madison.

Dots. Miller, John Barney.

Double No-Hit Kid. Vander Meer, John [Samuel].

Double X. Foxx, James Emory.

Doughboy's General. Bradley, Omar Nelson.

Douglas, Philip Brooks (1890–1952). Baseball pitcher: **Shufflin' Phil.**

Dour Scot. Sutherland, John Bain.

Dowell, Horace Kirby (born 1904). Jazz saxophonist and composer: **Saxie.**

Down East. 1. Maine. 2. Eastern coast of New England and Nova Scotia.

Down-Easter. 1. Native or resident of Maine. 2. Native or resident of the eastern coast of New England or Nova Scotia.

Down East State. Maine.

Downey, Morton (born 1902). Singer: **Irish Thrush.**

Downtown Connectors. Atlanta Flames' hockey line of Eric Vail, Willi Plett, and Tom Lysiak.

Dragonette, Jessica (active 1930s). Singer: **The Coca-Cola Girl, Little Angel of Radio.**

Dragon Lady. Wheeler, Helen Rippier.

Dragon Lady of Broadway. Wong, Pearl.

Dragons. Athletic teams of Moorhead State University, Moorhead, Minnesota.

Drake University, athletic teams of: **Bulldogs.**

Dr. Charlie. Mayo, Charles Horace.

Dream Singer. Kirbery, Ralph.

Dreiser, Theodore (1871–1945). Novelist: **Our Bitter Patriot.**

Dressler, Marie (1869–1933). Actress: **Grand Old Lady of the Movies, Old Trouper, Queen Marie of Hollywood.** Born: Leila Koerber.

Dr. Foghorn. Allen, Forrest Claire.

Dribblepuss. Lehr, Lew.

Driscoll, John Leo (1896–1968). Football back: **Paddy.**

Driving Force. Roosevelt, Theodore.

Dr. J. Erving, Julius.

Dr. Jazz. Zeitlin, Dennis.

Dr. No. Brown, Harold.

Drootin, Ben[jamin] (born 1920). Jazz drummer: **Buzzy.**

Dr. Rock. Schmitt, Jack.

Drummond [James] Roscoe (born 1902). Journalist: **Bulldog.**

Druze, Johnny (active 1930s). Football player. With other members of Fordham Team: **Seven Blocks of Granite.**

Dr. Will. Mayo, William James.

Dry Messiah. Cannon, James.

Dry Wind. Guyer, Ulysses Samuel.

Dual Cities. Minneapolis and St. Paul, Minnesota.

Dubofsky, Maurice (active 1929–31). Football guard: **Mush.**

Dubs, Adolph (1920–79). U.S. State Department official and ambassador: **Spike.**

Dubuque, Iowa. U.S. city: **Heidelberg of America, Key City.**

Duchess, The. Harding, Florence Kling DeWolfe; Spinelli, Ethel Leta Juanita.

Duchin, Eddie (1909–51). Jazz pianist: **Magic Fingers of Radio.** Legal name: Edwin Frank Duchin.

Duckboard. Butler, Smedley Darlington.

Duckie. Medwick, Joseph Michael.

Duckie Wuckie. Medwick, Joseph Michael.

Ducks. Athletic teams of the University of Oregon, Eugene.

Duffy. Lewis, George Edward.

Duffy, William J. (1883–1952). Speakeasy operator: **Big Bill.**

Dugout Doug. MacArthur, Douglas.

Duke. Derringer, Samuel Paul; Jordan, Irving Sidney; Markell, Harry [Duquesne]; Pearson, Columbus Calvin, Jr.; Slater, Fred[erick E.]; Wayne, John.

Duke, Doris (born 1912). Society glamour girl, 1930s. With Barbara Hutton: **The Gold Dust Twins, Poor Little Rich Girls.**

Duke, The. Cooney, Dennis; Ellington, Duke; Wayne, John.

Duke City. Albuquerque, New Mexico.

Duke E. Ellington, Duke.

Duke of Brooklyn. Snider, Duke.

Duke of Tralee. Bresnahan, Roger Philip.

Duke University, athletic teams of: **Blue Devils.**

Dulles, John Foster (1888–1959). U.S. Secretary of State: **Architect of the "Containing Communism" Policy.**

Duluth, Minnesota. U.S. city: **Zenith City of the Unsalted Sea, Air-conditioned City, Summer City.** With Superior, Wisconsin: **Twin Ports.**

Dumas from Ohio. Caniff, Milt[on Arthur].

Dumb Blonde. Milton, Vera.

Dumb Dan. Morgan, Daniel Francis.

Duncan, Isadora (1878–1927). Dancer: **First of the Modern Women.**

Duncan, Rosetta (1901?–59). Actress, singer, and composer: **Topsy.**

Dunne, Irene. (born 1904). Actress: **First Lady of Hollywood.**

Dupee. Shaw, Frederick L.

Dupontonia. Wilmington, Delaware.

Dupont Town. Wilmington, Delaware.

Durable Alcoholic. Malloy, Michael.

Durable Dane. Nelson, Oscar Matthew.

Durable Ned. Kalbfus, Edward Clifford.

Durant, William Crapo (1861–1947). Industrialist: **General of General Motors.**

Durante, Jimmy (born 1893). Comedian: **Ragtime Jimmy, The Schnozz, Schnozzola.** Legal name: James Francis Durante.

Durham, Edward Fant (1908–1976). Baseball pitcher: **Bull.**

Durham, Yancey (1921–73). Boxing manager: **Yank.**

Durocher, Leo Ernest (born 1906). Baseball shortstop and manager: **Leo the Lip, The Lip, Lippy, Lippy Leo, Little Shepherd of Coogan's Bluff.**

Duryea, Charles Edgar (1862–1938). Inventor and manufacturer: **Father of the Automobile.**

Duse of the Dance. Kaye, Nora.

Dust Bowl. Great Plains area west of the Mississippi River, esp. during droughts and dust storms in the 1930s.

Duster. Mails, Walter.

Dusty. Boggess, Lynton; Cooke, Allen Lindsey; Rhodes, James Lamar; Rhodes, John Gordon; Tuckerman, Earle.

Dutch. Clark, Earl Henry; Connor, Jack; Garfinkel, Jack; Harrison, Ernest Joe; Kindelberger, James Howard; Leonard, Hubert Benjamin; McIntosh, Russell; Meyer, Leo Robert; Ruether, Walter Henry; Schwab, Frank John; Sternaman, Ed[ward].

Dutch City. Holland, Michigan.

Dutchman. Schultz, Dutch.

Dutchman, The. Grunewald, Henry William.

Dutton, Mervyn (born 1898). Hockey defenseman, team manager, and association official: **Red.**

Dutz. Cohn, Julius.

Duumvirate, The (also called **The Duumvirs**). President Woodrow Wilson and his adviser Colonel Edward Mandell House.

Dwyer, William Vincent (1883–1946). Bootlegger and criminal: **Big Bill, King of the Bootleggers.**

DX. Bible, Dana Xenophon.

Dylan, Bob (born 1941). Poet, composer, and folk singer: **Radical Prophet of American Youth.** Born: Robert Zimmerman.

Dynamite. Post, Seraphim.

Dynamite Brooks. Brooks, Joseph.

Dynamite Joe. Bellino, Joseph.

Dynamo of Power. Roosevelt, Theodore.

E

Eagle. McDonnell Douglas F-15 tactical fighter plane.

Eagle, The. Baldelli, Ecola.

Eagle Eye. Beckley, Jake; Bitzer, Billy.

Eagles. Athletic teams of Boston College, Chestnut Hill, Massachuesetts.

Eagle Squadron. British Royal Air Force squadron of U.S. volunteers, World War II.

Eagle State. Mississippi.

Eagleton, Thomas Francis (born 1929). U.S. Senator from Missouri: **McGovern's Man from Missouri.**

Earhart, Amelia [Mary] (1897–1937). Aviator: **America's Premier Air Woman, First Lady of the Air.** Also known as Amelia Earhart Putnam.

Earl of Hanover. Blaik, Earl Henry.

Earl the Pearl. Monroe, Earl.

Earnshaw, George Livingston (1900–1976). Baseball pitcher: **Big Moose, Moose.**

Earpe, Francis (1897–1969). Football guard: **Jug.**

Earthquake. Dawkins, Daryl.

Earthquake City. Charleston, South Carolina.

East Carolina University, athletic teams of: **Pirates.**

Eastern Gateway to the Black Hills. Rapid City, South Dakota.

Eastern Michigan University, athletic teams of: **Hurons.**

Eastman, Edward (1873–1920). Gangster: **Monk.** Born: Edward Osterman.

Eastman, George (1854–1932). Inventor and industrialist: **Father of the Kodak.**

Eastmans, The. Gang of hoodlums led by Monk Eastman, early 1900s.

East Moline, Illinois. U.S. city. With Moline and Rock Island, Illinois, and Davenport, Iowa: **Quad Cities.**

Easy Ed. Macauley, Ed.

Eaton, Frank (1861–1958). U.S. Deputy Marshal: **Pistol Pete.**

Ebbets, Charles H. (1859–1925). Baseball promoter: **Father of the Brooklyn Dodgers.**

Eccentric Genius. Tesla, Nikola.

Eckstine, Billy (born 1914). Jazz musician, valve trombonist, and singer: **Mr. B., The Vibrato.** Legal name: William Clarence Eckstine.

Eddie. Award, established in 1951, by the Academy of Motion Picture Arts and Sciences for best editing of motion-picture and television films.

Edgar Award. Award, established in 1945 by Mystery Writers of America, Inc., and named after Edgar Allan Poe, for the best detective story of the year.

Edinburgh of America. Albany, New York.

Edison, Harry (born 1915). Jazz trumpeter: **Sweets.**

Edison, Thomas Alva (1847–1931). Inventor: **Father of the Phonograph, Wizard of Menlo Park, Wizard of the Wires.**

Edison of American Parachute Design. Irvin, Leslie Leroy.

Edison of Crime Detection. Heinrich, Edward Oscar.

Edmonton, Alberta. Canadian city: **Oil Capital of Canada.**

Edson, Merritt Austin (1897–1955). Major General, U.S. Marines: **Red Mike.**

Educational Center. Ithaca, New York.

Edwards, Albert Glen (1907?–73). Football tackle: **Turk.**

Edwards, Cliff (born 1895). Entertainer: **Ukelele Ike.**

Edwards, Eddie (1891–1963). Jazz trombonist: **Daddy.** Legal name: Edwin Branford Edwards.

Edwards, Webley (active 1920s and 1930s). Radio producer: **Hawaii's Music Man.**

Efron, Marshall (born c. 1938). Comedian: **Television's Tiny Terror.**

Egan, William (active 1910–20). Gangster: **Shorty.**

Egnor, Virginia Ruth (born 1927). Television actress: **Dagmar.** Also known as Jennie Lewis.

Eighth Armored Division. U.S. Army division, World War II: **Iron Snake.**

Eighth Infantry Division. U.S. Army division, World War II: **Golden Arrow.**

Eighth Wonder of the World. Temple, Shirley.

Eightieth Infantry Division. U.S. Army division, World War II: **Blue Ridge Division.**

Eighty-eighth Infrantry Division. U.S. Army division, World War II: **Blue Devil Division.**

Eighty-fifth Infantry Division. U.S. Army division, World War II: **Custer Division.**

Eighty-first Infantry Division. U.S. Army division, World War II: **Wildcat Division.**

Eighty-fourth Division. U.S. Army division, World War I: **Lincoln Division.**

Eighty-fourth Infantry Division. U.S. Army division, World War II: **Railsplitters.**

Eighty-ninth Division. U.S. Army division, World War I: **Middle West Division.**

Eighty-ninth Infantry Division. U.S. Army division, World War II: **Rolling W.**

Eighty-second Airborne Division. U.S. Army division, World War II: **All-American Division.**

Eighty-second Division. U.S. Army division, World War I: **All-American Division.**

Eighty-seventh Division. U.S. Army division, World War I: **Acorn Division.**

Eighty-seventh Infantry Division. U.S. Army division, World War II: **Golden Acorn Division.**

Eighty-sixth Division. U.S. Army division, World War I: **Black Hawk Division.**

Eighty-sixth Infantry Division. U.S. Army division, World War II: **Black Hawk Division.**

Eighty-third Division. U.S. Army division, World War I: **Ohio Division.**

Eighty-third Infantry Division. U.S. Army division, World War II: **Thunderbolt Division.**

Einstein's Editor. Stryfe, Paul.

Eisenhower, Dwight David (1890–1969). U.S. Army General and thirty-fourth President of the United States: **Ike.**

Eisenhower Doctrine. Policy of aid to the Middle East to forestall Communist influence; initiated by President Dwight D. Eisenhower, 1957.

El. Any of various elevated railroads in U.S. cities, such as the system in New York or Chicago.

Elberfeld, Norman Arthur (1875–1944). Baseball catcher: **Kid.**

Elbows. McFadden, George; Nesterenko, Eric.

Elder Statesman, The. Rogers, Shorty.

El Dorado State. California.

Eldridge, [David] Roy (born 1911). Jazz trumpeter and singer: **Little Jazz.**

Electra. Any of various airliners built by Lockheed, 1934–37.

Electrical Wizard. Steinmetz, Charles Proteus.

Electric Charlie. Wilson, Charles Edward.

Electric City. Schenectady, New York.

Elegant Hoosier Tunesmith. Porter, Cole.

Eleventh Airborne Division. U.S. Army division, World War II: **Angels.**

Eleventh Armored Division. U.S. Army division, World War II: **Thunderbolt Division.**

Eliot, Charles William (1834–1926). Educator and President of Harvard University: **America's First Citizen, Greatest Citizen in the United States.**

Eliot, T[homas] S[tearns] (1888–1965). Poet and man of letters: **Aged Eagle, Deliberate Pedant.**

Elis. Athletic teams, athletes, students, or alumni(ae) of Yale University, New Haven, Conneticut.

Elizabeth, New Jersey. U.S. city: **Betsytown.**

Elk. Elkins, Lawrence C.

Elkhart, Indiana. U.S. city: **Band City.**

Elkins, Lawrence C. (born 1943). Football end: **Elk.**

Ellington, Duke (1899–1974). Jazz bandleader, pianist, and composer: **America's Good Will Music Ambassador, Aristocrat of Swing, The Duke, Duke E., King of Jazz, King of Swing, Master of Jazz.** Born: Edward Kennedy Ellington.

Elliott, Edwin S. (1879–1913). Hockey player: **Chaucer.**

Elliott, Gordon [William] (1903–65). Motion picture actor: **Wild Bill.**

Elliott, James Thomas (born 1901) Baseball pitcher: **Jumbo.**

Ellsberg, Daniel (born 1930). Research associate and government official: **Last Great American Hero, Man Who Started It All.**

Elm City. New Haven, Connecticut.

Elmer the Great. Beck, Walter William.

Elmira, New York. U.S. city: **Glider Capital of America.**

El Paso, Texas. U.S. city: **Crossroads City, Gateway to Mexico.**

Elvis the Pelvis. Presley, Elvis Aron.

Emancipator of the Plater. Jacobs, Hirsch.

Embattled President. Nixon, Richard M[ilhous].

Emerald Empire. Northern Idaho.

Emerald Necklace. Park system of Boston; park system of Cleveland.

Emerging Industrial Center. Birmingham, Alabama.

Emmy. Statuette awarded by the Academy of Television Arts and Sciences for outstanding television work; named after the entertainer Faye Emerson.

Emory & Henry College, athletic teams of: **Wasps.**

Emperor of Newsprint. Hearst, William Randolph.

Emperor of the Caribbean. Keith, Minor Cooper.

Empire Builder. Hill, James Jerome.

110

Empire City. New York City.

Empire State. New York.

Empire State of the South. Georgia.

Empress of the Blues. Smith, Bessie.

Energy Czar. Simon, William E.

Enforcer, The. Nitti, Frank.

Engine Charlie. Wilson, Charles Erwin.

Engineer of Fantasy. Disney, Walt[er Elias].

Engineers. Athletic teams of Lehigh University, Bethlehem, Pennsylvania.

Enigmatic Angela. Davis, Angela [Yvonne].

Ennis, Edgar Clyde, Jr. (1907–63). Jazz musician, bandleader, and singer: **Skinnay.**

Ens, Jewel (born 1889). Baseball coach: **Mutt.**

Enterprise, **U.S.S.** Aircraft carrier: **Big E.**

Entertainer, The. Shack, Eddie.

Entertainment City. Los Angeles, California.

Ephmen. Athletic teams of Williams College, Williamstown, Massachusetts.

Eppie. Epstein, Charlotte.

Epstein, Charlotte (1885–1938). Swimming coach: **Eppie, Mother of American Women's Swimming.**

Equality State. Wyoming.

Equipoise (active 1930). Racehorse: **Chocolate Soldier.**

Equivocal Hero of Science. Oppenheimer, J[ulius] Robert.

Eraser, The. Barnes, Marvin.

Erie, Pennsylvania. U.S. city: **Harbor City.**

Ertle, Johnny (born 1896). Bantamweight boxer: **Kewpie.**

Ervin, Sam[uel James, Jr.] (born 1896). Lawyer and U.S. Senator from North Carolina: **Hyperbolic Historian, Po' Ol' Country Lawyer, Southern Sam, Uncle Sam.**

Erving, Julius (born 1950). Basketball player: **Dr. J.**

Erwin, George (born 1913). Jazz trumpeter: **Pee Wee.**

Escaper, The. Montos, Nick George.

Espo. Esposito, Phil[ip Anthony].

Esposito, Phil[ip Anthony] (born 1942). Hockey player: **Espo.**

Essick, William Earl (died 1951). Baseball scout: **Vinegar Bill.**

Essobees, The. O'Leary, Timothy J. and Sheridan, Elmo R.

Estes, Billie Sol (born 1925). Financier: **Billie Boy from Pecos.**

Esteves, Joseph (born 1921). Jazz musician: **Joe Loco.**

Eternal Flapper. Hopper, Edna Wallace.

Etting, Ruth (1898?–1978). Singer and actress: **Sweetheart of Columbia Records.**

Eureka State. California.

Eustis, Florida. U.S. town: **Orange Capital of the World.**

Evans, Charles (born 1890). Golfer: **Chick.**

Evans, Dale (born 1912). Singer and actress: **Queen of the Cowgirls, Queen of the West.** Born: Frances Octavia Smith.

Evans, Robley D[unglison] (1847–1912). Rear Admiral: **Fighting Bob, Old Gimpy.**

Evanston, Illinois. U.S. city: **Historical City of Homes.**

Evansville, Indiana. U.S. city: **City of Opportunity.**

Evansville, University of, athletic teams of: **Purple Aces.**

Everett, Robert A[shton] (1916–69). U.S. Representative from Tennessee: **Fats.**

Everglades, The. Swampy area of Florida: **River of Grass.**

Everglades Parkway. Florida road: **Alligator Alley.**

Everglade State. Florida.

Evergreen State. Washington.

Evers, John Joseph. (1883–1947). Baseball second baseman: **Crab, The Trojan.**

Evers, Walter Arthur (born 1921). Baseball outfielder: **Hoot.**

Evinrude, Ole (1877–1934). Inventor and manufacturer: **Father of the Outboard.**

Ewbank, Wilbur Charles (born 1907). Football coach: **Weeb.**

Ewing, John (born 1917). Jazz trombonist: **Streamline.**

Excelsior State. New York.

Executive City. Washington, D.C.

Ex-Im Bank. Export-Import Bank.

Expatriate, The. Miller, Henry.

Expatriate American Poet. Pound, Ezra [Loomis].

Explosive Mr. Brown. Brown, James.

Exponent of Futurism. Antheil, George.

Export-Import Bank. U.S. government-controlled bank: **Ex-Im Bank.**

Exterminator (active 1918). Racehorse: **Slim, Old Bones.**

F

Faber, Urban Charles (1888–1976). Baseball pitcher: **Red.**

Fabulous Babe. Hemingway, Margaux.

Fadiman, Clifton [Paul] (born 1904). Critic and radio and television master of ceremonies: **Kip.**

Fairbanks, Alaska. U.S. city: **Frostbite, Gateway to the Arctic, Golden Heart, Golden Heart of the North, Heart of Central Alaska, Tanana River City.**

Fairbanks, Charles Warren (1854–1918). Vice President of the United States: **Icebanks.**

Fairbanks, Douglas, Sr. (1883–1939). Motion-picture actor: **Fourth Musketeer.** Born: Julius Ullman.

Fair Deal. The policies of the liberals of the Democratic party under the leadership of President Harry S. Truman; first used in 1949.

Fair Little City. Tulsa, Oklahoma.

Fake Doctor. Phillips, Arthur Osborne.

Falconetto. Scott, [George] Ken[neth].

Falcons. Athletic teams of the United States Air Force Academy, Colorado Springs, Colorado, and Bowling Green State University, Bowling Green, Ohio.

Falk, Bibb August (born 1899). Baseball outfielder: **Jockey.**

Falkenberg, Frederick Peter (1880–1961). Baseball pitcher: **Cy.**

Fall, Albert Bacon (1861–1944). Lawyer, politician, rancher, and U.S.

114

Secretary of the Interior: **Decade's Arch Villain, Patriarch of Three Rivers.**

Fallon, William J. (1886–1927). Trial lawyer: **Great Mouthpiece.**

Fall River, Massachusetts. U.S. city: **Border City, City of Falling Water, Spindle City.**

Falls City. Louisville, Kentucky.

False Explorer. Cook, Frederick Albert.

Family City. Anaheim, California; St. Louis, Missouri.

Famous First. First Armored Division, World War II.

Faneuil Hall. Public hall in Boston, Massachusetts: **Cradle of Liberty.**

Fannie Mae. Federal National Mortgage Association (FNMA).

Fan-tastic Sally. Rand, Sally.

Far Away Island. Nantucket, Massachusetts.

Far Away Land. Nantucket, Massachusetts.

Farenthold, Frances [Tarlton] (born 1926). Lawyer, state legislator, and college president: **Sissy.**

Fargo Express. Petrolle, William.

Farley, James Aloysius (1888–1976). Politician: **Big Jim, Four-Job Farley, Political Thor, Smiling Jim, That Candid Spoilsman.**

Farmer Bob. Scott, Robert Walter.

Farmer's Friend. Capper, Arthur; Lowden, Frank Orren; Wallace, Henry [Cantwell].

Farmer's Holiday. Withholding of farm produce from the market, beginning October 1932, to raise prices.

Farm Machinery Capital of America. Moline, Illinois.

Farm Woman's Congresswoman. Knutson, Coya.

Farnsworth, Philo Taylor (1906–71). Inventor and electrical engineer: **Father of Television.**

Farrell, Edward Stephen (1902–66). Baseball second baseman and dentist: **Doc.**

Fashion Plate. Lewis, James Hamilton.

Fashion World's Most Irrepressible Master of Ceremonies. Cassini, Oleg [Loiewski].

Fast Talker from Pickens. Baker, Bobby.

Fat. Latham, George.

Fatha. Hines, Earl Kenneth.

Fathead. Newman, David.

Father Goose. Sennett, Mack.

Father of Amateur Trapshooting. McCarty, George S.

Father of American Forestry. Pinchot, Gifford.

Father of American Franchisers. Johnson, Howard.

Father of American Geophysics. Golyer, Everette Lee de.

Father of American Pragmatism. Peirce, Charles Sanders.

Father of American Psychology. James, William.

Father of American Radio. Bullard, William Hannum Grubb.

Father of American Rocketry. Goddard, Robert H.

Father of American Yacht Reporting. Stephens, William P.

Father of Automation. Wiener, Norbert.

Father of Basketball Tactics. Baum, Harry.

Father of Charlie Chan. Biggers, Earl Derr.

Father of Chemurgy. Carver, George Washington.

Father of Conservation. Pinchot, Gifford.

Father of Daylight Saving Time. Garland, Robert.

Father of Documentary Films. Flaherty, Robert Joseph.

Father of Dollar Diplomacy. Knox, Philander Chase.

Father of Ethyl Gasoline. Kettering, C[harles] F[ranklin].

Father of Football. Camp, Walter Chauncey.

Father of Frozen Foods. Birdseye, Clarence.

Father of Hot Rodding. Winfield, Ed[ward].

Father of Inside Baseball. McGraw, John Joseph.

Father of Modern American Gangsterdom. Torrio, John.

Father of Modern Amphibious Warfare. Smith, Holland McTyeire.

Father of Modern Dance. Shawn, Ted.

Father of Modern Education. Dewey, John.

Father of Modern Volleyball. Idell, A. Provost.

Father of Naval Aviation. Towers, John Henry.

Father of Night Baseball. Keyser, E. Lee.

Father of Oldsmobile and Reo. Olds, Ransome Eli.

Father of Our Modern Navy. Chandler, William Eaton.

Father of Power Steering. Davis, Francis W.

Father of Public Utility Regulation. Norris, George William.

Father of Radio. De Forest, Lee.

Father of Radio Broadcasting. Davis, Harry P[hillips].

Father of Rippling Rhythm. Fields, Shep[herd].

Father of Rock Culture. Dean, James.

Father of Rural Free Delivery. Stahl, John Meloy.

Father of Space Travel. Oberth, Hermann.

Father of Supersonic Flight. Von Karman, Theodore.

Father of Swing. Pollack, Ben[jamin].

Father of Syndication. Scripps, E[dward] W[yllis].

Father of Television. Farnsworth, Philo Taylor.

Father of the Aerial Camera. Folmer, William F.

Father of the American Foreign Service. Carr, Wilbur John.

Father of the Atom Bomb. Oppenheimer, J[ulius] Robert.

Father of the Atomic Submarine. Rickover, Hyman [George].

Father of the Automobile. Duryea, Charles Edgar.

Father of the Barge Canal. Symons, Thomas William.

Father of the Blues. Handy, W[illiam] C[hristopher].

Father of the Bonus. Patman, Wright; Van Zant, James E.

Father of the Brillo Pad. Loeb, Milton E.

Father of the Brooklyn Dodgers. Ebbets, Charles H.

Father of the Canvas Cofferdam. Meigs, Montgomery.

Father of the Catcher's Chest Protector. Sullivan, William J., Sr.

Father of the Civil Rights Movement. Randolph, A[sa] Philip.

Father of the Cosa Nostra. Maranzano, Salvatore.

Father of the Curve Ball. Cummings, William Arthur.

Father of the Davis Cup. Davis, Dwight F.

Father of the Dime Store. Woolworth, Frank Winfield.

Father of the Eighteenth Amendment. Sheppard, Morris.

Father of the Federal Probation System. McClintic, George W.

Father of the Federal Reserve System. Glass, Carter; Warburg, Paul Moritz.

Father of the Fiction Syndicate. McClure, Samuel Sidney.

Father of the Film Industry. Griffith, D[avid Lewelyn] W[ark].

Father of the Five and Ten. Woolworth, Frank Winfield.

Father of the Flivver. Ford, Henry.

Father of the 47 Workshop. Baker, George Peirce.

Father of the Forward Pass. Cochems, Edward B.

Father of the Graflex. Folmer, William F.

Father of the Helicopter. Sikorsky, Igor [Ivan].

Father of the Hershey Bar. Hershey, Milton Snavely.

Father of the Indianapolis Motor Speedway. Fisher, Carl Graham.

Father of the Kodak. Eastman, George.

Father of the Lasker Plan. Lasker, Albert Davis.

Father of the Modern Ballet. Fokine, Michael.

Father of the Modern Steam Automobile. Doble, Abner.

Father of the Modern Submarine. Lake, Simon.

Father of the M-1 Rifle. Garand, John Cantius.

Father of the Motor Car. Ford, Henry.

Father of the New Left. Marcuse, Herbert.

Father of the New York State Boxing Bill. Walker, James J[ohn].

Father of the One-Way Ride. Wajcieckowski, Earl.

Father of the Outboard. Evinrude, Ole.

Father of the Phonograph. Edison, Thomas Alva.

Father of the Rocky Mountain National Park. Mills, Enos Abijah.

Father of the Rubber Industry. Firestone, Harvey Samuel.

Father of the Safety Razor. Gillette, King Camp.

Father of the Seabees. Spaulding, E. Jack.

Father of the Self-Starter. Kettering, C[harles] F[ranklin].

Father of the Shell Manifesto. Tillman, Benjamin Ryan.

Father of the Skyscraper. Gilbert, Cass.

Father of the Tabloid. Patterson, Joseph Medill.

Father of the Telephone. Bell, Alexander Graham.

Father of the Tesla Turbine. Tesla, Nikola.

Father of the Tommy Gun. Thompson, John Taliaferro.

Father of the Townsend Plan. Townsend, Francis Everett.

Father of the Tucker Torpedo. Tucker, Preston [Thomas].

Father of the Twentieth Amendment to the Constitution. Norris, George William.

Father of the United Nations. Hull, Cordell.

Father of the U.S. Air Force. Arnold, Henry Harley.

Father of the Volstead Act. Volstead, Andrew J.

Father of the Western Story. Grey, Zane.

Father of U.S. Airborne Forces. Lee, William C.

Father of Waters. Mississippi River.

Fathers of the Bearcat. Stutz, Charles E. and Stutz, Harry C.

Fat Jack. Leonard, Jack E.

Fat Libitsky. Leonard, Jack E.

Fat Moe. Brown, Moe.

Fat One, The. Gleason, Jackie.

Fats. Domino, Antoine; Everett, Robert A[shton]; Henry, Wilbur F.; Heard, Eugene M.; Navarro, Theodore; Spears, Clarence Wiley; Waller, Thomas Wright.

Fatso Marco. Marcella, Marco.

Fat Tuesday. Tuesday before Ash Wednesday, climax of the Mardi Gras festivities, New Orleans.

Fatty. Arbuckle, Roscoe.

Faulkner, William (1897–1962). Writer: **American Balzac.**

Favorite Son of Texas. Garner, John Nance.

Fay, Larry (1889–1933). Gangster: **Beau Brummel of Broadway.**

FDR. Roosevelt, Franklin Delano.

Fearless Flynn. Flynn, Errol.

Fearless Frances. Perkins, Frances.

Fearsome Foursome. Defensive line of the Los Angeles Rams football team, mid-1960s, consisting of Lamar Lundy, Deacon Jones, Merlin Olsen, and Roosevelt Grier.

Fed. 1. Agent of the Federal Bureau of Investigation. 2. Agent of the U.S. Treasury Department.

Fed, The. The Federal Reserve System.

Federal City. Paterson, New Jersey; Washington, D.C.

Federal National Mortgage Association (FNMA). Government-sponsored private corporation: **Fannie Mae.**

Federal Reserve System. U.S. government agency: **The Fed.**

Feebie. Member of the Federal Bureau of Investigation.

Feinstein, Moshe (born 1895). Rabbi and authority on Jewish law: **Rev Moishe.**

Felix the Fixer. Rohatyn, Felix G.

Feller, Bob (born 1918). Baseball pitcher: **Rapid Robert.** Legal name: Robert William Andrew Feller.

Fellig, Arthur (1899–1968). Photographer: **Weegee.**

Fellowes, Mrs. Cornelius Peterkin (1884–1952). Theatrical performer: **Mademoiselle Dazie.**

Felsch, Oscar Emil (1891–1964). Baseball centerfielder: **Happy.**

Felton, Francis J. (1908–64). Jazz musician, singer, and radio personality: **Happy.**

Female Brain of the S.L.A. Soltysik, Patricia.

Fernandez, Humberto [Perez] (born 1932). Baseball shortstop: **Chico.**

Fernandez, Joachim Octave (born 1896). U.S. Representative from Louisiana: **Coroner.**

Ferns, Rube (1874–1952). Welterweight boxer: **Kansas Rube.** Also known as Jim Rube. Born: James Rube.

Fetchit, Stepin. Actor: **White Man's Negro.** Born: Lincoln Theodore Perry.

FFV's. 1. Natives or residents of Virginia. 2. First Families of Virginia.

Fiddler. Corridon, Frank J.

Fiddler Bill. McGee, William Henry.

Fiddling Bob. Taylor, Robert Love.

Fidgety. Collins, Phil Eugene.

Fidrych, Mark (born 1954). Baseball pitcher: **The Bird.**

Fiedler, Arthur (1894–1979). Symphony conductor: **Mr. Boston, Mr. Pops.**

Fielding, Temple [Hornaday] (born 1913). Writer of travel books: **King of European Guides.**

Fields, Carl Donnell (born 1915). Jazz drummer: **Kansas.**

Fields, George (active 1920s and 1930s). Radio comedian: **Honey Boy.**

Fields, Shep[herd] (born 1911). Jazz musician: **Father of Rippling Rhythm.**

Fields, W[illiam] C[laude] (1880–1946). Comedian, juggler, actor, and writer: **Whitey, World's Greatest Eccentric Juggler.** Also known as George Bogle, A. Pismo Clam, Otis Criblecoblis, Bill

Fields, Mahatma Kane Jeeves. Born: Claude William Dukenfield.

Fiesta Bowl. Football stadium in Tempe, Arizona; site of annual Fiesta Bowl college football game.

Fifi. Buccieri, Fiore.

Fifth Armored Division. U.S. Army division, World War II: **V for 5th and Victory.**

Fifth Estate. Organized crime.

Fifth Infantry Division. U.S. Army division, World War II: **Red Diamond Division.**

Fiftieth State. Hawaii.

Fifty-second Street. Section of street in New York City, between Fifth Avenue and Seventh Avenue, in which jazz nightclubs were located, late 1930s and 1940s: **The Street, Street of Swing, Swing Alley, Swing Street.**

Fighter, The. McFadden, Bernarr.

Fightin' Blue Hens. Athletic teams of the University of Delaware, Newark.

Fighting Angel. Sydenstricker, Absalom.

Fighting Bob. La Follette, Robert [Marion, Sr.]; Evans, Robley Dunglison.

Fighting First. First Infantry Division.

Fighting Gamecocks. Athletic teams of the University of South Carolina, Columbia.

Fighting Illini. Athletic teams of the University of Illinois, Urbana.

Fighting Irish. Athletic teams of the University of Notre Dame, Notre Dame, Indiana.

Fighting Irishman from South Boston. McCormack, John W[illiam].

Fighting Marine. Tunney, Gene.

Fighting Scots. Athletic teams of the College of Wooster, Wooster, Ohio.

Fighting Sixty-ninth, The. Sixty-ninth Regiment.

Fighting Tigers. Athletic teams of Louisiana State University, Baton Rouge.

Fightin' Hoosiers. Athletic teams of the Indiana University, Bloomington.

Filipino Libertarian. Aguinaldo, Emilio.

Film Capital of the World. Hollywood, California.

Filmland. Hollywood, California.

Final Authority on Etiquette. Post, Emily Price.

Financial Capital of the World. New York City.

Financial Center of the West. San Francisco, California.

Financial Wizard. Koretz, Leo.

Financial Wizard of Hobcaw Barony. Baruch, Bernard M[annes].

Finn. Niemi, Laurie.

Finn, Neal Francis (born 1903). Baseball second baseman: **Mickey.** Born: Cornelius Francis Finn.

Firebrand, The. Marcantonio, Vito.

Fire Chief. Carley, Patrick J.

Fireman. Page, Joe.

Fireside Chat. Friendly, warm talk by the U.S. President, keeping the American people informed of what he is doing and instilling confidence in government policy; originally one of the radio talks given by President Franklin D. Roosevelt to reassure the public about the strength of the economy and the war effort, 1933–45.

Firestone, Harvey Samuel (1868–1938). Industrialist: **Father of the Rubber Industry.**

Firp. Greene, Waldo.

Firpo. Marberry, Fred; Morrison, Lake.

First American in Orbit. Glenn, John [Herschel].

First American in Space. Shepard, Alan B[artlett]. Jr.

First Armored Division. U.S. Army Division, World War II: **Famous First.**

First Avon Lady. Albee, Mrs. P. F. E.

First Automobile Bandit. Jackson, Frank.

First Cavalry Division. U.S. Army division, World War II: **Cavalry Troopers.**

First City of the First State. Wilmington, Delaware.

First Families of Virginia. Descendants of the first permanent settlers of the Tidewater area of Virginia: **FFV's**

First City of the South. Savannah, Georgia.

First Great Racer, The. Robertson, George Hepburn.
First Indy Four-Hour Winner. Wallard, Lee.
First Infantry Division. U.S. Army division, World War II. **Fighting First, Red One.**
First Lady, The. Wife of the U.S. President.
First Lady of Baseball. Day, Laraine.
First Lady of Hollywood. Dunne, Irene.
First Lady of Radio. Brainard, Bertha; Smith, Kate.
First Lady of Song. Fitzgerald, Ella.
First Lady of Supper Clubs. Hildegarde.
First Lady of Talk. Walters, Barbara.
First Lady of the Air. Earhart, Amelia [Mary].
First Lady of the American Stage. Cornell, Katharine.
First Lady of the American Theater. Hayes, Helen.
First Lady of the Screen. Gish, Lillian.
First Lady of the World. Roosevelt, [Anna] Eleanor [Roosevelt]; Wilson, Edith Bolling Galt.
First Lady of Vermont. Canfield, Dorothy.
First Lawyer of the Land. Attorney General of the United States.
First Man on the Moon. Armstrong, Neil A.
First of the Beautiful People. Nast, Condé.
First of the Modern Women. Duncan, Isadora.
First of the Nixon Men. Haldeman, H[arry] R[obbins].
First Scientist in Space. Schmitt, Jack.
First State. Delaware.
First Super End. Hutson, Don[ald Montgomery].
Fischer, Bobby (born 1943). Chess player: **Boy Robot, Corduroy Killer, Sweatshirt Kid.** Legal name: Robert James Fischer.
Fish, Hamilton, Jr. (born 1888). Football player, U.S. Army captain, and U.S. Representative from New York: **Great All American, One-Man Patriot.**
Fish Bait. Miller, William Mosley.
Fisher, Carl Graham (1874–1939). Promoter: **Father of the Indianapolis Motor Speedway.**
Fisherman's Paradise of the North Atlantic. Block Island, Rhode Island.

Fish Hook. Stout, Allyn McClelland.

Fisk, Carlton [Ernest] (born 1947). Baseball player: **Pudge.**

Fistic Harlequin. Baer, Max[imilian Adelbert].

Fitzgerald, Ella (born 1918). Jazz singer and composer: **First Lady of Song.**

Fitzgerald, John F[rancis] (1863–1950). Politician: **Honey Fitz.**

Fitzsimmons, James Edward (1874–1966). Racehorse trainer: **Dean of American Trainers, Grand Old Man of Racing, Mr. Fitz, Sunny Jim.**

Five-year-old Child Wonder. Rose Marie, Baby.

Flag of the United States: Stars and Stripes, Old Glory.

Flaherty, Patrick Joseph (1876–1968). Baseball pitcher: **Patsy.**

Flaherty, Ray (active 1920s and 1930s). Football coach: **Red.**

Flaherty, Robert Joseph (1884–1951). Explorer and motion-picture producer: **Father of Documentary Films.**

Flak Highway. Route to Berlin for American bombers based in Britain, World War II.

Flash. Gordon, Joe; Suther, John.

Flea. Clifton, Herman E.; Roberts, Walter.

Fleagle, Jacob Roger (born 1906). Jazz guitarist: **Brick.**

Fleetster. Any of various twin-float passenger and cargo seaplanes built by Consolidated Aircraft Corporation, 1929–32.

Fleischer, Nat[haniel S.] (1888–1972). Publisher, journalist, and boxing authority: **Mr. Boxing, Dean of Boxing Writers.**

Flicka. Von Stade, Frederica.

Flickertail. Native or resident of North Dakota.

Flickertail State. North Dakota.

Flim-flam Man. Mastriana, Louis P.

Flint, Michigan. U.S. city: **Vehicle City.**

Flip. Phillips, Joseph Edward; Rosen, Al[bert Leonard].

Flivver King. Ford, Henry.

Flood, Daniel J. (born 1903). U.S. Representative from Pennsylvania: **Dapper Dan.**

Flood City. Johnstown, Pennsylvania.

Florida. Twenty-seventh U.S. state: **Alligator State, Cane Sugar State, Everglades State, Gulf State, Land of Flowers, Land of Sunshine, Live Oak State, Orange State, Peninsula State, Peninsular State, Sunshine State.**

Florida, University of, athletic teams of: **Gators.**

Florida A & M University, athletic teams of: **Rattlers.**

Florida Keys. Chain of islands below southern Florida: **Wet Tortugas.**

Florida's Showcase Community. Coral Gables, Florida.

Florida State University, athletic teams of: **Seminoles.**

Florida's Vacation Capital. Daytona Beach, Florida.

Flory, Meredith Irwin (born 1926). Jazz saxophonist and leader: **Med.**

Flossie. Harding, Florence Kling DeWolfe.

Flour City. Buffalo, New York; Minneapolis, Minnesota; Rochester, New York.

Flower City. Rochester, New York.

Flowers, Theodore (1895–1927). Middleweight boxer: **Tiger, Georgia Deacon.**

Floyd, Charles (1904–34). Gangster: **Pretty Boy.**

Flyer, The. Biplane used by the Wright Brothers in 1903; the first successful airplane.

Flyers. Athletic teams of the University of Dayton, Dayton, Ohio.

Flying Admiral. Sherman, Forrest Percival.

Flying Boxcar. C-82 military cargo plane, World War II.

Flying Dutchman. Long, Herman C.; Wagner, John Peter.

Flying Fortress. B-17 bombing plane, World War II

Flying Norseman. Tokle, Torger D.

Flying Parson. Dodds, Gilbert Lothair.

Flying Saucer. Flat, often illuminated, unidentified flying object.

Flying Tiger. Chennault, Claire Lee.

Flying Tigers. P-40 fighter planes of the American Volunteer Group in China, World War II; pilots of the planes.

Flynn, Errol (1909–59). Motion-picture actor: **Fearless Flynn.**

Foam City. Milwaukee, Wisconsin.

Fob. James, Forrest Hood, Jr.

Fo'c'sle Joe. Curran, Joseph Edwin.

Foggy Bottom. 1. The United States Department of State. 2. Area of Washington, D.C. near Potomac River.

Foghorn. Allen, Forrest Claire; Funston, Edward Hogue.

Foist Lieutenant. Schaffel, Albert S.

Fokine, Michael (1880–1942). Choreographer: **Father of the Modern Ballet.**

Foley, John (active 1920–30). Gangster: **Mitters.**

Folmer, William F. (1862–1936). Inventor: **Father of the Graflex, Father of the Aerial Camera.**

Folsom, James E[lisha] (born 1908). Governor of Alabama: **Kissing Jim.**

Fonda, Jane (born 1937). Actress and political activist: **Mr. Fonda's Baby Jane, Non-Stop Activist.**

Fontaine, Frank (1920–78). Singer and entertainer: **Crazy Guggenheim.** Also known as John L. C. Sivoney.

Football Capital of the South. Birmingham, Alabama; New Orleans, Louisiana.

Football Classicist. Bible, Dana Xenophon.

Football Doctor. Anderson, Edward N.

Football Scholar. Snavely, Carl Grey.

Football's Greatest Coach. Neyland, Robert Reese, Jr.

Football's Old Man River. Stagg, Amos Alonzo.

Football Statesman. Crisler, Fritz.

Foots. Thomas, Walter Purl.

Ford, Edward Charles (born 1928). Baseball pitcher: **Whitey.**

Ford, Ernest Jennings (born 1919). Entertainer and singer: **Cousin Ern, King of the Tennessee Pea Pickers, Tennessee Ernie.**

Ford, Gerald [Rudolph, Jr.] (born 1913). Vice President and thirty-eighth President of the United States: **Mr. Clean, Mr. Middle America.** Born: Leslie Lynch King.

Ford, Henry (1863–1947). Automobile manufacturer: **Automobile Wizard, Father of the Flivver, Father of the Motor Car, Flivver King, Genius of Motordom.**

Fordham Flash. Frisch, Frank Francis.

Fordham University, athletic teams of: **Rams.**

Fordtown. Detroit, Michigan.

Foreman, George (born 1949). Heavyweight boxer: **Big George, Instant Champion, Lightning Destroyer.**

Forest City. Cleveland, Ohio; Portland, Maine; Savannah, Georgia.

Forgotten Man, The. The ordinary U.S. worker during the Depression; Braddock, James J.

Forgotten Man of American Music, The. Warren, Harry.

Forrester, Elijah Lewis (1896–1970). U.S. Representative from Georgia: **Tic.**

Fort Dodge, Iowa. U.S. town: **Queen of the Cowtowns.**

Fortieth Division. U.S. Army division, World War I: **Sunshine Division.**

Fortieth Infantry Division. U.S. Army division, World War II: **Sunburst Division.**

Fort Lauderdale, Florida. U.S. city: **Boating Capital of the World, Gateway to the Everglades, Venice of America.**

Fort Myers, Florida. U.S. city: **City of Palms.**

Fortress America. America, regarded as immune to foreign aggression, 1930s.

Fort Town. Fort Worth, Texas.

Fortunate Island. Monhegan, Maine.

Fortunato, Angelo (active 1937). Football player: **Butch.**

Fort Worth, Texas. U.S. city: **Arsenal of Democracy, Cowtown, Fort Town, Lake City, Panther City, Stagecoach Town.**

Forty-fifth Infantry Division. U.S. Army division, World War II: **Thunderbird Division.**

Forty-first Division. U.S. Army division, World War I: **Sunset Division.**

Forty-first Infantry Division. U.S. Army Division, World War II: **Jungleers Division.**

.44-Caliber Killer. Berkowitz, David Richard.

Forty Niners. Athletic teams of California State University, Long Beach.

Forty-second Division, American Expeditionary Forces. U.S. Army division, World War I: **Rainbow Division.**

Forty-second Infantry Division. U.S. Army division, World War II: **Rainbow Division.**

Forty-seventh Street. Street in New York City occupied by jewelers: **Diamond Street.**

Forty-third Infantry Division. U.S. Army division, World War II: **Winged Victory Division.**

Foster, George Murphy (1892–1969). Jazz bass player: **Pops.**

Foster, Harold (born 1906). Basketball forward and center: **Bud.**

Founder of Behaviorism. Watson, John Broadus.

Founder of Functionalism. Sullivan, Louis Henri.

Founder of Humanistic Psychology. Maslow, Abraham.

Founder of Rum Row. McCoy, William.

Founder of the Birth Control Movement. Sanger, Margaret [Higgins].

Founding Father of the Kennedy Clan. Kennedy, Joseph Patrick.

Fountain, The. Ashurst, Henry Fountain.

Fountain City. Pueblo, Colorado.

Fountain of Youth City. St. Augustine, Florida.

Four Eyes. Roosevelt, Theodore.

Four Horsemen. Backfield members of the University of Notre Dame football team, 1920s: Jim Crowley, Elmer Layden, Don Miller, and Harry Stuhldreher.

Four Hundred, The. Body of socially prominent persons, 1890s–1930s, esp. in New York City.

Four-Job Farley. Farley, James Aloysius.

Four Lake City. Madison, Wisconsin.

Four Season City. Superior, Wisconsin.

Four Straight Jake. Ruppert, Jacob, Sr.

Fourth Infantry Division. U.S. Army division, World War II: **Ivy Division.**

Fourth Musketeer. Fairbanks, Douglas, Sr.

Four Undertakers, The. Modern Jazz Quartet.

Fox. Williams, George Dale.

Fox, The. Torrio, John.

Fox, Ervin (1909–66). Baseball outfielder: **Pete.**

Fox, Jacob Nelson (1927–75). Baseball second baseman: **Nellie.**

Fox, John J. (1897–1956). Bobsledder: **Donna.**

Fox, John Linwood (1907–54). Light-heavyweight boxer: **Tiger Jack.**

Fox, William (1879–1952). Motion-picture producer: **Greatest Fox of Them All.**

Foxe, Fanne (born 1937). Dancer: **Argentine Firecracker, Tidal Basin Bombshell.** Legal name: Annabel Battistella.

Foxx, James Emory (1907–67). Baseball first baseman and catcher: **Double X, Beast.**

Foxx, Redd (born 1922). Television actor and comedian: **Chicago Red.** Born: John Elroy Sanford.

Foxy Harry. Daugherty, Harry.

Foyt, A[nthony] J[oseph, Jr.] (born 1935). Racing driver: **Hard-nosed Demon of the Ovals, Houston Hurricane.**

FPA. Adams, Franklin Pierce.

Franchise, The. Thompson, David.

Francis, Clarence (born 1932). Basketball player: **Bevo.**

Francis, Emile [Percy] (born 1926). Hockey goalie: **The Cat.**

Franco, Ed (active 1930s). Football player. With other members of Fordham team: **Seven Blocks of Granite.**

Frank. Hogan, James Francis.

Frankfort, Kentucky. U.S. city: **Bluegrass Capital, Heart of Kentucky.**

Frankie. Carbo, Paul John.

Franklin, Aretha (born 1942). Singer: **Lady Soul.**

Franklin, James (born c. 1945). Cartoonist: **Armadillo Man.**

Franklin, Murray Asher (born 1914). Baseball shortstop: **Moe.**

Franklin, **U.S.S.** Aircraft carrier: **Big Ben.**

Frank Swoonatra. Sinatra, Frank.

Frank the Just. Murphy, Frank.

Frazier, Joe (born 1944). Heavyweight boxer: **Smokin' Joe.**

Frazier, Walt (born 1945). Basketball guard: **Clyde.**

Freck. Owen, Marvin James.

Freckles. Barry, Wesley.

Fredericksburg, Virginia. U.S. city: **America's Most Historic City, Cockpit of the Civil War.**

Free. Hoffman, Abbie.

Freedom Marchers. Blacks and whites marching and demonstrating for racial integration, early 1960s.

Freedom Riders. Interracial groups riding to the South to stop segregation of blacks, early 1960s.

Freeman, John F. (1871–1949). Baseball pitcher and outfielder: **Buck.**

Free State. Maryland; West Virginia.

Freestone State. Connecticut.

Freeway City. Los Angeles, California.

French Chef. Child, Julia [McWilliams].

French Connection. Buffalo Sabres' hockey line of Gil Perreault, Rick Martin, and René Robert.

French Shore. Northern and western coasts of Newfoundland.

Frenchy. Demoisey, John; Mader, Fred.

Fresno, California. U.S. city: **Raisin Center of the World, Sweet Wine Capital of the World.**

Fried Chicken King. Sanders, Harland.

Friedman, Irving (born 1903). Jazz musician: **Izzy.**

Friendliest City. Rochester, New York.

Friendly Island. Martha's Vineyard, Massachusetts.

Friend of Helpless Children. Hoover, Herbert [Clark].

Friend of Presidents. Sullivan, Mark.

Friganza, Trixie (1871–1955). Vaudeville star: **Champagne Girl.** Born: Brigid O'Callaghan.

Frisch, Frank Francis (1898–1973). Baseball second baseman and manager: **Fordham Flash.**

Frisco. San Francisco; not used by natives.

Fritz. Crisler, Herbert Orrin; Knothe, Wilfred Edgar; Mondale, Walter Frederick; Ostermueller, Frederick Raymond.

Fritz and Grits. Mondale, Walter Frederick and Carter, Jimmy.

Fritzie. Zivic, Ferdinand Henry John.

Frog Man. Sykowski, Abram.

Frog Prince. Reynolds, Burt.

Fromme, Lynette Alice (born 1948). Conspirator, convicted of attempting to assassinate President Gerald R. Ford: **Squeaky.**

Frost, Robert [Lee] (1874–1963). Poet: **Voice of New England.**

Frost Belt. Northeast and Midwest of the United States.

Frostbite. Fairbanks, Alaska.

Frozen Wilderness. Alaska.

Fruit Bowl of the Nation. Yakima, Washington.

Fud. Livingston, Joseph A.

Fuel State. West Virginia.

Fulkerson, Ralph Clayburn (1905–49). Rodeo clown: **Jazbo.**

Fuller, Alfred C. (1885?–1973). Brush manufacturer and retailer: **Brush King.**

Fuller, R[ichard] Buckminster (born 1895). Architect, engineer, and author: **Bucky.**

Fulmer, Hampton Pitts (1875–1944). U.S. Representative from South Carolina: **Horsepower.**

Fulton, John (born 1932). Bullfighter and painter: **Yanqui Matador.** Born: John Fulton Short.

Fun City. New York City.

Fungus Corners. Bremerton, Washington.

Funniest Woman of the Silent Screen. Normand, Mabel.

Funston, Edward Hogue (1836–1911). U.S. Representative from Kansas: **Foghorn.**

Funston, George Keith (born 1910). President of the New York Stock Exchange: **Mr. Shareowner.**

Fur. Sammons, James.

Furman University, athletic teams of: **Paladins.**

Furniture City. Grand Rapids, Michigan.

Futurity King. Marsch, John.

Fuzzy. Kallet, Aaron Harry; Zoeller, Frank Urban.

G

Gabby. Hartnett, Charles Leo; Hayes, George Francis; Roseboro, John H.; Street, Charles Evard.

Gabby Lithuanian. Sharkey, Jack.

Gabe. Gabriel, Roman.

Gable, Daniel (born c. 1949). Wrestler: **Gorgeous Dan.**

Gable, [William] Clark (1901–60). Motion-picture actor: **King of Hollywood.**

Gabriel, Roman (born 1940). Football quarterback: **Gabe.**

Gadge. Kazan, Elia.

Gafford, Roy (active 1940s). Football back: **Monk.**

Gaines, Clarence (born 1923). Basketball player: **Big House.**

Gainesville, Florida. U.S. city: **University City.**

Galante, Carmine (1910–79). Gangster: **The Cigar, Lilo.**

Galaxy. Lockheed C-5 large cargo plane.

Galbraith, John Kenneth (born 1909). Economist, author, diplomat, and professor: **Great Mogul, The World's Tallest Economist.**

Gale, Lauren (born 1916). Basketball forward: **Laddie.**

Galena, Illinois. U.S. town: **City Time Forgot.**

Galento, Tony (1910–79). Heavyweight boxer and wrestler: **Battling Barkeep, Two-Ton Tony.**

Gallagher, John (born 1904). Basketball player: **Taps.**

Gallagher, Richard S. (1891–1955). Stage and motion-picture comedian: **Skeets.**

Gallatin, Harry (born 1928). Basketball player: **Horse.**

Gallo, Joseph (1927–72). Racketeer and gangster: **Crazy Joe, Joe the Blond.**

Galloping Gertie. Suspension bridge over the Narrows of Puget Sound, Tacoma, Washington, destroyed by wind in 1940.

Galloping Ghost. Grange, Harold E[dward]; Wheatley, Bill.

Galloping Sprafka. Sprafka, Joseph.

Galveston, Texas. U.S. city: **Oleander City, Seaport of the West, Space Port U.S.A.**

Galveston Giant, The. Johnson, Jack.

Game Kid. Crowley, Francis.

Gandil, Charles Arnold (1887–1970). Baseball first baseman: **Chick.**

Gangdom's Favorite Florist. O'Banion, Dion.

Gangland. Chicago, Illinois.

Gans, Joe (1874–1910). Lightweight boxer: **Old Master.** Born: Joseph Gaines.

Gap. Mangione, Chuck.

Gap, The. Petrelli, Dominick.

Garand, John Cantius (1888–1974). Canadian-American gun designer: **Father of the M-1 Rifle.**

Gar Bait. Miller, William Mosley.

Garden City. San Jose, California; Savannah, Georgia.

Garden City, New York. U.S. city: **Cathedral Town.**

Garden City of Georgia. Augusta, Georgia.

Garden Grove, California. U.S. city: **Planned Growing City.**

Gardenia Grover. Whalen, Grover Aloysius.

Garden Island. Kauai.

Garden of Canada. Ontario.

Garden of Maine. Aroostook County.

Garden of the Caribbean. Puerto Rico.

Garden of the Gulf. Prince Edward Island.

Garden of the West. Illinois; Kansas.

Garden of the World. Mississippi River Valley.

Garden Province. Prince Edward Island.

Garden State. New Jersey; Kansas.

133

Gardner, Ed (1901?–63). Radio performer: **Archie the Manager.** Born: Edward Francis Gardner Poggenburg.

Gardner, Roy (active 1921). Train robber: **King of Escape Artists.**

Garfield Gunner. Larkin, Tippy.

Garfinkel, Jack (born 1920). Basketball player: **Dutch.**

Garland, Judy (1922–69). Singer and motion picture actress: **Lady Lazarus, Triple-Threat Girl.** Born: Frances Gumm.

Garland, Robert (1863–1949). Industrialist: **Father of Daylight Saving Time.**

Garlits, Donald Glenn (born 1933). Automobile racing driver: **Big Daddy.**

Garms, Debs G. (born 1908). Baseball third baseman and outfielder: **Tex.**

Garner, John Nance (1869–1967). U.S. Vice President: **Cactus Jack, Favorite Son of Texas, Mohair Jack, The Owl, Poker Face, Sage of Uvalde, Uvalde Jack.**

Garr, Ralph Allen (born 1945). Baseball outfielder: **Road Runner.**

Garvey, Marcus M[oziah] (1887–1940). Editor, lecturer, and leader of black nationalist movement: **Black Nationalist, Provisional President of Africa.**

Gary, Indiana. U.S. city: **Steel City.**

Gaseous Cassius. Ali, Muhammad.

Gas House Gang. St. Louis Cardinals, 1930s.

Gastown. Waterfront neighborhood of Vancouver, British Columbia.

Gate City. Atlanta, Georgia; Chattanooga, Tennessee; Nashua, New Hampshire; San Bernardino, California.

Gate City of Florida. Jacksonville, Florida.

Gate City of the South. Atlanta, Georgia.

Gate City of the West. Omaha, Nebraska.

Gatemouth. Armstrong, Louis.

Gates, John Warne (1855–1911). Industrialist: **Bet-a-Million Gates, Moonshine Gates, Wire King of America.**

Gateway Arch City. St. Louis, Missouri.

Gateway City. Louisville, Kentucky; Minneapolis, Minnesota.

Gateway City of the Hills. Rapid City, South Dakota.
Gateway City to Canada. Buffalo, New York.
Gateway State. Ohio.
Gateway to Alaska. Seattle, Washington.
Gateway to America. New York City.
Gateway to California. San Diego, California.
Gateway to Latin America. Miami, Florida.
Gateway to Mexico. El Paso, Texas; Laredo, Texas.
Gateway to Mount Rainier. Tacoma, Washington.
Gateway to the Arctic. Fairbanks, Alaska.
Gateway to the Black Hills. Pierre, South Dakota.
Gateway to the Dakotas. Sioux Falls, South Dakota.
Gateway to the Everglades. Fort Lauderdale, Florida.
Gateway to the Famed Northwoods. St. Paul, Minnesota.
Gateway to the Great Seaway. Green Bay, Wisconsin.
Gateway to the Midwest. Canton, Ohio.
Gateway to the Orient. Hawaii.
Gateway to the Rockies. Denver, Colorado.
Gateway to the Smokies. Knoxville, Tennessee.
Gateway to the West. Independence, Missouri; Pittsburgh, Pennsyl-
vania; St. Louis, Missouri.
Gator Bowl. Football stadium in Jacksonville, Florida; site of annual
Gator Bowl college football game.
Gators. Athletic teams of the University of Florida, Gainesville.
Gavilan, Kid (born 1926). Welterweight boxer: **The Hawk.** Born:
Geraldo Gonzalez.
Gavvy. Cravath, Clifford Carlton.
Gay. Bromberg, Gabriel.
Gay, Hobart Raymond (born 1894). U.S. Army Lieutenant General:
Hap.
Gay White Way. Broadway.
Gebardi, Vincent (1904–36). Gangster: **Machine Gun Jack McGurn.**
Born: James Vincenzo de Mora.
Gee. Whitney, Gwladys [Crosby Hopkins].
Gehrig, Lou (1903–41). Baseball first baseman: **Biscuit Pants, Iron
Horse, Iron Man of Baseball, Larruping Lou, Pride of the Yan-
kees.** Legal name: Henry Louis Gehrig.

135

Gem City. Dayton, Ohio.

Gem of Beaches. Long Beach, California.

Gem of the Mountains. Idaho.

Gem of the Ozone. Kaltenborn, H[ans] V[on].

Gem of the Pacific. Hawaii.

Gem State. Idaho.

Gem Stater. Native or resident of Idaho.

General. Crowder, Alvin Floyd.

General, The. Neyland, Robert Reese, Jr.; Sinatra, Frank.

General Manager of the War. Smith, Walter Bedell.

General of General Motors. Durant, William Crapo.

General-Purpose Vehicle. Light car originally developed for use by the U.S. Army: **Jeep.**

Generals. Athletic teams of Washington & Lee University, Lexington, Virginia.

Genero, Joseph (active 1930s). Criminal: **Peppy.**

Generous Lender, The. Rose, William.

Gene the Machine. Littler, Eugene.

Genius of Motordom. Ford, Henry.

Genius of Racing. Weil, Joseph R.

Genius of the Negative Approach. Nader, Ralph.

Genius on a Low Budget. Kramer, Stanley E.

Genna Gang. Group of illicit distillers and brewers in Chicago.

Genovese, Vito (1898–1969). Leader of the Mafia: **Don Vitone.**

Gentle Ben. Crenshaw, Benjamin.

Gentle Grafter. Remus, George B.

Gentle Guru of the Flower People. Ginsberg, Allen.

Gentleman from Indianapolis. Tarkington, [Newton] Booth.

Gentleman Jim. Corbett, James John.

Gentleman Jimmy. Walker, James J[ohn].

Gentlemen's Agreement. Agreement of Japan, 1907, to forbid laborers to migrate to the United States.

Geoffrion, Bernie (born 1931). Hockey player: **Boom Boom.**

George, Charlie (born 1912). Baseball catcher: **The Greek.**

George, Harold H. U.S. Army Air Corps General: **Pursuit.**

George Washington Bloom. Bloom, Sol.

Georgia. Fourth U.S. state: **Buzzard State, Cracker State, Empire State of the South, Goober State, Land of the Peanuts, Peach State.**

Georgia, University of, athletic teams of: **Bulldogs.**

Georgia Deacon. Flowers, Theodore.

Georgia Institute of Technology, athletic teams of: **Yellow Jackets.**

Georgia Mafia. Group of influential men who helped secure the Democratic presidential nomination for Jimmy Carter in 1976 and who later served in his administration, among them Bert Lance, Griffin Bell, Hamilton Jordan, and Jody Powell.

Georgia Peach. Cobb, Ty[rus Raymond].

Georgia's Oldest City. Savannah, Georgia.

Gerber, Walter (1891–1951). Baseball shortstop: **Spooks.**

German Agent E-13. Means, Gaston Bullock.

Germans, The. H. R. Haldeman and John Erlichman, associates of President Richard M. Nixon.

Germany. Long, Herman C.; Schaefer, Herman A.; Schulz, Adolph George; Smith, Harry.

Gerry, Peter Goelet (1879–1957). U.S. Representative and Senator from Rhode Island: **The Millionaire.**

Gershwin, George (1898–1937). Composer and pianist: **Mr. Big of Tin Pan Alley.** Also known as James Baker, Fred Murtha, Bert Wynn. Born: Jacob Gershvin.

Gertrude Stein of the Musical Underground. Kaufman, Murray.

Getty, J[ean] Paul, Sr. (1892–1976). Billionaire oil operator: **Richest Man in the World.**

Gettysburg, Pennsylvania. U.S. town: **Battlefield City.**

Getz, Stan[ley] (born 1927). Jazz saxophonist: **The Sound.**

Ghetto Wizard. Leonard, Benny.

Ghost of the Ghetto. Terris, Sid.

Giancana, Sam (1894?–1975). Gangster: **Momo, Mooney.** Born: Salvatore Giancana.

Giant. Conroy, Jack.

Giant Killer. Covelski, Harry Frank.

Gibbons, Euell (1911–75). Wild food proponent and author: **The Wild Hickory Nut.**

Gibbons, Mike (1887–1956). Middleweight boxer: **The St. Paul Phantom, The Wizard.** Legal name: Michael J. Gibbons.

Gibbs, Georgia (born c. 1923). Singer: **Her Nibs Miss Gibbs.** Born: Freda Gibbson.

GI Bill of Rights. Servicemen's Readjustment Act.

Gibraltar of Democracy. Hoboken, New Jersey.

Gibson, George (1880–1967). Baseball catcher and manager: **Mooney.**

Gibson, Hoot (1892–1962). Rodeo champion and actor in motion-picture Westerns; with three other stars: **Big Four.** Legal name: Edward Richard Gibson.

Gibson, Joshua (1911–47). Baseball player: **The Black Babe Ruth.**

Gibson, Robert (born 1935). Baseball pitcher: **Hoot, Old Master.**

Gibson, Samuel Braxton (1900–62). Baseball pitcher: **Hoot.**

Gifford, Charles L. (1871–1947). U.S. Representative from Massachusetts: **Cranberry.**

Gifford, Frank (born 1930). Football back and sports announcer: **Golden Boy.**

Giggles. Von Zell, Harry.

GI Jane. Enlisted woman in the U.S. Army, esp. in World War II.

GI Joe. Enlisted man in the U.S. Army, esp. in World War II.

Gilbert, Cass (1859–1934). Architect: **Father of the Skyscraper.**

Gilbert, John (1895–1936). Motion-picture actor: **Great Lover.** Born: John Pringle.

Gilbert, Rod[rique] (born 1941). Hockey player: **Hot Rod, Mr. Ranger, Rocky.**

Gilchrist, Carlton C. (born 1935). Football back: **Cookie.**

Gill, Amory Tingle (1901–66). Basketball player, coach, and athletic director: **Slats.**

Gill, Ralph (born 1919). Composer and singer: **Rusty.**

Gillars, Mildred Elizabeth (born 1900). Radio propagandist for the Nazis: **Axis Sally, Midge at the Mike.** Born: Mildred Elizabeth Sisk.

Gillespie, John [Birks] (born 1917). Jazz trumpeter: **Dizzy.**

Gillette, King Camp (1855–1932). Inventor and industrialist: **Father of the Safety Razor.**

Gilliam, Jim (1928–78). Baseball second and third baseman: **Junior.** Legal name: James William Gilliam.

Gilliam, John [Rally] (born 1945). Football end: **Tally.**

Gillis, Lester M. (1903–34). Gangster: **Baby Face Nelson.** Also known as George Nelson.

Gimp, The. Snyder, Martin.

Gimpy. Pappas, Milt.

Ginger. Beaumont, Clarence Howeth.

Gink. Hendrick, Harvey.

Ginnie Mae. Government National Mortgage Association (GNMA).

Ginsberg, Allen (born 1926). Hippie poet: **Gentle Guru of the Flower People, Wild Shaman of the Beat Generation.**

Gints, The. New York Giants.

Gioe, Charlie (active 1930s). Gangster: **Cherry Nose.**

Gipp, George (1895–1920). Football back: **Gipper.**

Gipper. Gipp, George; Locke, Roland A.

Girl in the Red Velvet Swing. Nesbit, Evelyn.

Girl in the Swing. Nesbit, Evelyn.

Girl on the Piano. Morgan, Helen.

Girl We Would Like to Take a Slow Boat Back to the States With. Day, Doris.

Girl with the Ginger Snap Name. Pitts, ZaSu.

Gish, Dorothy (1898–1968). Motion-picture actress: **Miss Apprehension.** Born: Dorothy de Guiche.

Gish, Lillian (born 1896). Motion-picture actress: **Carrots, First Lady of the Screen, Iron Horse, Miss Lillian, Potato.** Born: Lillian de Guiche.

Giunta, Giuseppe (active 1930s). Gangster: **Hop Toad.**

Give 'Em Hell Harry. Truman, Harry S.

Glacier Priest. Hubbard, Bernhard Rosecrans.

Gladding, Fred Earl (born 1936). Baseball pitcher: **Bear.**

Glamor Boy of the Race Drivers. Revson, Peter.

Glass, Carter (1858–1946). U.S. Senator from Virginia: **Father of the Federal Reserve System, Snapping Turtle, Sound Money Glass, Unreconstructed Rebel.**

Glass Capital of New York. Corning, New York.

Glass Capital of Ohio. Toledo, Ohio.

Glass City. Toledo, Ohio.

Glass Menagerie on the East River. United Nations headquarters, New York City.

Gleason, Jackie (born 1916). Comedian and televison personality: **The Fat One, The Great One, Mr. Saturday Night.** Legal name: Herbert John Gleason.

Gleason, William (1866–1933). Baseball coach: **Kid.**

Glendale, California. U.S. city: **Jewel City, Queen of the Valley.**

Glenn, John [Herschel] (born 1921). Astronaut, businessman, and U.S. Senator from Ohio: **First American in Orbit, The Original Astronaut.**

Glider Capital of America. Elmira, New York.

Glitter Gulch. Reno, Nevada; Main Street of Las Vegas, Nevada.

Gloomy. Dobie, Gil[mour].

Gloomy Dean of Broadway. Kaufman, George S.

Glorious Fifty. The states of the United States.

Gluck, Edward (1902?–73). Basketball player: **Sonny.**

G-Man. Agent of the Federal Bureau of Investigation.

Goat of the Wets. Volstead, Andrew J.

Gobblers. Athletic teams of Virginia Polytechnic Institute & State University, (VPI) Blacksburg.

Gobel, George [Leslie] (born 1920). Television comedian: **Lonesome George.**

Goddard, Robert H. (1882–1945). Scientist: **Father of American Rocketry.**

Godfather, The. Nixon, Richard M[ilhous].

Godfrey, Arthur [Michael] (born 1903). Radio and television star: **Red, Red Head.**

Godfrey, Warren Edward (born 1931). Hockey player: **Rocky.**

God of Hollywood. Griffith, D[avid Lewelyn] W[ark].

God's Country. United States of America (or one's favorite part of it).

Goldberg, Rube (1883–1970). Cartoonist, author, and comic strip artist: **The Dean, Wizard of Wacky Inventions.** Legal name: Reuben Lucius Goldberg.

Gold Coast. Shore area of wealthy homes, esp. those of southeastern Florida or the northern part of Chicago.

Gold Coast City. Miami Beach, Florida.

Gold Dust Twins, The. 1. Duke, Doris and Hutton, Barbara. 2. Hindermyer, Harvey and Tuckerman, Earle.

Golden Acorn Division. Eighty-seventh Infantry Division.

Golden Arches, The. McDonald's.

Golden Arrow. Eighth Infantry Division.

Golden Bear. Nicklaus, Jack [William].

Golden Bears. Athletic teams of the University of California, Berkeley.

Golden Boy. Gifford, Frank; Hornung, Paul [Vernon]; Hull, Bobby.

Golden City of the Gold Coast. Boca Raton, Florida.

Golden Eagles. Athletic teams of the University of Southern Mississippi, Hattiesburg.

Golden Flashes. Athletic teams of Kent State University, Kent, Ohio.

Golden Gate City. San Francisco.

Golden Heart. Fairbanks, Alaska.

Golden Heart of the North. Fairbanks, Alaska.

Golden Horseshoe. 1. Industrial shoreline in the area of Toronto, Canada. 2. Two lowermost tiers of boxes at the former Metropolitan Opera House, New York City.

Golden Hurricane. Athletic teams of the University of Tulsa, Tulsa, Oklahoma.

Golden Hussey. Chadwick, Cassie.

Golden Hyphen. Winston-Salem, North Carolina.

Golden Isles. Islands of Jekyll, Saint Simons, and Sea Island off the coast of Georgia.

Golden Jet. Hull, Bobby.

141

Golden Lion Division. One Hundred and Sixth Infantry Division.

Golden Province. Ontario.

Golden Rule Fellow. Steffens, [Joseph] Lincoln.

Golden State. California.

Golden Talon Division. Seventeenth Airborne Division.

Golden Tonsil. Day, Doris.

Golden Triangle. Triangular downtown business district of Pittsburgh, Pennsylvania.

Golden Twenties. The 1920s, seen as a time of prosperity.

Golden Voice of Radio. Munn, Frank.

Goldie. Hindermyer, Harvey.

Goldilocks. Temple, Shirley.

Gold Medal County. Alameda County, California.

Gold Rush Town. Nome, Alaska.

Goldstein, Martin (died 1941). Gangster: **Bugsy.**

Goldstein, Ruby (born 1907). Lightweight boxer and referee: **Jewel of the Ghetto.** Legal name: Reuben Goldstein.

Goldwater, Barry [Morris] (born 1909). Politician and U.S. Senator from Arizona: **Beelzebub M. Goldwater, Monster from Arizona.**

Gold Capital of the World. Palm Springs, California.

Golfdom's Mighty Mite. Hogan, [William] Ben[jamin].

Golyer, Everette Lee de (1886–1956). Geologist and geophysicist: **Father of American Geophysics.**

Gomer. Osteen, Claude Wilson.

Gomez, Vernon Louis (born 1908). Baseball pitcher: **Lefty.**

Gompers, Samuel (1850–1924). U.S. labor leader: **Grand Old Man of Labor.**

Gonsoulin, Austin (born 1938). Football back: **Goose.**

Gonzales, Richard [Alonzo] (born 1928). Tennis player: **Pancho.**

Goober. Native or resident of Alabama, Georgia, or North Carolina.

Goober State. Georgia.

Gooch, Wayne R. (active 1906). Bootlegger: **King of Moonshiners.**

Good Citizen. Schuster, Arnold.

Goodman, Benny (born 1909). Clarinetist and bandleader: **BG, King of Swing.** Legal name; Benjamin David Goodman.

Good Neighbor Policy. Policy, initiated by President Franklin D. Roosevelt in 1933, of nonintervention in the affairs of other nations of the Western Hemisphere.

Good News. Barnes, Marvin.

Good News Tonight Man, The. Heatter, Gabriel.

Goodrich, Gail (born 1943). Basketball forward: **Stumpy.**

Good Roads Cartwright. Cartwright, Wilburn.

Goodson, Mark (born 1915). Television producer. With William Todman: **Maharajahs of Paneldom.**

Good Witch of the West, The. Huebner, Louise.

Goo-Goo. Abusive epithet for a political reformer calling for "good government."

Gooney Bird. Douglas DC-3 airliner.

Goose. Gonsoulin, Austin; Goslin, Leon Allen; Grumman A-21 amphibian plane, World War II; Tatum, Reese.

Goose Capital of the World. Cairo, Illinois.

GOP. Grand Old Party, i.e., the Republican Party.

Gophers. Athletic teams of the University of Minnesota, Minneapolis.

Gopher State. Minnesota.

Gordon, Joe (born 1915). Baseball second baseman and manager: **Flash.** Legal name: Joseph Lowell Gordon.

Gore, Thomas Pryor (1870–1949). U.S. Senator from Oklahoma: **Blind Savant.**

Gorgas, William Crawford (1854–1920). Sanitation expert and U.S. Surgeon General: **Conqueror of Yellow Fever.**

Gorgeous Cassie. Chadwick, Cassie.

Gorgeous Dan. Gable, Daniel.

Gorgeous George. Wagner, George Raymond.

Gorgeous Georgeous. Wagner, George Raymond.

Gorgeous Greeter, The. Whalen, Grover Aloysius.

Gorgeous Gussie. Moran, Gertrude Augusta.

Gorilla. Jones, William.

Gorilla Murderer. Wilson, Roger.

Goring, Robert Thomas (born 1949). Hockey player: **Butch, Seed.**

Goslin, Leon Allen (1900–71). Baseball outfielder: **Goose.**

Gospel Singer. McHugh, Edward.

Gotham. New York City.

Gothamite. Native or resident of New York City.

Gould, Joe (1889–1957). Greenwich Village character: **Professor Seagull.**

Gould, Laurence M[cKinley] (born 1896). Educator and polar explorer: **Chips.**

Government National Mortgage Association (GNMA). Federal agency: **Ginnie Mae.**

Grable, Betty (1916–73). Motion-picture actress and sex symbol: **No. 1 Pinup Girl, Soldier's Inspiration, Undisputed Queen of the Movies.**

Grace, Charles Manuel (1881–1960). Evangelist: **Daddy.**

Grady, Billy (born 1890). Theatrical agent: **The Irish Peacock.**

Graham, Billy (born 1918). Baptist clergyman, evangelist, and author: **The Cadillac Evangelist, Most Admired Man in America.** Legal name: William Franklin Graham.

Graham, Bonnie (born 1914). Basketball player: **Country.**

Grainger, Percy Aldridge (1882–1961). Pianist and composer: **The Joyous Musician.**

Grambling University, athletic teams of: **Tigers.**

Grand Canyon State. Arizona.

Grandma. Burright, Neva; Moses, Anna Mary Robertson.

Grandma Flapper. Hopper, Edna Wallace.

Grand Old Lady of American Art. Moses, Anna Mary Robertson.

Grand Old Lady of Opera. Schumann-Heink, Ernestine [Rössler].

Grand Old Lady of the Movies. Dressler, Marie.

Grand Old Man, The. Rayburn, Sam.

Grand Old Man of Football. Stagg, Amos Alonzo.

Grand Old Man of Labor. Gompers, Samuel.

Grand Old Man of Racing. Fitzsimmons, James Edward.

144

Grand Old Man of Six-shooterology. McGivern, Edward.

Grand Old Man of the Aw Shucks School. Stewart, James [Maitland].

Grand Old Man of the Screen. Roberts, Theodore.

Grand Old Novelist. Wilder, Thornton [Niven].

Grand Old Party. The Republican Party.

Grandpa. Jones, Louis.

Grand Rapids, Michigan. U.S. city: **Furniture City.**

Grand Slam. The winning by one person of the most prestigious tournaments (as in golf or tennis) in one year.

Grand Veteran. Johnson, Walter Perry.

Grange, Harold E[dward] (born 1903). Football player and sports commentator: **Galloping Ghost, Red, Wheaton Iceman.**

Granger. Member of the National Grange.

Granite Center. Barre, Vermont.

Granite City. Quincy, Massachusetts.

Granite State. New Hampshire.

Granite Woman. Snyder, Ruth.

Granny. Rice, [Henry] Grantland.

Grant, Edward Leslie (1883–1918). Baseball third baseman: **Harvard Eddie.**

Grant, Travis (born 1950). Basketball player: **The Machine.**

Grantham, George Farley (1900–54). Baseball first and second baseman: **Boots.**

Grape Juice. Johnson, Greg.

Grape State. California.

Grasshopper State. Kansas.

Graves, Ernest (1880–1953). Football player: **Pot.**

Graves, Perry Ivia (born 1892). Welterweight boxer: **Kid.**

Gray, Gilda (1898?–1959). Dancer: **Box Office Girl.** Born: Marianne Michaelska.

Gray, Glen (1906–63). Jazz bandleader: **Spike.** Legal name: Glen Gray Knoblaugh.

Gray, Sam[uel David] (1897–1953). Baseball pitcher: **Dolly.**

Gray-Crested Flycatcher. Burroughs, John.

Gray Eagle. Speaker, Tristram.

Gray Ghost. Native Dancer.

Gray Gold. Molybdenum.

Gray Power. Political solidarity and power of the Gray Panthers, a group organized to fight discrimination against old people.

Graziano, Rocky (born 1922). Middleweight boxer and actor: **Atomic Puncher, The Rock, Rockabye Rocky.** Born: Rocco Barbella.

Greaseball. Maloney, Tom.

Greasy. Neale, Earle.

Greasy Thumb Guzik. Guzik, Jack.

Greasy Thumb Jake. Guzik, Jack.

Great Agnostic. Ingersoll, Robert Green.

Great All American. Fish, Hamilton, Jr.

Great Carsoni, The. Carson, Johnny.

Great Central State. North Dakota.

Great Commoner. Bryan, William Jennings; Hogg, James Stephen.

Great Debunker. Mencken, H[enry] L[ouis].

Great Depression. Economic depression, in the U.S. lasting from October 1929 until the late 1930s.

Great Dissenter. Roberts, Owen Josephus.

Great Engineer. Hoover, Herbert [Clark].

Greatest, The. Ali, Muhammad.

Greatest Bowler in History. Carter, Donald James.

Greatest Citizen in the United States. Eliot, Charles William.

Greatest Criminal Lawyer of His Time. Stever, Max D.

Greatest Fox of Them All. Fox, William.

Greatest Gambler. Canfield, Richard A.

Greatest Hog Caller East of the Rockies. Kaufman, Morris.

Greatest Man-About-Town Any Town Ever Had. Mizner, Wilson.

Greatest Player of Hockey. Orr, Bobby.

Greatest Practicing Literary Journalist. Mencken, H[enry] L[ouis].

Greatest Showman Since Barnum. North, John Ringling.

Great Imposter. Weinberg, Stephen Jacob.

Great Jockey of the Golden Age of Sports. Sande, Earl H.

Great John L. Sullivan, John Lawrence.
Great Lakes Province. Ontario.
Great Lake State. Michigan.
Great Land. Alaska.
Great Left-handed Press Agent. Mails, Walter.
Great Liberal. Wheeler, Burton K[endall].
Great Lover. Gilbert, John.
Great Mails, The. Mails, Walter.
Great Man, The. Dean, Jay Hanna; Rockne, Knute Kenneth.
Great Merlini, The. Towne, Stuart.
Great Mick, The. Mantle, Mickey [Charles].
Great Mogul. Galbraith, John Kenneth.
Great Mouthpiece. Fallon, William J.
Great One, The Gleason, Jackie.
Great Profile, The. Barrymore, John.
Great Raymond, The. Raymond, Maurice.
Great Repealer, The. Barton, Bruce.
Great River City. St. Louis, Missouri.
Great Smoky Mountains. Appalachian mountain range in North Carolina and Tennessee: **Smokies.**
Great Society, The. President Lyndon B. Johnson's vision of a society with an improved quality of life for all.
Great Stone Face. Sullivan Ed[ward Vincent].
Great Thundering Rooster. Johnson, Hugh Samuel.
Great Tooth Tycoon. Parker, Edgar Rudolph Randolph.
Great Uncompromiser, The. Clay, Lucius DuBignon.
Great White Chief. Roosevelt, Theodore.
Great White Father. President of the United States.
Great White Fleet. Group of U.S. warships on a good-will mission around the world, 1907–09.
Great White Way. Broadway.
Greb, Edward Henry (1894–1926). Middleweight boxer: **The Human Windmill, The Pittsburgh Windmill.**
Greek, The. George, Charlie.
Greek Purist. Norris, George William.

Green, Hetty (1834–1916). Financier and miser: **Witch of Wall Street.** Legal name: Henrietta Howland Green.

Green, Joe (born 1946). Football tackle: **Mean Joe Green.**

Green, John (born 1933). Basketball player: **Jumpin' Johnny.**

Green, Vernice, Jr. (born 1935). Jazz musician: **Bunky.**

Green, Wilfred Thomas (1896–1960). Hockey player: **Shorty.**

Green Bay, Wisconsin. U.S. city: **Gateway to the Great Seaway, Packers' Town, Titletown, U.S.A., Port of Distinction.**

Green Bay Packers. Team of the Green Bay National Football Club, Inc.

Green Berets. U.S. special troops trained to combat guerrillas in Vietnam.

Greenberg, David (born 1943). New York City policeman: **Batman.** With Robert Hantz: **Batman and Robin.**

Greenberg, Hank (born 1911). Baseball player: **Hammering Hank.** Born: Henry Benjamin Greenberg.

Greenberg, Harry (died 1939). Gangster: **Big Greenie.**

Greenberg, Max (died 1928). Gangster: **Big Maxey.**

Greene, Waldo (active 1927). Football player: **Firp.**

Green Hornet. Patton, George Smith, Jr.

Green Knights. Athletic teams of St. Norbert College, De Pere, Wisconsin.

Green Man. DeSalvo, Albert H.

Green Max. Palevsky, Max.

Green Mountain Boys. Natives or residents of Vermont.

Green Mountain City. Montpelier, Vermont.

Green Mountain State. Vermont.

Greensboro, North Carolina. U.S. city. **City of Charm.**

Greenstein, Joseph L. (1883–1977). Wrestler and vaudeville showman: **Mighty Atom.**

Green Wave. Athletic teams of Tulane University, New Orleans, Louisiana.

Greenwich Village. District in Manhattan, New York City, traditionally an area of artists and writers: **The Village.**

Gregory, Francis Arnold (born 1926). Advertising executive: **Stretch.**

Gregory the Great. Ratoff, Gregory.

Grey, Zane (1875–1939). Writer: **Father of the Western Story.**

Grey Lady of the "*Times*." Sulzberger, Iphigene Ochs.

Grich, Robert Anthony (born 1949). Baseball second baseman: **Bird.**

Gridiron Brigadier. Neyland, Robert Reese, Jr.

Griebling, Otto (1897–1972). Circus clown: **The Sour-Faced Clown.**

Grier, Jimmie (1902–59). Jazz musician: **Host to the Coast.** Legal name: James W. Grier.

Grier, Roosevelt (born 1932). Football tackle and entertainer: **Rosey.**

Griffis, Silas Seth (1880?–1950). Hockey player: **Sox.**

Griffith, Clark Calvin (1869–1955). Baseball pitcher and manager: **Old Fox.**

Griffith, Corinne (1906–79). Motion-picture actress: **Orchid of the Screen.**

Griffith, D[avid Lewelyn] W[ark] (1875–1948). Motion-picture actor, director, and producer: **American Shakespeare, Father of the Film Industry, God of Hollywood.** Also known as David Brayington, Lawrence Griffith, Granville Warwick.

Grim, Joe (1881–1939). Boxer: **Iron Man.** Born: Saverio Giannone.

Grimes, Burleigh Arland (born 1893). Baseball pitcher: **Last of the Spitball Pitchers, Old Stubblebeard, Senator.**

Grimes, Lloyd (born 1915). Jazz guitarist: **Tiny.**

Grissom, Virgil I[van] (1926–67). Astronaut: **Gus.**

Grizzlies. Athletic teams of the University of Montana, Missoula.

Groaner, The. Crosby, Bing.

Groh, Henry Knight (1889–1968). Baseball second and third baseman: **Heinie.**

Grooms, Charles Roger (born 1937). Artist and motion-picture maker: **Red.**

Groove. Holmes, Richard Arnold.

Gros Bill, Le. Beliveau, Jean.

Gross, H. R. (born 1899). U.S. Representative from Iowa: **Congress' Lovable Curmudgeon.**

Groundhog State. Mississippi.

Grove, Robert Moses (1900–75). Baseball pitcher: **Lefty.**

Groza, Alex (born 1926). Basketball player: **Weed.**

Groza, Lou[is] (born 1924). Football tackle and kicker: **The Toe.**

Gruenther, Alfred M[aximilian] (born 1899). U.S. Army General, adviser to governmental military agencies, businessman, and authority on contract bridge: **Brain of the Army.**

Grunewald, Henry William (1893–1958). Convicted criminal: **The Dutchman.**

Guadalcanal General. Vandegrift, Alexander Archer.

Guardian of the Government. Seymour, Whitney North.

Guest, Edgar A[lbert] (1881–1959). Verse writer: **Poet of the People.**

Guffer. Murphy, John T.

Guffey, Joseph F. (1875–1959). U.S. Senator from Pennsylvania: **King-Maker.**

Guidolin, Armand (born 1925). Hockey player: **Bep.**

Guinan, Mary Louise Cecelia (1884–1933). Nightclub entertainer and film actress: **Nightclub Queen, Two-Gun Girl, Queen of the Speakeasies, Texas.**

Guinea Pig State. Arkansas.

Gulf City. Mobile, Alabama; New Orleans, Louisiana.

Gulf Coast City. Pensacola, Florida.

Gulf of Alaska. Body of water off the southern coast of Alaska: **Home of Storms.**

Gulf Oil Corporation. Business organization; with six other oil companies: **Seven Sisters.**

Gulf State. Florida.

Gulf States. States bordering on the Gulf of Mexico—Florida, Alabama, Mississippi, Louisiana, and Texas.

Gump. Worsley, Lorne John.

Gunboat. Hudson, Walter.

Gunboat Smith. Smyth, Edward J.

Gunflint. Native or resident of Rhode Island.

Gung-Ho Battalion. Special U.S. Marine force in World War II under the leadership of Colonel Evans Fordyce Carlson. Also known as **Carlson's Raiders.**

150

Gunner, The. Smyth, Edward J.

Gurrah Jake. Shapiro, Jacob.

Gus. Dorais, Charles E.; Grissom, Virgil I[van]; Mancuso, Ronald Bernard; Wynn, Early.

Gussie. Moran, Gertrude Augusta.

Gutierrez, Cesar Dario (born 1943). Baseball shortstop, second, and third baseman: **Cocoa.**

Gutter Nietzschean. Penrose, Boies.

Guttero, Lee (born 1912). Basketball player: **Rubberlegs.**

Guyer, Ulysses Samuel (1863–1943). U.S. Representative from Kansas: **Dry Wind, Kansas Dry.**

Guyon, Joseph (1892–1971). Baseball player: **Indian Joe.**

Guzik, Jack (1886–1956). Gangster: **Greasy Thumb Guzik, Greasy Thumb Jake.**

Gyp. DeCarlo, Angelo.

H

Haas, George William (1903–1974). Baseball outfielder: **Mule.**

Haas, Oscar P. (1908–57). Test pilot and aviation official: **Bud.**

Haberdasher Harry. Truman, Harry S.

Habitant. Rural French Canadian.

Hack. Wilson, Lewis Robert.

Hadley, Irving Darius (1904–63). Baseball pitcher: **Bump.**

Hagberg, Rudolf (1907–60). Football center: **Swede.**

Hagen, Walter Charles (1892–1969). Golfer: **The Haig.**

Hague, Frank (1876–1956). Political boss: **Boss Hague, Dictator of Jersey City.**

Hahn, Frank George (1879–1960). Baseball pitcher: **Noodles.**

Haig, Alexander Meigs, Jr. (born 1924). U.S. Army General and government official: **Mr. Inside, The Sir Laurence Olivier of the White House.**

Haig, The. Hagen, Walter Charles.

Haight-Ashbury. Section of San Francisco, California, formerly occupied by hippies: **Hashbury, Psychedelphia, Tripsville.**

Haines, William C. (1887–1956). Meteorologist: **Cyclone.**

Haldeman, H[arry] R[obbins] (born 1926). Advertising executive and presidential aide: **First of the Nixon Men, Nixon's Alter Ego, President's Rasputin, Pride of Pragmatists.** Also known as Bob Haldeman.

152

Hale, Arvel Odell (born 1908). Baseball second and third baseman: **Chief, Bad News.**

Haley, Bill (born 1927). Rock 'n' roll musician, guitarist, and singer: **The Rambling Yodeler, Rock Around the Clock Haley.** Legal name: William Haley.

Half-Breed Logger. Pennier, Henry George.

Hall, Alfred (1895–1946). Jazz drummer: **Tubby.**

Hall, Howard (active 1925–35). Jazz musician and pianist: **Joe the Horse.**

Hall, Wendell Woods (born 1896). Composer and entertainer: **Redheaded Music-Maker.**

Halsey, William F[rederick], Jr. (1882–1959). Admiral of the Fleet: **Bull.**

Hamburger King. McDonald, Maurice James.

Hamilton, Foreststorn (born 1921). Jazz drummer and composer: **Chico.**

Hamilton, George (1901–57). Jazz composer and leader: **Spike.**

Hamlet of the Halls. Lewis, Ted.

Hammer, Armand (born 1898). Entrepreneur and business executive: **Boy Wonder, Russian Connection, Salesman De Luxe.**

Hammer, The. Kostka, Stanley; Schultz, David.

Hammering Hank. Greenberg, Hank.

Hammer of the North. Bierman, Bernard William.

Hammer of Thor. Townsend, Francis Everett.

Hamp, The. Hampton, Lionel Leo.

Hampton, Lionel [Leo] (born 1914). Jazz musician: **The Hamp.**

Hampton, Locksley Wellington (born 1932). Jazz trombonist, tuba player, and composer: **Slide.**

Hampton, Virginia. U.S. city: **Crabtown.**

Hampton Roads, Virginia. U.S. town: **World's Greatest Harbor.**

Hamtramck, Michigan. U.S. city: **Polish City.**

Hancock, Clarence Eugene (1885–1948). U.S. Representative from New York: **Banty.**

Handcuff King. Houdini, Harry.

Handsome Charley. Becker, Charles.

Handsome Harry. Daugherty, Harry [Micajah].

Handsome Johnny. Barend, John.

Handsome One. Barend, John.

Handy, W[illiam] C[hristopher] (1873–1958). Jazz composer: **Father of the Blues.**

Hanging Prosecutor. McSwiggin, William H.

Hangman. Cantonwine, Howard.

Hank. Crawford, Benny Ross, Jr.

Hanna, Richard (born 1914). Politician and U.S. Representative from California: **Capitol Hill's Premier Junketeer.**

Hanneford, Edwin (1892–1967). Circus clown: **Poodles.**

Hannibal, Missouri. U.S. city: **Bluff City, Capital of Youth, Mark Twain Town.**

Hans. Lobert, John Bernard; Wagner, John Peter.

Hansen, Roy Emil (born 1910). Baseball player: **Snipe.**

Hantz, Robert (born 1943). New York City policeman: **Robin.** With David Greenberg: **Batman and Robin.**

Hap. Arnold, Henry Harley; Day, Clarence Henry; Gay, Hobart Raymond; O'Donnell, John.

Hapless Hooker. Vecchio, Mary.

Happy. Chandler, Albert Benjamin; Caldwell, Albert; Day, Clarence Henry; Felton, Francis J.; Maloney, Patrick; Rockefeller, Margaretta [Fitler]; Turner, John C.

Happy Home of the Bulldozer. Los Angeles, California.

Happy Hooker, The. Hollander, Xaviera.

Happy Jack. Chesbro, John Dwight.

Happy Talker. Cavett, Dick.

Happy Warrior. Humphrey, Hubert Horatio; Roosevelt, Theodore; Smith, Alfred Emanuel.

Harbor City. Erie, Pennsylvania

Harburg, E. Y. (born 1898). Librettist and author: **Yip.**

Hard-Case State. Oregon.

Harder, Melvin Leroy (born 1909). Baseball pitcher: **Chief.**

Hardin, Louis Thomas (born 1916). Jazz musician: **Moondog.**

Harding, Florence Kling DeWolfe (1860–1929). Wife of U.S. President Warren G. Harding: **Boss, The Duchess, Flossie, Ma.**

Harding, Warren Gamaliel (1865–1923). Twenty-ninth President of the United States: **Dark Horse Candidate, Winnie.**

Harding Enthusiast. Smoot, Reed.

Hard Luck Bruder. Bruder, Henry.

Hard-nosed Demon of the Ovals. Foyt, A[nthony] J[oseph, Jr.].

Hard Rock. American Broadcasting Company.

Hardrock. Shoun, Clyde Mitchell.

Hardrock Kid. Mislen, John.

Hard-Shell Baptist. Primitive Baptist.

Hardwicke, Otto (born 1904). Jazz saxophonist: **Toby.**

Hargrave, Eugene Franklin (1892–1969). Baseball catcher: **Bubbles.**

Hargrave, William McKinley (born 1900). Baseball catcher: **Pinkey.**

Harlan County, Kentucky. Coal mining area and scene of labor violence, 1930s: **Bloody Harlan.**

Harlem. District in Manhattan, New York City, with a very large black population: **Soul City.**

Harlow, Jean (1911–37). Motion-picture actress: **Blonde Bombshell.** Born: Harlean Carpenter.

Harmon, Ernest N[ason] (born 1894). U.S. Army Major General and president of Norwich University: **Old Gravel Voice.**

Harmonica Rascal. Minevich, Borrah.

Haroun-al-Roosevelt. Roosevelt, Theodore.

Harrelson, Ken[neth Smith] (born 1941). Baseball outfielder and first baseman: **Hawk.**

Harriman, Edward H. (1848–1909). Businessman and financier: **Colossus of the Roads.**

Harriman, [William] Averell (born 1891). U.S. diplomat and businessman: **The Crocodile.**

Harrington, Francis C. (1887–1940). U.S. Army officer and politician: **Pinky.**

Harris, Arlene (active 1925–35). Radio actress: **Human Chatterbox.**

Harris, Benjamin (born 1919). Jazz trumpeter: **Little Benny.**

Harris, David Stanley (born 1903). Baseball outfielder: **Sheriff.**

Harris, Emily (born c. 1947). Member of the Symbionese Liberation Army: **Yolanda.**

Harris, James Armstrong (1847–1921). Promoter of orange growing in Florida: **Orange King.**

Harris, Jed (born 1900). Theatrical producer: **Boy Wonder of Broadway.**

Harris, Stanley Raymond (1896–1977). Baseball second baseman and manager: **Boy Wonder, Bucky.**

Harris, William (born c. 1945). Member of the Symbionese Liberation Army: **Tico.**

Harrisburg, Pennsylvania. U.S. city: **Courteous Capital City, State City.**

Harrisburg Seven, The. Eqbal Ahmed, Rev. Philip Berrigan, Sister Elizabeth McAlister, Rev. Neil McLaughlin, Anthony Scoblick, Mary Cain Scoblick, and Rev. Joseph Wenderoth, antiwar demonstrators accused of subversive activities, 1960s and 1970s.

Harrison, Ernest Joe (born 1910). Golfer: **Dutch.**

Harry. Bridges, Alfred Bryant Renton.

Harry Hussey. Tourbillon, Robert Arthur.

Harry the Hop. Hopkins, Harry Lloyd.

Hart, Philip A[loysius] (1912–76). U.S. Senator from Michigan: **Conscience of the Senate.**

Harter, Down Watters (1885–1971). U.S. Representative from Ohio: **Rubber King.**

Hartford, Connecticut. U.S. city: **Charter Oak City, Insurance City.**

Hartline, Mary (born 1926). Television personality and circus band leader: **Super Circus Girl.**

Hartnett, Charles Leo (1900–72). Baseball catcher: **Gabby, Man in the Iron Mask.**

Harvard Eddie. Grant, Edward Leslie.

Harvard's Gift to the West. Cutting, Bronson.

Harvard University. 1. Athletic teams of: **Cantabs, Crimson.** 2. Athletic teams of, with teams of Yale and Princeton: **Big Three.** 3.

Athletic teams of, with seven other teams in college conference: **Ivy League.**

Hashbury. Haight-Ashbury.

Hastings, William Wirt (1866–1938). U.S. Representative from Oklahoma: **Cherokee Bill.**

Hat, The. Walker, Harry William.

Hatch, Carl Atwood (1889–1963). U.S. Senator from New Mexico: **Cowboy Carl.**

Hatfield, Charles Folsom (1862–1939). Advertising executive: **Dean of Community Advertising.**

Hat-in-the-Ring Squadron. Ninety-fourth Aero Pursuit Squadron.

Haughton, Percy Duncan (1876–1924). Football coach: **Haughton of Harvard, PD.**

Haughton of Harvard. Haughton, Percy Duncan.

Hauptmann, Bruno Richard (1899–1936). Convicted kidnaper and murderer of Charles A. Lindbergh's infant son: **Cemetery John.**

Havlicek, John (born 1940). Basketball player: **Hondo.**

Havoc, June (born 1916). Dancer and actress: **Dainty Baby June, the Pocket-sized Pavlova.** Born: June Hovick.

Hawaii. Fiftieth U.S. state: **Aloha State, Cane Sugar State, Fiftieth State, Gateway to the Orient, Gem of the Pacific, Island Paradise, Island State, Paradise of the Pacific, Orchid Isle, Pineapple State, Youngest State.**

Hawaii. Island in the state of Hawaii: **Big Island.**

Hawaii, University of, athletic teams of: **Rainbow Warriors.**

Hawaiian Giant. Kuhaulua, Jesse.

Hawaiian Pineapple King. Dole, James Drummond.

Hawaii's Music Man. Edwards, Webley.

Hawk. Curtiss P-36 fighter plane, World War II; Harrelson, Ken[neth Smith]; Hawkins, Coleman; Taylor, Robert Dale.

Hawk, The. Charles, Ezzard; Hawkins, Coleman; Hawkins, Connie; Hogan, [William] Ben[jamin]; Gavilan, Kid.

Hawkeye. Native or resident of Iowa.

Hawkeyes. Athletic teams of the University of Iowa, Iowa City.

Hawkeye State. Iowa.

Hawkins, Coleman (1904–69). Jazz saxophonist: **Hawk, Bean, The Hawk.**

Hawkins, Connie (born 1944). Basketball player: **The Hawk.**

Hawkins, Erskine (born 1914). Jazz musician: **Twentieth Century Gabriel.**

Hawley, Roy M. (1901–54). College athletic director: **Legs.**

Hayakawa, S[amuel] I[chiye] (born 1906). U.S. Senator from California and semanticist: **Samurai in a Tam O'Shanter.**

Hayes, Edward Brian (born 1935). Jazz saxophonist: **Tubby.**

Hayes, Elvin (born 1945). Basketball center: **The Big E.**

Hayes, E. O. (1906–73). Basketball coach: **Doc.**

Hayes, George Francis (1885–1969). Motion-picture actor: **Gabby.**

Hayes, Helen (born 1900). Actress: **First Lady of the American Theater.** Born: Helen Hayes Brown.

Hayes, Isaac (born 1942). Singer and composer: **Black Moses.**

Hayes, Sam[uel] (born 1904). Radio news commentator: **The Richfield Reporter.**

Hayes, Wayne Woodrow (born 1913). Football coach: **Woody.**

Haywood, William D[udley] (1869–1928). Labor leader: **Big Bill, Wild Bill.**

Hayworth, Myron Claude (born 1915). Baseball catcher: **Red.**

Hayworth, Rita (born 1918). Motion-picture actress: **Love Goddess.** Born: Margarita Carmen Cansino.

Hazel, Arthur (1903–68). Jazz musician: **Monk.**

Head Hunter. Bailey, F[rancis] Lee.

Headless Horseman. Wallace, George [Corley].

Head of the White House Plumbers. Krogh, Egil, Jr.

Health City. Battle Creek, Michigan.

Heard, Eugene M. (born 1923). Jazz drummer: **Fats.**

Hearst, Patricia [Campbell] (born 1954). Heiress, victim of kidnaping by Symbionese Liberation Army, and convicted bank robber: **Renegade Newspaper Heiress, Tania.**

Hearst, William Randolph (1863–1951). Publisher: **Emperor of**

Newsprint, Lord of San Simeon, The People's Democrat, Poor Little Rich Boy.

Heartland City. Kansas City, Missouri.

Heartland of America. Midwest, The.

Heart of America. Kansas City, Missouri.

Heart of California. Sacramento, California.

Heart of Canada. Ontario.

Heart of Central Alaska. Fairbanks, Alaska.

Heart of Dixie. Alabama; New Orleans, Louisiana.

Heart of Georgia. Macon, Georgia.

Heart of Historic Virginia. Charlottesville, Virginia.

Heart of Kentucky. Frankfort, Kentucky.

Heart of Polynesia. American Samoa.

Heart of the Cow Country. Oklahoma.

Heart of the Gold Coast. Hollywood, Florida.

Heart of the Inland Empire. Spokane, Washington.

Heart of the Nation. Illinois

Heart of the Nation's Heritage. Alexandria, Virginia.

Heart of the New Industrial South. Alabama.

Heart of the Old Southwest. Tucson, Arizona.

Heart of the Sun Country. Phoenix, Arizona.

Heath, Albert (born 1935). Jazz drummer: **Tootie.**

Heath, James Edward (born 1926). Jazz saxophonist: **Little Bird.**

Heatter, Gabriel (1890–1972). News announcer and analyst: **The Good News Tonight Man.**

Heffelfinger, William Walter (1868–1954). Football guard: **Pudge.**

Heff Lee. Bailey, F[rancis] Lee.

Hefner, Hugh [Marston] (born 1926). Publisher: **Boss of the Bunny Empire, Mr. Playboy of the Western World, Prince of Sophisticated Pornography.**

Heidelberg of America. Dubuque, Iowa.

Heidt, Horace Murray (born 1901). Jazz musician and bandleader. **The Heidt of Entertainment, The Money Maestro, Musical Copy-Cat.**

159

Heidt of Entertainment, The. Heidt, Horace Murray.

Heinie. Groh, Henry Knight; Manush, Henry Emmett; Meine, Henry William; Mueller, Clarence Franklin; Peitz, Henry Clement; Scheer, Henry William; Schuble, Henry George, Jr.; Zimmerman, Henry.

Heinrich, Edward Oscar (active 1916–23). Detective: **Edison of Crime Detection.**

Helena, Montana, U.S. city: **Queen of the Mountains.**

Hell and Maria Dawes. Dawes, Charles Gates.

Hellcat. Grumman F6F fighter plane, World War II.

Hellcat Division. Twelfth Armored Division.

Hell in the Hills. Pittsburgh, Pennsylvania.

Hell on Wheels Division. Second Armored Division.

Hell's Devil Butler. Butler, Smedley Darlington.

Hell's Kitchen. Unsavory tenement district in Manhattan, New York City, around lower 10th Avenue, once the home of many thieves and gunmen, first half of 20th century.

Hemingway, Ernest (1899–1961). Writer: **Papa Hemingway, Spokesman for the Lost Generation.**

Hemingway, Margaux (born 1955). Model, actress, and granddaughter of Ernest Hemingway: **Fabulous Babe.**

Hemp State. Kentucky.

Henderson, [James] Fletcher (1898–1952). Jazz pianist and bandleader: **Smack.**

Henderson, Lyle Cedric (born 1918). Jazz musician, pianist, and composer: **Skitch.** Also known as Sydney Ferguson.

Henderson, Thomas (born 1953). Football linebacker. **Hollywood.**

Hendrick, Harvey (1897–1941). Baseball outfielder: **Gink.**

Hendricks, Joseph Edward (born 1903). U.S. Representative from Florida: **Doc Townsend of Florida.**

Henline, Walter John (1898–1957). Baseball catcher and umpire: **Butch.**

Henry, O. (1862–1910). Writer: **American Maupassant.** Legal name: William Sydney Porter.

Henry, Wilbur F. (1897–1952). Football player: **Fats.**

Henry Ford of Aviation. Piper, William Thomas.

Henry Ford of the Movies. Zukor, Adolph.

Henry J. Kaiser, Henry J.

Henry the K. Kissinger, Henry A[lfred].

Henry You-Know-Who. Kissinger, Henry A[lfred].

Henson, Matthew (1866–1955). Polar explorer: **Black Explorer, Negro Explorer.**

Herbert, Victor (1859–1924). Composer and conductor: **The American Music-Master.**

Herblock. Block, Herb.

Hercules, Lockheed HC–130 transport plane.

Hercules Mary. Promitis, Mary.

Herkimer Hurricane. Ambers, Lou.

Herman, Floyd Caves (born 1903). Baseball outfielder: **Babe.**

Hermit Author of Palo Alto. Hoover, Herbert [Clark].

Hermit of Slabsides. Burroughs, John.

Her Nibs Miss Gibbs. Gibbs, Georgia.

Hero. Calley, William Laws.

Hero Husband. Wanderer, Carl.

Heroine of Bald Mountain. Morrow, Anne McIntyre.

Hero of Chappaquiddick. Kennedy, Edward M[oore].

Hero of San Juan Hill. Roosevelt, Theodore.

Hero of Squaw Island. Kennedy, Edward M[oore].

Hero of the Cities. Smith, Alfred Emanuel.

Hero of Wall Street. Whitney, Richard.

Herr Henry. Kissinger, Henry A[lfred].

Herring, Arthur L. (born 1907). Baseball pitcher: **Red, Sandy.**

Her Sexellency. Rand, Sally.

Hershey, Milton Snavely (1857–1945). Chocolate manufacturer and philanthropist: **The Chocolate King, The Cocoa King, Father of the Hershey Bar.**

Hershey, Pennsylvania. U.S. city: **Chocolate City.**

Herzog, Charles Lincoln (1885–1953). Baseball second and third baseman: **Buck.**

Heston, William Martin (1878–1963). Football halfback and lawyer: **The Michigan Terror.**

Hezzie. Trietsch, Paul.

HHH. Humphrey, Hubert Horatio.

Hialeah, Florida. U.S. city: Taxpayer's Haven.

Hibben, Paxton Pattison (1880–1928). Journalist and diplomat. **Hoosier Quixote.**

Hick. Cady, Forrest Leroy.

Hickey, Howard (active after 1940). Football end and coach: **Red.**

Hickory. Solomon, Moses.

Hi De Ho Man. Calloway, Cab.

Higginbotham, Jack (born 1906). Jazz trombonist: **Jay C, JC.**

Higgins, Andrew Jackson (born 1886). Shipbuilder: **America's Number One Boatbuilder, Money-Maker and Hoopla Artist, Shipyard Bunyan.**

Higgins, Mike (1909–69). Baseball third baseman and manager: **Pinkey.** Legal name: Michael Franklin Higgins.

Highest State. Colorado.

High-hatted Tragedian of Jazz. Lewis, Ted.

High Priest of Bebop. Monk, Thelonious Sphere.

High Tax Harry. Truman, Harry S.

Hiker. Joy, William P.

Hildegarde (born 1906). Entertainer: **First Lady of Supper Clubs, Incomparable Hildegarde.** Legal name: Hildegarde Loretta Sell.

Hill, Bertha (1905–50). Blues singer: **Chippie.**

Hill, James Jerome (1838–1916). Railway executive and financier: **Empire Builder.**

Hill, The. 1. Capitol Hill. 2. Poor district of Pittsburgh.

Hill, Walter Barnard (1851–1905). Lawyer: **Apostle of Temperance.**

Hillbilly Cat. Presley, Elvis [Aron].

Hillbilly Country. Backwoods or remote region, esp. the mountainous regions in the southern United States.

Hill City. Portland, Maine.

Hilltoppers. Athletic teams of Western Kentucky University, Bowling Green.

Hilton, Conrad, Jr. (1927–69). Hotel executive and playboy: **Nicky.**

Hilton, Conrad [Nicholson] (1887–1979). Hotel executive: **Biggest Hotel Man in the World, Number One Innkeeper.**

Hindermyer, Harvey (active 1920s and 1930s). Radio singer: **Goldie.** With Earle Tuckerman: **The Gold Dust Twins.**

Hines, Earl Kenneth (born 1905). Jazz pianist: **Fatha.**

Hink, The. Kenna, Michael.

Hinky Dink. Kenna, Michael.

Hip Harpsichordist. Newman, Anthony.

Hippieland's Court Chemist. Stanley, Augustus Owsley, III.

Hippie Murderer. Manson, Charles M.

Hippo. Vaugh, James Leslie.

Hired Man on Horseback. Rhodes, Eugene Manlove.

Hireling of the Anti-Saloon League. Wheeler, Wayne Bidwell.

Hirsch, Elroy (born 1923). Football end and back: **Crazylegs.**

Hirt, Al[ois Maxwell] (born 1922). Jazz trumpeter: **Trumpeting Behemoth.**

Historical City of Homes. Evanston, Illinois.

Historic Center of North Carolina. New Bern, North Carolina.

Hitchcock, Alfred (born 1899). Motion-picture director: **The Cherubic, The Portly Master of the Involuntary Scream, Master of Suspense.**

Hitchcock, Thomas, Jr. (1900–44). Polo player and military flyer: **Babe Ruth of Polo.**

Hoak, Donald Albert (1928–69). Baseball third baseman: **Tiger.**

Hobey. Baker, Hobart Amory Hare.

Hobohemia. Any of a number of neighborhoods frequented by outcasts.

Hoboken, New Jersey. U.S. city: **Gibraltar of Democracy, Little Eden, Mile-Square City.**

Hobson, Richmond Pearson (1870–1937). Naval hero: **Kissing-Bug Hobson, Parson Hobson.**

Hodges, John Cornelius (1906–70). Jazz saxophonist: **Rabbit.**

Hoernschemeyer, Bob (active 1940s and 1950s). Football back: **Hunchy.**

Hoff, Max (active 1930s). Racketeer and bootlegger: **Boo Boo.**

Hoffman, Abbie (born 1936). Civil rights demonstrator: **Free.**

Hoffman, Clare E. (1875–1967). U.S. Representative from Michigan: **CIO Hoffman, Sit-down Striker.**

Hoffman, Dustin (born 1937). Actor: **The Little Big Man, The Man Behind the Smile, The Midnight Cowboy.**

Hoffman, Frank (active 1930s). Football player: **Nordy.**

Hogan, Frank (1906–67). Baseball catcher: **Shanty.** Legal name: James Francis Hogan.

Hogan, Frank S[mithwick] (born 1902). District attorney in Manhattan: **Mr. District Attorney.**

Hogan, [William] Ben[jamin] (born 1912). Golfer: **Bantam Ben, Golfdom's Mighty Mite, The Hawk, The Iceman.**

Hog and Hominy State. Tennessee.

Hogarth of Manhattan, The. Marsh, Reginald.

Hog Butcher for the World. Chicago.

Hogg, James Stephen (1851–1906). Politician: **Great Commoner.**

Hogsett, Elon Chester (born 1903). Baseball pitcher: **Chief.**

Ho-Jo. Howard Johnson's.

Hold That Line. Blanton, Thomas Lindsay.

Holiday, Billie (1915–59). Jazz singer: **Lady, Lady Day.** Born: Eleanora Fagan.

Holland, Herbert Lee (born 1910). Jazz trumpeter: **Peanuts.**

Holland, Michigan. U.S. city: **Dutch City.**

Hollander, Xaviera (active 1950–73). Brothel proprietor and author: **The Happy Hooker.**

Hollandersky, Abraham (active early 1900s). Boxing champion: **Abe the Newsboy.**

Holley, Major [Quincy, Jr.] (born 1924). Jazz bass player: **Mule.**

Hollywood. Henderson, Thomas.

Hollywood, California. U.S. community, section of the city of Los Angeles: **Celluloid City, Film Capital of the World, Filmland, Illusion Factory, Movie Capital, Movieland, Studioland, Television City, Tinsel City.**

Hollywood, Florida. U.S. city: **Heart of the Gold Coast.**

Hollywood Pilot, Mantz, [Albert] Paul.

Hollywood Plutarch, Dieterle, Wilhelm.

Hollywood's Busiest and Most Versatile Woman. Hopper, Hedda.

Hollywood's Grand Old Man. Barrymore, Lionel.

Hollywood's Melancholy Blonde. Novak, Kim.

Hollywood's Number One Glamor Boy. Mature, Victor [John].

Hollywood Ten. Group of motion-picture producers, directors, and writers who in 1947 refused to tell the House Committee on Un-American Activities whether or not they were Communists.

Holman, Nat (born 1896). Basketball player and coach: **Mr. Basketball.**

Holmes, Richard Arnold (born 1931). Jazz organist: **Groove.**

Holtzman, Elizabeth (born 1942). U.S. Representative from New York: **Liz the Lion Killer.**

Holy City. Charleston, South Carolina.

Holy Cross, College of the, athletic teams of: **Crusaders.**

Holy Rollers. Church of God.

Holy Terror from Texas. McClendon, Sarah.

Home City. Charlotte, North Carolina.

Home of Abraham Lincoln. Springfield, Illinois.

Home of Baseball. Cooperstown, New York.

Home of Diamond Walnuts. Stockton, California.

Home of Disneyland. Anaheim, California.

Home of Frontier Days. Cheyenne, Wyoming.

Home of Storms. Gulf of Alaska.

Home of the Alamo. San Antonio, Texas.

Home of the Blues. Memphis, Tennessee.

Home of the Cotton Carnival. Memphis, Tennessee.

Home of the Kentucky Derby. Louisville, Kentucky.

Home of the Mining Barons. Spokane, Washington.

Home of the Orange. Riverside, California.

Home of the Pacific Fleet. Bremerton, Washington.

Home of the Peach, Strawberry, and Vine. Arkansas.

Home of the U.S. Naval Academy. Annapolis, Maryland.

Home of Vulcan. Birmingham, Alabama.

Home Run. Baker, [John] Frank[lin].

Homicide Hank. Jackson, Henry.

Hondo. Havlicek, John.

Honest George. McGovern, George [Stanley].

Honest Harold, Ickes, Harold LeClaire.

Honest Hero of the Black Sox Scandal. Kerr, Dickie.

Honest John. 1. Bricker, John William. 2. Surface-to-surface ballistic missile.

Honey. Russell, John.

Honey Bear. Sedric, Eugene Paul.

Honey Boy. Fields, George.

Honey Fitz. Fitzgerald, John Francis.

Honeymoon City. Niagara Falls, New York.

Honey State. Utah.

Honolulu, Hawaii. U.S. city: **Crossroads of the Pacific.**

Honorable Rosenfeld. Rosenfeld, Sigmund.

Honored Society. The Mafia

Honus. Wagner, John Peter.

Hoodlum Priest. Clark, Charles Dismas.

Hooey Long. Long, Huey [Pierce].

Hooks. Dauss, George August; Mylin, Edward; Wiltse, George L.

Hooley. Ahola, Sylvester.

Hooper, Nesbert (born 1938). Jazz drummer: **Sticks, Stix.**

Hoosier. Native or resident of Indiana.

Hoosier Capital. Indianapolis, Indiana.

Hoosier Hotshot. Shriner, Herb[ert].

Hoosier Poet. Riley, James Whitcomb.

Hoosier Quixote. Hibben, Paxton Pattison.

Hoosier State. Indiana.

Hoosier Statesman. Marshall, Thomas Riley.

Hoosier Thunderbolt. Rusie, Amor Wilson.

Hoot. Evers, Walter Arthur; Gibson, Robert; Gibson, Samuel Braxton.

Hootie. McShann, Jay.

Hoover, Herbert [Clark] (1874–1964). Thirty-first President of the

United States: **Friend of Helpless Children, Great Engineer, Hermit Author of Palo Alto, Man of Great Heart.**

Hoover, J[ohn] Edgar (1895–1972). Lawyer, criminologist, and director of the F.B.I.: **The Modern Knight Errant.**

Hooverville. Ramshackle settlement of homeless, unemployed workers during the Great Depression.

Hopalong. Cassady, Howard.

Hope, Bob (born 1904). Entertainer: **Ski-nose.** Born: Leslie Townes Hope.

Hopkins, Harry Lloyd (1890–1946). Politician and presidential aide: **Harry the Hop.**

Hopkins, Sam (born 1912). Jazz singer and guitarist: **Lightnin'.**

Hoppe, Willie (1889–1959). Billiards champion: **Boy Wonder, Old Master.** Legal name: William Frederick Hoppe.

Hopper, Edna Wallace (1864–1959). Actress and beauty specialist: **Eternal Flapper, Grandma Flapper.**

Hopper, Edward (1882–1967). Artist: **Painter of Loneliness.**

Hopper, Hedda (1890–1966). Columnist: **Hollywood's Busiest and Most Versatile Woman.** Born: Elda Furry.

Hop Toad. Giunta, Giuseppe.

Horn, Ted (1910–48). Racing driver: **Racing Legend.** Born: Eyland Theodore Von Horn.

Horned Frogs. Athletic teams of Texas Christian University, Fort Worth.

Hornsby, Rogers (1896–1963). Baseball short stop, second baseman, and manager: **Rajah, Rajah of Swat.**

Hornung, Paul [Vernon] (born 1935). Football back: **Golden Boy.**

Horr, Marquis Franklin (1880–1955). Football player and Olympic champion: **Bill.**

Horse. Gallatin, Harry; Mehre, Harry J.

Horse, The. Ameche, Alan; Danning, Harry.

Horsepower. Fulmer, Hampton Pitts.

Horseshoe Curve. Altoona, Pennsylvania.

Hospitality State. Mississippi.

Hostess with the Mostest. Mesta, Perle.

Host to the Coast. Grier, Jimmie.

Host with the Most. Wilson, Charles Kemmons.

Hotcake Baron. Childs, William.

Hothouse Champion. Jaffe, Irving B.

Hot Line. Telephone connection between the White House and the Kremlin.

Hot Lips. Burnett, Carol; Levine, Henry; Page, Oran.

Hot Oil Marland. Marland, Ernest Whitworth.

Hot Rod. Gilbert, Rod[rique]; Hundley, Rod.

Hot Springs, Arkansas. U.S. city: **America's Own Spa, Baden-Baden of America, Carlsbad of America, Nation's Health Resort, Vapor City.**

Hottelet, Richard C[urt] (born 1917). Foreign correspondent and news commentator. With seven other broadcasters: **Murrow's Boys.**

Hot Water State. Arkansas.

Houdini, Harry (1874–1926). Magician and escape artist: **Champion Jail Breaker, Handcuff King, Houdini the Great, King of Escapologists, King of Handcuffs, Monarch of Leg Shackles, Prince of the Air, Syllable-accenting American, Undisputed King of Handcuffs.**

Houdini in the White House. Roosevelt, Franklin D[elano].

Houdini of the Hardwood. Cousy, Bob.

Houdini the Great. Houdini, Harry.

Houk, Ralph [George] (born 1919). Baseball club manager: **Major.**

Hound Dog. Taylor, Theodore.

Hourglass Division. Seventh Infantry Division.

House, Eddie James, Jr. (born 1902). Jazz singer and guitarist: **Son.**

House, The. U.S. House of Representatives.

House That Ruth Built. Yankee Stadium.

Houston, Texas. U.S. city: **Bayou City, Magnolia City, Land of the Big Rich, Space Center, Space City.**

Houston Hurricane. Foyt, A[nthony] J[oseph, Jr.].

Houston, University of, athletic teams of: **Cougars.**

168

How, James Eads (1868–1930). Heir to great wealth: **Millionaire Hobo, Millionaire Tramp.**

Howard, Avery (1908–66). Jazz trumpeter: **Kid.**

Howard Johnson's. Restaurant chain: **Ho-Jo's.**

Howe, Edgar Watson (1853–1937). Newspaper editor and publisher: **Sage of Potato Hill.**

Howe, Gordie (born 1928). Hockey player: **Best Player in Hockey.** Legal name: Gordon Howe.

Howell, Millard (1913–71). College football back and coach: **Dixie.**

Howie the Horse. Samuels, Howard J.

Howlin' Mad. Smith, Holland M[cTyeire].

Howlin' Wolf. Burnett, Chester Arthur.

HST. Truman, Harry S.

Hub, The. Boston, Massachusetts.

Hubbard, Bernhard Rosecrans (1888–1962). Catholic priest and explorer: **Glacier Priest.**

Hubbard, Elbert [Green] (1856–1915). Writer and philosopher: **Philosopher Freethinker.**

Hubby. Kimmel, Husband Edward.

Hub City. Anchorage, Alaska.

Hub City of the South Plains. Lubbock, Texas.

Hub of American Culture. Boston, Massachusetts.

Hub of New England. Boston, Massachusetts.

Hub of North America. Superior, Wisconsin.

Hub of the Solar System. Boston, Massachusetts.

Hub of the Southeast. Atlanta, Georgia.

Hub of the Universe. Boston, Massachusetts.

Huck. Betts, Walter M.

Hucko, Michael Andrew (born 1918). Jazz musician: **Peanuts.**

Huckster of the Tabernacle. Sunday, Billy.

Hudkins, Ace (1905–73). Boxer and rancher: **The Nebraska Wildcat.**

Hudson, Walter (born 1898). Baseball writer: **Gunboat.**

Hudson's Bay Company, The. Business organization: **The Bay.**

Huebner, Louise (active 1960s and 1970s). Columnist: **The Official Witch of Los Angeles, The Good Witch of the West.**

Huey. Helicopter, Utility Model 1-B, Vietnam War; UH1 helicopter, Vietnam War.

Hug. Huggins, Miller James.

Huggins, Miller James (1879–1929). Baseball second baseman and manager: **Hug, The Mighty Mite.**

Hughes, Charles Evans (1862–1948). U.S. Secretary of State, later Chief Justice: **The Bearded Iceberg.**

Hughes, Howard [R.] (1905–77). Airplane manufacturer, aviator, industrialist, and recluse: **Billionaire Recluse, Mysterious Billionaire, Phantom Billionaire.**

Hugo the Victor. Bezdek, Hugo Frank.

Hula Bowl. Major collegiate all-star football game, Honolulu, Hawaii.

Hull, Bobby (born 1939). Canadian hockey player: **Golden Boy, Golden Jet.** Legal name: Robert Marvin Hull, Jr.

Hull, Cordell (1871–1955). U.S. Secretary of State: **Cord, Father of the United Nations, Old H'ar'-Thar'-and-Ev'ry-Whar'.**

Human Chatterbox. Harris, Arlene.

Human Fly, The. Willig, George H.

Human Frog. Sykowski, Abram.

Human Gagometer. Williams, Gurney.

Human Windmill, The. Greb, Edward Henry.

Hump. Campbell, Bruce Douglas; Richards, George.

Hump, The. Humphrey, Hubert Horatio; Humphreys, Murray.

Humphrey, Hubert Horatio (1911–78). Vice President of the United States: **HHH, Happy Warrior, The Hump, Pinky.**

Humphreys, Murray (died 1965). Criminal: **The Camel, The Hump.**

Humpty. Richards, George.

Hunchy. Hoernschemeyer, Bob.

Hundley, Rod (born 1934). Basketball guard: **Hot Rod.**

Hundred Days. March 9–June 16, 1933, period during which 73d Congress passed the most important acts of the New Deal.

Hundred-Million-Dollar Baby. McLean, Vinson Walsh.

Hungry Gulliver. Wolfe, Thomas [Clayton].

Hunk. Anderson, Heartley.

Hunk, The. Mature, Victor [John].

Hunt, Bobby (active 1965–70). Wrestler: **The Pittsburgh Hurricane.**

Hunt, E[verette] Howard, [Jr.] (born 1918). Author, White House consultant, and convicted defendant in the Watergate trial: **The Master Storyteller.** Also known as John Baxter, Robert Dietrich, David St. John, Gordon Davis.

Hunt, Frazier (1885–1967). Author, newspaperman, and war correspondent: **Spike.**

Hunt, Walter (born 1907). Jazz singer and trombonist: **Pee Wee.**

Hunter, James Augustus (born 1946). Baseball pitcher: **Cat, The Cat, Catfish.**

Huntsville, Alabama. U.S. city: **City of Contrasts, City of Governors, City of Gracious Living, Rocket Capital of the Nation, Rocket City, U.S.A., Space Capital of the Nation, Space Capital of the World.**

Hurons. Athletic teams of Eastern Michigan University, Ypsilanti.

Hurricane. Carter, Rubin; Jackson, Tommy.

Hurricane Bella. Abzug, Bella S[avitsky].

Hurricane Henry. Armstrong, Henry.

Hurricanes. Athletic teams of the University of Miami, Coral Gables, Florida.

Hurry Up. Yost, Fielding Harris.

Hurry-up Henry. Kaiser, Henry J.

Hurtling Habitant. Morenz, Howie.

Husk. Chance, Frank LeRoy; Mathewson, Christy.

Huskies. Athletic teams of the University of Connecticut, Storrs; Northern Illinois University, DeKalb; and the University of Washington, Seattle.

Husky Territory. The Yukon.

Hustler. B-58 bombing plane.

Hustling Henry. Kissinger, Henry A[lfred].

Hutcheson, William Levi (1874–1953). Labor leader: **Big Bill.**

Hutchins, Robert Maynard (1899–1977). President of the University of Chicago: **Boy President.**

Hutson, Don[ald Montgomery] (born 1913). Football end: **First Super End.**

Hutton, Barbara (1912–79). Society glamour girl, 1930. With Doris Duke: **The Gold Dust Twins, Poor Little Rich Girls.**

Hyland, Richard (active 1926–27). Football guard, center, and tackle: **Tricky Dick.**

Hymie the Polack. Wajcieckowski, Earl.

Hype. Igoe, Herbert A.

Hyperbolic Historian. Ervin, Sam[uel James, Jr.]

Hypnotic Hippie. Manson, Charles M.

I

Icebanks. Fairbanks, Charles Warren.

Ice Box. Chamberlain, Elton P.

Ice King. Morse, Charles Wyman.

Iceman, The. Hogan, [William] Ben[jamin].

Ickes, Harold LeClaire (1874–1952). U.S. Secretary of the Interior and writer: **Curmudgeon, Honest Harold, Old Curmudgeon.**

Idaho. Forty-third U.S. state: **Gem of the Mountains, Gem State, Land of the Shining Mountains, Little Ida, Panhandle State, Spud State.**

Idaho, University of, athletic teams of: **Vandals.**

Idaho Lion. Borah, William Edgar.

Idell, A. Provost (1889–1965). Volleyball player, coach, and official: **Father of Modern Volleyball, Pop.**

Idol of Baseball Fandom. Cobb, Ty[rus Raymond].

Idol of the American Boy. Ruth, Babe.

Igoe, Herbert A. (1877–1945). Sports writer and cartoonist: **Hype.**

Ike. Eisenhower, Dwight David; Samuels, Samuel Earl.

Ike's Kissinger. Nixon, Richard M[ilhous].

Illinois. Twenty-first U.S. state: **Corn State, Garden of the West, Heart of the Nation, Land of the Illini, Land of Lincoln, Lincoln's State, Inland Empire, Prairie State, Sucker State, Tall State.**

Illinois, University of. 1. Athletic teams of: **Fighting Illini.** 2. Athletic teams, with other teams in regional conference: **Big Ten.**

Illinois Division. Thirty-third Infantry Division.

Illinois River City. Peoria, Illinois.

Illinois State University, athletic teams of: **Redbirds.**

Illinois Thunderbolt. Overlin, Ken.

Illusion Factory. Hollywood, California.

Illustrator of Early Twentieth-Century America. Rockwell, Norman.

Illustrious Infidel. Ingersoll, Robert G.

Immortal Jolson, The. Jolson, Al.

Immune, The. Torrio, John.

Impeachment Thomas. Thomas, J[ohn] Parnell

Imperial Valley. Valley in California: **America's Great Winter Garden.**

Imposter's Imposter. Weinberg, Stephen Jacob.

Impulsive Innovator. Colombo, Joseph Anthony.

Incomparable Hildegarde. Hildegarde.

Independence, Missouri. U.S. city: **Gateway to the West, Queen City of the Trails.**

Independence Hall. Old State House, Philadelphia, Pennsylvania.

Indestructible Mike Malloy. Malloy, Michael.

Indiana. Nineteenth U.S. state: **Crossroads of America, Hoosier State, State of Surprises.**

Indianapolis, Indiana. U.S. city: **Circle City, Hoosier Capital, Indy, Railroad City.**

Indianapolis 500. Automobile race held at Indianapolis, Indiana: **Indy, Indy 500.**

Indianapolis Potato Mayor. Shank, Samuel Lewis.

Indiana's Songbird. Bucher, Helen.

Indiana State University, athletic teams of: **Sycamores.**

Indiana University. 1. Athletic teams of: **Fightin' Hoosiers.** 2. Athletic teams of, with other teams in regional conference: **Big Ten.**

Indian Bob. Johnson, Robert Lee.

Indian Head Division. Second Infantry Division.

Indian Joe. Guyon, Joseph.

Indians. Athletic teams of Arkansas State University, State University; Northeast Louisiana University, Monroe; and College of William & Mary, Williamsburg, Virginia.

India Rubber Man. Wooden, John [Robert].

Indomitable Bronk. Nagurski, Bronislau.

Industrial Capital of Connecticut. Bridgeport, Connecticut.

Industrial Center of the Great South. Birmingham, Alabama.

Industrial City of Dixie. Birmingham, Alabama.

Industrial City of Iowa. Sioux City, Iowa.

Industrial City of The South. Birmingham, Alabama.

Industrial Park State. New Jersey.

Industrial Workers of the World. U.S. revolutionary labor organization, founded 1905; **Wobblies.**

Indy. 1. Indianapolis, Indiana. 2. Indianapolis 500.

Indy 500. Indianapolis 500.

Inevitable General. Westmoreland, William Childs.

Inevitable Spa City. Saratoga Springs, New York.

Infant Prodigy. Mantle, Mickey [Charles].

Ingersoll, Robert G[reen] (1833–99). Lawyer, orator, lecturer, politician, statesman: **Great Agnostic, Illustrious Infidel.**

Ingram, William (1897–1943). Football player and coach: **Navy Bill.**

Inland Empire. Illinois.

Inland Metropolis. Birmingham, Alabama.

Instant Champion. Foreman, George.

Insurance Capital. Hartford, Connecticut; Omaha, Nebraska.

Insurance Center of the South. Jacksonville, Florida.

Insurance City. Hartford, Connecticut; Atlanta, Georgia.

Insurance State. Connecticut.

Intellectual Aristocrat of the Screen. Pringle, Aileen.

International Capital. New York City.

International City. Long Beach, California.

International King of Cards. Leipzig, Nat.

International Women's Air Race. Annual 2,500-mile race: **Powder Puff Derby.**

Interstate State. Tennessee.

Intrepid Four. First four draft evaders in the Vietnam war to arrive in Sweden, via the *Intrepid,* a U.S. aircraft.

Iodine State. South Carolina.

Iowa. Twenty-ninth U.S. state: **Hawkeye State, Land of the Rolling Prairie, Peerless State.**

Iowa, University of. 1. Athletic teams of: **Hawkeyes.** 2. Athletic teams of, with other teams in regional conference: **Big Ten.**

Iowa State University. 1. Athletic teams of: **Cyclones.** 2. Athletic teams of, with other teams in regional conference: **Big Eight.**

Irascible Easterner. Valiant, James.

Irascible Patrician. Adams, Charles Francis.

Iris City. Nashville, Tennessee.

Irish. Meusel, Emil Frederick.

Irish Channel. Waterfront slum area of New Orleans, Louisiana.

Irish Peacock, The. Grady, Billy.

Irish Thrush. Downey, Morton.

Iron Butterfly, The. MacDonald, Jeanette [Anna]; Young, Loretta.

Iron City. Bessemer, Alabama; Pittsburgh, Pennsylvania.

Iron Horse. Gehrig, [Henry] Lou[is]; Gish, Lillian; Schulmerich, [Edward] Wes[ley].

Ironic Prophet. West, Nathanael.

Iron Jack. Walton, J. C.

Iron Major. Cavanaugh, Frank William.

Iron Man. Grim, Joe; McGinnity, Joseph Jerome; Starr, Ray[mond Francis]; Wetzel, Damon.

Iron Man of Baseball. Gehrig, [Henry] Lou[is].

Iron Men of Metz. Ninety-fifth Infantry Division.

Iron Mike. O'Daniel, John W.

Iron Mountain State. Missouri.

Ironside, Henry Allan (1876–1951). Clergyman: **Archbishop of Fundamentalism.**

Iron Snake. Eighth Armored Division.

Iroquois Division. Ninety-eighth Infantry Division.

Irrepressible Egoist. Stuart, Richard Lee.

Irvin, Leslie Leroy (1895–1966). Parachute inventor and manufacturer: **Edison of American Parachute Design, Sky High Irvin.**

Irvine, Harry (died 1951). Actor: **Bishop of Broadway.**

Island-and-Mainland Province. Newfoundland.

Island City. Montreal, Quebec; Manhattan.

Island City of Old World Charm. Key West, Florida.

Island Paradise. Hawaii.

Island State. Hawaii.

Isles, The. New York Islanders.

Italy of America. Arizona.

Itch. Schoenhaus, Isadore.

It Girl. Bow, Clara.

Ithaca, New York. U.S. city: **Educational Center.**

I.T.T.'s Memo Writer. Beard, Dita [Davis].

Ivan the Terrible. Johnson, Ivan Willard.

Ivory Soap King. Procter, William Cooper.

Ivy. Olson, Ivan Massie.

Ivy, Frank (active after 1940). Football end and coach: **Pop.**

Ivy Division. Fourth Infantry Division.

Ivy League. College athletic conference composed of eight old Eastern institutions—Brown University, Columbia University, Cornell University, Dartmouth College, Harvard University, University of Pennsylvania, Princeton University, and Yale University; reputation for high scholastic achievement and social prestige; characteristics of Ivy League students **(Ivy Leaguers)** in clothing and manners.

Izzy. Friedman, Irving.

Izzy the Rat. Buchalsky, Isidore.

J

Jabbo. Smith, Cladys.

Jackie O. Onassis, Jacqueline Bouvier Kennedy.

Jackie Robinson of Golf. Sifford, Charles.

Jackie the Lackie. Cerone, John Philip.

Jackpine Jim. Corcoran, James A.

Jackrabbit. Abbit, Jim; Smith, J. R.

Jackrabbits. Athletic teams of South Dakota State University, Brookings.

Jackson, Frank (died 1921). Bank robber: **First Automobile Bandit, King of the Bank Robbers.** Born: Henry Starr.

Jackson, George Pullen (1874–1953). Musicologist: **Black Giant of White Spirituals, Judge.**

Jackson, Greig [Stewart] (born 1918). Jazz bass player and songwriter: **Chubby.**

Jackson, Harvey (born 1911). Hockey player: **Busher.**

Jackson, Henry (born 1912). Featherweight, welterweight, and lightweight boxer: **Homicide Hank.** Also known as Henry Armstrong.

Jackson, Henry [Martin] (born 1912). U.S. Senator from Washington: **Last of the Cold War Liberals, Scoop.**

Jackson, Joseph Jefferson (1888–1951). Baseball outfielder: **Shoeless Joe.**

Jackson, Leonard (born 1931). Gangster: **Red.**

Jackson, Mahalia (1911–1972). Singer: **Queen of the Gospel Song, Sister Mahalia.**

Jackson, Milt[on] (born 1923). Jazz musician: **Bags.**

Jackson, Mississippi. U.S. city: **Crape Myrtle City.**

Jackson, Phil (born 1945). Basketball forward: **Spider.**

Jackson, Quentin [Leonard] (born 1909). Jazz trombonist: **Butter.**

Jackson, Robert Houghwout (1892–1954). Assistant Attorney General of the United States: **Jack the Giant Killer.**

Jackson, Tommy (born 1933). Light heavyweight boxer: **Hurricane.**

Jackson State University, athletic teams of: **Tigers.**

Jacksonville, Florida. U.S. city: **Gate City of Florida, Insurance Center of the South, Jax.**

Jack's Pack. Fans of Jack Nicklaus.

Jack the Dripper. Pollock, Jackson.

Jack the Dropper. Kaplan, Nathan.

Jack the Giant Killer. Dempsey, Jack; Dillon, Jack; Jackson, Robert Houghwout.

Jack the Ripper. Roberts, Jack.

Jacobs, Hirsch (1904–70). Racehorse breeder and trainer: **Emancipator of the Plater.**

Jacobs, Joe (1896–1940). Prizefight manager: **Yussel the Muscle.** Legal name: Joseph Jacobs.

Jaffe, Irving B. (born 1906). Ice skating champion: **Hothouse Champion.**

Jagade, Herry (1928–68). Football back: **Chick.**

Jaguars. Athletic teams of Southern University, Baton Rouge, Louisiana.

Jake. Cann, Howard G.; Kramer, Jack; Lingle, Alfred; Swirbul, Leon A.

Jake the Barber. Factor, John.

Jaki. Byard, John A., Jr.

James, Cornelius (born 1927). Jazz singer: **Pinocchio.**

James, Daniel, Jr. (1920–78). U.S. Air Force General: **Chappie.**

James, Forrest Hood, Jr. (born 1934). Industrialist and governor of Alabama: **Fob.**

James, George (active 1920s and 1930s). Football coach: **Lefty.**

James, Nehemiah (born 1902). Jazz singer, guitarist, and pianist: **Skip.**

James, Robert (1896–1935). Murderer: **Rattlesnake Murderer.**

James, William (1842–1910). Philosopher and psychologist: **Father of American Psychology, Pragmatist Philosopher.**

James, William Henry (1887–1942). Baseball pitcher: **Big Bill.**

JaMi. Urbanized area between Jacksonville and Miami, Florida.

Jammy. Moskowitz, Harry.

Janis, Elsie (1889–1956). Variety performer and songwriter: **Sweetheart of the A.E.F.** Born: Elsie Bierbower.

Jax. Jacksonville, Florida.

Jay C. Higginbotham, Jack.

Jayhawker. Native or resident of Kansas.

Jayhawks. Athletic teams of the University of Kansas, Lawrence.

Jayhawk State. Kansas.

Jay Jay. Johnson, James Louis.

Jazbo. Fulkerson, Ralph Clayburn.

Jazz Age. The 1920s in the United States, in their more frenetic aspects.

Jazz's Angry Man. Mingus, Charles.

JB. Barr, Jim.

JC. Higginbotham, Jack.

Jean Baptiste. Any male French Canadian.

Jeep. 1. General-purpose vehicle, World War II and after. 2. Parise, J. P.

Jeff. Tesreau, Charles Monroe.

Jeff City. Jefferson City, Missouri.

Jeffers, [John] Robinson (1887–1962). Poet: **Stone Mason of Tor House.**

Jefferson, Cliff[ord] (born 1926). Convict: **Death Row Jeff.**

Jefferson City, Missouri. Capital of Missouri: **Jeff City.**

Jefferson's Country. Albemarle County, Virginia.

Jeffries, Jim (1875–1953). Heavyweight boxer: **Big Jeff, Boilermaker, The California Hercules.** Legal name: James J. Jeffries.

Jelly Roll. Morton, Ferdinand Joseph.

Jenckes, Virginia Ellis (1882–1975). U.S. Representative from Indiana: **Cherry-Trees Nemesis.**

Jenkins, David Abbot, Jr. (1883–1956). Racing car driver: **Ab.**

Jenkins, Freddy (born 1906). Jazz trumpeter: **Posey.**

Jenny. 1. Curtiss JN-4 training biplane, World War I. 2. Short, Dewey Jackson.

Jensen, Forrest Ducenus (born 1909). Baseball outfielder: **Woody.**

Jensen, Mrs. Owen (died 1953). Circus fat lady: **Dainty Dotty.**

Jephtha. Rixey, Eppa, Jr.

Jerry. Brown, Edmund Gerald, Jr.

Jersey Joe. Stripp, Joseph Valentine; Walcott, Joe.

Jeru. Mulligan, Gerry.

Jessel, Georgie (born 1898). Entertainer: **Boy Monologuist.** Legal name: George Albert Jessel.

Jet, The. Walker, Chet.

Jet Age Renaissance Man. Tilmon, James.

Jet Age Super-Sleuth. Peloquin, Robert Dolan.

Jetsam. McEarchan, Malcolm.

Jet Set, The. The fast-living, moneyed, and chic people of the 1960s and 1970s, especially those noted for frequent international trips.

Jetstar. Lockheed C-140 cargo plane.

Jetstream. Smith, James.

Jew Ben. Newmark, Benjamin.

Jewel City. Glendale, California.

Jewel City of California. San Diego, California.

Jewel of the Ghetto. Goldstein, Ruby.

JFK. Kennedy, John Fitzgerald.

Jiggs. Whigham, Haydn.

Jim. Crow, Floyd.

Jimbo. Connors, Jimmy.

Jim Crow Law. Law enforcing racial segregation in public places and transportation.

Jiménez, José (born 1949). Revolutionary: **Cha Cha.**

Jimmy Three Sticks. Robinson, James D., III.

Jingle Money Smith. Smith, James Monroe.

Jitterbug. Kellogg, Bobby.

JJ. Johnson, James Louis.

Jo. Jones, Jonathan.

Joan of Art(s). Mondale, Joan [Adams].

Jock. Sutherland, John Bain; Whitney, John Hay; Yablonski, Joseph
    A.

Jockey. Falk, Bibb August; Kolp, Raymond Carl.

Joe Bananas. Bonanno, Joseph.

Joe Batty. Accardo, Anthony Joseph.

Joe Blow. Any ordinary American man.

Joe D. DiMaggio, Joe.

Joe Doakes. Any ordinary American man.

Joe Loca. Esteves, Joseph.

Joe Pass. Passalaqua, Joseph Anthony.

Joe the Blond. Gallo, Joseph.

Joe the Boss. Masseria, Giuseppe.

Joe the Horse. Hall, Howard.

Joe the Jet. Bellino, Joseph.

Joe Willie. Namath, Joseph William.

Joe Zilch. Any ordinary American man.

John Barleycorn. Liquor personified.

John Carroll University, athletic teams of: **Blue Streaks.**

John D. Rockefeller, John D[avison].

John L. Sullivan, John Lawrence.

Johnny Buff. Lesky, John.

Johnny Eggs. Lansky, Meyer.

Johnny Hammond. Smith, John Robert.

John O' Birds. Burroughs, John.

Johnson, Byron Bancroft (1864–1931). President of the American
    Baseball League: **Ban.**

Johnson, Claudia Alta Taylor (born 1912). Wife of President Lyndon
    Baines Johnson: **Lady Bird.**

Johnson, Curtis Lee (born 1928). Journalist and writer: **Walter Whiz.**
    Also known as Lee Wallek.

Johnson, Don (active 1920s and 1930s). Radio comedian: **Professor Figgsbottle.**

Johnson, Enoch L. (active 1930s). Political boss and racketeer: **Nucky.**

Johnson, Frederic H. (born 1908). Jazz trombonist: **Keg.**

Johnson, Greg (born 1950). Track star: **Grape Juice.**

Johnson, Harold Ogden (1891–1962). Vaudeville and motion picture comedian: **Chic.**

Johnson, Howard (1897–1972). Restaurateur: **Father of American Franchisers.**

Johnson, Howard W. (1910–45). Football guard: **Smiley.**

Johnson, Hugh Samuel (1882–1943). Federal administrator: **Babe Ruth of the New Deal, Crack-down Johnson, Crack-down Czar of the N.R.A., Great Thundering Rooster, King of the Never-Made-Good Crack Downs, N.R.A. Czar, Old Iron Pants.**

Johnson, Ivan Willard (1897–1979). Hockey player: **Ching, Ivan the Terrible.**

Johnson, Jack (1878–1946). Heavyweight boxer: **The Galveston Giant, Li'l Arthur.** Legal name: John Arthur Johnson.

Johnson, James Joy (1876–1946). Boxing manager and promoter: **Boy Bandit.**

Johnson, James Louis (born 1924). Jazz trombonist: **JJ, Jay Jay.**

Johnson, Lyndon Baines (1908–73). Thirty-sixth President of the United States: **The Accidental President, Landslide Johnson, Landslide Lyndon, LBJ, Light Bulb Lyndon, The Prodigious Spender, Uncle Cornpone.**

Johnson, Robert Lee (born 1908). Baseball outfielder: **Cherokee, Indian Bob.**

Johnson, Walter Perry (1887–1946). Baseball pitcher and manager: **Barney, Best Pitcher in Baseball, Big Train, Grand Veteran, Swede.**

Johnson, William (born 1911). Basketball player: **Skinny.**

Johnson, William Eugene (1862–1945). Prohibition enforcement officer: **Booze Buster, Pussyfoot.**

Johnson, William Geary (1879–1949). Jazz cornetist and trumpeter: **Bunk.**

Johnston, Velma (1911–77). Advocate for the preservation of wild horse herds in the West: **Wild Horse Annie.**

Johnston, Wheeler Rogers (1887–1961). Baseball first baseman: **Doc.**

Johnston, William M. (1895–1946). Tennis player: **Little Bill.**

Johnstown, Pennsylvania. U.S. city: **Cradle of the Steel Industry, Flood City.**

Joiner, Columbus H. (1859–1947). Promoter of Texas oil: **Dad.**

Jo-Jo. White, Joyner Clifford.

Jolie. Jolson, Al.

Jolly Green Giant. Sikorsky CH/HH-3E helicopter.

Jolson, Al (1886–1950). Actor and singer: **Jolie, The Immortal Jolson.** Born: Asa Yoelson.

Joltin' Joe. DiMaggio, Joe.

Jonah. Jones, Robert Elliot.

Jones, Bobby (1902–71). Golfer: **King of the Links.** Legal name: Robert Tyre Jones.

Jones, Buck (1889–1942). Actor in motion-picture Westerns; with three other stars: **Big Four.** Legal name: Charles Jones.

Jones, Charles Jesse (1844–1919). Author, big game hunter, and business executive: **Buffalo, Colonel, Lord of the Beasts.**

Jones, Ed[ward] (born c. 1951). Football end: **Too Tall Jones.**

Jones, Henry (born 1912). Actor and musician: **Broadway Jones.**

Jones, Howard [Harding] (1886–1941). Football coach: **Thunder Maker.**

Jones, Isham (1894–1956). Jazz saxophonist, pianist, violinist, and composer: **The Composer's Composer.**

Jones, [John] Marvin (1886–1976). U.S. Representative from Texas, judge, food administrator: **Agricultural Jones.**

Jones, Jonathan (born 1911). Jazz drummer: **Jo.**

Jones, Joseph Rudolph (born 1923). Jazz drummer: **Philly Joe.**

Jones, Kathleen (born 1948). Dancer: **Kandi Kisses.**

Jones, Lawrence McCeney (born 1895). Football player and coach: **Biff, Captain of Excitement.**

Jones, Louis (active 1960s and 1970s). Country and western singer and entertainer: **Grandpa.**

Jones, Quincy [Delight] (born 1933). Band leader and musical director: **Man Behind the Music.**

Jones, Robert Elliot (born 1909). Jazz trumpeter and bandleader: **Jonah.**

Jones, Rufus (born 1936). Jazz drummer: **Speedy.**

Jones, Samuel Pond (1892–1966). Baseball pitcher: **Sad Sam, Toothpick.**

Jones, Thomas Albert Dwight (1887–1957). Football quarterback and coach: **Tad.**

Jones, Virgil (active 1939). Football player: **Brahma.**

Jones, Wallace (born 1926). Basketball player: **Wah Wah.**

Jones, William (born 1906). Middleweight boxer: **Gorilla.**

Jones, Wilmore (born 1907). Jazz drummer: **Slick.**

Joplin, Janis (1943–70). Singer: **Pearl, Queen of the Hippies.**

Joplin, Scott (1868–1917). Ragtime pianist and composer: **King of the Ragtime Composers.**

Jordan, Baxter Byerly (born 1908). Baseball first baseman: **Bucky.**

Jordan, Irving Sidney (born 1922). Jazz pianist and composer: **Duke.**

Jordan, [William] Hamilton [McWhorter] (born 1944). Presidential adviser and administrative assistant. With other members of President Jimmy Carter's administration: **Georgia Mafia.**

Joy, William P. (active 1932). Football coach: **Hiker.**

Joyce, William (1906–46). U.S. radio propagandist for the Nazis: **Lord Haw Haw.**

Joyous Musician, The. Grainger, Percy Aldridge.

JP. Morgan, John Pierpont.

Judge. Jackson, George Pullen; Landis, Kenesaw Mountain.

Judge Louis. Buchalter, Louis.

Judge of the North. Morrow, William G.

Judge Perez. Perez, Leander H., Sr.

Jug. Ammons, Eugene; Earpe, Francis; Republic P-47 fighter plane, World War II.

Juice, The. Simpson, O[renthal] J[ames].

Julian, Alvin F. (1901–67). Basketball coach: **Doggie.**

Jumbo. Elliott, James Thomas; Nash, Jim.

Jumbos. Athletic teams of Tufts University, Medford, Massachusetts.

Jumbo State. Texas.

Jumping Jack. McCracken, Jack D.

Jumping Joe. Savoldi, Joseph.

Jumpin' Johnny. Green, John.

Juneau, Alaska. U.S. city: **Alaska's Scenic Capital.**

June Bug. Curtiss biplane, 1908.

Jungleers Division. Forty-first Infantry Division.

Jungle Jim. Lewis, James Wilson.

Junior. Cook, Herman; Davis, Glenn W.; Gilliam, Jim; Kline, Robert George; McEnroe, John [Patrick, Jr.]; Mance, Julian Clifford, Jr.; Raglin, Alvin [Redrick]; Stephens, Vern[on Decatur, Jr.]; Wells, Amos, Jr.

Junior Circuit. American League of Professional Baseball Clubs.

Jupiter of Wall Street. Morgan, John Pierpont.

Justice, Charlie (active 1948–49). Football back: **Choo-Choo.**

Just Society, The. Ideal of the administration of Canadian Prime Minister Pierre Elliott Trudeau.

Jymie. Merritt, James.

K

Kahn, Albert (1869–1942). Architect: **World's No. 1 Industrial Architect.**

Kahn, Eddie (1911–45). Football player: **King Kong Kahn.** Legal name: Edwin Bernard Kahn.

Kahn, Norman (1924–53). Jazz drummer and arranger: **Tiny.**

Kahoolawe, Hawaii. U.S. island: **Target Island.**

Kaiser. Wilhelm, Irving Key.

Kaiser, Henry J. (1882–1967). Industrialist: **Hurry-up Henry, Henry J.**

Kalamazoo, Michigan. U.S. city: **Celery City.**

Kalbfus, Edward Clifford (1877–1954). U.S. Admiral: **Durable Ned.**

Kallet, Aaron Harry (1887–1965). Football player: **Fuzzy.**

Kaltenborn, H[ans] V[on] (1879–1965). Editor and radio commentator: **Columbia's Gem of the Ozone, Dean of Commentators, Gem of the Ozone, Radio's Greatest Commentator.**

Kanawha River City. Charleston, West Virginia.

Kandi Kisses. Jones, Kathleen.

Kane, Harry (1883–1932). Baseball pitcher: **Klondike.** Born: Harry Cohen.

Kane, Helen (1904–66). Singer and actress: **Boop-Boop-a-Doop Girl.**

Kane, W. R. (1911–57). U.S. Navy Commander and fighter pilot: **Killer.**

Kangaroo. Cunningham, Billy.

Kangaroo Kid. Pollard, Jim.

Kansas. Fields, Carl Donnell.

Kansas. Thirty-fourth U.S. state: **Battleground of Freedom, Breadbasket of the Nation, Central State, Cyclone State, Garden of the West, Garden State, Grasshopper State, Jayhawk State, Midway U.S.A., Squatter State, Sunflower State, Wheat State.**

Kansas, University of. 1. Athletic teams of: **Jayhawks.** 2. Athletic teams of, with other teams in regional conference: **Big Eight.**

Kansas City, Missouri. U.S. city: **Cosmopolis of the Heartland, Heartland City, Heart of America, KC, Metropolis of the Missouri Valley.**

Kansas Coolidge. Landon, Alf[red Mossman].

Kansas Dry. Guyer, Ulysses Samuel.

Kansas Giant. Willard, Jess.

Kansas Rube. Ferns, Rube.

Kansas State University. 1. Athletic teams of: **Wildcats.** 2. Athletic teams of, with other teams in regional conference: **Big Eight.**

Kaplan, Eddie (1907?-64). Theatrical performer and talent representative: **Nuts Kaplan.** Legal name: Edward Kaplan.

Kaplan, Harriet Jan (born 1933). Radio executive: **Sis.**

Kaplan, Louis (born 1902). Featherweight boxer: **Kid.**

Kaplan, Nathan (died 1923). Gangster and racketeer: **Jack the Dropper, Kid Dropper.**

Karamatic, George (born 1917). Football back: **Automatic.**

Karate Poet. Reid, Joseph.

Karilivacz, Carl F. (1930-69). Football back: **Kava.**

Karpis, Alvin (1907-79). Canadian criminal: **Old Creepy, Slim.** Born: Francis Albin Karpoviecz.

Kastel, Phil (1894-1962). Underworld gambling operator: **Dandy Phil.**

Kate. Japanese torpedo bomber, World War II.

Katy. Missouri-Kansas-Texas Railroad.

Kauai. Island of Hawaii: **Garden Island.**

Kaufman, George S. (1889–1961). Playwright, theatrical director, and producer: **Gloomy Dean of Broadway.**

Kaufman, Irving (born 1900). Radio singer, announcer, and recording artist: **Lazy Dan.**

Kaufman, Julian (active 1920–30). Criminal: **Potatoes.**

Kaufman, Martin Ellis (born 1899). Conductor and composer: **Whitey.**

Kaufman, Morris (born c. 1911). Square-dance caller: **Greatest Hog Caller East of the Rockies, Piute Pete.**

Kaufman, Murray (born 1930). Disc jockey: **Murray the K, Gertrude Stein of the Musical Underground.**

Kaufman, Wallace (born 1939). Writer and columnist: **Vickers.**

Kava. Karilivacz, Carl F.

Kaye, Nora (born 1920). Ballerina: **Duse of the Dance.** Born: Nora Koreff.

Kazan, Elia (born 1919). Writer and director: **Gadge.** Born: Elia Kazanjoglous.

KC. 1. Kansas City, Missouri. 2. Kansas City style of jazz.

K₁C₃. Korea, Crime, Communism, Corruption: formula provided by Karl Mundt for Republican victory in the 1952 presidential election.

Keane, Ellsworth McGranahan (born 1927). Jazz trumpeter: **Shake.**

Kearns, Jack (1862–1963). Boxing manager: **Doc, Perfume Jack.** Legal name: John Leo McKernon.

Keeler, Oscar Bane (1882–1950). Golf writer: **Pop.**

Keeler, William Henry (1872–1923). Baseball outfielder: **Wee Willie.**

Keenan, Dorothy (1884?–1923). Mistress of John Kearsley Mitchell: **Broadway Butterfly.** Also known as Dot King.

Keg. Johnson, Frederic H.; Purnell, William.

Keiser, Robert (1862–1932). Composer: **Bobo King.**

Keith, Minor Cooper (1848–1929). Railroad builder and founder of the United Fruit Company: **Emperor of the Caribbean.**

Kellems, Vivien (1896–1975). Manufacturer and opponent of tax withholding: **Connecticut Tax Lady.**

Keller, Kent Ellsworth (1867–1954). U.S. Representative from Illinois: **Big Man from Little Egypt.**

Kellogg, Bobby (active 1940). Football back: **Jitterbug.**

Kellogg, John Harvey (1852–1943). Manufacturer of breakfast cereals: **Corn Flake King.**

Kelly, Alvin Anthony (1885–1952). Stunt man famous for flagpole sitting : **Shipwreck, Sailor, Luckiest Fool Alive.**

Kelly, Bob (born 1950). Hockey forward: **Battleship.** Legal name: Robert James Kelly.

Kelly, Clinton Wayne (1844–1923). Physician: **Big Medicine.**

Kelly, Colin P[urdie] (1915–41). U.S. Army Air Forces Captain: **America's First World War II Hero.**

Kelly, Edward Austin, (1892–1969). U.S. Representative from Illinois: **Baseball Eddy.**

Kelly, Emmett (1898–1979). Circus clown: **Weary Willie.**

Kelly, George (1887–1974). Playwright and actor: **King of Comedy.**

Kelly, George R. (1897–1954). Bootlegger, kidnaper, and murderer: **Machine Gun Kelly.**

Kelly, John Simms (active 1930s). Football back: **Shipwreck.**

Kelly, Leonard Patrick (born 1927). Hockey forward and defenseman: **Red.**

Kemp, Harry Hibbard (1883–1960). Poet and writer: **Tramp Poet.** Born: Hibbard Kemp.

Kendall, Donald McIntosh (born 1934). Soft drink manufacturing executive: **Super Soda Pop Peddler.**

Kenna, Michael (1857–1946). Political boss in Chicago: **Hinky Dink, The Dink, The Hink.**

Kenneally, George V. (born 1902). Football end and coach: **Old Man of the Gridiron.**

Kennedy, Edward M[oore] (born 1932). U.S. Senator from Massachusetts: **Chappaquiddick Kid, Democrat Albatross, Hero of Chappaquiddick, Hero of Squaw Island, Last of the Kennedy Brothers.**

Kennedy, John F[itzgerald] (1917–63). Thirty-fifth President of the United States: **JFK.**

Kennedy, Joseph Patrick (1888–1969). Business executive and statesman: **Founding Father of the Kennedy Clan.**

Kennedy, Matthew Patrick (1908–57). Basketball referee: **Wild Man of Hoboken.**

Kennedy, Minnie (died 1948). Evangelist: **Ma.**

Kennedy, Robert F[rancis] (1925–68). U.S. Attorney General and U.S. Senator from New York: **RFK.**

Kent State University, athletic teams of: **Golden Flashes.**

Kentucky. Fifteenth U.S. state: **Bluegrass State, Corncracker State, Dark and Bloody Ground, Hemp State, Tobacco State.**

Kentucky, University of, athletic teams of: **Wildcats.**

Kentucky Lion. Showalter, Jackson Whipps.

Kenyon College, athletic teams of: **Lords.**

Kern, Jerome [David] (1885–1945). Composer: **Dean of America's Show Music Composers.**

Kerr, Dickie (1893–1963). Baseball pitcher: **Honest Hero of the Black Sox Scandal.** Legal name: Richard Henry Kerr.

Kerry. Mills, Frederick Allen.

Ket. Kettering, Charles Franklin.

Ketchel, Stanley (1887–1910). Middleweight boxer: **Michigan Assassin.** Born: Stanislaus Kiechal.

Kettering, C[harles] F[ranklin] (1876–1958). Engineer and industrialist: **Boss Kettering, Father of Ethyl Gasoline, Father of the Self-Starter, Ket.**

Kewpie. Dahl, Percival Rollo; Ertle, Johnny.

Kewpie Doll Lady. O'Neill, Rose Cecil.

Key City. Dubuque, Iowa.

Keydets. Athletic teams of Virginia Military Institute (VMI), Lexington.

Keydoozler. Saunders, Clarence.

Keyser, E. Lee (1886–1950). Baseball official: **Father of Night Baseball.**

Keystone Division. Twenty-eighth Infantry Division.

Keystone Province. Manitoba.

Keystoner. Native or resident of Pennsylvania.

Keystone State. Pennsylvania.

Key West, Florida. U.S. city: **America's Singapore, Island City of Old World Charm.**

Khaury, Herbert Buckingham (born c. 1923). Singer and entertainer: **Tiny Tim.** Also known as Darry Dover.

Khaury, Victoria B. (born 1952). Actress and entertainer: **Miss Vicky, Mrs. Tiny Tim.** Also known as Mrs. Herbert Buckingham Khaury. Born: Victoria May Budinger.

Kid. Bassey, Hogan; Elberfeld, Norman Arthur; Gleason, William; Graves, Perry Ivia; Howard, Avery; Kaplan, Louis; Lambert, Charles Frederick; McPartland, William Lawrence; Nichols, Charles Augustus; Ory, Edward; Rena, Henry; Roy, Leo; Sullivan, Steve.

Kid, The. Cauthen, Steve; Muehfeldt, Freddie; Rizzuto, Phil[ip Francis]; Williams, Ted.

Kid Blackie. Jack Dempsey.

Kiddo. Davis, George Willis.

Kid Dropper. Kaplan, Nathan.

Kid from Brooklyn. Copland, Aaron.

Kid from Sweetwater. Turner, Clyde Douglas.

Kid Line. Toronto Maple Leafs' hockey line of Joe Primeau, Bucher Jackson, and Charlie Conacher, 1930s.

Kid McCoy. McCoy, Charles; Selby, Norman.

Kid Norfolk. Ward, Willie.

Kid Shots. Madison, Louis.

Kid Tiger. Sykowski, Abram.

Kid Twist. Reles, Abe.

Kiki. Cuyler, Hazen Shirley.

Kilgallen, Dorothy (1913–65). Journalist, television panelist, and actress: **Voice of Broadway.** Also known as Mrs. Richard Kollmar.

Kill Crazy Dillinger. Dillinger, John Herbert.

Killefer, William Lavier (1888–1960). Baseball catcher and manager: **Reindeer Bill.**

Killer. Kane, W. R; Madden, Owen.

Killer, The. Rankin, John Elliott.

Killer Bees. Twelve Texas state senators who absented themselves from the legislature to prevent a quorum on a controversial bill, 1979.

Kilpatrick, Benjamin (died 1912). Western outlaw: **Tall Texan.**

Kimmel, Husband E[dward] (1882–1968). Admiral, World War II: **Hubby.**

Kimsey, Clyde Elias (born 1906). Baseball pitcher: **Chad.**

Kindelberger, James Howard (1895–1962). Businessman and chairman of North American Aviation: **Dutch.**

Kiner, Ralph [McPherran] (born 1922). Baseball outfielder: **Mr. Home Run.**

King. Armstrong, Louis; Bolden, Buddy; Cole, Leonard Leslie; Keppard, Freddie; Larouche, Pierre; Oliver, Joe.

King, B. B. (born 1925). Jazz singer and guitarist: **Blues Boy.** Born: Riley B. King.

King, Billie Jean [Moffitt] (born 1943). Tennis player: **King of the Courts, Old Lady, Tennis Tycoon.**

King, Martin Luther, Jr. (1929–68). Baptist minister and civil rights advocate: **Peaceful Warrior.** Born: Michael Luther King, Jr.

King, Moses (1884–1956). Boxing coach: **Mosey.**

King, Wayne [Harold] (born 1901). Bandleader: **Waltz King.**

King, William Henry (1863–1949). U.S. Representative and Senator from Utah: **King of the District, King of Investigators, Mormon Bishop.**

King County Stadium. Sports center, Seattle: **Kingdome.**

King Crab Capital. Kodiak, Alaska.

Kingdome. King County Stadium.

Kingfish. Long, Huey [Pierce].

King Johnny. Cash, Johnny.

King Kong. Kline, Robert George; Korab, Jerry.

King Kong Kahn. Kahn, Eddie.

King Levinsky. Williams, Barney.

King-Maker. Guffey, Joseph F.

King of Acid. Stanley, Augustus Owsley, III.

King of Amateur Swimming. Spitz, Mark Andrew.

King of Broadway. Cohan, George M[ichael].

King of Comedy. Kelly, George; Sennett, Mack.

King of Corn. Lombardo, Guy [Albert].

King of Country Music. Acuff, Roy [Claxton]; Williams, Hank.

King of Escape Artists. Gardner, Roy.

King of Escapologists. Houdini, Harry.

King of European Guides. Fielding, Temple [Hornaday].

King of Gamblers. Rothstein, Arnold.

King of Graft. Becker, Charles.

King of Handcuffs. Houdini, Harry.

King of Harlem. Powell, Adam Clayton.

King of Hi De Ho. Calloway, Cab.

King of Hobos. Park, Arthur.

King of Hollywood. Gable, [William] Clark; Mayer, Louis Burt.

King of Investigators. King, William Henry,

King of Jazz. Ellington, Duke; Whiteman, Paul.

King of Kings. Mails, Walter.

King of Little Men. Arcaro, Eddie.

King of Moonshiners. Gooch, Wayne R.

King of Musical Corn. Welk, Lawrence [LeRoy].

King of Power. Niagara Falls, New York.

King of Rivers. Colorado River.

King of Rum Runners. McCoy, William.

King of Soul. Brown, James.

King of Speculators. Livermore, Jesse Lauriston.

King of Sports Promoters. Rickard, Tex.

King of Steel. Carnegie, Andrew.

King of Stunt Men. Canutt, Yakima.

King of Swat. Ruth, Babe.

King of Swing. Ellington, Duke; Goodman, Benny.

King of Swoon. Sinatra, Frank.

King of Television Gamesmanship. Barris, Charles.

King of the Banjo. Peabody, Edward.

King of the Bank Robbers. Jackson, Frank; Zavada, Joseph.

King of the Bombers. Belcastro, James.

King of the Bootleggers. Dwyer, William Vincent; Remus, George B.

King of the Canebrakes. Stribling, William Lawrence, Jr.

King of the Courts. King, Billie Jean [Moffitt].

King of the Daredevils. Knievel, Evel.

King of the District. King, William Henry.

King of the Drums. Krupa, [Eu]gene [Bertram].

King of the Electric Guitar. Rey, Alvino.

King of the Grain Dealers. Cutten, Arthur W.

King of the Harmonica. Minevich, Borrah.

King of the Hill. Miller, William Mosley.

King of the Hillbillies. Acuff, Roy [Claxton].

King of the Hoboes. Mislen, John.

King of the Hollywood Air Devils. Mantz, [Albert] Paul.

King of the Jukes. Como, Perry.

King of the Links. Jones, Bobby.

King of the Muckrakers. Steffens, [Joseph] Lincoln.

King of the Never-Made-Good Crack Downs. Johnson, Hugh Samuel.

King of the New Dealers. Minton, Sherman.

King of the New York Rackets. Luciano, Charles.

King of the Nonbooks. Sloan, Harry.

King of the Nudie Movie. Meyer, Russ.

King of the Quick Quip. Allen, Fred.

King of the Ragtime Composers. Joplin, Scott.

King of the Road. Petty, Richard.

King of the Stakes Riders. Arcaro, Eddie.

King of the Strikebreakers. Bergoff, Pearl L.

King of the Tennessee Pea Pickers. Ford, Ernest Jennings.

King of the Texas Wildcatters. Cullen, Hugh Troy.

King of the Wildcatters. Benedum, Michael.

King of Western Swing. Cooley, Donald.

King Richard. Nixon, Richard M[ilhous].

Kinsey Reports. Two studies by Alfred C. Kinsey, *The Sexual Behavior of the Human Male* (1948) and *The Sexual Behavior of the Human Female* (1953).

Kip. Cohen, Gerald Bruce; Fadiman, Clifton.

Kirberg, Ralph (active 1925–35). Radio singer: **Dream Singer.**

Kirby, Allan Price (born 1892). Financier: **Proxy Fighter by Proxy.**

Kirk, Ronald T. (born 1936). Jazz musician and composer: **Roland.**

Kissing-Bug Hobson. Hobson, Richmond Pearson.

Kissinger, Henry A[lfred] (born 1923). Educator and U.S. Secretary of State: **Administration's Marco Polo, Henry the K, Henry You-Know-Who, Herr Henry, Hustling Henry, Nixon's Svengali, Sammy Glick of the Cold War, Superhenry.**

Kissing Jim. Folsom, James E[lisha].

Kiss-of-Death Oliver. Oliver, Eli L.

Kit. Cornell, Katharine.

Kitchen Debate. Political exchange between U.S. Vice President Richard M. Nixon and Soviet Premier Nikita S. Khrushchev at the opening of U.S. Exhibition in Moscow (1959).

Kitt, Eartha [Mae] (born 1930). Actress, singer, and dancer: **That Bad Eartha, Thursday's Child.**

Kittredge, George Lyman (1860–1941). Professor of literature: **Kitty.**

Kitty, Bransfield, William Edward; Kittredge, George Lyman.

KKK. Ku Klux Klan.

Klan, The. Ku Klux Klan.

Kleberg, Richard Miffin (1887–1955). U.S. Representative from Texas: **Cattle King.**

Klein, Alex (active 1922–26). Football player: **Shon.**

Klem, William J. (1874–1951). Baseball umpire: **Old Arbitrator.**

Klimek, Tillie (born 1865). Murderer: **Chicago's Constant Widow, The Prophet.**

Kline, Robert George (born 1909). Baseball pitcher: **King Kong, Junior.**

Klondike. Kane, Harry; O'Donnell, William

Klondike Kate. Van Duren, Kathleen Rockwell Waner Matson.

Klook, Clark, Kenneth Spearman.

Klotz, Herman (born 1921). Basketball player: **Reds.**

Knickerbocker. Resident of New York City, especially one of old native stock.

Knickerbocker State. New York

Knievel, Evel (born 1938). Stunt motorcycle rider: **King of the Daredevils.** Born: Robert Craig Knievel.

Knight of the Red Rose. Taylor, Alfred Alexander.

Knight of the White Rose. Taylor, Robert Love.

Knight with the Rueful Countenance. Stryker, Lloyd Paul.

Knipschield, Edward Henry (1907?–64). Aerialist: **Captain Eddie.**

Knitting Hattie. Caraway, Hattie Wyatt.

Knobby. Totah, Nabil Marshall; Warwick, Grant David.

Knockout Brown. Braun, Valentine.

Knopf, Alfred A. (born 1892). Publisher: **Perfect Publisher.**

Knothe, Wilfred Edgar (1904–63). Baseball third baseman: **Fritz.**

Knox, Philander Chase (1853–1921). Lawyer and statesman: **Sleepy Phil, Father of Dollar Diplomacy.**

Knox College, athletic teams of: **Siwash.**

Knoxville, Tennessee. U.S. city: **Gateway to the Smokies, Marble City, Queen City of the Mountains.**

Knudsen, Semon E. (born 1913). Automobile manufacturing executive: **Bunkie.**

Knudsen, William S. (1879–1948). Industrialist: **Big Bill.** Born: Signius Wilhelm Paul Knudsen.

Knutson, Coya (born 1912). U.S. Representative from Minnesota: **Farm Woman's Congresswoman.** Legal name: Cornelia Gjesdal Knutson.

Knutson, Harold (1880–1953). U.S. Representative from Minnesota and journalist: **Anti-war Knutson.**

Koch, Barton (1906–64). Football player: **Botchey.**

Kodak City. Rochester, New York.

Kodiak, Alaska. U.S. city: **King Crab Capital.**

Kohawks. Athletic teams of Coe College, Cedar Rapids, Iowa.

Kolp, Raymond Carl (1894–1967). Baseball pitcher: **Jockey.**

Koncil, Frank (died 1927). Gangster: **Lefty.**

Konetchy, Edward Joseph (1885–1947). Baseball first baseman: **Big Ed.**

Korab, Jerry (born 1948). Hockey defenseman: **King Kong.** Legal name: Gerald Joseph Korab.

Koretz, Leo (1880–1925). Stockbroker and swindler: **Financial Wizard, New Rockefeller, Oil King, Swindler of the Century, Wonder Boy of the Financial District.**

Korngold, Erich Wolfgang (1897–1958). Composer: **Modern Mozart.**

Kossack, N.E. (active 1931–33). Football player: **Tully.**

Kostka, Stanley (active 1934). Football back: **The Hammer.** Born: Stanislaus Kostka.

Koufax, Sandy (born 1935). Baseball pitcher: **Man with the Golden Arm.** Legal name: Sanford Koufax.

Kramer, Benjamin (born 1913). Basketball player: **Red.**

Kramer, Jack (born 1921). Tennis player: **Big Jake, Jake.** Legal name: John Albert Kramer.

Kramer, Stanley E. (born 1913). Motion-picture producer: **Genius on a Low Budget, Wonder Boy.**

Kraut Line. Boston Bruins' hockey line of Milt Schmidt, Woody Dumart, and Bobby Bauer, 1940s.

Kress, Ralph (1907–62). Baseball shortstop: **red.**

Kringleville. Racine, Wisconsin.

Krogh, Egil, Jr. (born 1939). Government official imprisoned for role in Nixon administration scandals: **Bud, Head of the White House Plumbers.**

Krohn, John Albert (active 1908–10). Transcontinental walker: **Colonel Jack.**

Krug, Julius Albert (1907–70). U.S. Secretary of the Interior: **Cap.**

Kruger, Harold (1897?–1965). Swimming champion and motion-picture stunt man: **Stubby.**

Krulak, Victor H. (born 1913). U.S. Marine Corps General: **Brute.**

Krupa, [Eu]gene [Bertram] (1909–73). Jazz drummer: **Ace Drummer Man, King of the Drums.**

Kuhaulua, Jesse (born c. 1944). Sumo wrestler: **Hawaiian Giant.**

Ku Kluxer. Member of the Ku Klux Klan.

Ku Klux Klan. Secret organization advocating the supremacy of native Protestant whites and aiming to suppress the rights of other groups, especially blacks: **KKK, The Klan.**

Kunstler, William [Moses] (born 1919). Educator, lawyer, and writer: **Wild Bill.**

Kyner, Sylvester (born 1932). Jazz saxophonist: **Sonny Red.**
Kyser, Kay (born 1906). Bandleader: **Old Professor.** Legal name:
James King Kern Kyser.

L

L.A. Los Angeles.

Labor's Rugged Individualist. Reuther, Walter [Philip].

LaChance, George J. (1870–1932). Baseball first baseman: **Candy.**

Laddie. Gale, Lauren.

Lady. Holiday, Billie.

Lady, The. 1. Mount Emmons; 2. Statue of Liberty.

Lady Bird. Johnson, Claudia Alta Taylor.

Lady Day. Holiday, Billie.

Lady from Philadelphia. Anderson, Marian.

Lady Lazarus. Garland, Judy.

Lady of Fifty-seventh Street. Carnegie Hall.

Lady Soul. Franklin, Aretha.

Lady South. Charleston, South Carolina

Lady with the Hatchet. Nation, Carry or Carrie [Amelia Moore Gloyd].

Lady with the Lamp. Statue of Liberty.

Lafayette College, athletic teams of: **Leopards.**

Lafayette Escadrille. French air force squadron of U.S. volunteers, started 1916. Also known as Lafayette Squadron.

La Follette, Robert Marion, Sr. (1855–1925). Governor, U.S. Representative, and U.S. Senator from Wisconsin: **Battling Bob, Fighting Bob.**

La Guardia, Fiorello H[enry] (1882–1947). Mayor of New York City: **Butch, Little Flower.**

Laguna Beach, California. U.S. city: **City of Serene Living.**

Laine, Albert (active 1917). Jazz musician: **Baby.**

Laine, Frankie (born 1913). Singer: **Mr. Rhythm.** Born: Frank Paul Lo Vecchio.

Laine, George [Vitelle] (1873–1966). Jazz drummer: **Papa Jack.**

Laird of Skibo Castle. Carnegie, Andrew.

Laird of Woodstock Lodge. Burroughs, John.

Lajoie, Napoleon (1875–1959). Baseball second baseman and manager: **Larry.**

Lake, Simon (1865–1945). Naval architect and mechanical engineer: **Father of the Modern Submarine.**

Lake City. Chicago, Illinois; Fort Worth, Texas; Madison, Wisconsin.

Lake George. Lake in New York state: **Queen of American Lakes.**

Lake Placid. Lake in New York state: **America's Switzerland.**

Lake State. Michigan; Minnesota.

Lake Tahoe, California-Nevada. U.S. town: **America's All-Year Playground, Coming Vegas, Recreational Slum.**

Lalo. Schifrin, Boris.

Lamare, Hilton (born 1910). Jazz guitarist, banjo player, and singer: **Nappy.**

Lamar University, athletic teams of: **Cardinals.**

Lambeau, Earl L. (1898–1965). Football back and coach: **Curly.**

Lambert, Basil Garwood (1891–1950). Xylophonist: **Professor Lamberti.**

Lambert, Charles Frederick (born 1887). Western peace officer: **Kid.**

Lambert, Ward L. (1888–1958). Basketball coach: **Piggy.**

Lame Deer (born c. 1902). Indian medicine man: **Seeker of Visions.**

Lame Duck Alley. A screened-off corridor in the White House offices where politicians who were defeated in elections met; used c. 1910.

Lame Duck Amendment. Twentieth Amendment.

La Motta, Jacob (born 1921). Middleweight boxer: **Bronx Bull.**

Lamour, Dorothy (born 1914). Film actress and singer: **Mary Pickford of This War, Paratrooper Pet, Sarong Girl, Sweetheart of**

the Foxholes, Uncle Sam's Favorite Niece. Born: Dorothy
Kaumeyer.

Lanai, Hawaii. Island of Hawaii: Pineapple Island.

Lancaster, Burt[on Stephen] (born 1913). Motion-picture actor and
producer: Lang.

Lancaster, Pennsylvania. U.S. city: Pretzel City.

Lance, [Thomas] Bert[ram] (born 1931). Banker and presidential
aide. With other members of President Jimmy Carter's administration: Georgia Mafia.

Land God Gave Cain. The Arctic regions of Canada.

Landis, Kenesaw Mountain (1866–1944). Baseball commissioner:
Czar of American Baseball, Czar of Baseball, Czar of the National Pastime, Judge.

Land of Beginnings. North Carolina.

Land of Enchantment. New Mexico.

Land of Evangeline. Coastal Maine, New Brunswick, and Nova
Scotia; coastal Louisiana.

Land of Exciting Contrasts. Oregon.

Land of Flowers. Alabama; Florida.

Land of Fresh Horizons. North Dakota.

Land of Gold. California.

Land of Grass Roots. South Dakota.

Land of History. Ohio.

Land of Legend. Yukon Territory.

Land of Opportunity. Arkansas.

Land of Peanuts. Georgia.

Land of Plenty. South Dakota.

Land of Roger Williams. Rhode Island.

Land of Romance. Virginia.

Land of Shining Mountains. Idaho.

Land of Spring. Coastal southern California.

Land of Steady Habits. Connecticut.

Land of Sunshine. Florida; New Mexico; southern California.

Land of 10,000 Lakes. Minnesota.

Land of the Big Rich. Houston, Texas.

Land of the Dakotas. North Dakota.

Land of the Free. United States of America.

Land of the Honey Bees. Utah.

Land of the Illini. Illinois.

Land of the Long North Furrow. North Dakota.

Land of the Midnight Sun. Alaska.

Land of the Mormons. Utah.

Land of the Purple Sage. Wyoming.

Land of the Red People. Oklahoma.

Land of the Rolling Prairie. Iowa.

Land of the Saints. Utah.

Land of the Sky. North Carolina.

Land of the Trade Winds. Virgin Islands.

Land o' Lakes. Wisconsin.

Landon, Alf[red Mossman] (born 1887). Governor of Kansas and Republican candidate for U.S. President: **Coolidge of the West, Kansas Coolidge.**

Landslide Johnson. Johnson, Lyndon Baines.

Landslide Lyndon. Johnson, Lyndon Baines.

Lane, Franklin Knight (1864–1921). Politician and statesman: **Despoiler of Public Lands, Mystic Materialist.**

Lane, Richard (born 1928). Football halfback: **Night Train.**

Lang. Lancaster, Burt[on Stephen].

Langdon, Harry (1884–1944). Motion-picture comedian: **Baby.**

Lange, William Alexander (1871–1950). Baseball outfielder: **Big Bill, Little Eva.**

Langer, John (active 1912). Gambler: **Dollar John.**

Langford, Sam (1886–1956). Canadian-American heavyweight boxer: **Boston Tar Baby, Tar Baby.**

Lank. Leonard, Frank E.

Lanny. Morgan, Harold Lansford.

Lansky, Meyer (born 1902). Crime syndicate chief: **Johnny Eggs, Meyer the Bug.** Born: Maier Suchowljansky.

Lanson, Roy (born 1919). Popular singer: **Snooky.**

Lanza, John (born c. 1940). Wrestler: **Black Jack, Cowboy Jack.**

Laredo, Texas. U.S. city: **Gateway to Mexico.**

Largest City in the Largest State. Anchorage, Alaska.

Larkin, Tippy (born 1917). Welterweight boxer: **Garfield Gunner.** Born: Tony Pilleteri.

La Rocca, Nick (1889–1961). Jazz musician: **Assassinator of Syncopation.** Legal name: Dominick James La Rocca.

Larouche, Pierre (born 1955). Hockey player: **King.**

Larruping Lothario of Pugilism. Baer, Max[imilian Adelbert].

Larruping Lou. Gehrig, [Henry] Lou[is].

Larry. Lajoie, Napoleon; McPhail, Leland Stanford.

Larry the Aviator. Banghart, Basil.

Larson, Emery Ellsworth (1899–1945). Football coach and U.S. Colonel: **Swede.**

La Salle College, basketball team of, with other Philadelphia area teams: **Big Five.**

Lasha, William B. (born 1929). Jazz flutist and composer: **Prince.**

Lasker, Albert Davis (1880–1952). Baseball official: **Advertising Wizard, Father of the Lasker Plan.**

Last Frontier. Northwest Territories; Alaska.

Last Great American Hero. Ellsberg, Daniel.

Last Lovely City. San Francisco, California.

Last of the Big-City Bosses. Daley, Richard Joseph.

Last of the Big Time Grafters. Sullivan, Timothy Daniel.

Last of the Cold War Liberals. Jackson, Henry [Martin].

Last of the Great New York Bosses. De Sapio, Carmine.

Last of the Great Southern Belles. Mitchell, Martha.

Last of the Kennedy Brothers, Kennedy, Edward M[oore].

Last of the Oldtime Gangsters. Orger, Jacob.

Last of the Red-Hot Mamas. Tucker, Sophie.

Last of the Spitball Pitchers. Grimes, Burleigh Arland.

Last of the Western Train Robbers. Carlile, William L.

Las Vegas, Nevada. U.S. city: **City of Chance, City Without Clocks, Gambling Capital of the Far West, Playground of the Desert, Playtown U.S.A., Punk's Paradise, Sin City, Vegas.**

Latham, Dwight (active 1920s and 1930s). Radio singer: **Red.**

Latham, George (active 1921–23). Football player: **Fat.**

Latman, Arnold Barry (born 1936). Baseball pitcher: **Shoulders.**

Lattimore, Owen (born 1900). Author and historian: **China Lobby Man.**

Laubach, Frank Charles (1884–1970). Missionary and educator: **Teacher of Millions.**

Laughing-Gas Man. Short, Dewey Jackson.

Laughing Lady. O'Neil, Kitty.

Lavagetto, Harry Arthur (born 1912). Baseball second and third baseman and manager: **Cookie.**

Lavelle, Mike (born c. 1933). Columnist: **Blue Collar Pundit.**

Lavigne, Kid (1869–1936). Lightweight boxer: **Saginaw Kid.** Legal name: George Lavigne.

Lawnmower. Csonka, Larry.

Lawrence University, athetic teams of: **Vikings.**

Lawson, Andrew Cowper (1861–1952). Geologist and educator: **Doc.**

Lawson, John R. (born 1911). Jazz trumpeter: **Yank.**

Lawyer. Sorrell, Victor Garland.

Layden, Elmer [Francis] (1903–73). Football fullback, coach, and professional league official. With other members of Notre Dame backfield: **Four Horsemen.**

Layne, Robert Lawrence (born 1926). Football quarterback: **Built-in Timepiece.**

Lazy Dan. Kaufman, Irving.

Lazzeri, Anthony Michael (1903–46). Baseball second baseman: **Push-'em-up Lazzeri.**

LBJ. Johnson, Lyndon Baines.

Lea, Langdon (1874–1937). Football tackle: **Biffy.**

Lea, Luke (1879–1945). U.S. Senator from Tennessee: **Young Thunderbolt.**

Leach, Felix (active 1930). Football player: **Lefty.**

Leach, Thomas William (1877–1969). Baseball outfielder and third baseman: **Wee Tommy.**

Leadbelly. Ledbetter, Huddie.

Leader, The. Sinatra, Frank.

Leader of Men, Pelley, William Dudley.

Leading Figure of the Yiddish Theater. Schwartz, Maurice.

Leading Muckraker of His Time. Pearson, Drew.

Lead State. Colorado; Missouri; Montana.

Leadville, Colorado. U.S. town: **Cloud City.**

Leahy, Francis William (1908–73). Football coach: **Prussian Leprechaun.**

Leary, Timothy [Francis] (born 1920). Psychologist; drug cult leader: **Messiah of LSD, Uncle Tim.**

Leathernecks. 1. United States Marine Corps. 2. Athletic teams of Western Illinois University, Macomb.

Leavenworth, Kansas. U.S. city: **Cottonwood City.**

Leavitt, Frank S. (1890–1953). Wrestler: **Man-Mountain Dean.**

LeBlanc, Dudley J. (born 1894). Politician and patent medicine manufacturing executive: **Couzin Dud, Uncle Dud, Mr. Hadacol.**

Lebrowitz, Barney (1891–1949). Light heavyweight boxer: **Battling Levinsky.**

Ledbetter, Huddie (1888–1949). Blues singer and guitarist: **Leadbelly.**

Lee, Hal Burnham (born 1907). Baseball outfielder: **Sheriff.**

Lee, Ivy Ledbetter (1877–1934). Public relations consultant: **Public Relations Genius.**

Lee, John Clifford Hodges (1887–1958). U.S. Army Lieutenant General: **Court House.**

Lee, Joshua Bryan (1892–1967). U.S. Represenative and Senator from Oklahoma: **Boy Orator, Boy Wonder, One Speech Lee, Second William Jennings Bryan, Silver-tongued Josh.**

Lee, Peggy (born 1920). Popular singer: **Queen of American Pop Music.** Born: Norma Dolores Jean Engstrom.

Lee, Pincus (born 1916). Actor and television performer: **Pinky.** Born: Pincus Leff.

Lee, William C. (1895–1948). U.S. Army Major General: **Father of U.S. Airborne Forces.**

Leemans, Alphonse (born 1913). Baseball player: **Tuffy.**

Leeteg, Edgar (1904–53). Artist: **American Gauguin, The Master.**

Left's Lawyer's Lawyer. Boudin, Leonard.

Lefty. Gomez, Vernon Louis; Grove, Robert Moses; James, George; Koncil, Frank; Leach, Felix; O'Doul, Frank Joseph; Phillips, Harold Ross; Shaute, Joseph Benjamin; Tyler, George Albert; Williams, Claude Preston.

Legal Successor of Houdini. Weiss, Theo.

Le Gros Bill. Beliveau, Jean.

Legs. Diamond, Jack; Hawley, Roy M.

Lehigh University, athletic teams of: **Engineers.**

Lehr, Lew (1895–1950). Radio and newsreel comedian: **Dribblepuss.**

Leibrook, Wilfred (1903–43). Jazz musician: **Min.**

Leipzig, Nat (1873–1939). Magician and hypnotist: **International King of Cards.** Born: Nathan Leipziger.

Lema, Tony (1934–66). Golfer: **Champagne Tony.** Legal name: Anthony Lema.

Lemke, William (1878–1950). U.S. Representative from North Dakota: **Moratorium Bill, Liberty Bill.**

Lemon, Meadow George (born 1933). Basketball player: **Clown Prince of Basketball, Meadowlark.**

Lemons. Solters, Julius Joseph.

Lena. Blackburne, Russell.

Leonard, Benny (1896–1947). Lightweight boxer: **Ghetto Wizard.** Born: Benjamin Leiner.

Leonard, Frank E. (died 1974). Cartoonist: **Lank.**

Leonard, Hubert Benjamin (1892–1952). Baseball pitcher: **Dutch.**

Leonard, Jack E. (1911–73). Comedian: **Fat Jack, Fat Libitsky, Master of the Oneliner, Mean Mr. Clean, Mr. Insult.** Born: John Libitsky.

Leopards. Athletic teams of Lafayette College, Easton, Pennsylvania.

Leopold, Nathan F., Jr. (1906–71). Murderer, ornithologist, and writer: **Babe.**

Leo the Lip. Durocher, Leo Ernest.

Lepine, Alfred (1901–55). Canadian hockey player: **Pit.**

Lepke. Buchalter, Louis.

Lesky, John (1888–1955). Flyweight and bantamweight boxer: **Johnny Buff.**

LeSueur, Larry (born 1909). News commentator. With seven other broadcasters: **Murrow's Boys.** Legal name: Lawrence Edward LeSueur.

Lettuce Bowl. 1. Salinas Valley, California. 2. Stadium of the Salinas Packers Football Club, Salinas, California.

Levine, Henry (born 1907). Jazz trumpeter: **Hot Lips.**

Levine, Hymie (active 1920–30). Criminal: **Loud Mouth.**

Levine, Lou (born c. 1939). Marksman and television news director: **Mr. Nice Gun.**

Levinsky, Alexander H. (born 1912). Hockey player: **Mein Boy.**

Levy, Leonard (active 1939–48). Football guard and wrestler: **Butch.**

Levy, Walter James (born 1911). Economist: **Dean of Petroleum Analysts, Dean of Petroleum Consultants.**

Lewis, Art[hur] (1911–62). Football tackle and coach: **Pappy.**

Lewis, David John (1869–1952). Coal miner and politician: **Little Davey, Little Giant.**

Lewis, Ed (1890–1966). Heavyweight wrestler: **The Strangler.** Born: Robert H. Friedrich.

Lewis, George Edward (born 1888). Baseball outfielder: **Duffy.**

Lewis, [Harry] Sinclair (1885–1951). Author: **Red.**

Lewis, James Hamilton (1863–1939). U.S. Senator from Illinois: **Beau Brummel of the Senate, Fashion Plate, Pink Whiskers.**

Lewis, James Wilson (born 1915). U.S. Army officer: **Big Jim, Jungle Jim.**

Lewis, Ted (1891–1971). Jazz musician, clarinetist, singer, composer, and bandleader: **Hamlet of the Halls, Lonely Troubadour, Medicine Man for Your Blues, Top-hatted Tragedian of Jazz.** Born: Theodore Leopold Friedman.

Lewis, Vach (died 1908). Ganster: **Cyclone Louie.**

Lexington, Kentucky. U.S. city: **Athens of the West, Belle City of the Bluegrass Regions, Bluegrass Capital, Capital of the Horse World.**

Lexington, Massachusetts. U.S. town: **Birthplace of American Liberty, Cradle of Liberty.**

Liberace, George J. (born 1911). Violinist and bandleader: **Brother George.**

Liberace of the Accordion. Welk, Lawrence [LeRoy].

Liberal Politician. Perkins, Frances.

Liberator. Consolidated B-24 bombing plane, World War II.

Liberty Bell. Bell of the Old State House (Independence Hall), Philadelphia; first cast 1752.

Liberty Bell Division. Seventy-sixth Division.

Libertybellsville, Philadelphia, Pennsylvania.

Liberty Bill. Lemke, William,

Liberty Bowl. Football stadium in Memphis, Tennessee; site of annual Liberty Bowl college football game.

Liberty Division. Seventy-ninth Division.

Librarian, The. Pearson, Edmund Lester.

Library Builder. Carnegie, Andrew.

Library of Congress. Federal institution: **Slumbering Giant of Capitol Hill.**

Licavoli, Thomas (1904–73). Gangster: **Yonnie.**

L.I.E., The

Lieb, John William (1860–1929). Inventor: **Apostle of Light and Power.**

Light, Ben (1894–1965). Jazz pianist: **Lightning Fingers.**

Light Bulb Lyndon. Johnson, Lyndon Baines.

Lighthorse Harry. Wilson, Harry E.

Lightnin'. Hopkins, Sam.

Lightning. Lockheed P-38 fighter plane, World War II.

Lightning Destroyer. Foreman, George.

Lightning Division. Seventy-eighth Infantry Division.

Lightning Fingers. Light, Ben.

Lilac City. Lincoln, Nebraska.

Li'l Arthur. Johnson, Jack.

Lillie, Gordon W. (1860–1942). Frontier scout and showman: **Pawnee Bill, White Chief of the Pawnees.**

Lilo. Galante, Carmine.

Lily-White. Advocate of segregation and inferior status for blacks.

Lincoln, Nebraska. U.S. city: **Cornhusker Capital City, Lilac City.**

Lincoln, Warren (died 1941). Criminal lawyer, horticulturist, and murderer: **Scot Free Lincoln.**

Lincoln Division. Eighty-fourth Division.

Lincoln's State. Illinois.

Lindbergh, Charles A[ugustus] (1902–74). Aviator: **Ambassador of Good Will, Ambassador of the Air, Lindy, Lone Eagle, Lucky Lindy.**

Lindemann, Leo (1888–1957). Restaurateur: **Lindy.**

Lindsay, Donald (born c. 1946) Bagpipe player and teacher: **Dean of the Bagpipers.**

Lindy. Boggs, Corinne C[laiborne]; Lindbergh, Charles A[ugustus]; Lindemann, Leo.

Ling, James Joseph (born 1922). Manufacturer: **Texas Titan.**

Lingle, Alfred (1892?–1930). Police reporter and murder victim: **Jake.**

Lingley, William (died 1915). Gangster: **Big Bill.**

Lion Hunter. Tinkham, George Holden.

Lion of the Senate, The. Borah, William Edgar.

Lions. Athletic teams of Columbia University, New York City.

Lion's Den State. Tennessee.

Lion's Gate. Entrance to Vancouver harbor.

Lip, The. Durocher, Leo Ernest.

Lippman, Sally (born 1901). Lawyer and habitué of New York City discotheques, late 1970s: **Disco Sally.**

Lippy, Durocher, Leo Ernest.

Lippy Leo. Durocher, Leo Ernest.

Lipscomb, Gene (1931–63). Football tackle: **Big Daddy.** Legal name: Eugene Lipscomb.

Liquor Czar. Morgan, William Forbes.

Literary Emporium. Boston, Massachusetts.

Literary Radical. Bourne, Randolph Silliman.

Lithuanian, The. Sharkey, Jack.

Littauer, Emmuel Victor (born 1895). Football player: **Manny.**

Little, Dudley (born 1930). Jazz pianist, bandleader, and singer: **Big Tiny.**

Little, John (1900–56). Entertainer and composer: **Little Jack Little, Radio's Cheerful Little Earful.**

Little, Lou[is Lawrence] (1893–1979). Football coach: **Big-Nose Louie, Caesar of Football.** Born: Luigi Piccolo.

Little Alby. Barkley, Alben William.

Little Angel of Radio. Dragonette, Jessica.

Little Augie. Orgen, Jacob; Pisano, Augie.

Little Beaver. Dionne, Marcel Elphege.

Little Benny. Harris, Benjamin.

Little Big Man. Archibald, Nate; Hoffman, Dustin.

Little Big Man from Brooklyn. Weinberg, Stephen Jacob.

Little Bill. Johnston, William M.

Little Bird. Heath, James Edward.

Little Boy Blue. Booth, Albie.

Little Caesar. Petrillo, James Caesar; Varco, Joseph Vincent Di.

Little Chocolate. Dixon, George.

Little Church Around the Corner. Church of the Transfiguration, New York City.

Little Clipper. Smith, John Philip.

Little Davey. Lewis, David John.

Little David. O'Brien, David.

Little Dixie. Missouri; Southeastern part of Oklahoma.

Little Doc. Severinsen, Doc.

Little Doctor. Meanwell, Walter E.

Little Eden. Hoboken, New Jersey.

Little Egypt. Region around Cairo, Illinois.

Little Elsie. Morgan, Helen.

Little Eva. Lange, William Alexander.

Little Evalyn. McLean, Evalyn Walsh.

Little Flower. La Guardia, Fiorello H[enry].

Little Giant. Lewis, David John.

Little Hatchet. Nation, Carry or Carrie [Amelia Moore Gloyd].

Little Havana. Cuban section of Miami.

Little Hebrew. Attell, Abe.

Little Ida. Idaho.

Little Indian. Moore, Wilbur.

Little Italy. Any city neighborhood of people of Italian descent.

Little Jack Little. Little, John.
Little Jazz. Eldridge, David Roy.
Little Joe. 1. Montoya, Joseph M. 2. Type of spacecraft booster.
Little John. 1. Torrio, John. 2. Type of surface-to-surface rocket.
Little Lunnon. Colorado Springs, Colorado.
Little Major. Corum, Bill
Little Man in Pro Football. Walker, [Ewell] Doak, [Jr.].
Little Miss Poker Face. Wills, Helen [Newington].
Little Miss Roosevelt. Longworth, Alice Roosevelt.
Little Missy. Oakley, Annie.
Little Mo. Connolly, Maureen Catherine.
Little Monkey. Rizzuto, Phil[ip Francis].
Little Mountain State. West Virginia.
Little Napoleon. McGraw, John Joseph.
Little New York. Campagna, Louis.
Little Nick. Montos, Nick George.
Little Pearl Harbor. Clark Field, Philippine Islands, after a Japanese bombing raid of December 7, 1941.
Little Poison. Waner, Lloyd James.
Little Quakers. Athletic teams of Swarthmore College, Swarthmore, Pennsylvania.
Littler, Eugene (born 1930). Golfer: **Gene the Machine.**
Little Red. Rudd, W. L.; Starkweather, Charles.
Little Rhody. Rhode Island.
Little Rock, Arkansas. U.S. city: **Arkopolis, City of Roses, City of Three Capitols.**
Little Round Man. Butts, Wally.
Little Shepherd of Coogan's Bluff. Durocher, Leo Ernest.
Little Slug of the Boston Red Sox. Stephens, Vern[on Decatur, Jr.].
Little Songbird from Italy. Van Dine, Harvey.
Little Sure Shot. Oakley, Annie.
Little Three. 1. Basketball teams of Canisius College, Buffalo, New York; Niagara University, Buffalo, New York; and St. Bonaventure University, Olean, New York. 2. Amherst College, Amherst, Massachusetts; Wesleyan University, Middletown,

Connecticut; and Williams College, Williamstown, Massachusetts.

Little Tokyo. Any city neighborhood of people of Japanese descent.

Little Tramp. Chaplin, Charles.

Little Tubby. Raskin, Julius.

Little White House. Home of President Franklin D. Roosevelt at Warm Springs, Georgia.

Little White House City. Warm Springs, Georgia.

Live Oak State. Florida.

Livermore, Jesse Lauriston (1877–1940). Broker and speculator: **King of Speculators, Speculator King.**

Livermore Butcher Boy. Baer, Max[imilian Adelbert].

Livermore Larruper. Baer, Max[imilian Adelbert].

Livingston, Joseph A. (1906–57). Jazz saxophonist: **Fud.**

Lizard. Native or resident of Alabama.

Lizard State. Alabama.

Liz the Lion Killer. Holtzman, Elizabeth.

Lloyd, Harold [Clayton] (1893–1971). Motion picture comedian: **Lonesome Luke.**

Lloyd, John Henry (1884–1965). Baseball shortstop and manager: **Black Honus Wagner, Pop.**

Lobert, John Bernard (1881–1968). Baseball third baseman and coach: **Hans.**

Lobos. Athletic teams of the University of New Mexico, Albuquerque.

Lobsterland. Maine.

Lock City. Stamford, Connecticut

Locke, Roland A. (1903?–52). Track runner: **Gipper.**

Lockjaw. Davis, Eddie.

Locklear, Omar (died 1920). Exhibition flier: **Man Who Walked on Wings.**

Lodge, Henry Cabot (1850–1924). U.S. Senator from Massachusetts and author: **Destroyer of the League of Nations.**

Loeb, Milton E. (1888–1972). Manufacturing executive and inventor: **Father of the Brillo Pad.**

Lofton, Lawrence (born 1930). Jazz trombonist: **Tricky.**

Loggers. Athletic teams of the University of Puget Sound, Tacoma, Washington.

Lolly. Parsons, Louella.

Lombardi, Ernest Natali (1908–77). Baseball catcher: **Snozz.**

Lombardi, Vince[nt Thomas] (1913–70). Football player and coach. With other members of Fordham team: **Seven Blocks of Granite.**

Lombardo, Guy [Albert] (1902–77). Bandleader: **King of Corn, Mr. New Year's Eve, Prince of Wails, Schmaltz King.**

Lombardo, Thomas A. (1922–50). Football back, quarterback, and U.S. Army officer: **Lombo.**

Lombard Street Curlicue. Length of street on Russian Hill, San Francisco, that climbs a steep slope in eight hairpin turns.

Lombo. Lombardo, Thomas A.

Lonardo, Joseph (born 1927). Gangster: **Big Joe.**

London, Jack (1876–1916). Author and sailor: **American Kipling, Prince of the Oyster Pirates, Prophet of The Strenuous Life.** Legal name: John Griffith London.

London's Rose of Texas. Armstrong, Anne [Legendre].

Lone Eagle. Lindbergh, Charles A[ugustus].

Lone Lion, The. Borah, William Edgar.

Lonely Troubadour. Lewis, Ted.

Lonergan, Richard (active 1920–30). Gangster: **Pegleg.**

Lonesome George. Gobel, George [Leslie]; Romney, George; Wallace, George [Corley].

Lonesome Luke. Lloyd, Harold Clayton.

Lonesome Singer of the Air. Marvin, Johnny.

Lone Star. Dietz, William H.

Lone Star Division. Thirty-sixth Division.

Lone Star State. Texas.

Lone Wolf of the Senate. Morse, Wayne [Lyman].

Lone Wolf of the Underworld. Millman, Harry.

Long, Clair (active 1916). Football player: **Shorty.**

Long, Herman C. (1866–1909). Baseball shortstop: **Germany, Flying Dutchman.**

Long, Huey [Pierce] (1893–1935). Governor of Louisiana and U.S. Senator from Louisiana: **Dictator of Louisiana, Hooey Long, Kingfish, Louisiana's Loud Speaker.**

Longbaugh, Robert (1901–72). Outlaw: **Cimarron Kid.**

Long Beach, California. U.S. city: **City by the Sea, Gem of Beaches, International City, Pride of the Pacific, Queen of Beaches, Star of the Southland.**

Longest Day, The. June 6, 1944, the day on which the Allied invasion of Normandy, France, began; Also known as D-Day.

Long Gone. Miles, Luke.

Long-haired Wonder. Clark, Steve.

Longhorns. Athletic teams of the University of Texas, Austin.

Long Island Expressway. Superhighway on Long Island, New York: **The Big LIE, The L.I.E., World's Longest Parking Lot.**

Long Jim. Barnes, James M.

Long John. Nebel, John.

Long Tom. Self-propelled cannon, Korean War.

Longworth, Alice Roosevelt (born 1884). Social leader: **Little Miss Roosevelt, Princess Alice, Queen Alice.**

Longy. Zwillman, Abner.

Lonnie. Stagg, Amos Alonzo.

Loop, The. Shopping area of Chicago, characterized by a looplike junction of elevated railroad tracks.

Lopez, Vincent (1895–75). Jazz pianist and bandleader: **Pianner Kid.**

Loquacious Linguist Whom Labor Loves. Perkins, Frances.

Lorber, Max J. (active 1923–24). Football player: **Mugs.**

Lord. Nelson, [John] Byron, [Jr.].

Lord, The. Crisler, Fritz.

Lord Haw Haw. Joyce, William.

Lord High Executioner. Anastasia, Albert.

Lord Jeffs. Athletic teams of Amherst College, Amherst, Massachusetts.

Lord of San Simeon. Hearst, William Randolph.

Lord of the Beasts. Jones, Charles Jesse.

Lords. Athletic teams of Kenyon College, Gambier, Ohio.

Lorenzo the Magnificent of the Stage, Ziegfeld, Flo[renz, Jr.].

Los Alamos, New Mexico, U.S. city: **Atomic City, Capital of the Atomic Age.**

Los Angeles, California. U.S. city; **Angel City, City of Angels, El-Ay, Entertainment City, Freeway City, Happy Home of the Bulldozer, L.A., Metropolis of the West, Movie City, Music Capital of America, Old Pueblo, Smog City, Solar Energy Capital.**

Los Angeles State University, athletic teams of: **Diablos.**

Lost Battalion. 308th Infantry Battalion, 77th Division, World War I, cut off behind German lines during the Meuse-Argonne offensive; second battalion of the 131st Field Artillery, captured by the Japanese in 1942 during World War II.

Lost Generation. Group of writers who came of age after World War I, including Ernest Hemingway, F. Scott Fitzgerald, and John Dos Passos, and also their contemporaries, viewed as spiritually and culturally lost in the social turmoil of the times.

Lost Leader. Cannon, James.

Loud Larry. McPhail, Leland Stanford.

Loud Mouth. Levine, Hymie.

Louie the Lump. Pioggi, Louis.

Louis, Joe (born 1914). Heavyweight boxer: **Brown Bomber, Dark Destroyer, Superman of the Prize Ring.** Born: Joseph Louis Barrow.

Louisa May Woollcott. Woollcott, Alexander Humphreys.

Louisiana. Eighteenth U.S. state: **Alligator State, Bayou State, Cane Sugar State, Creole State, Nature's Cornucopia, Pelican State, Sugar State.**

Louisiana Ram. Mouton, Robert L.

Louisiana's Loud Speaker. Long, Huey [Pierce].

Louisiana State University, athletic teams of: **Bengals, Fighting Tigers, Ole War Skule.**

Louisiana Tech University, athletic teams of: **Bulldogs.**

Louisville, Kentucky. U.S. city: **City by the Falls, Derby City, Falls City, Gateway City, Home of the Kentucky Derby.**

Louisville, University of, athletic teams of: **Cardinals.**

Louisville Lip. Ali, Muhammad.

Lovebird, Allen, William Franklin.

Love Goddess. Hayworth, Rita.

Lovelorn Killer. Ray, James Earl.

Lovett, William (died 1923). Gangster: **Wild Bill.**

Lovin' Putty. Annixter, Julius.

Lowden, Frank Orren (1861–1943). U.S. Representative from Illinois and Governor of Illinois: **Farmer's Friend.**

Lowell, Massachusetts. U.S. city: **City of Spindles, Manchester of America, Spindle City.**

Lowell of the South. Augusta, Georgia.

Lower Case Cummings. cummings, e.e.

Lower 48. In Alaska, the 48 contiguous states.

Loyal Hard Hat. Brennan, Peter J.

Loyalist Province. New Brunswick.

LP. The "long-playing" phonograph record, turning at 33⅓ revolutions per minute, introduced in 1948.

LSD King. Stanley, Augustus Owsley, III.

LSD Tycoon. Stanley, Augustus Owsley, III.

Lu. Blue, Luzerne A.

Lubbock, Texas. U.S. city: **Hub City of the South Plains.**

Lucas, Nick (born 1897). Singer and guitarist: **Crooning Troubadour.** Born: Nick Lucanese.

Luce, Robert (1862–1946). U.S. Representative from Massachusetts: **The Parliamentarian.**

Luchese, Thomas (1899–1967). Mafia leader and criminal: **Three-Finger Brown.** Born: Thomas Gaetano Luchese.

Luciano, Charles (1897–1962). Racketeer: **Charlie Lucky, King of the New York Rackets, Lucky, The Man, Three-Twelve.** Legal name: Salvatore Luciana.

Luckey. Roberts, C. Luckeyth.

Luckiest Fool Alive. Kelly, Alvin Anthony.

Lucky. Luciano, Charles; Millinder, Lucius; Thompson, Eli.

Lucky Lindy. Lindbergh, Charles A[ugustus].

Lucky Seventh. Seventh Armored Division.

Ludlow, Louis Leon (1873–1950). U.S. Representative from Indiana and journalist: **Peace Ludlow.**

Lugar, John (1900–54). Gangster: **Buddy.**

Lugar, Richard G[reen] (born 1932). Mayor of Indianpolis and U.S. Senator from Indiana: **President Nixon's Favorite Mayor.**

Luke. Sewell, James Luther.

Luke, Frank, Jr. (1897–1918). World War I aviator: **Balloon Buster.**

Lulu. Bender, Louis.

Lumber Capital. Tacoma, Washington.

Lumber City. Bangor, Maine.

Lumberjacks. Athletic teams of Northern Arizona University, Flagstaff.

Lumber King. Weyerhaeuser, Frederick.

Lumber State. Maine.

Luscious Lucius. Beebe, Lucius.

Lyle, Albert Walter (born 1944). Baseball pitcher: **Sparky.**

Lynch, James (1904–58). Gambler: **Piggy.**

Lyon, David Gordon (born 1911). Advertising executive and author: **Campus Radical, Soggy.**

M

Ma. Barker, Kate Clark; Beland, Lucy; Bethune, Mary McLeod; Harding, Florence Kling DeWolfe; Kennedy, Minnie; Rainey, Gertrude.

Maas, Melvin Joseph (1898–1964). U.S. Representative from Minnesota and aviator: **Marine Aviator.**

Ma Bell. Bell telephone system.

Macaroni. Capone, Al[phonse].

MacArthur, Douglas (1880–1964). U.S. Army General: **Beau Brummel of the Army, Buck Private's Gary Cooper, D'Artagnan of the AEF, Disraeli of the Chiefs of Staff, Dugout Doug, The Magnificent, The Napoleon of Luzon.**

Macauley, Ed (born 1928). Basketball center and coach: **Easy Ed.**

MacDonald, Jeanette [Anna] (1907–65). Singer and motion-picture actress: **The Iron Butterfly.** Also known as Mrs. Gene Raymond.

Machine, The. Grant, Travis.

Machine-gun Frank. Thompson, Russell.

Machine Gun Jack McGurn. Gebardi, Vincent.

Machine Gun Kelly. Kelly, George.

Mack, Connie (1862–1956). Baseball club founder and manager: **Mr. Baseball.** Born: Cornelius McGillicuddy.

MacLeish, Rick (born 1950). Hockey player: **Chuckles.**

Macon, Georgia. U.S. city: **Heart of Georgia.**

Mad Austrian. Bluhdorn, Charles.

Mad Av. Madison Avenue.

Mad Bomber, The. Metesky, George [Peter].

Mad Canadian. Carter, Ken.

Madcap Maxie. Baer, Max[imilian Adelbert].

Madden, Owen (1892–1965). Gangster: **Killer, Owney, Owney the Killer.**

Mad Dog. Coll, Vincent.

Mad Dog of Gangland. Coll, Vincent.

Maddox, Lester [Garfield] (born 1915). Restaurateur, politician, and Governor of Georgia: **Mr. White Backlash.**

Mademoiselle Dazie. Fellowes, Mrs. Cornelius Peterkin.

Mader, Fred (active 1920–30). Labor union racketeer: **Frenchy.**

Madison, Louis (1899–1948). Jazz cornetist: **Kid Shots.**

Madison, Wisconsin. U.S. city: **City of Four Lakes, Four Lake City, Lake City.**

Madison Avenue. The advertising industry and its characteristic attitudes; after a section of a street in New York City near which the executive offices of the advertising and communications industries are located.

Mad Pittsburgh Playboy, The. Thaw, Harry Kendall.

Mad Russian. Vukovich, William.

Maestro, The. Toscanini, Arturo.

Maestro of the Omelet. Stanish, Rudolph.

Mafia. Group of criminal organizations: **Cosa Nostra, Honored Society, The Syndicate.**

Maggie. Magnavox Corporation.

Magic. Sayers, Gale.

Magical Maker of Mobiles. Calder, Alexander.

Magic City. Billings, Montana; Birmingham, Alabama; Miami, Florida.

Magic City of the South, Birmingham, Alabama.

Magic Fingers of Radio. Duchin, Eddie.

Magic Maker. cummings, e. e.

Maglie, Sal[vatore Anthony] (born 1917). Baseball pitcher: **The Barber.**

Magnavox Corporation. U.S. company: **Maggie.**

Magnificent, The. Barnes, Marvin; MacArthur, Douglas.

Magnificent Mile, The. North Michigan Avenue, Chicago.

Magnificent Mongoose. Moore, Archie.

Magnificent Rube. Rickard, Tex.

Magnificent Screwball. Baer, Max[imilian Adelbert].

Magnificent Skeptic. Dobie, Gil[mour].

Magnolia. Native or resident of Mississippi.

Magnolia City. Houston, Texas.

Magnolia Mafia. Group of assistants to President Jimmy Carter.

Magnolia State. Mississippi.

Magnum, Leo Allan (born 1900). Baseball player: **Blacky.**

Maharajahs of Paneldom. Goodson, Mark and Todman, William [Selden].

Mahatma, The. Rickey, Branch [Wesley].

Mails, Walter (born 1896). Baseball player and press agent: **Big Lip, Cock o' the Walk of Baseball, Duster, Great Left-handed Press Agent, The Great Mails, King of Kings.**

Main Drag. Principal street of any town.

Main Drag of Many Tears. One Hundred Twenty-fifth Street, New York City.

Maine. Twenty-third U.S. state: **Border State, Down East, Down East State, Lobsterland, Lumber State, Old Dirigo State, Pine Tree State, Polar Star State, Vacationland.**

Maine, University of, athletic teams of: **Black Bears.**

Main Line. Chain of wealthy Philadelphia suburbs from Overbrook to Paoli, along the former Pennsylvania Railroad main line to Pittsburgh.

Main Street of America. Route 66.

Major. Bowes, Edward; Houk, Ralph George.

Maker of Stars. Bonesteele, Jessie.

Malcolm X (1925–65). Black power advocate: **Big Red, Detroit Red.** Also known as Malik El-Shabazz. Born: Malcolm Little.

Mallon, Mary (1870–1938). Typhoid carrier, active c. 1904–15: **Typhoid Mary.**

Mallory, William Neely (1901–45). Football back: **Bull, Memphis Bill.**

Malloy, Michael (died 1932). Victim of Murder Trust gang: **Durable Alcoholic, Indestructible Mike Malloy, Somniferous Malloy.**

Malone, James H. (1887–1955). Detective: **Shooey.**

Malone, Percy Lay (born 1903). Soldier and baseball player: **Black Knight of the Border; Pat.**

Maloney, Patrick (active 1920–30). Gangster: **Happy.**

Maloney, Tom (active 1930s). Heavyweight boxer: **Greaseball.**

Man, The. Bilbo, Theodore Gilmore; Luciano, Charles; Sinatra, Frank.

Manassa Mauler. Dempsey, Jack.

Man Behind the Music. Jones, Quincy [Delight].

Man Behind the $64,000 Question. March, Hal.

Man Behind the Smile. Hoffman, Dustin.

Mance, Julian Clifford, Jr. (born 1928). Jazz pianist: **Junior.**

Manchester, New Hampshire: U.S. city: **Four Seasons Crossroad of New England, Queen City of the Merrimack Valley.**

Manchester of America. Lowell, Massachusetts.

Mancuso, August Rodney (born 1905). Baseball player: **Blackie.**

Mancuso, Ronald Bernard (born 1933). Jazz musician: **Gus.**

Manders, Jack (born 1909). Football back: **Automatic.**

Man from Missouri. Truman, Harry S.

Man from Steamtown. Blount, Francis Nelson.

Mangano, Lawrence (active 1920–30). Criminal: **Dago Lawrence.**

Mangione, Chuck (born 1938). Jazz pianist and composer: **Gap.** Born: Gaspare Charles Mangione.

Mangrove Coast. Southernmost coast of Florida.

Manhattan. Borough of New York City: **Island City.**

Manhattan Project. Research and development of the atomic bomb, early 1940s.

Manhattan's Mad Bomber. Metesky, George [Peter].

Man in the Iron Mask. Hartnett, Charles Leo; Moody, William Vaughn.

Manion, Clyde Jennings (born 1896). Baseball player: **Pete.**

Manitoba. Canadian province: **Canada's Heartland, Keystone Province.**

Man-Mountain Dean. Leavitt, Frank S.

Man of a Thousand Faces. Chaney, Lon.

Man of Dimenson. Connors, Kevin Joseph Aloysius.

Man of Great Heart. Hoover, Herbert [Clark].

Man of Independence. Truman, Harry S.

Man of Many Faces. Muni, Paul.

Man of Steel. Zale, Tony.

Man of the Migrants. Chávez, César.

Manone, Joseph Mathews (born 1904). Jazz trumpeter, bandleader, and singer: **Wingy.**

Man on Horseback. Roosevelt, Theodore.

Man o' War (1917–47). Racehorse: **Big Red.**

Mansfield, Mike (born 1903). U.S. Senator from Montana and ambassador: **Montana Mike.** Legal name: Michael Joseph Mansfield.

Manson, Charles M. (born 1934). Murderer and leader of "hippie family": **Demon of Death Valley, Hippie Murderer, Hypnotic Hippie.**

Manson Girls. Group (Susan Denise Atkins, Linda Kasabian, Patricia Krenwinkle, and Leslie Van Houton) that followed Charles Manson as members of his "hippie family."

Mantle, Mickey [Charles] (born 1931). Baseball outfielder: **The Great Mick, Infant Prodigy, Million Dollar Invalid, Wounded Hero.**

Mantle, [Robert] Burns (1873–1948). Drama critic: **Dean of American Dramatic Critics.**

Man to See, The. Rothstein, Arnold.

Mantz, [Albert] Paul (1903–65). Stunt aviator: **Hollywood Pilot, King of the Hollywood Air Devils.**

Man Uptown, The. Rothstein, Arnold.

Manush, Henry Emmett (1902–71). Baseball outfielder: **Heinie.**

Man Who Broke a Thousand Chains. Burns, Robert Elliott.

Man Who Bumped Fulbright. Bumpers, Dale.

Man Who Can Say Anything and Make Everybody Like It. Rogers, Will.

Man Who Is Always Somebody Else. Muni, Paul.

Man Who Killed Kennedy. Oswald, Lee Harvey.

Man Who Made the Trombone Laugh. Raderman, Harry.

Man Who Owned Broadway. Cohan, George M[ichael].

Man Who Started It All. Ellsberg, Daniel.

Man Who Walked on Wings. Locklear, Omar.

Man Who Would Not Die. Young, James Arthur.

Man with a Message. Carnegie, Dale.

Man with the Golden Arm. Koufax, Sandy.

Man with the Mustache. Rose, Mauri.

Man You Love to Hate. Von Stroheim, Erich [Oswald Hans Carl Maria von Nordenwall].

Maramen. New York Giants.

Maranville, Walter James Vincent (1891–1954). Baseball shortstop: **Rabbit.**

Maranzano, Salvatore (1868–1931). Mafia leader: **Boss of All Bosses, Father of Cosa Nostra.**

Maravich, Peter (born 1949). Basketball player: **Pistol Pete.**

Marberry, Fred (born 1899). Baseball pitcher: **Firpo.**

Marble City. Knoxville, Tennessee; Rutland, Vermont.

Marblehead, Massachusetts. U.S. town: **Birthplace of the American Navy.**

Marcantonio, Vito (1902–54). U.S. Representative from New York: **The Firebrand.**

Marcella, Marco (1909?–62). Theatrical performer: **Fatso Marco.**

Marcel Marceau of Television. Skelton, Red.

March, Hal (1920–70). Television personality and motion picture actor: **Man Behind The $64,000 Question.** Born: Harold Mendelsohn.

Marcher, The. Chávez, César.

March King. Sousa, John Philip.

Marciano, Rocky (1923–69). Heavyweight boxer: **Brockton Block-**

buster, Brockton Bull, Brockton Buster. Born: Rocco Francis Marchegiano.

Marcus, David (1902–48). New York City Commissioner of Corrections, U.S. Army Colonel, and military government adviser: **Mickey.**

Marcuse, Herbert (1898–1979). Philosopher: **Father of the New Left.**

Mardi Gras Metropolis. New Orleans, Louisiana.

Marianas Turkey Shoot. Battle of the Philippine Sea.

Marine Aviator. Maas, Melvin Joseph.

Marine Bob. Mouton, Robert L.

Marine Division. Third Infantry Division.

Markell, Harry [Duquesne] (born 1923). Baseball pitcher: **Duke.** Born: Harry Duquesne Makowski.

Market Street. Street in San Francisco: **Path of Gold.**

Markewich, Maurice (born 1936). Jazz pianist and flutist: **Reese.**

Markham, Edwin (1852–1940). Poet: **Dean of American Poetry.**

Mark Twain of Cartoonists. Webster, Harold Tucker.

Marland, Ernest Whitworth (1874–1941). U.S. Representative from Oklahoma: **Hot Oil Marland.**

Marlowe, Julia (1866–1950). Actress: **Queen of the American Stage.** Born: Sarah Frances Frost.

Marmarosa, Michael (born 1925). Jazz pianist: **Dodo.**

Marne Division. Third Division, Third Infantry Division.

Marquardt, Richard Wilham (born 1889). Baseball pitcher. **Rube.**

Marsch, John (1869–1954). Industrialist and race horse owner: **Futurity King.**

Marse Henry. Watterson, Henry.

Marse Joe. McCarthy, Joe.

Marsh, Reginald (1898–1954). Artist: **The Hogarth of Manhattan.**

Marshall, Thomas Riley (1854–1925). Lawyer and Vice President of the U.S.: **Advocate of the Five Cent Cigar, Hoosier Statesman.**

Marshall Plan. European Recovery Program suggested by General George C. Marshall, U.S. Secretary of State, to supply money and material to rebuild Europe after World War II.

Marshall University, athletic teams of: **Thundering Herd.**

Martha's Vineyard. Island off the coast of Cape Cod, Massachusetts: **Friendly Island.**

Martin, Anne (born 1920). Statistician: **Pride of Pittsburgh, Savior of Terre Haute.**

Martin, Freddy (born c. 1907) Jazz musician: **Mr. Silvertone.**

Martin, John Leonard (1904–65). Baseball outfielder: **Pepper, Wild Hoss of the Osage.**

Martin, Lloyd (born 1916). Jazz musician: **Skip.**

Martino, Edward Vittorio (born 1903). Bantamweight boxer: **Cannonball Martin.**

Marvel, Louise (active 1960s). Cattle rancher: **Cattle Lady.**

Marvin, Johnny (1897–1944). Musician and singer: **Lonesome Singer of the Air, Ukelele Ace.** Legal name: John Marvin.

Mary Garden of Ragtime. Tucker, Sophie.

Maryland. Seventh U.S. state: **Cockade State, Delightful Land, Free State, Monumental State, Old Line State, Oyster State, Queen State, Star-spangled Banner State, Terrapin State.** With Delaware and Virginia: **Del-Mar-Va, Delmarva.**

Maryland, University of, athletic teams of: **Terps.**

Mary Pickford of This War. Lamour, Dorothy.

Masha. Stern, Marie Simchow.

Masked Marvel of Modern Letters. Vidal, Gore.

Maslow, Abraham (1908–70). Psychologist: **Founder of Humanistic Psychology.**

Massachusetts. Sixth U.S. state: **Baked Bean State, Bay State, Bean State, Birthplace of American Freedom, Old Colony State, Puritan State.**

Massachusetts, University of, athletic teams of: **Minutemen.**

Massachusetts, U.S.S. Battleship: **Big Mamie.**

Masseria, Giuseppe (died 1931). Gangster: **Joe the Boss.**

Master, The. Arcaro, Eddie; Leeteg, Edgar.

Master Money Manager. Templeton, John Marks.

Master of Crime. Rothstein, Arnold.

Master of Jazz. Ellington, Duke.

Master of Magic. Raymond, Maurice.

Master of Suspense. Hitchcock, Alfred.

Master of the Aerial Circus. Morrison, [Jesse] Ray.

Master of the Monumentalists. Smith, Tony.

Master of the Oneliner. Leonard, Jack E.

Master of the Tenderloin. Becker, Charles.

Master of the Typographical Art. Rogers, Bruce.

Master of Undergraduate Humor. Shulman, Max.

Master of Violence. Peckinpah, Sam[uel].

Master of White House Dirty Tricks. Colson, Charles W[endell].

Master of Words and Guardian of Magazines. Anselm, Felix.

Master Photographer. Steichen, Edward.

Masters, Edgar Lee (1869–1950). Poet: **Spoon River Poet.**

Master Storyteller, The. Hunt, E[verette] Howard [Jr.]

Master Wrecker. McGovern, George [Stanley].

Mastriana, Louis P. (born c. 1922). Swindler: **Flim-flam Man.**

Matal, Tony (active 1933–34). Football player: **Red.**

Match, Pincus (1904–44). Basketball player: **Pinky.**

Match of the Century. Defeat by Suzanne Lenglen of France of Helen Wills of the United States in tennis, 1926.

Mathewson, Christy (1880–1925). Baseball pitcher: **Matty the Great, Bix Six, Husk.** Legal name: Christopher Mathewson.

Mathias, Robert Bruce (born 1930). Athlete: **Champion of Champions.**

Matinee Burglar. Williams, Albert.

Matlock, Julian Clifton (born 1909). Jazz clarinetist: **Matty.**

Matriarch of Anthropology. Mead, Margaret.

Matson, James Randel (born 1945). Athlete: **Randy.**

Matsumoto, Hidehiko (born 1926). Jazz saxophonist and flutist: **Sleepy.**

Matthews, Raymond (born 1905). Football end: **Rags.**

Matthews, William R. (1873–1948). Welterweight boxer: **Matty.**

Matty. Matthews, William R.; Matlock, Julian Clifton.

Matty the Great. Mathewson, Christy.

Mature, Victor [John] (born 1916). Motion-picture actor: **Hollywood's Number One Glamor Boy, The Hunk.**

Maui, Hawaii. U.S. island: **Valley Isle.**

Mavericks. Athletic teams of the University of Texas, Arlington.

Maximum John. Sirica, John [Joseph].

Maxwell, Anna Caroline (1851–1929). Nurse: **American Florence Nightingale.**

Maxwell, Elsa (1883–1963). Party-giver: **America's No. 1 Hostess.**

Mayer, Erskine John (1891–1957). Baseball pitcher: **Scissors.** Born: James Erskine.

Mayer, Louis B[urt] (1885–1957). Motion-picture producer: **King of Hollywood.**

Maynard, Ken (1895-1973). Actor in motion-picture Westerns; with three other stars: **Big Four.**

Mayo, Charles Horace (1865–1939). Co-founder of the Mayo Clinic: **Dr. Charlie.**

Mayo, William James (1861–1939). Co-founder of the Mayo Clinic: **Dr. Will.**

Mayor Jimmy. Walker, James J[ohn].

Mayor of Broadway. Connors, Kevin Joseph Aloysius.

Mays, Willie [Howard] (born 1931). Baseball outfielder: **Amazing Mays, Buckduck, Willie the Wallop, Say Hey Kid.**

Mazziotta, John (born c. 1916). Racketeer: **Choppy.**

McAdoo, William Gibbs (1863–1941). U.S. Secretary of the Treasury and U.S. Senator from California: **Bill the Builder, Crown Prince, Daddy Longlegs, Dancing Fool, World War Croesus.**

McAlexander, Ulysses Grant (1864–1936). Army officer, World War I: **Rock of the Marne.**

McAuliffe, Anthony Clement (1898–1975). U.S. Army General: **Old Crock.**

McBride, Arthur (1887–1972). Football manager and team owner: **Mickey.**

McBride, Arthur B. (born 1886). Gangster: **Mickey**

McCaffrey, Frank (active 1920s). Football player: **Bull.**

McCarthy, Joe (1887–1978). Baseball manager: **Marse Joe.** Legal name: Joseph Vincent McCarthy.

McCarthy, Joseph R[aymond] (1908–57). U.S. Senator from Wisconsin: **Tail Gunner Joe.**

McCarty, George S. (1868–1945). Trapshooter: **Father of Amateur Trapshooting.**

McCarty, Luther (1892–1913). Heavyweight boxer: **White Hope Champion.**

McClendon, Sarah (born 1913). Journalist: **Holy Terror from Texas.**

McClintic, George W. (1866–1942). U.S. District Court Judge: **Father of the Federal Probation System.**

McClintic, James Vernon (1878–1948). U.S. Representative from Oklahoma: **Rivet.**

McClung, Thomas Lee (1870–1914). Football back and politician: **Bum.**

McClure, Samuel Sidney (1857–1949). Editor and publisher: **Father of the Fiction Syndicate.**

McComb, Robert (active 1920s). Stunt flier: **Uncle Fudd.**

McConnell, James Ed (1892–1954). Radio and television singer: **Smilin' Ed.**

McCormack, Jack W[illiam] (born 1891). U.S. Representative from Massachusetts and Speaker of the House: **The Archbishop, Fighting Irishman from South Boston.**

McCormick, Robert Rutherford (1880–1955). Newspaper publisher: **Bertie.**

McCoy, Charles (1873–1940). Welterweight boxer: **Corkscrew Kid, Kid McCoy, Real McCoy.** Born: Norman Selby.

McCoy, William (1877–1948). Prohibition-era liquor smuggler: **Founder of Rum Row, King of Rum Runners, Real McCoy.**

McCracken, Jack D. (1911–58). Basketball player: **Jumping Jack.**

McDaniel, Hattie (1895–1952). Actress: **Beulah.**

McDaniel, Robert Hyatt (1911–55). Racehorse trainer: **Red.**

McDermott, Maurice Joseph (born 1928). Baseball pitcher: **Mickey.**

McDonald, Marie (1923–65). Motion-picture actress: **The Body.** Born: Marie Frye.

McDonald, Maurice James (1902?–71). Food executive: **Hamburger King.**

McDonald's. Fast-food chain: **The Golden Arches.**

McDougald, Gilbert James (born 1928). Basketball player: **Casey's Kid.**

McDuffy, Eugene (born 1926). Jazz organist and composer: **Brother Jack McDuff.**

McEarchan, Malcolm (1884?–1945). Theatrical performer: **Jetsam.**

McEnroe, John [Patrick, Jr.] (born 1958). Tennis player: **Junior, Mr. Sourpuss.**

McErlane, Frank (active 1920–30). Gangster: **Most Brutal Gunman in Chicago.**

McFadden, Bernarr (1868–1955). Publisher and physical culturist: **The Body, The Fighter.**

McFadden, George (1872–1951). Lightweight boxer: **Elbows.**

McFarland, George Emmett (born 1928). Child motion-picture actor: **Spanky.**

McFarland, Patrick (1888–1936). Lightweight boxer: **Packy.**

McFarlane, William Dodridge (born 1894). U.S. Representative from Texas: **Anti-McFarlane.**

McGee, William Henry (born 1911). Baseball pitcher: **Fiddler Bill.**

McGhee, Walter (born 1915). Jazz singer and guitarist: **Brownie.**

McGinnity, Joseph Jerome (1871–1929). Baseball pitcher: **Iron Man.**

McGivern, Edward (died 1957). Trick pistol shooter: **Grand Old Man of Six-shooterology.**

McGovern, George [Stanley] (born 1922). Educator, politician, and U.S. Senator from South Dakota: **Honest George, Master Wrecker, St. George.**

McGovern, Hugh (active 1920–30). Gambler and criminal: **Stubby.**

McGovern, John Terrence (1880–1918). Lightweight boxer: **Terrible Terry.**

McGovern's Man from Missouri. Eagleton, Thomas Francis.

McGraw, Frank Edwin (born 1944). Baseball pitcher: **Tug.**

McGraw, John Joseph (1873–1934). Baseball third baseman and manager: **Father of Inside Baseball, Little Napoleon.**

McGregor, Douglas Murray (1906–64). College president: **Chairman Mac.**

McGuire, James Thomas (1863–1936). Baseball catcher and manager: **Deacon.**

McGuire, William [Joseph, Jr.] (born 1926). Actor and playwright: **Biff.**

McHargue, James Eugene (born 1907). Jazz clarinetist: **Rosy.**

McHugh, Edward (active 1920s and 1930s). Radio singer: **Gospel Singer.**

McInnis, John Phelan (1890–1960). Baseball first baseman: **Stuffy.**

McIntire, Carl (born 1906). Clergyman: **Pirate Preacher.**

McIntosh, Russell (active 1921). Football player: **Dutch.**

McKeever, Ed[ward Clark] (born 1910). Football coach: **Big Ed.**

McKeithen, John Julian (born 1918). Governor of Louisiana: **Big John.**

McLaglen, Victor (1886–1959). Motion-picture actor: **Beloved Brute.**

McLaren, George W. (died 1967). Football back: **Tank.**

McLarnin, James (born 1905). Welterweight boxer: **Baby Face.**

McLaughry, De Ormond (born 1893). Football player and coach: **Tuss.**

McLean, Evalyn Walsh (1886–1947). Society woman: **Little Evalyn, Washington's Cinderella Woman.**

McLean, Ray[mond] (1915–64). Football back: **Scooter.**

McLean, Vinson Walsh (1909–19). Son of Evalyn Walsh McLean and Edward Beale McLean: **Hundred-Million-Dollar Baby.**

McLendon, Gordon (active 1925–35). Radio sports announcer: **Old Scotsman.**

McLinn, George E. (1884–1953). Sports broadcaster and writer: **Stoney.**

McLoughlin, Maurice (1889–1956). Tennis player: **California Comet.**

McMahon, William (active 1929–32). Football player: **Bingo.**

McMillan, John Lanneau (born 1898). Politician and U.S. Representative from South Carolina: **Mr. Mac.**

McMillin, Alvin Nugent (1895–1952). Football quarterback, coach, and athletic director: **Bo.**

McNair, Donald Erie (1909–49). Baseball shortstop and second baseman: **Boob, Rabbit.**

McNally, John V. (born 1904). Football back: **Blood.**

McNary, Charles Linza (1874–1944). U.S. Senator from Oregon: **Wise Charley.**

McNeese State University, athletic teams of: **Cowboys.**

McNutt, Paul Vories (1891–1955). Politician: **Boob.**

McPartland, William Lawrence (1878–1953). Lightweight boxer and referee: **Kid.**

McPhail, Leland Stanford (1890–1975). Businessman, army officer, and baseball club president: **Larry, Lord Larry, Wizard of Baseball.**

McPhee, John Alexander (1859–1943). Baseball second baseman and manager: **Bid.**

McPherson, Aimee Semple (1890–1944). Evangelist: **Sister Aimee, World's Most Pulchritudinous Evangelist.**

McShann, Jay (born 1909). Jazz bandleader and pianist: **Hootie.**

McSwiggin, William H. (died 1926). Assistant state's attorney in Illinois: **Hanging Prosecutor.**

McWeeny, Douglas Lawrence (1896–1953). Baseball pitcher: **Buzz.**

Meachum, James H. (1893?–1963). Theatrical performer: **Dad.**

Mead, Margaret (1901–78). Anthropologist: **Matriarch of Anthropology.**

Meadowlark. Lemon, Meadow George.

Mean Green. Athletic teams of North Texas State University, Denton.

Mean Joe Green. Green, Joe.

Mean Mr. Clean. Leonard, Jack E.

Means, Gaston Bullock (1879–1938). Investigator and swindler: **German Agent E-13, Münchausen in Modern Dress, Spectacular Rogue, Swindler of the Century.**

Meanwell, Walter E. (1884–1953). Basketball coach and physician: **Doc, Little Doctor.**

Meany, George (born 1894). Labor leader: **Silver-haired Elderly Statesman of American Labor.**

Measuring Man. DeSalvo, Albert H.

Med. Flory, Meredith Irwin.

Meddler, The. Roosevelt, Theodore.

Medicine Man for Your Blues. Lewis, Ted.

Medici of the Minimals. Scull, Robert C.

Medwick, Joseph Michael (1911–75). Baseball outfielder: **Duckie, Duckie Wuckie, Mickey.**

Meehan, John Francis (1893–1972). Football coach: **Chick.**

Megalomaniac. Clarke, Norham Pfardt.

Mehaffey, Leroy (born 1904). Baseball player: **Pop-eye.**

Mehre, Harry J. (active 1928–45). Football coach: **Horse, True Athenian.**

Meier, Sally (born 1928). Animal lover and protector of stray cats: **Cat Lady of San Francisco.**

Meigs, Montgomery (1847–1931). Civil engineer and inventor: **Father of the Canvas Cofferdam.**

Mein Boy. Levinsky, Alexander H.

Meine, Henry William (1896–1968). Baseball pitcher: **Heinie.**

Mele, Sabath Anthony (born 1923). Baseball first baseman, outfielder, coach, and manager: **Sam.**

Melillo, Oscar Donald (1899–1963). Baseball second baseman: **Ski.**

Mellon, Andrew William (1855–1937). Financier, business executive, and U.S. Secretary of The Treasury: **Mentor of Aluminum, Ubiquitous Financier of the Universe, World's Second Richest Man.**

Melting Pot. The United States as an assimilator of immigrants from various countries.

Melting Pot Division. Seventy-seventh Division, American Expeditionary Force, World War I.

Memorial Day Massacre. Incident, 1937, in which union demonstrators outside the Republic Steel plant in South Chicago were fired on by police.

Memphis, Tennessee. U.S. city: **Babylon on the Bluff, Bluff City, City of the Blues, Cotton Center, Home of the Blues, Home of the Cotton Carnival, Tri-State Capital.**

Memphis Bill. Mallory, William Neely; Terry, Bill.

Memphis Pal. Moore, Thomas Wilson.

Memphis Slim. Chatman, Peter.

Memphis State University, athletic teams of: **Tigers.**

Mencken, H[enry] L[ouis] (1880–1956). Editor, essayist, newspaperman, and author: **Disturber of the Peace, Great Debunker, Greatest Practicing Literary Journalist, Private Secretary of God Almighty, The Ringmaster, Sage of Baltimore.**

Mendy. Rudolph, Marvin.

Mentor of Aluminum. Mellon, Andrew William.

Mentor of the Algonquin. Case, Frank.

Mentor of the Rule of Reason. White, Edward Douglass.

Merchant of Venom. Rickles, Don.

Mercury. Morris, Eugene.

Meredith, Burgess (born 1907). Actor: **Bugs, Buzz.**

Merkle, Frederick Charles (1888–1956). Baseball first baseman: **Bonehead.**

Merrick, David (born 1912). Theatrical producer: **Barnum of Broadway Producers.** Born: David Margulies.

Merrill Lynch, Pierce, Fenner & Smith: Brokerage company. **Thundering Herd.**

Merrill's Marauders. U.S. military group, World War II, led by Brigadier General Frank D. Merrill, active in Burma behind Japanese lines in 1944.

Merritt, James (born 1926). Jazz bass player: **Jymie.**

Mescalero. Cessna T-41A small training plane.

Mesirow, Milton (1899–1973). Jazz clarinetist and saxophonist: **Ananias of Jazz, Mezz.** Also known as Milton Mezzrow.

Messiah of LSD. Leary, Timothy [Francis].

Messino, William (born 1917). Gangster: **Wee Willie.**

Mesta, Perle (born 1891). Arbiter-hostess in Washington, D.C.: **Call Me Madam, Hostess with the Mostest, World's No. 1 Party-Giver.** Born: Pearl Skirvin.

Met, The. 1. Metropolitan Life Insurance Company. 2. Metropolitan Museum of Art. 3. Metropolitan Opera House.

Metesky, George [Peter] (born 1900). Planter of bombs in New York City: **The Mad Bomber, Manhattan's Mad Bomber.**

Me-Too-ism. Republican acceptance of Democratic economic and foreign policies, 1940s.

Metro. Urban and surrounding area; urbanized stretch between Jacksonville and Miami, Florida.

Metropolis of America. New York City.

Metropolis of New England. Boston.

Metropolis of Oregon. Portland.

Metropolis of the Desert. Phoenix, Arizona.

Metropolis of the Missouri Valley. Kansas City, Missouri.

Metropolis of the Northeast. Bangor, Maine.

Metropolis of the Panhandle. Amarillo, Texas.

Metropolis of the West. Los Angeles, California.

Metropolitan Division. Seventy-seventh Division, American Expeditionary Force, World War I.

Metropolitan Life Insurance Company. U.S. corporation: **The Met.**

Metropolitan Museum of Art. Art museum, New York City: **The Met.**

Metropolitan Opera House. Theater of the Metropolitan Opera Company, New York City: **The Met.**

Met's Second Caruso. Tucker, Richard.

Meusel, Emil Frederick (1893–1963). Baseball outfielder: **Irish.**

Meyer, Leo Robert (born 1898). Football coach: **Dutch, Old Iron Pants, Saturday Fox.**

Meyer, Lou[is] (born c. 1905). Racing driver: **Office Builder.**

Meyer, Russ (born 1922). Motion-picture producer and director: **King of the Nudie Movie, Mr. X.**

Meyers, Bruce (born c. 1927). Racing driver: **Buggymaster of the Roaring Dunes.**

Meyer the Bug. Lansky, Meyer.

Mezz. Mesirow, Milton.

Miami, Florida. U.S. city: **Bikini City, Gateway to Latin America, Magic City, Playground of the Americas, Tropic Metropolis.** With Miami Beach, Florida: **Twin Cities.**

Miami, University of, athletic teams of: **Hurricanes.**

Miami and Miami Beach, Florida. U.S. cities: **Twin Cities.**

Miami Beach, Florida. U.S. city: **Gold Coast City, Playground of the Americas, Riviera of America.** With Miami, Florida: **Twin Cities.**

Miami's Unmiraculous Miracle Worker. Shula, Don[ald Francis].

Miami University, athletic teams of: **Redskins.**

Michael, Moina (1870–1944). Deviser of the American Legion poppy: **Poppy Lady.**

Michigan. Twenty-sixth U.S. state: **Auto State, Big Fish State, Great Lake State, Lake State, Peninsula State, Wolverine State.**

Michigan, University of. 1. Athletic teams of: **Wolverines.** 2. Athletic teams of, with other teams in regional conference: **Big Ten.**

Michigan Assassin. Ketchel, Stanley.

Michigan State University. 1. Athletic teams of: **Spartans.** 2. Athletic teams of, with other teams in regional conference: **Big Ten.**

Michigan Terror, The. Heston, William Martin.

Michigan Wildcat. Wolgast, Ad[olph].

Mickey. Cochrane, Gordon Stanley; Cohen, Meyer Harris; Finn, Neal Francis; McBride, Arthur; McBride, Arthur B.; McDermott, Maurice Joseph; Marcus, David; Medwick, Joseph Michael; Owen, Arnold Malcolm; Thomson, [Marion] Lee.

Mickey Mouse. Walt Disney Productions.

Midas of Mutual Funds. Cornfeld, Bernard.

Middies. Athletic teams of the United States Naval Academy, Annapolis, Maryland.

Middle America. Conservative middle-class America.

Middlebury College, athletic teams of: **Panthers.**

Middle West Division. Eighty-ninth Division.

Midge. Costanza, Margaret.

Midge at the Mike. Gillars, Mildred Elizabeth.

Midget. Smith, William Joseph.

Midgett, Elwin W. (born 1911). Educator and writer: **Wink.**

Midnight Cowboy, The. Hoffman, Dustin.

Midnight Express. Tolan, Edward.

Midshipmen. Athletic teams of United States Naval Academy, Annapolis, Maryland.

Midway U.S.A. Kansas.

Midwest, The. North central area of the United States: **Heartland of America.**

Midwest Metropolis. Chicago, Illinois.

Miff. Mole, Irving Alfred.

MIG Alley. Mountain valley area frequented by MIG fighter planes, Korean War.

Mighty Atom. Booth, Albie; Greenstein, Joseph L.

Mighty Jack. Dempsey, Jack.

Mighty Mike. Booth, Albie; Huggins, Miller James; Ott, Melvin Thomas.

Mike. Berger, Meyer; Casteel, Miles W.; Moser, William J.

Milan, Jesse Clyde (1887–1953). Baseball outfielder and manager: **Deerfoot.**

Mile-a-Minute Harry. Selfridge, Harry Gordon.

Mile-a-Minute Murphy. Murphy, Charles M.

Mile-High City. Denver, Colorado.

Miles, Luke (born 1925). Jazz singer: **Long Gone.**

Mile-Square City. Hoboken, New Jersey.

Miley, James (1903–32). Jazz trumpeter: **Bubber.**

Military Expedients, The. O'Leary, Timothy J. and Sheridan, Elmo R.

Milk of Magnesia Phillips. Phillips, Alfred Noroton, Jr.

Millard, Edward R. (died 1963). Theatrical performer: **Rocky.**

Miller, Clarence H. (born 1923). Jazz singer and bass player: **Big Miller.**

Miller, Don[ald C.] (1902–79). Football halfback, U.S. district attorney, and judge. With other members of Notre Dame backfield: **Four Horsemen.**

Miller, Edmund John (1894–1966). Baseball outfielder: **Bing.**

Miller, Ernest (born 1897). Jazz trumpeter and singer: **Punch.**

Miller, George (1893–1957). Racketeer, bootlegger, and burglar: **Bugs.** Born: George Moran.

Miller, Harry Willis (1880-1977). Surgeon, nutritionist, and medical missionary: **China Doctor.**

Miller, Henry (born 1891). Author: **The Expatriate.**

Miller, John Barney (1886–1923). Baseball first and second baseman: **Dots.**

Miller, John E. (1903–64). Football player: **Bing.**

Miller, [Lowell] Otto (1889–1962). Baseball catcher: **Moonie.**

Miller, Mitch[ell William] (born 1911). Oboist, conductor, and recording executive: **The Beard.**

Miller, Vern[al Philip] (born 1928). Choreographer and dancer: **Buzz.**

Miller, William Mosley (born 1909). Doorkeeper of the U.S. House of Representatives: **Alligator Bait, Crab Bait, Fish Bait, Gar Bait, King of the Hill, Shrimp Bait.**

Millikan, Robert Andrews (1863–1953). Physicist and educator: **Conquerer of the Electron.**

Millinder, Lucius (born 1900). Bandleader: **Lucky.**

Million-Acre Farm. Prince Edward Island.

Millionaire, The. Gerry, Peter Goelet.

Millionaire Gorilla. Capone Al[phonse].

Millionaire Hobo. How, James Eads.

Millionaire Maestro. Davis, Meyer.

Millionaire Sheriff, The. Baker, Anderson Yancey.

Millionaire Tramp. How, James Eads.

Million Dollar Invalid. Mantle, Mickey [Charles].

Millman, Harry (died 1937). Gangster: **Lone Wolf of the Underworld.**

Mills, Enos Abijah (1870–1922). Mountaineer and naturalist: **Columbus of the Rockies, Father of Rocky Mountain National Park.**

Mills, Frederick Allen (1869–1948). Composer and song publisher: **Kerry.**

Mills, Wilbur [Daigh] (born 1909). U.S. Representative from Arkansas: **The Arkansas Hunkerer, Mr. Taxes.**

Milton, Vera (1909–52). Ziegfeld Follies dancer: **Dumb Blonde.**

Milwaukee, Wisconsin. U.S. city: **Beer Capital of America, Beer City, City of Fountains, Cream City, Foam City, Suds City.**

Milwaukee Phil. Alderisio, Felix Anthony.

Mimi. Capone, Amadeo Ermino; Baker, Gloria.

Min. Leibrook, Wilfred.

Mineral City of the South. Birmingham, Alabama.

Mineral Springs City. Altoona, Pennsylvania.

Mineral Storehouse of the Nation. Hudson Bay area of Canada.

Miners. Athletic teams of the University of Texas, El Paso.

Minevich, Borrah (1902–55). Harmonica player and entertainer: **King of the Harmonica, Harmonica Rascal.**

Mingus, Charles (1922–79). Jazz bass player: **Jazz's Angry Man.**

Mining Baron. Clark, William Andrews.

Mining State. Nevada.

Minneapolis, Minnesota. U.S. city: **City of Lakes, Flour City, Gateway City, Minnie, Sawdust City.** With St. Paul, Minnesota: **Twin Cities, Twin City.**

Minnesota. Thirty-second U.S. state: **Bread and Butter State, Gopher State, Lake State, Land of 10,000 Lakes, Minnie, New England of the West, North Star State, Wheat State.**

Minnesota, University of. 1. Athletic teams of: **Gophers.** 2. Athletic teams of, with other teams in regional conference: **Big Ten.**

Minnesota Fats. Wanderone, Rudolf Walter, Jr.

Minnesota Strip. Area near Times Square, New York City, where teenage prostitutes from Middle West congregated, 1970s.

Minnesota Vikings. Football team: **The Purple Gang.**

Minnie. 1. German mine-throwing device, World War I. 2. Minneapolis, Minnesota. 3. Minoso, Saturnino Orestes Arrieta.

Minoso, Saturnino Orestes Arrieta (born 1922). Baseball outfielder: **Minnie.**

Minton, Sherman (1890–1965). U.S. Senator from Indiana: **King of the New Dealers, Shay.**

Minton, Yvonne (born c. 1942). Singer: **Strawberry Blonde.**

Minutemen. Athletic teams of the University of Massachusetts, Amherst.

Minx of the Movies. Compson, Betty.

Miracle Man of Virginia Beach. Cayce, Edgar.

Misanthrope, The. Bremer, Arthur Herman.

Mislen, John (active 1970s). Hobo: **Hardrock Kid, King of the Hoboes.**

Miss Apprehension. Gish, Dorothy.

Missie. Mississippi.

Miss Independent. Thomas, Marlo.

Missing Witness. Schepps, Samuel.

Mission City. Riverside, California; San Antonio, Texas.

Mission Street. Street in San Francisco: **The Slot.**

Mississippi. Twentieth U.S. state; **Alligator State, Bayou State, Border Eagle State, Cotton Kingdom, Eagle State, Groundhog State, Hospitality State, Magnolia State, Missie, Mudcat State, Mud Waddler State, Tadpole State.**

Mississippi, University of. Educational institution: **Old Miss, Ole Miss.**

Mississippi, University of, athletic teams of: **Rebels.**

Mississippi River. U.S. river: **Father of Waters, Big Muddy, Big Miss.**

Mississippi River Valley: Garden of the World.

Mississippi State University, athletic teams of: **Bulldogs.**

Miss Lil. Prado, Katie.

Miss Lillian. Carter, [Bessie] Lillian; Gish, Lillian.

Missouri. Twenty-fourth U.S. state: **Bullion State, Cave State, Iron Mountain State, Lead State, Little Dixie, Mother of the West, Ozark State, Pennsylvania of the West, Show-Me State.**

Missouri, University of. 1. Athletic teams of: **Tigers.** 2. Athletic teams of, with other teams in regional conference: **Big Eight.**

Missouri, **U.S.S.** Battleship, World War II: **Big Mo, Big M.**

Missouri-Kansas-Texas Railroad. U.S. railroad: **Katy.**

Miss Tarbarrel. Tarbell, Ida Minerva.

Miss Vicky. Khaury, Victoria B.

Mitchel, John Purroy (1879–1918). Investigator and mayor of New York City: **Young Torquemada.**

Mitchell. B-25 bombing plane, World War II.

Mitchell, Gordon B. (born 1932). Jazz bass player: **Whitey.**

Mitchell, John [Newton] (born 1913). Lawyer, politician, and U.S. Attorney General: **Phantom President of the United States, President's Worst Friend.**

Mitchell, Martha [Beall] (1918–1976). Wife of U.S. Attorney General John Newton Mitchell: **Last of the Great Southern Belles, Mouth That Roared, Watergate's Warbler.**

Mitchell, Martha M. (born 1940). Assistant to President Jimmy Carter for special projects: **Bunny.**

Mitchell, Richard Allen (1930–79). Jazz trumpeter: **Blue.**

Mitchell, William (1879–1936). Military aviator and U.S. Army Air Forces General: **Angry Eagle of Aviation, Pioneer of Air Power.**

Mitchell Meteor. Morenz, Howie.

Mitters. Foley, John.

Mix, Tom (1880–1940). Motion-picture and radio actor: **America's Favorite Cowboy, Ralston Straight Shooter, World's Champion Cowboy.** With three other Western stars: **Big Four.** Legal name: Thomas Edwin Mix.

Mixey. Callahan, James Joseph.

Mize, John Robert (born 1913). Baseball first baseman: **Big Cat.**

Mizmoon. Soltysik, Patricia.

Mizner, Wilson (1876–1933). Gambler, entrepreneur, playwright, and short story writer: **Greatest Man-About-Town Any Town Ever Had.**

MJQ. Modern Jazz Quartet.

Mo. Udall, Morris K.

Mobile, Alabama. U.S. city: **Alabama's Only Port, City of Five Flags, City of Six Flags, Gulf City, Picnic City, Port City.**

Mobil Oil Corporation. Business organization; with six other oil companies: **Seven Sisters.**

Moccasins. Athletic teams of the University of Tennessee, Chattanooga.

Mo City. Detroit, Michigan.

Mockingbird. Native or resident of Arkansas.

Model-T Ford. Early Ford automobile: **Tin Lizzie.**

Modern Athens. Boston, Massachusetts.

Modern Cagliostro. Sykowski, Abram.

Modern Generation's Rudy Vallee. Monroe, Vaughn [Wilton].

Modern Jazz Quartet (active 1950s and 1960s). Jazz group consisting of John Lewis, Milt Jackson, Connie Kay, and Percy Heath: **The Four Undertakers, MJQ.**

Modern King of Swing. Rogers, Shorty.

Modern Knight Errant, The. Hoover, J[ohn] Edgar.

Modern Mercury. Roosevelt, James.

241

Modern Mother of Presidents. Ohio.

Modern Mozart. Korngold, Erich Wolfgang.

Modern Muckraker. Anderson, Jack[son Northman].

Moe. Berg, Morris; Franklin, Murray Asher; Roberts, Maurice; Savransky, Morris; Snyder, Martin.

Mohair Jack. Garner, John Nance.

Mole, Irving Milfred (1898–1961). Jazz trombonist: **Miff.**

Molesworth, Keith F. (1906–66). Football quarterback; **Rabbit.**

Moline, Illinois. U.S. city: **Farm Machinery Capital of America, Plow City.** With East Moline and Rock Island, Illinois, and Davenport, Iowa: **Quad Cities.**

Molink. Teletype connection between the White House and the Kremlin.

Molybdenum. Silver-white metal element: **Gray Gold.**

Momo. Giancana, Sam[uel].

Momsie. Snyder, Ruth.

Monarch of Leg Shackles. Houdini, Harry.

Monarch of Mastication. Wrigley, William, Jr.

Mondale, Joan [Adams] (born 1930). Wife of Vice President Walter Frederick Mondale and Carter administration advocate for arts and culture: **Joan of Art(s).**

Mondale, Walter Frederick (born 1928). Vice President of the United States: **Fritz.** With Jimmy Carter in 1976 election campaign: **Fritz and Grits.**

Mondello, Nuncio (born 1912). Jazz saxophonist: **Toots.**

Mondschein, Irving (born 1925). Track runner: **Moon.**

Money King of Saigon. Crum, William J.

Money Maestro, The. Heidt, Horace Murray.

Money-Maker and Hoopla Artist. Higgins, Andrew Jackson.

Monhegan. Maine island: **Fortunate Island.**

Monk. Campbell, John; Eastman, Edward; Gafford, Roy; Hazel, Arthur; Montgomery, William [Howard]; Pierce, Marvin; Sibbett, Morgan.

Monk, Thelonious [Sphere] (born 1920). Jazz pianist and composer: **High Priest of Bebop.**

Monkey Trial. Trial of John T. Scopes, 1925, to test a Tennessee law against the teaching of the Darwinian theory of evolution.

Monkey Trial Defendant. Scopes, John Thomas.

Monkey Ward. Montgomery Ward and Company.

Monomail. Any of various monoplanes built by Boeing Air Transport in the early 1930s.

Monroe, Earl (born 1944). Basketball guard: **Earl the Pearl.**

Monroe, Vaughn [Wilton] (1912–73). Bandleader and singer: **Modern Generation's Rudy Vallee, Voice of R.C.A.**

Monster from Arizona. Goldwater, Barry [Morris].

Montana. Forty-first U.S. state: **Big Ski Country, Big Sky Country, Bonanza State, Lead State, Mountain State, Singed Cat State, Stub Toe State, Treasure State.**

Montana, Louis (1885–1950). Wrestler and motion picture actor: **Bull.** Born: Luigi Montagna.

Montana, University of, athletic teams of: **Grizzlies.**

Montana Mike. Mansfield, Mike.

Monterey, California. U.S. city: **Capital of Old California, City of History and Romance.**

Montezuma's Revenge. Diarrhea or dysentery, suffered by travelers in foreign lands.

Montgomery, Alabama. U.S. city: **Birthplace of Dixie, City of Opportunity, Cow Town of the South, Cradle of the Confederacy.**

Montgomery, Peggy (born 1918). Motion picture child actress: **Baby Peggy.**

Montgomery, William [Howard] (born 1921). Jazz bass player: **Monk.**

Montgomery Ward and Company. Mail order business: **Monkey Ward.**

Montos, Nick George (born 1916). Burglar and jail breaker: **The Escaper, Little Nick.**

Montoya, Joseph M. (born 1915). U.S. Representative from New Mexico: **Little Joe.**

Montpelier, Vermont. U.S. town: **Green Mountain City.**

Montreal, Quebec. Canadian city: **Air Capital of the World, City of Saints, Island City.**

Monumental City. Baltimore, Maryland.

Monumental State. Maryland.

Monument City. Baltimore, Maryland.

Moody, Orville (born c. 1934). Golfer: **The Sarge, Unknown Soldier.**

Moody, William Vaughn (1869-1910). Educator and author: **Man in the Iron Mask.**

Moon. Baker, Ralph; Mondschein, Irving; Mullins, Lawrence A.

Moondog. Hardin, Louis Thomas.

Mooney. Giancana, Sam[uel]; Gibson, George.

Moonie. 1. Follower of Sun Myung Moon, Korean preacher, mid-1970s. 2. Miller, [Lowell] Otto.

Moon Maniac. Cook, DeWitt Clinton.

Moon over the Mountain Girl. Smith, Kate.

Moonshine Gates. Gates, John Warne.

Moore, Archie (born 1916). Light heavyweight boxer: **Old Mongoose, Magnificent Mongoose.** Born: Archibald Lee Wright.

Moore, Carl (active 1920s and 1930s). Jazz musician and singer: **Deacon.**

Moore, Harold (born 1915). Petty thief: **The Chiseler.**

Moore, James H. (1869?-1953). Restaurateur: **Dinty.**

Moore, John Edward (active 1920-30). Gangster: **Screwey.**

Moore, Russell (born 1913). Jazz trombonist: **Big Chief.**

Moore, Thomas Wilson (1894-1953). Boxer: **Memphis Pal.**

Moore, Wilbur (1916-65). Football back: **Little Indian.**

Moore, William A. (born 1924). Jazz saxophonist; **Brew.**

Moore, William Henry (1848-1923). Capitalist and promoter: **Sphinx of the Rock Island.**

Moore, William Wilcy (1897-1963). Baseball pitcher: **Cy.**

Moorhead State University, athletic teams of: **Dragons.**

Moose. Charlap, Morris; Earnshaw, George Livingston; Solters, Julius Joseph.

Mops. Ricca, Paul; Volpe, Anthony.

Moran, Charles B. (1879-1949). Baseball umpire and football coach: **Uncle Charlie.**

Moran, George (1896-1957). Gangster: **Bugs.**

Moran, Gertrude Augusta (born 1923). Tennis player and sports commentator: **Gorgeous Gussie, Gussie.**

Moratorium Bill. Lemke, William.

Morello, Peter (active 1920–30). Mafia leader: **Boss of Bosses, Clutching Hand.** Also known as Piddu Morello.

Morenz, Howie (1902–37). Canadian hockey player: **Babe Ruth of Hockey, Stratford Streak, Canadien Comet, Hurtling Habitant, Mitchell Meteor.** Legal name; Howard William Morenz.

Moretti, Salvatore (1906–52). Gambler: **Solly Moore.**

Moretti, Willie (1894?–1951). Gangster and gambler: **Willing Willie.**

Morgan, Daniel Francis (1873–1955). Boxing manager; **Dumb Dan.**

Morgan, Harold Lansford (born 1934). Jazz saxophonist: **Lanny.**

Morgan, Harry Richard (1878–1962). Baseball pitcher: **Cy.**

Morgan, Helen (1900–41). Singer and actress: **Girl on the Piano, Little Elsie, Queen of the Torch Singers.**

Morgan, John Pierpont (1837–1913). Industrialist and financier; **Commodore, JP, Jupiter of Wall Street.**

Morgan, William Forbes (1879–1937). Banker and politician: **Czar of the Liquor Industry, Liquor Czar.**

Moriarty, Joseph Vincent (1910?–79). Gambler: **Newsboy.**

Mormon Bishop. King, William Henry.

Mormon City. Salt Lake City, Utah.

Mormon's Mecca. Salt Lake City, Utah.

Mormon State. Utah.

Morningside Heights. Neighborhood of New York City: **Acropolis of America.**

Morris, Carl (1887–1951). Heavyweight boxer: **Original White Hope, Sadulpa Giant.**

Morris, [Eu]gene (born 1947). Football back: **Mercury.**

Morris, [John] Chester [Brooks] (1901–70). Actor: **Boston Blackie.**

Morris, Leonard Carter (born 1915). Jazz trumpeter and singer: **Skeets.**

Morrison, DeLesseps Story (1912–64). Mayor of New Orleans and U.S. Representative to the Organization of American States: **Chep.**

Morrison, [Jesse] Ray (active 1915–51). Football coach: **Master of the Aerial Circus.**

Morrison, Lake (active 1921). Football player: **Firpo.**

Morrison, Richard C. (born 1937). Burglar: **Babbling Burglar.**

Morrow, Anne McIntyre (1860?–1935). Pioneer and prostitute: **Heroine of Bald Mountain, Pegleg.**

Morrow, William G. (born c. 1916). Canadian jurist: **Judge of the North.**

Morse, Alfreda Theodora Strandberg (1883–1953). Lyricist: **Dolly.**

Morse, Charles Wyman (1856–1933). Businessman: **Ice King.**

Morse, Clinton R. (active 1920s and 1930s). Sports writer; **Brick.**

Morse, Wayne [Lyman] (1900–74). Lawyer, educator, and U.S. Senator from Oregon: **Lone Wolf of the Senate, The Wrecker.**

Morton, Ferdinand Joseph (1885–1941). Jazz pianist and composer: **Jelly Roll.** Born: Ferdinand Joseph La Menthe.

Morton, Henry Sterling (born 1907). Jazz trombonist: **Benny.**

Morton, Samuel J. (active 1920–30). U.S. Army officer and gangster: **Nails.**

Mosbacher, Emil, Jr. (born 1922). Yachtsman: **Bus, Buster.**

Moser, William J. (1916–53). Television producer: **Mike.**

Moses, Anna Mary Robertson (1860–1961). Artist; **Grandma, Grand Old Lady of American Art.**

Mosey. King, Moses.

Moskowitz, Harry (born 1904). Basketball coach and player: **Jammy.**

Mosley, Lawrence Leo (born 1909). Jazz musician: **Snub.**

Mosquito. Fighter plane used in World War II.

Mosquito State. New Jersey.

Most Admired Man in America. Graham, Billy.

Most Brutal Gunman in Chicago. McErlane, Frank.

Most Famous Folk Singer of His Race. White, Joshua Daniel.

Most Happy Fellow, The. Reagan, Ronald.

Most Northern Southern City. Tulsa, Oklahoma.

Mother Bloor. Omholt, Ella Reeve Bloor.

Mother Cabrini. Cabrini, St. Frances Xavier.

Mother City of Georgia. Savannah, Georgia.

Mother Courage. Abzug, Bella S[avitsky].
Mother of All the Doughboys. Schumann-Heink, Ernestine Rössler.
Mother of American Women's Swimming. Epstein, Charlotte.
Mother of Exiles. Statue of Liberty.
Mother of Flag Day. Prisk, Laura B.
Mother of Muckrakers. Tarbell, Ida Minerva.
Mother of Presidents. Virginia.
Mother of Rivers. New Hampshire.
Mother of States. Virginia.
Mother of the American Legion. Schumann-Heink, Ernestine Rössler.
Mother of the West. Missouri.
Mother of Trusts. Standard Oil Company.
Mother Waddles. Waddles, Charleszetta.
Motion Picture Palace Potentate. Rothafel, Samuel Lionel.
Motivation Mentor. Packard, Vance Oakley.
Motor Town. Detroit, Michigan.
Motown. Detroit, Michigan.
Motown Sound. Rock music in the style of Detroit, usually by black performers.
Mott, James Wheaton (1883–1945). U.S. Representative from Oregon: **Tonguepoint Mott.**
Mound City. St. Louis, Missouri.
Mountain City. Altoona, Pennsylvania; Chattanooga, Tennessee.
Mountaineer Division. Tenth Mountain Division.
Mountaineers. Athletic teams of Appalachian State University, Boone, North Carolina, and West Virginia University, Morgantown.
Mountain State. Montana; West Virginia.
Mount Emmons. Large mountain near Crested Butte, Colorado, known for its rich deposits of molybdenum: **The Lady, Red Lady Mountain.**
Mount Holyoke College. Educational institution; with six other women's colleges: **Seven Sisters.**
Mouse. Randolph, Irving.

247

Mouth, The. Clarke, Norman Pfardt; Cosell, Howard.

Mouth of the South, The. Turner, Ted.

Mouth That Roared. Mitchell, Martha.

Mouton, Robert L. (1892–1956). U.S. Representative from Louisiana: **Louisiana Ram, Marine Bob.**

Movement, The. New Left.

Movie Capital. Hollywood, California.

Movie City. Los Angeles, California.

Movieland. Hollywood, California.

Moyse, Alphonse (1898?–1973). Bridge player and columnist: **Sonny.**

Mr. A.A.R. Rothstein, Arnold.

Mr. America. Cooper, Alice.

Mr. American. Tugwell, Rexford Guy.

Mr. Attack. Taylor, Maxwell Davenport.

Mr. B. Eckstine, Billy.

Mr. Baseball. Mack, Connie.

Mr. Basketball. Holman, Nat.

Mr. Big. Rothstein, Arnold.

Mr. Big in Crime. Accardo, Anthony Joseph.

Mr. Big of Tin Pan Alley. Gershwin, George.

Mr. Black Labor. Randolph, A[sa] Philip.

Mr. Boston. Fiedler, Arthur.

Mr. Boxing. Fleischer, Nat[haniel S.].

Mr. Broadway. Cohan, George M[ichael].

Mr. Charlie. Cannon, Charles A.

Mr. Clean. Boone, Pat; Dean, John III; Ford, Gerald [Rudolph, Jr.]; Reagan, Ronald; Richardson, Elliot Lee; Rockefeller, Nelson [Aldrich].

Mr. Conductor. Ormandy, Eugene.

Mr. Dirty Words. Colson, Charles W[endell].

Mr. District Attorney. Hogan, Frank S[mithwick].

Mr. Dynamite. Brown, James.

Mr. Economy. Byrd, Harry Flood.

Mr. Fitz. Fitzsimmons, James Edward.

Mr. Five by Five. Rushing, Jimmy.

Mr. Fonda's Baby Jane. Fonda, Jane.

Mr. Grow-it-all. Baker, Jerry.

Mr. Guitar. Atkins, Chet.

Mr. Hadacol. LeBlanc, Dudley J.

Mr. Home Run. Kiner, Ralph McPherran.

Mr. How-About-That. Allen, Mel.

Mr. Impeccable. Cox, Archibald.

Mr. Impossible. Robinson, Brooks [Calbert, Jr.].

Mr. Inside. Blanchard, Doc; Haig, Alexander [Meigs, Jr.]; Wilson, Robert C.

Mr. Insult. Leonard, Jack E.

Mr. Lawyer. Davis, John William.

Mr. LSD. Stanley, Augustus Owsley, III.

Mr. Mac. McMillan, John Lanneau.

Mr. Middle America. Ford, Gerald [Rudolph, Jr.].

Mr. Music Maker. Welk, Lawrence [LeRoy].

Mr. New Year's Eve. Lombardo, Guy [Albert].

Mr. Nice Gun. Levine, Lou.

Mr. Outside. Davis, Glenn W.

Mr. Perseverance. Tickner, Charlie.

Mr. Playboy of the Western World. Hefner, Hugh.

Mr. Pops. Fiedler, Arthur.

Mr. President. Shaw, [Warren] Wilbur.

Mr. Ranger. Gilbert, Rod[rique].

Mr. Relaxation. Como, Perry; Oosterbaan, Benjamin Gaylord.

Mr. Republican. Taft, Robert A[lphonso].

Mr. Rhythm. Laine, Frankie.

Mr. Sam. Rayburn, Sam.

Mr. San Diego. Smith, C. Arnholt.

Mr. Saturday Night. Gleason, Jackie.

Mr. Shareowner. Funston, George Keith.

Mr. Silvertone. Martin, Freddy.

Mrs. Tiny Tim. Khaury, Victoria B.

Mr. Stork Club. Billingsley, [John] Sherman.

Mr. Taxes. Mills, Wilbur [Daigh].

Mr. Television. Berle, Milton.

Mr. Unpredictable. Patton, Billy Joe.

Mr. Untouchable. Barnes, Leroy.

Mr. Warmth. Rickles, Don.

Mr. White Backlash. Maddox, Lester [Garfield].

Mr. Wonderful. Davis, Sammy, Jr.

Mr. X. Meyer, Russ.

Muckraker. Investigator of corrupt business practices, early 20th century.

Muckraker with a Mission. Anderson, Jack[son Northman].

Mudcat. Native or resident of Mississippi.

Mudcat State. Mississippi.

Muddy. Ruel, Herold D.

Mud Hen City. Toledo, Ohio.

Mud Waddler State. Mississippi.

Muehfeldt, Freddie (active 1910–20). Gangster: **The Kid.**

Mueller, Clarence Franklin (1899–1975). Baseball outfielder: **Heinie.**

Muggsy. Spanier, Francis Joseph.

Mugs. Lorber, Max J.

Mule. Bradford, Perry; Haas, George William; Holley, Mayor [Quincy, Jr.]; Watson, Milton W.

Mules. Athletic teams of Muhlenberg College, Allentown, Pennsylvania.

Muller, Donald (active 1930s). Football player: **Mush.**

Muller, Harold P. (1901–62). Football end: **Brick.**

Mulligan, Gerry (born 1927). Jazz saxophonist, pianist, and composer: **Jeru.** Legal name: Gerald Joseph Mulligan.

Mullins, Lawrence A. (1908–68). Football coach: **Moon.**

Münchausen in Modern Dress. Means, Gaston Bullock.

Muni, Paul (1895–1967). Actor: **Man of Many Faces, Man Who Is Always Somebody Else.** Born: Muni Weisenfreund.

Municipal Assistance Corporation. Agency established during financial crisis to handle New York City borrowing, 1970s: **Big Mac.**

Municipal Muckraker. Steffens, [Joseph] Lincoln.

Munn, Clarence Lester (1908–75). Football coach: **Biggie.**

Munn, Frank (1895–1953). Singer: **Golden Voice of Radio.**

Munson, Thurman [Lee] (1947–79). Baseball catcher: **Pudge, Squatty, Round Man, Bad Body.**

Murderers Row. New York Yankees team of 1927, including Babe Ruth, Lou Gehrig, Bob Meusel, and Tony Lazzeri.

Murder Incorporated. Group of professional criminals, New York City, c. 1940.

Murdering Policeman. Becker, Charles.

Murder Paymaster. Schepps, Samuel.

Murder Trust. Group consisting of Harry Green, Dan Kreisberg, Tony Marino, Joe Murphy, and Frank Pasque that murdered Michael Malloy, 1932.

Murphy, Audie (1924–71). Army officer and actor; **America's Most Decorated Soldier, Baby.**

Murphy, Charles Francis (1858–1924). Politician: **Silent Charley.**

Murphy, Charles M. (1870–1950). Bicycle racer: **Mile-a-Minute Murphy.**

Murphy, Frank (1893–1949). U.S. Attorney General and Associate Justice of the Supreme Court: **Frank the Just, New Deal's Tom Dewey.**

Murphy, James (died 1924). Mechanic and racing driver: **The Natural.**

Murphy, John T. (1900?–64). Theatrical performer: **Guffer.**

Murphy, Lyle (born 1908). Jazz composer and saxophonist: **Spud.**

Murphy, Mel[vin E.] (born 1915). Jazz trombonist, composer, and bandleader: **Turk.**

Murphy, Timothy (died 1928). Labor racketeer: **Big Tim.**

Murray, James [Arthur] (born 1937). Jazz drummer: **Sunny.**

Murray, John Joseph (1884–1958). Baseball outfielder: **Red.**

Murray, William (1877–1954). Singer and entertainer: **Camden Budgerigar, Denver Nightingale.**

Murray, William Henry (1869–1956). Governor of Oklahoma: **Alfalfa Bill, Cockle-Bur Bill, Sage of Tishomingo.**

Murray the K. Kaufman, Murray.

Murrow's Boys. Eight CBS newsmen who worked with newscaster-commentator-interviewer Edward R[oscoe] Murrow (1908–65): Cecil Brown, Winston M. Burdett, Charles Collingwood, Richard C. Hottelet, Larry LeSueur, Eric Sevareid, William L. Shirer, and Howard K. Smith.

Muscles. Upton, Thomas Herbert; Waner, Lloyd James.

Mush. Muller, Donald; Dubofsky, Maurice.

Musial, Stan (born 1920). Baseball outfielder and first baseman: **Stan the Man.** Legal name: Stanley Frank Musial.

Musical Copy-Cat. Heidt, Horace Murray.

Music Capital of America. Los. Angeles, California; New York City.

Music City. Nashville, Tennessee.

Musicianly Boxer. Calhoun, Rory.

Mussulli, Henry W. (born 1917). Jazz saxophonist: **Boots.**

Mustang. North American P-51 fighter plane, World War II.

Mustangs. Athletic teams of Southern Methodist University, Dallas, Texas.

Mutt. Carey, Thomas; Ens, Jewel.

Muttle. Brescher, Max.

Muttonleg. Donnelly, Theodore.

Myers, Hubert Maxwell (1912–68). Jazz musician: **Bumps.**

Myers, Theodore E. (1874–1954). Automobile racing executive: **Pop.**

Myers, Wilson Ernest (born 1906). Jazz musician: **Serious.**

Mylin, Edward (1895–1975). Football coach: **Hooks.**

Mysterious Billionaire. Hughes, Howard [R.]

Mystic Materialist. Lane, Franklin Knight.

N

Nader, Ralph (born 1934). Lawyer, reformer, and author: **Consumer Advocate, Genius of the Negative Approach, National Ombudsman, Open Issue Ralph, People's Lawyer.**

Nader's Raiders. Investigative team of Ralph Nader.

Nagurski, Bronislau (born 1908). Canadian football player and wrestler: **Big Ukrainian, The Bronk, Bronko, Indomitable Bronk.**

Nail City. Wheeling, West Virginia.

Nails. Morton, Samuel J.

Namath, Joseph William (born 1943). Football quarterback: **Broadway Joe, Joe Willie.**

Nance, Willis (born 1913). Jazz cornetist, violinist, and singer: **Ray.**

Nanton, Joseph (1904–48). Jazz trombonist: **Tricky Sam.**

Nantucket. Island off the coast of Cape Cod, Massachusetts: **Far Away Island, Far Away Land.**

Nap. Rucker, George Napoleon.

Napoleon of Luzon, The. MacArthur, Douglas.

Napoleon of Promoters. Rickard, Tex.

Nappy. Lamare, Hilton.

Nash, [Frederic] Ogden (1902–71). Poet and versifier: **Undisputed Master of Light Verse.**

Nash, Jim (born 1945). Baseball pitcher: **Jumbo.** Legal name: James Edwin Nash.

Nashua, New Hampshire. U.S. city: **Gate City.**

Nashville, Tennessee. U.S. city: **Athens of the South, City Beautiful, City of Rocks, Cumberland River City, Dimple of the Universe, Iris City, Music City, Rock City.**

Nast, Condé (1874–1942). Publisher: **First of the Beautiful People.**

Natchez, Mississippi. U.S. city: **Bluff City.**

Nathan, George Jean (1882–1958). Theatrical critic, editor, and author: **Dean of Theatrical Criticism, Thersites of American Drama Critics.**

Nation, Carry or **Carrie [Amelia Moore Gloyd]** (1846–1911). Temperance agitator: **Advocate of Hatchetation, Lady with the Hatchet, Little Hatchet.**

National Anthem City. Baltimore, Maryland.

National Broadcasting Company, The. Television and radio organization: **Thirty Rock.**

National League of Professional Baseball Clubs. Organization of major league baseball teams: **Senior Circuit.**

National Ombudsman. Nader, Ralph.

National Packing Company. Organization formed by the Armour, Morris, and Swift companies, 1902, for monopolistic purposes: **Beef Trust.**

National Pastime. The game of baseball in America.

Nation of Cities. United States of America.

Nation's Birthplace. Plymouth, Massachusetts.

Nation's Health Resort. Hot Springs, Arkansas.

Nation's Most Redoubtable Criminal Lawyer. Stryker, Lloyd Paul.

Nation's No. 1. Football Fan. Nixon, Richard M[ilhous].

Nation's Seafood Center. Biloxi, Mississippi.

Nation's State. Washington, D.C.

Native Dancer (active 1953). Racehorse: **Gray Ghost.**

Nats, The. Washington Senators.

Natural, The. Murphy, James.

Natural Force. Swope, Herbert Bayard.

Nature Boy from Brooklyn. Ahbez, Eden.

Nature's Cornucopia. Louisiana.

Naughtiest Boys on Television. Smothers, Dick and Smothers, Tom.

Navarro, Theodore (1923–50). Jazz trumpeter: **Fats.**

Navel of the Nation. Butte County, South Dakota.

Navy Bill. Ingram, William.

Navy's Destroyer. Bellino, Joseph.

Navy's First City of the Sea. Portsmouth, Virginia.

Nazim of Necromantic Nudity. Todd, Michael.

Neale, Earle (1892–1973). Football coach: **Greasy.**

Nebel, John (1900–78). Radio talk-show host: **Long John.** Born: John Zimmerman.

Nebraska. Thirty-seven U.S. state: **Antelope State, Beef State, Big Country, Black Water State, Bug-eating State, Cornhusker State, Nebraskaland, Tall Corn State, Tree Planters' State.**

Nebraska, University of. 1. Athletic teams of: **Cornhuskers.** 2. Athletic teams of, with other teams in regional conference: **Big Eight.**

Nebraskaland. Nebraska.

Nebraska Wildcat, The. Hudkins, Ace.

Negro Burbank. Carver, George Washington.

Negro Explorer. Henson, Matthew.

Nehemiah, Renaldo (born 1959). High hurdler: **Skeets.**

Nellie. Fox, Jacob Nelson.

Nelson, Glenn Richard (born 1924). Baseball first baseman: **Rocky.**

Nelson, [John] Byron, [Jr.] (born 1912). Golfer: **Lord.**

Nelson, Louis Delisle (1885–1949). Jazz clarinetist: **Big Eye Louis.**

Nelson, Oscar Matthew (1882–1954). Lightweight boxer: **Battling Nelson, The Battler, Durable Dane.**

Nelson, Roger Eugene (born 1944). Baseball pitcher: **Spider.**

Nerve Center of Alaska. Anchorage, Alaska.

Nesbit, Evelyn (1884–1967). Dancer and wife of Harry Kendall Thaw: **Girl in the Red Velvet Swing, Girl in the Swing.** Legal name: Evelyn Nesbit Thaw.

Nesterenko, Eric (born 1935). Hockey player: **Elbows.**

Nevada. Thirty-sixth U.S. state: **Battle Born State, Mining State, Sagebrush State, Sage Hen State, Sage State, Silver State, Vacation State.**

Nevers, Ernest A. (born 1902). Football back: **Big Dog.**

Newark, New Jersey. U.S. city: **Birmingham of America, City of Industry.**

New Bedford, Massachusetts. U.S. city: **Whaling City.**

New Bern, North Carolina. U.S. city: **Historic Center of North Carolina.**

New Brunswick. Canadian province: **Loyalist Province, Picture Province.**

Newburyport, Massachusetts. U.S. town: **City of Captains' Houses, Yankee City.**

New Colossus. Statue of Liberty.

Newcombe, Don[ald] (born 1926). Baseball pitcher: **Newk.**

New David. Wheeler, Wayne Bidwell.

New Deal. Economic policy of the administration of President Franklin D. Roosevelt, beginning 1933.

New Dealer. A believer in the policies of President Franklin D. Roosevelt.

New Deal's Tom Dewey. Murphy, Frank.

New England of the West. Minnesota.

New England's Mafia Boss. Patriarca, Raymond L. S.

New England's Treasure House. Salem, Massachusetts.

Newfie. Native or resident of Newfoundland.

New Foundation. Ideal of the administration of President Jimmy Carter.

Newfoundland. Canadian province: **Island-and-Mainland Province, Pitcher Plant Province.**

New Freedom. Ideal of the administration of President Woodrow Wilson.

New Frontier. Ideal of the administration of President John F. Kennedy.

New Hampshire. Ninth U.S. state: **Granite State, Mother of Rivers,**

Old Man of the Mountain State, Scenic State, White Mountain State. With Vermont: **Twin States.**

New Hampshire, University of, athletic teams of: **Wildcats.**

New Haven, Connecticut. U.S. city: **City of Elms, Elm City, Yankee Athens.**

New Jersey. Third U.S. state: **Adaptable State, Clam State, Corridor State, Cockpit of History, Crossroads State, Garden State, Industrial Park State, Mosquito State, Pathway of the Revolution, Sharpbacks State.**

New Jersey, **U.S.S.** Battleship: **Big J.**

New Jerusalem. Salt Lake City, Utah.

Newk. Newcombe, Donald.

New Left. Radical movement rejecting the policies of both the U.S. and the U.S.S.R., active 1960s.

New Majority. Those Americans whom President Richard M. Nixon perceived as beneficiaries of his administration, 1972.

Newman, Anthony (born 1941). Musician and composer: **Hip Harpsichordist.**

Newman, David (born 1933). Jazz saxophonist: **Fathead.**

Newmark, Benjamin (active 1920–30). Politician and criminal: **Jew Ben.**

New Mexico. Forty-seventh U.S. state: **Cactus Land, Land of Enchantment, Land of Sunshine, Spanish State, Sunshine State, Unspoiled Empire.** With Texas: **Texico.**

New Mexico, University of, athletic teams of: **Lobos.**

New Mexico State University, athletic teams of: **Aggies.**

New Mobe. New Mobilization Committee to End the War in Vietnam.

New Mobilization Committee to End the War in Vietnam. Peace organization, 1969–71: **New Mobe.**

New Orleans, Louisiana. U.S. city: **Crawfish Town, City of Jazz and the Mardi Gras, City That Care Forgot, Crescent City, Football Capital of the South, Gulf City, Heart of Dixie, Mardi Gras Metropolis, Queen of the South.**

New Populist. Bumpers, Dale.

Newport, Rhode Island. U.S. city: **America's City of History, America's Society Capital, City of Contrasts, Queen of Summer Resorts, Yachting Capital of the World.**

Newport News, Virginia. U.S. city: **City of Ships and Shipbuilding.**

Newport of the Pacific. Santa Barbara, California.

New Radicals. Radical movement rejecting the policies of both the U.S. and the U.S.S.R., active 1960s.

New Rochelle, New York. U.S. city: **City of Huguenots, Park City.**

New Rockefeller. Koretz, Leo.

Newsboy. Moriarty, Joseph Vincent.

New S.O.B., The. The Dirksen Senate Office Building, Washington, D.C.

Newsom, Louis Norman (1907–62). Baseball pitcher: **Bobo, Buck.**

Newspaper Cabinet. Corps of journalists covering the White House in the administration of President Theodore Roosevelt, 1901–09.

New Sultan of Swat. Aaron, Hank.

New Yorican. Puerto Rican living in New York.

New York. Eleventh U.S. state: **Empire State, Excelsior State, Knickerbocker State, Seat of Empire.**

New York, Chicago and St. Louis Railroad. U.S. railroad: **Nickel Plate.**

New York City. U.S. city: **The Apple, The Big Apple, Baghdad on the Hudson, Baghdad on the Subway, Big Burg, Big Town, Capital of the World, City of Islands, City of Towers, City That Never Sleeps, Empire City, Financial Capital of the World, Fun City, Gateway to America, Gotham, International Capital, Metropolis of America, Music Capital of America, United Nations Capital, Wonder City of the World.**

New York Division. Twenty-seventh Division.

New York Fats. Wanderone, Rudolf Walter, Jr.

New York Giants. Football team: **Maramen.**

New York Giants. National League baseball team: **The Gints.**

New York Islanders. Hockey team: **The Isles.**

New York of the South. Atlanta, Georgia.

New York Review of Books. Periodical: **Parlor Panther.**

New York's Own. Seventy-seventh Infantry Division.

New York Stock Exchange. Stock exchange: **Big Board.**

New York Yankees. American League baseball team: **Bronx Bombers, Yanks.**

New Ziegfeld, The. Todd, Michael.

Neyland, Robert Reese, Jr. (1892–1962). U.S. Army General and football coach: **Football's Greatest Coach, The General, Gridiron Brigadier.**

Niagara Falls, New York. U.S. city: **Cataract City, Honeymoon City, King of Power, Power City.**

Niagara University, basketball teams of. With teams of Canisius College and St. Bonaventure University: **Little Three.**

Nibs. Price, Clarence.

Nicholas, Joe (born 1883). Jazz cornetist and clarinetist: **Wooden Joe.**

Nichols, Charles Augustus (1869–1953). Baseball pitcher and manager: **Kid.**

Nichols, John Conover (1896–1945). U.S. Representative from Oklahoma: **Oklahoma Jack.**

Nicholson, Alexandra (born c. 1957). Gymnast: **Tramp Champ.**

Nick. Carter, Vincent Michael; Cullop, Norman Andrew.

Nickelplate. Arndstein, Jules Arnold.

Nickel Plate. New York, Chicago and St. Louis Railroad.

Nicklaus, Jack [William] (born 1940). Golf player: **Golden Bear, Ohio Fats.**

Nick the Greek. Dandolos, Nicholas Andrea; Zographos, Nicholas.

Nicky. Barnes, Leroy; Hilton, Conrad, Jr.

Niemi, Laurie (1925–68). Football tackle: **Finn.**

Nig. Siegel, Benjamin.

Niggy. Rutkin, James.

Nightclub Queen. Guinan, Mary Louise Cecelia.

Nightingale. McDonnell Douglas C-9A cargo plane.

Night Train. Lane, Dick.

Nine Old Men, The. The Chief Justice and eight Associate Justices of the U.S. Supreme Court; coined during administration of President Franklin D. Roosevelt, who proposed reorganization of the Court (1937).

Ninetieth Infantry Division. U.S. Army division, World War II: **Tough Ombres.**

Ninety-eighth Infantry Division. U.S. Army division, World War II: **Iroquois Division.**

Ninety-fifth Infantry Division. U.S. Army division, World War II: **Iron Men of Metz, Victory and OK Division.**

Ninety-first Division. U.S. Army division, World War I: **Wild West Division.**

Ninety-first Infantry Division. U.S. Army division, World War II: **Powder River Division.**

Ninety-fourth Aero Pursuit Squadron. U.S. aerial squadron, World War I: **Hat-in-the-Ring Squadron.**

Ninety-ninth Infantry Division. U.S. Army division, World War II: **Checkerboard Division.**

Ninety-second Infantry Division. U.S. Army division, World War II: **Buffalo Division.**

Ninety-sixth Infantry Division. U.S. Army division, World War II: **Deadeye Division.**

Ninth Armored Division. U.S. Army division, World War II: **Phantom Division.**

Nittany Lions. Athletic teams of Pennsylvania State University, University Park.

Nitti, Frank (1885–1943). Chicago gangster: **The Enforcer.** Also known as Frank Nitto.

Nixon, Richard M[ilhous] (born 1913). Thirty-seventh President of the United States. **The Czar, Embattled President, The Godfather, Ike's Kissinger, King Richard, Nation's No. 1 Football Fan, Tarnished President, Tricky Dick.**

Nixon Family's Closest Friend, The. Rebozo, Charles Gregory.

Nixon's Alter Ego. Haldeman, H[arry] R[obbins].

Nixon's Keen Scythe. Brinegar, Claude Strout.

Nixon's Nixon. Agnew, Spiro [Theodore].

Nixon's Svengali. Kissinger, Henry A[lfred].

Nob Hill Terror. Attell, Monte.

Noble, Clem (1832–1954). Former slave and oldest person in the U.S., 1950s: **Uncle Pike.**

Nodak. Native or resident of North Dakota.

Nome, Alaska. U.S. city: **Gold Rush Town.**

No Neck. William, Walt[er Allen].

Non-Stop Activist. Fonda, Jane.

Non-Violent Singer. Baez, Joan.

Noodles. Hahn, Frank G.

No. 1 Pinup Girl. Grable, Betty.

Nordy. Hoffman, Frank.

Norfolk, Virginia. U.S. city: **City by the Sea, Dismal Swamp City, Sailor Town.**

Normal Bean. Burroughs, Edgar Rice.

Norman. Simmons, Sarney.

Norman, Karyl (1896?–1947). Female impersonator: **Creole Fashion Plate.** Born: George Norman.

Normand, Mabel (1898–1930). Motion picture actress: **Funniest Woman of the Silent Screen.**

Norris, George William (1861–1944). U.S. Senator from Nebraska: **Dean of the Liberals, Father of Public Utility Regulation, Father of the Twentieth Amendment to the Constitution, Greek Purist.**

North, John Ringling (born 1903). Circus impresario: **Greatest Showman Since Barnum.**

North Carolina. Twelfth U.S. state: **Land of Beginnings, Land of the Sky, Old North State, Second Nazareth, Tarheel State, Turpentine State.** With South Carolina: **Carolinas.**

North Carolina, University of, athletic teams of: **Tarheels.**

North Carolina State University, athletic teams of: **Wolfpack.**

North Dakota. Thirty-ninth U.S. state: **Flickertail State, Great Central State, Land of Fresh Horizons, Land of the Dakotas, Land of the Long North Furrow, Peace Garden State, Sioux State.** With South Dakota: **Dakotas, Nosodak, Twin Sisters.** With South Dakota and Wyoming: **Dakoming.**

North Dakota, University of, athletic teams of: **Sioux.**

Northeast Louisiana University, athletic teams of: **Indians.**

Northern Arizona University, athletic teams of: **Lumberjacks.**

Northern Illinois University, athletic teams of: **Huskies.**

Northerns. The Burlington, Great Northern, and Northern Pacific railroads.

North Star City. St. Paul, Minnesota.

North Star State. Minnesota.

North Texas State University, athletic teams of: **Mean Green.**

North Western Line. Chicago and North Western Railway.

Northwestern State University, athletic teams of: **Demons.**

Northwestern University. 1. Athletic teams of: **Wildcats.** 2. Athletic teams of, with other teams in regional conference: **Big Ten.**

Northwest Mystic. Callahan, Kenneth.

Northwest Territories. Canadian territory: **Last Frontier.**

Norton, Homer Hill (1895–1965). Football coach: **Showdown Man.**

Norwalk, Connecticut. U.S. city: **Clam Town.**

Nosodak. North and South Dakota.

Noto, John J. (active 1952). Gangster: **Rabbit.**

Notre Dame, University of, athletic teams of: **Fighting Irish.**

Not-So-Favorite Son, The. Reagan, Ronald.

Novak, Kim (born 1933). Motion picture actress: **Hollywood's Melancholy Blonde.** Born: Marilyn Pauline Novak.

Nova Scotia. Canadian province: **Bluenose Province, Canada's Doorstep, Doorstep to Canada, Sea-girt Province, Wharf of North America.**

Novelist of the Cattle Kingdom. Rhodes, Eugene Manlove.

Now Generation. Generation coming of age in or shortly after the 1960s.

N.R.A. Czar. Johnson, Hugh Samuel.

Nucky. Johnson, Enoch L.

Number-One Host of the Jersey Coast. Atlantic City, New Jersey.

Number One Innkeeper. Hilton, Conrad [Nicholson].

Nuñez, Alcide (1884–1934). Jazz clarinetist: **Yellow.**

Nutmeg. Native or resident of Connecticut.

Nutmeg State. Connecticut.

Nuts Kaplan. Kaplan, Eddie.

O

Oahu. Island in the state of Hawaii: **Capital Island.**

Oak City. Raleigh, North Carolina.

Oakland, California. U.S. city: **Detroit of the West, Western City of Ships.**

Oakland Athletics. American League baseball team: **A's, The.**

Oakland Redhead. Budge, [John] Don[ald].

Oakley, Annie (1860–1926). Markswoman and vaudeville actress who starred in Buffalo Bill's "Wild West" Show: **Little Missy, Little Sure Shot, Peerless Lady Wing Shot.** Legal name: Phoebe Anne Oakley Moses (later Mozee).

Oak Park, Illinois. U.S. city: **Saints' Rest.**

Oak Ridge, Tennessee. U.S. city: **Atomic City, Atomic Energy City.**

Oasis in the Desert. Palm Springs, California.

O'Banion, [Charles] Dion (1892–1924). Gangster and florist: **Chicago's Arch Criminal, Deany, Gangdom's Favorite Florist.**

Oberlander, Andrew J. (1905–68). Football player: **Swede.**

Oberta, John (active 1920–30). Politician and labor racketeer: **Dingbat.**

Oberth, Hermann (born 1894). Scientist: **Father of Space Travel, Pioneer of Modern Astronautics.**

Obici, Amadeo (1877–1947). Promoter of peanut growing: **Peanut King.**

Obie Award. Award given by the *Village Voice* (New York City) for the best Off-Broadway show of American origin.

O'Brien, David (active 1938). Football tackle: **Little David, Slingshot.**

O'Brien, Jack (1878–1942). Light heavyweight boxer: **Philadelphia Jack.**

O'Brien, James C. (active 1920s). Lawyer and assistant state's attorney in Illinois: **Rope.**

O'Brien, John T. (1895–1967). Labor leader (Teamsters union): **Sandy.**

Obscure Mr. Volstead, The. Volstead, Andrew J.

Ocean State. Rhode Island.

Ochs, Adolph Simon (1858–1935). Newspaper publisher: **Builder of Chattanooga, Watchdog of Central Park.**

O'Connor, Herbert William (born 1916). Hockey forward: **Buddy.**

O'Daniel, John W. (1895–1975). U.S. Army Lieutenant General: **Iron Mike.**

O'Daniel, W. Lee (1890–1969). Governor of Texas and U.S. Senator: **Pappy.**

O'Day, Caroline Goodwin (1875–1943). U.S. Representative from New York: **White House Pet.**

Odom, Johnny Lee (born 1945). Baseball pitcher: **Blue Moon.**

O'Donnell, Edward (active 1920–30). Bootlegger: **Spike.**

O'Donnell, Emmett, Jr. (1906–71). Football player and U.S. Air Force officer: **Rosy.**

O'Donnell, John (1868?–1944). Theatrical performer and producer: **Hap.**

O'Donnell, William (active 1920–30). Bootlegger: **Klondike.**

O'Doul, Frank Joseph (1897–1969). Baseball pitcher and outfielder: **Lefty.**

O'Dowd, Mike (1895–1957). Middleweight boxer: **Paul Cyclone.** Legal name: Michael O'Dowd.

Office Builder. Meyer, Lou[is].

Officer Mama. Schnabel, Martha.

Official Witch of Los Angeles, The. Huebner, Louise.

O'Hara, John [Henry] (1905–70). Writer: **Voice of the Hangover Generation.**

O'Hara, Maureen (born 1921). Motion pitcture actress: **Queen of Technicolor.** Born: Maureen Fitzsimons Brown.

O. Henry Girl, The. Ayres, Agnes.

Ohio. Seventeenth U.S. state: **Buckeye State, Gateway State, Land of History, Modern Mother of Presidents, Tomato State, "You-Name-It-We-Make-It" State.**

Ohio Division. Eighty-third Division.

Ohio Fats. Nicklaus, Jack [William].

Ohio Gang. Group of politicians during the administration of President Warren G. Harding found to have used their power and offices for personal gain and accused or convicted of fraud, bribery, and conspiracy, 1920s.

Ohio Northern University, athletic teams of: **Polar Bears.**

Ohio's Beautiful Capital. Columbus, Ohio.

Ohio State University. 1. Athletic teams of: **Buckeyes.** 2. Athletic teams of, with other teams in regional conference: **Big Ten.**

Ohio University, athletic teams of: **Bobcats.**

Ohio Wesleyan University, athletic teams of: **Battling Bishops.**

Oil Baron. Rockefeller, John D[avison].

Oil Capital of Canada. Edmonton, Alberta.

Oil Capital of the Rockies. Casper, Wyoming.

Oil Capital of the World. Tulsa, Oklahoma.

Oil City. Bayonne, New Jersey.

Oil City, Pennsylvania. U.S. city: **Derrick City.**

Oil Dorado. Oil country of northwestern Pennsylvania.

Oil King. Koretz, Leo.

Oil Province. Alberta.

OJ. Simpson, O[renthal] J[ames].

O'Keefe, Joseph J. (born 1907). Suspect in Brink's robbery in Boston, 1950: **Specs.**

O'Keeffe, Georgia (born 1887). Artist: **Desert and Prairie Painter.**

Okie. Migrant agricultural worker, 1930s, esp. one from Oklahoma; native or resident of Oklahoma.

Oklahoma. Forty-sixth U.S. state: **Heart of the Cow Country, Land of the Red People, Sooner State.** With Texas: **Texhoma, Texola.**

Oklahoma, University of. 1. Athletic teams of: **Sooners.** 2. Athletic teams of, with other teams in regional conference: **Big Eight.**

Oklahoma City, Oklahoma. U.S. city: **Capital of Soonerland, City of 1000 Lakes, Sedate Capital of the Bible Belt, Soonerland.**

Oklahoma Jack. Nichols, John Conover.

Oklahoma State University. 1. Athletic teams of: **Cowboys.** 2. Athletic teams of, with other teams in regional conference: **Big Eight.**

Oklahoma's Yodeling Cowboy. Autry, Gene [Orvon].

Ol' Arkansas. Warnecke, Lonnie.

Ol' Blue Eyes. Sinatra, Frank.

Old Aches and Pains. Appling, Luke.

Old Alex. Alexander, William Anderson.

Old Arbitrator. Klem, William J.

Old Blood and Butts. Whitney, Bartholomew Reynolds.

Old Blunderbuss. Saxbe, William B[art].

Old Bones. 1. Brown, Joe. 2. Exterminator.

Old Bucko. Tracy, Spencer.

Old Colonel, The. Arnheim, Gus.

Old Colony State. Massachusetts.

Old Creepy. Karpis, Alvin.

Old Crock. McAuliffe, Anthony Clement.

Old Curmudgeon. Ickes, Harold LeClaire.

Old Dad. Crosby, Bing

Old Dino. Rusk, [David] Dean.

Old Dirigo State. Maine.

Old Dominion. Virginia.

Old Dorp. Schenectady, New York.

Old Double Dome. Brisbane, Arthur.

Oldfield, Barney (1878–1946). Pioneer automobile racing driver: **America's Legendary Speed King.** Born: Berna Eli Oldfield.

Old Fox. Griffith, Clark Calvin.

Old Fritz. Zivic, Ferdinand Henry John.

Old Garrison. San Antonio, Texas.

Old Gene. Talmadge, Eugene.

Old Gimlet Eye. Butler, Smedley Darlington.

Old Gimpy. Evans, Robley Dunglison.

Old Glory. The flag of the United States of America.

Old Gravel Voice. Harmon, Ernest N[ason].

Old Guard. Managers of the Republican Party.

Old H'ar-Thar'-and Ev'ry-Whar'. Hull, Cordell.

Old Harve. Bailey, Harvey.

Old Hermit of Journalism. Scripps, E[dward] W[illis].

Old Hickory Division. Thirtieth Division, American Expeditionary Force.

Old Indian. Wynn, Early.

Old Iron Pants. Johnson, Hugh Samuel; Meyer, Leo Robert; Patton, George Smith, Jr.

Ol' Diz. Dean, Jerome Herman.

Old Lady. King, Billie Jean [Moffitt].

Old Leather Face. Chennault, Claire Lee.

Old Lefthander. Sanders, Joseph L.

Old Line State. Maryland.

Old Lion. Darrow, Clarence [Seward]; Roosevelt, Theodore.

Old Lou. Athletic teams of Louisiana State University, Baton Rouge.

Old Maestro. Bernie, Ben.

Old Man. Alexander, William Anderson.

Old Man Cottrell. Cottrell, Louis.

Old Man of the Gridiron. Kenneally, George V.

Old Man of the Mountain State. New Hampshire.

Old Man River. Mississippi River.

Old Master. Butts, Joseph Sarfuss; Gans, Joe; Gibson, Robert; Pep, Willie.

Old Master, The. Hoppe, Willie.

Old Miss. Mississippi, University of.

Old Mongoose. Moore, Archie.

Old Nels. Rockefeller, Nelson [Aldrich].

Old North State. North Carolina.

Old Pete. Alexander, Grover Cleveland.

Old Poison. Stewart, Nels.

Old Professor. Kyser, Kay.

Old Pueblo. Los Angeles, California; Tucson, Arizona.

Old Reliable. Carlson, Jules.

Old Right-Hander. Coon, Carleton A.

Olds, Ransom Eli (1864–1950). Automobile manufacturer: **Father of Oldsmobile and Reo.**

Old Scotsman. McLendon, Gordon.

Old S.O.B., The. The Russell Senate Office Building, Washington, D.C.

Old Stonefingers. Stuart, Richard Lee.

Old Stubblebeard. Grimes, Burleigh Arland.

Old Tomcat of the Keys. Zurke, Robert.

Old Trouper. Dressler, Marie.

Old Tu'key Neck. Stilwell, Joseph Warren.

Old Zeb. Weaver, Zebulon.

Old Zeke. Count Fleet.

Oleander City. Galveston, Texas.

O'Leary, Timothy J. (born 1909). U.S. Army officer, World War II. With Elmo R. Sheridan: **The Essobbees, The Military Expedients.**

Ole Miss. Mississippi, University of.

Oles. Athletic teams of St. Olaf College, Northfield, Minnesota.

Ole War Skule. Athletic teams of Louisiana State University, Baton Rouge (1908).

Ol' Hummon. Talmadge, Herman Eugene.

Oliver, Edna May (1883–1942). Actress: **Woman Who Always Speaks Her Mind.** Born: Edna May Cox-Oliver.

Oliver, Eli L. (born 1899). Labor leader: **Kiss-of-Death Oliver.**

Oliver, Joseph (1885–1938). Jazz cornetist: **King.**

Oliver, Melvin James (born 1910). Jazz composer, bandleader, singer, and trumpeter: **Sy.**

Oliver, Thomas Noble (born 1904). Baseball outfielder: **Rebel.**

Ol' Redhead, The. Barber, Red.

Olson, Carl (born 1928). Middleweight boxer: **Bobo.**

Olson, Ivan Massie (1885–1965). Baseball shortstop, second, and third baseman: **Ivy.**

Omaha, Nebraska. U.S. city: **Gate City of the West, Insurance Capital.**

Omholt, Ella Reeve Bloor (1862–1951). Communist militant: **Mother Bloor.**

Onassis, Jacqueline Bouvier Kennedy (born 1929). Widow of President John F. Kennedy and socialite: **Jackie O.**

Onaway Division. Seventy-sixth Infantry Division.

One-armed Scout. Crisp, Henry.

One-eyed Connelly. Connelly, James Leo.

One Hundred and First Airborne Division. U.S. Army division, World War II: **Screaming Eagle Division.**

One Hundred and Fourth Infantry Division. U.S. Army division, World War II: **Timberwolf Division.**

One Hundred and Second Infantry Division. U.S. Army division, World War II: **Ozark Division.**

One Hundred and Sixth Infantry Division. U.S. Army division, World War II: **Golden Lion Division.**

One Hundred and Third Infantry Division. U.S. Army division, World War II: **Cactus Division.**

One Hundredth Infantry Division. U.S. Army division, World War II: **Century Division.**

O'Neil, John Francis (born 1921). Baseball shortstop and coach: **Buck.**

O'Neil, Kitty (active 1925–35). Radio comedienne: **Laughing Lady.**

O'Neill, Frank J. (1876–1958). Football player and coach: **Buck.**

O'Neill, Rose Cecil (1874–1944). Illustrator and author: **Kewpie Doll Lady.**

O'Neill, Thomas P., Jr. (born 1912). U.S. Representative from Massachusetts and Speaker of the House: **Tip.**

One-Man Patriot. Fish, Hamilton, Jr.

One Ship Fleet. *Salt Lake City*, U.S.S.

One Speech Lee. Lee, Joshua Bryan.

Ontario. Canadian province: **Capital Province, Garden of Canada, Golden Province, Great Lakes Province, Heart of Canada.**

Onward Christian Cagle. Cagle, Christian Keener.

Oomph Girl. Sheridan, Ann.

Oosterbaan, Benjamin Gaylord (born 1906). Football coach: **Mr. Relaxation.**

Op Art. Optical Art.

Open Issue Ralph. Nader, Ralph.

Open Skies. Proposal made by the United States during the Geneva Summit Talks of July 1955, whereby the United States and the U.S.S.R. would exchange blueprints of each other's military establishments and allow each other aerial reconnaissance of those establishments.

Operation Keelhaul. Forcible return to Communist countries of refugees.

Operations Man. Baker, Bobby.

Opinion Forecaster, The. Roper, Elmo.

Oppenheimer, J[ulius] Robert (1904–67). Physicist: **Equivocal Hero of Science, Father of the Atom Bomb, Troubled Pied Piper of Los Alamos.**

Optical Art: Op Art. Non-objective art based on optical illusions.

Orange Bowl. Roddey Burdine Memorial Stadium.

Orange Capital of the World. Eustis, Florida.

Orange Crush. Defensive unit of the Denver Broncos football team.

Orange Juice. Simpson, O[renthal] J[ames].

Orange King. Harris, James Armstrong.

Orangemen. Athletic teams of Syracuse University, Syracuse, New York.

Orange State. California; Florida; Texas.

Orchard City. Burlington, Iowa.

Orchid Isle. Hawaii.

Orchid of the Screen. Griffith, Corinne.

Oregon. Thirty-third U.S. state: **Beaver State, Hard-Case State, Land of Exciting Contrasts, Sunset State, Webfoot State.**

Oregon, University of. 1. Athletic teams of: **Ducks.** 2. Athletic teams of, with other teams in regional conference: **Pacific Ten.**

Oregon State University. 1. Athletic teams of: **Beavers.** 2. Athletic teams of, with other teams in regional conference: **Pacific Ten.**

Organ Town. Brattleboro, Vermont.

Orgen, Jacob (1894-1927). Gangster: **Last of the Oldtime Gangsters, Little Augie.**

Original, The. Watson, Billy.

Original Astronaut, The. Glenn, John [Herschel].

Original Bathing Girl. Steadman, Vera.

Original Glamour Girl. Bara, Theda.

Original Radio Girl. De Leath, Vaughn.

Original White Hope. Morris, Carl.

Oriole. 1. Curtiss biplane, 1920. 2. Native or resident of Maryland.

Orion. Any of various monoplanes built by Lockheed in the early 1930s.

Ormandy, Eugene (born 1899). Symphony orchestra conductor: **Mr. Conductor, Uncle Gene.**

O'Rourke, Charles C. (born 1917). Football quarterback: **Chuckin' Charley.**

Orr, Bobby (born 1948). Hockey player: **Greatest Player of Hockey.**

Orsi, John F. (active after 1930). Football player and coach: **Count.**

Orstein, Honora (1883-1975). Alaskan dance hall queen: **Diamond Tooth Lil.**

Ortega, Tony (born 1928). Jazz musician: **Batman.** Legal name: Anthony Robert Ortega.

Ory, Edward (1886-1973). Jazz trombonist and composer: **Kid.**

Oscar. Statuette given as an award by the Academy of Motion Picture Arts and Sciences.

Oscar of the Waldorf. Tschirky, Oscar.

Osteen, Claude Wilson (born 1939). Baseball pitcher: **Gomer.**

Ostermueller, Frederick Raymond (1907-57). Baseball pitcher: **Fritz.**

Oswald, Lee Harvey (1939-63). Assassin of President John F. Kennedy: **Man Who Killed Kennedy, The Psychopath.**

O.T.B. Czar. Samuels, Howard J.

Ott, Mel[vin Thomas] (1909-58). Baseball outfielder: **Mighty Mite.**

Our Bitter Patriot. Dreiser, Theodore.

Our Bob. Reynolds, Robert Rice; Taylor, Robert Love.

Outdoor Girl of the Films. Valli, Virginia.

Overland Man. Sutherland, John Bain.

Overlin, Ken (born 1910). All-Navy middleweight boxing champion: **Illinois Thunderbolt.**

Owen, Arnold Malcolm (born 1916). Baseball catcher: **Mickey.**

Owen, Marv[in James] (born 1908). Baseball third baseman: **Freck.**

Owen, Stephen Joseph (born 1898). Football coach: **Big Steve.**

Owens, Clarence B. (1885?–1949). Baseball umpire: **Brick.**

Owens, Jack (active 1930s). Radio singer: **Cruising Crooner.**

Owens, Jesse (born 1913). Olympic athlete. **Brown Bombshell, Buckeye Bullet.** Born: James Cleveland Owens.

Owens, Steve (born 1947). Football back: **Booming Sooner.**

Owens, Thomas Llewellyn (1874–1952). Baseball second baseman: **Red.**

Owl. The. Banghart, Basil; Garner, John Nance; Polizzi, Al.

Owls. Athletic teams of Rice University, Houston, Texas, and Temple University, Philadelphia, Pennsylvania.

Owney. Madden, Owen.

Owney the Killer. Madden, Owen.

Ownie. Carroll, Owen T.

Owski. Dingell, John David.

Ox. Da Grosa, John.

Oyster. Burns, Thomas P.

Oyster State. Maryland.

Oz. Robertson, Oscar [Palmer].

Ozark Division. One Hundred and Second Infantry Division.

Ozark Ike. Zernial, Gus [Edward].

Ozark State. Missouri.

Ozarks' Western Gateway. Tulsa, Oklahoma.

P

Pa. Corbin, William H.; Watson, Edwin Martin.

Pacific, University of, athletic teams of: **Tigers.**

Pacific Coast Province. British Columbia.

Pacific Cyclone. Smith, Holland McTyeire.

Pacific Province. British Columbia.

Pacific Ten (originally **Pacific Eight**). College athletic conference composed of University of California (Berkeley), University of California at Los Angeles, University of Oregon, Oregon State University, University of Southern California, Stanford University, University of Washington, Washington State University, and (since 1978) University of Arizona and Arizona State University: **Pac Ten** (originally **Pac Eight**).

Packard, Vance Oakley (born 1914). Journalist, lecturer, and author: **Motivation Mentor.**

Packers. Athletic teams of Armour Institute of Technology, Chicago, Illinois.

Packers' Town. Green Bay, Wisconsin.

Packy. McFarland, Patrick.

Pac Ten (originally **Pac Eight**). **Pacific Ten** (originally **Pacific Eight**).

Paddles. Butkus, Dick.

Paddock, Charles W. (1900–43). Sprint champion: **World's Fastest Human.**

Paddy. DeMarco, Pat; Driscoll, John Leo; Smithwick, A.P.

Padrone, Il. Sinatra, Frank.

Page, Joe (born 1917). Baseball pitcher: **Fireman.** Legal name: Joseph Francis Page.

Page, Oran (1908–54). Jazz trumpeter: **Hot Lips.**

Paige, Leroy Robert (born 1906). Baseball pitcher: **Satchel.**

Painless Parker. Parker, Edgar Rudolph Randolph.

Painter of Loneliness. Hopper, Edward.

Palace of King Cotton. Waco, Texas.

Palevsky, Max (born 1924). Electronics executive: **Green Max.**

Paladins. Athletic teams of Furman University, Greenville, South Carolina.

Palm Beach, Florida. U.S. town: **World's Premier Winter Resort.**

Palm City. Phoenix, Arizona.

Palm Coast. East coast of Florida between Jacksonville and Daytona.

Palmer, Thomas (1876–1949). Bantamweight boxer: **Pedlar.**

Palmetto. Native or resident of South Carolina.

Palmetto City. Charleston, South Carolina.

Palmetto State. South Carolina.

Palm Springs, California. U.S. town: **America's Desert Resort, Capital of Sunshine, Golf Capital of the World, Oasis in the Desert, Swimming Pool City.**

Panama Canal. Interoceanic canal in Panama: **Big Ditch, The Ditch.**

Pancho. Barnes, Florence Lowe; Gonzales, Richard [Alonzo]; Segura, Francisco; Snyder, Frank J.

Pancoast, Asa (born 1905). Composer and organist: **Ace.**

Panhandle State. Idaho; West Virginia.

Panther. Grumman F9F-2 fighting plane, Korean War.

Panther City. Fort Worth, Texas.

Panther Division. Thirty-sixth Division.

Panthers. Athletic teams of Middlebury College, Middlebury, Vermont, and the University of Pittsburgh, Pittsburgh, Pennsylvania.

Pants. Rowland, Clarence H.

Papa. Bell, James Thomas.

Papa Hemingway. Hemingway, Ernest.

Papa Jac. Assunto, Jacob.

Papa Jack. Laine, George [Vitelle].

Papa Mutt. Carey, Thomas.

Papke, Billy (1886–1936). Middleweight boxer: **The Thunderbolt.** Born: William Herman Papke.

Papp, Joe (born 1921). Theatrical director and producer: **Populist and Imperialist.** Born: Joseph Papirofsky.

Pappas, Milt (born 1939). Baseball pitcher: **Gimpy.** Legal name: Milton Steven Pappas.

Pappy. Lewis, Art[hur]; O'Daniel W. Lee; Waldorf, Lynn O.

Paquin, Leo (active 1930s). Football player. With other members of Fordham team: **Seven Blocks of Granite.**

Paradise of the Pacific. Hawaii.

Paratrooper Pet. Lamour, Dorothy.

Parham, Charles Valdez (born 1913). Jazz bass player: **Truck.**

Parise, J. P. (born 1941). Hockey player: **Jeep.** Legal name: Jean Paul Parise.

Paris of America. San Francisco, California.

Parity John. Bankhead, John Hollis.

Park, Arthur (active 1940–73). Hobo: **King of Hobos, Slow Motion Shorty Park.**

Park Avenue Hillbilly. Shay, Dorothy.

Park City. Bridgeport, Connecticut; New Rochelle, New York.

Parker, Buddy (born 1913). Football coach: **Top Football Coach in America.** Legal name: Raymond Klein Parker.

Parker, Charlie (1920–55). Jazz saxophonist: **Bird, Yardbird.**

Parker, Clarence (born 1913). Football quarterback: **Ace.**

Parker, Edgar Rudolph Randolph (1872–1952) Canadian dentist: **Great Tooth Tycoon, Painless Parker.**

Parker, Francis James (born 1913). Baseball shortstop and manager: **Salty.**

Parking Lot City. St. Louis, Missouri.

Parliamentarian, The. Luce, Robert.

Parlor City. Cedar Rapids, Iowa.

Parlor Panther. *New York Review of Books.*

Parson. Sunday, Billy.

Parson Hobson. Hobson, Richmond Pearson.

Parsons, Louella (1881–1972). Journalist: **Lolly.**

Partisan of the Unpopular. Darrow, Clarence [Seward].

Pasadena, California. U.S. city: **City of Roses, Crown City, Town That Roses Built.**

Pasadena Stadium. Stadium in Pasadena, California; site of annual Rose Bowl college football game: **Rose Bowl.**

Paskert, George Henry (1881–1959). Baseball outfielder: **Dode.**

Passalaqua, Joseph Anthony (born 1929). Jazz guitarist: **Joe Pass.**

Passamaquoddy Bay. Bay between Maine and New Brunswick: **Quoddy.**

Pastor. Russell, Charles Taze.

Pat. Ballard, Francis Drake; Brown, Edmund Gerald; Crawford, Clifford Rankin; Malone, Percy Lay.

Paterson, New Jersey. U.S. city: **American Lyons, Cradle of American Industry, Federal City, Silk City.**

Path of Gold. Market Street, San Francisco.

Pathway of the Revolution. New Jersey.

Patman, Wright (1893–1976). Farmer and U.S. Representative from Texas: **Anti-Chain-Store Patman, Father of the Bonus.**

Patriarca, Raymond L. S. (born 1908). Syndicate gangster: **New England's Mafia Boss.**

Patriarch of Three Rivers. Fall, Albert Bacon.

Patsy. Donovan, Patrick Joseph; Flaherty, Patrick Joseph; Tebeau, Oliver W.

Patt, Maurice (active 1934–42). Football end: **Babe.**

Patterson, Eleanor Medill (1884–1948). Newspaper publisher: **Cissy.** Also known as Eleanor M. Gizycka.

Patterson, Floyd (born 1935). Heavyweight boxer: **The Rabbit.**

Patterson, Joseph Medill (1879–1946). Newspaper publisher: **Father of the Tabloid.**

Patton, Billy Joe (born 1922). Golfer: **Mr. Unpredictable.**

Patton, George Smith, Jr. (1885–1945). U.S. Army General, World War II: **Blood and Guts, Old Iron Pants, Green Hornet.**

Patton, John (1883–1956). Gangster: **Boy Mayor of Burnham** [Illinois].

Patton, John (born 1936). Jazz organist: **Big John.**

Patton's Peer. Abrams, Creighton William.

Paul Revere of Ecology. Commoner, Barry.

Pavageau, Alcide (1888–1969). Jazz bass player: **Slow Drag.**

Pawnee Bill. Lillie, Gordon W.

Pawtucket, Rhode Island. U.S. city: **Birthplace of the American Cotton Industry.**

PD. Haughton, Percy Duncan.

Peabody, Edward (active 1925–70). Musician: **King of the Banjo.**

Peabody, Endicott T. (born 1920). Football guard: **Chub.**

Peaceful Warrior. King, Martin Luther, Jr.

Peace Garden State. North Dakota.

Peace Ludlow. Ludlow, Louis Leon.

Peach, The. Depew, Chauncey Mitchell.

Peach Bowl. Football stadium in Atlanta, Georgia; site of annual Peach Bowl college football game.

Peach State. Georgia.

Peacock Alley. Corridor of the Waldorf-Astoria Hotel, New York City, frequented by persons of fashion.

Peanut King. Obici, Amadeo.

Peanut Man. Carver, George Washington.

Peanuts. Holland, Herbert Lee; Hucko, Michael Andrew.

Pearl. 1. Joplin, Janis. 2. Pearl Harbor.

Pearl, Minnie (born 1912). Comedienne: **Queen of Country Corn.** Born: Sarah Ophelia Colley Cannon.

Pearl Harbor. Naval base on Oahu, Hawaii: **Pearl.**

Pearlie Mae. Bailey, Pearl.

Pearl King of the World. Rosenthal, Leonard.

Pearson, Arnett (active 1921): Football player: **Chink.**

Pearson, Charles M. (1920–44). Football player: **Stubby.**

Pearson, Columbus Calvin, Jr. (born 1932). Jazz pianist and composer: **Duke.**

Pearson, Drew (1897–1969). Journalist and newspaper columnist: **Leading Muckraker of His Time, Pugnacious Pearson, Tenacious Muckraker.** Legal name: Andrew Russell Pearson.

Pearson, Edmund Lester (1880–1937). Editor, biographer, and librarian: **The Librarian.**

Pearson, Madison (active 1929–37). Football center: **Bert.**

Pearson, Walter Clyde (born 1929). Poker champion: **Pug.**

Peck. Pieculewicz, Charles.

Peckinpah, Sam[uel] (born 1925). Motion picture director: **Master of Violence.**

Pedantic Professor. Sherman, Allie.

Pedlar. Palmer, Thomas.

Peerless Lady Wing-Shot. Oakley, Annie.

Peerless Leader. Chance, Frank LeRoy.

Peerless State. Iowa.

Pee Wee. Erwin, George; Hunt, Walter; Reece, Harold Henry; Russell, Charles [Ellsworth]; Spitelara, Joe.

Peg. Pegler, [James] Westbrook; Vaughn, Miles W.

Pegleg. Lonergan, Richard; Morrow, Anne McIntyre.

Pegler, [James] Westbrook (1894–1969). Newspaper columnist: **Angry Man of the Press, Peg.**

Peirce, Charles Sanders (1839–1914). Philosopher: **Father of American Pragmatism.**

Peirce, Waldo (1884–1970). Artist and author: **American Renoir.**

Peitz, Henry Clement (1872–1943). Baseball catcher: **Heinie.**

Pelican. Native or resident of Louisiana.

Pelican State. Louisiana.

Pelley, William Dudley (1890–1965). Nazi sympathizer and author: **Leader of Men, Smelly Pelley.**

Peloquin, Robert Dolan (born c. 1928). Detective: **Jet Age Super-Sleuth.**

Pelty, Barney (1880–1939). Baseball pitcher: **Yiddish Curver.**

Pelvis, The. Presley, Elvis [Aron].

Penamite. Native or resident of Pennsylvania.

Pendergast, Thomas J. (1872–1945). Political boss in Missouri: **Boss Pendergast.**

Peninsular State. Florida.

Peninsula State. Florida; Michigan.

Pennier, Henry George (born 1904). Canadian logger: **Half-Breed Logger.**

Pennington, Ann (1893–1971). Dancer and actress: **Shimmie Queen.**

Penn's Town. Reading, Pennsylvania.

Pennsy. Pennsylvania Railroad.

Pennsylvania. Second U.S. state: **Birthplace of a Nation, Coal State, Keystone State, Quaker State, Steel State, Workshop of the World.**

Pennsylvania, University of. 1. Athletic teams of: **Quakers.** 2. Athletic teams of, with seven other teams in college conference: **Ivy League.** 3. Basketball team of, with other Philadelphia area teams: **Big Five.**

Pennsylvania Dutch. Clark, Thomas.

Pennsylvania of the West. Missouri.

Pennsylvania Railraod. U.S. railroad: **Pennsy.**

Pennsylvania's Boss of Bosses. Penrose, Boies.

Pennsylvania State University, athletic teams of: **Nittany Lions.**

Penny. Bjorkland, Rosemarie Diane.

Penobscot River City. Bangor, Maine.

Penrose, Boies (1860–1921). Politician and Republican boss of Pennsylvania: **Boss, Gutter Nietzschean, Pennsylvania's Boss of Bosses.**

Pensacola, Florida. U.S. city: **Annapolis of the Air, City of Camellias, City of Five Flags, Cradle of Naval Aviation, Gulf Coast City, Pensy.**

Pensy. Pensacola, Florida.

Pentagon Papers. Official history of U.S. involvement in Vietnam, published without authorization in 1971.

People's Attorney. Brandeis, Louis Dembitz.

People's Democrat. Hearst, William Randolph.

279

People's Lawyer. Brandeis, Louis Dembitz; Nader, Ralph.

People's Poet. Wilcox, Ella Wheeler.

Peoria, Illinois. U.S. city: **Center of Midwest Friendliness, Illinois River City, Peory, Whiskey Town.**

Peory. Peoria, Illinois.

Pep. Tobey, David; Young, Lemuel Floyd.

Pep, Willie (born 1922). Featherweight boxer: **Old Master, Will-o'-the-Wisp.** Born: William Gugliermo Papaleo.

Pepi. Pepitone, Joseph Anthony.

Pepitone, Joseph Anthony (born 1940). Baseball first baseman and outfielder: **Pepi.**

Pepper. Adams, Park; Austin, James Philip; Martin, John Leonard.

Pepper Box. Bartell, Richard.

Peppy. Genero, Joseph.

Perez, Leander H., Sr. (1892–1969). Louisiana segregationist and political boss: **Judge.**

Perfecter of Opalescent Glass. Tiffany, Louis Comfort.

Perfect Fool. Wynn, Ed.

Perfect Publisher. Knopf, Alfred A.

Perfume Jack. Kearns, Jack.

Perkins, Frances (1882–1965). U.S. Secretary of Labor: **Fearless Frances, Liberal Politician, Loquacious Linguist Whom Labor Loves.**

Perot, H. Ross (born 1930). Business executive and philanthropist: **Texas Computer Millionaire.**

Perpetual Adolescent of American Poetry. Pound, Ezra [Loomis].

Perry, Gaylord Jackson (born 1938). Baseball pitcher: **Spitball Pitcher.**

Pershing, John Joseph (1860–1948). U.S. Army General, World War I: **Black Jack.**

Pessimist with Hope. Darrow, Clarence [Seward].

Pete. Alexander, Grover Cleveland; Fox, Ervin; Conrad, Charles, Jr.; Manion, Clyde Jennings; Quesada, Elwood Richard.

Peter McGill. Pedro Miguel locks of the Panama Canal.

Petrelli, Dominick (1900–53). Gangster: **The Gap.**

Petrillo, James Caesar (born 1892). Labor leader and president of the musicians' union: **Little Caesar.**

Petrocelli, Americo Peter (born 1943). Baseball third baseman: **Rico.**

Petrolle, William (born 1905). Welterweight boxer: **Fargo Express.**

Petty, Richard (born 1937). Automobile racing driver: **King of the Road.**

Pfirman, Charles H. (born 1891). Baseball umpire: **Cy.**

Phantom. McDonnell Douglas F-4B tactical fighter plane.

Phantom Billionaire. Hughes, Howard [R.]

Phantom Division. Ninth Armored Division.

Phantom President of the United States. Mitchell, John [Newton].

Pharaoh. Sanders, Farrell.

Phelps, Ernest Gordon (born 1908). Baseball catcher: **Babe, Blimp.**

Philadelphia, Pennsylvania. U.S. city: **Birthplace of American Liberty, City of Brotherly Love, City of Homes, City of Penn, Cradle of Liberty, Cradle of the American Revolution, Libertybellsville, Philly, Quaker City, Quaker Town.**

Philadelphia Jack. O'Brien, Jack.

Philadelphia's Murdering Faith Healer. Bolber, Morris.

Phillippe, Charles Louis (1872–1952). Baseball pitcher: **Deacon.**

Phillips, Alfred Noroton, Jr. (1894–1970). U.S. Representative from Connecticut and manufacturer: **Milk of Magnesia Phillips.**

Phillips, Arthur Osborne (born 1894). Self-taught surgeon and impostor: **Doc, Fake Doctor.**

Phillips, Barton (active 1920–30). Bank robber: **Whitey.**

Phillips, Harold Ross (1919–72). Baseball manager: **Lefty.**

Phillips, John Melvin (born 1930). Baseball third baseman and outfielder: **Bubba.**

Phillips, Joseph Edward (born 1915). Jazz saxophonist: **Flip.**

Philly. Philadelphia, Pennsylvania.

Philly Jilly. Carlton, Steven Norman.

Philly Joe. Jones, Joseph Rudolph.

Philosopher, The. Sorrell, Victor Garland.

Philosopher Freethinker. Hubbard, Elbert.

Philosophy Smith. Smith, Thomas Vernon.

Phoenix, Arizona. U.S. city: **City Where Summer Winters, Heart of the Sun Country, Metropolis of the Desert, Palm City, Profit Center of the Southwest, Youngest Big City in the United States.**

Phoenix City. Chicago, Illinois.

Phog. Allen, Forrest Claire.

Photographic Purist. Adams, Ansel.

Photography Capital. Rochester, New York.

Photo Reportress. Bourke-White, Margaret.

Phrasemaker. Wilson, [Thomas] Woodrow.

Phrasemaker of Versailles. Wilson, [Thomas] Woodrow.

Pianner Kid. Lopez, Vincent.

Picasso of Children's Books. Sendak, Maurice.

Picasso of the Camera. Weston, Edward.

Pick. Dehner, Lou[is].

Pickford, Mary (1894–1979). Motion-picture actress: **America's Sweetheart, America's Sweetheart Emeritus, Queen of the Movies, World's Sweetheart.** Born: Gladys Mary Smith.

Pickle Works. Building of the Central Intelligence Agency, Langley, Virginia.

Picnic City. Mobile, Alabama.

Picon, Molly (born 1898). Actress: **Baby Margaret, Sweetheart of Second Avenue.** Also known as Mrs. Jacob Kalich.

Picture Province. New Brunswick.

Pie. Traynor, Harold Joseph.

Pieculewicz, Charles (active 1929–32). Football player: **Peck.**

Pied Piper of Broadway. Preston, Robert.

Pierce, Joseph De Lacrois (1904–73). Jazz trumpeter and cornetist: **Dede.**

Pierce, Marvin (active 1916). Football player: **Monk.**

Pierce, Nat (1913–75). Football player. With other members of Fordham team: **Seven Blocks of Granite.**

Pierre, South Dakota. U.S. city: **A Real Western Town, Gateway to the Black Hills.**

Piet, Tony (born 1906). Baseball second and third baseman: **Tony the Silent, Whitey.** Legal name: Anthony Francis Pietruszka.

Piggly Wiggly Man. Saunders, Clarence.

Piggy. Lambert, Ward L.; Lynch, James.

Pinchot, Gifford (1865–1946). Forestry expert, politician, and Governor of Pennsylvania: **Father of American Forestry, Father of Conservation.**

Pineapple Bowl. Football stadium at Honolulu, Hawaii.

Pineapple Division. Twenty-fifth Infantry Division.

Pineapple Island. Lanai, Hawaii.

Pineapple State. Hawaii.

Pinetop. Smith, Clarence.

Pine Tree State. Maine.

Pink. Baker, Harlan F.

Pinkey. Hargrave, William McKinley; Higgins, Mike; Whitney, Arthur Carter.

Pink Whiskers. Lewis, James Hamilton.

Pinky. Clarke, Louis Albert; Harrington, Francis C.; Humphrey, Hubert Horatio; Lee, Pincus; Match, Pincus; Tomlin, Truman.

Pinocchio. James, Cornelius.

Pioggi, Louis (active 1908–12). Gangster: **Louie the Lump.**

Pioneer Mormon City. Provo, Utah.

Pioneer of Air Power. Mitchell, William.

Pioneer of Modern Astronautics. Oberth, Hermann.

Pious John. Wanamaker, John.

Pipeline Disney. Disney, Wesley Ernest.

Piper, W[illiam] Thomas (1881–1970). Airplane manufacturer: **Henry Ford of Aviation.**

Pirate City. Tampa, Florida.

Pirate Preacher. McIntire, Carl.

Pirates. Athletic teams of East Carolina University, Greenville, North Carolina.

Pisano, Augie (1897–1959). Gangster: **Little Augie.** Born: August Carfano.

Pistol Pete. Brennan, Peter J.; Eaton, Frank; Maravich, Peter; Wisniewski, Henry.

Pit. Bourque, Napoleon; Lepine, Alfred.

Pitcher Plant Province. Newfoundland.

Pitchfork Ben. Tillman, Benjamin Ryan.

Pittinger, Charles R. (1871–1909). Baseball pitcher: **Togie.**

Pittman, Key (1872–1940). Miner and U.S. Senator from Nevada: **Voice of Silver.**

Pitts, Edwin Collins (1911–41). Baseball player and athlete: **Alabama.**

Pitts, ZaSu (1900–63). Motion-picture actress **Girl with the Ginger Snap Name.**

Pittsburgh, Pennsylvania. U.S. city: **Big Smoke, City of Bridges, Gateway to the West, Hell in the Hills, Iron City, Renaissance City of America, Smoky City, Steel City, World's Workshop.**

Pittsburgh, University of, athletic teams of: **Panthers.**

Pittsburgh Hurricane, The. Hunt, Bobby.

Pittsburgh Kid. Conn, William.

Pittsburgh of the South. Birmingham, Alabama.

Pittsburgh Phil. Strauss, Harry.

Pittsburgh Pirates. National League baseball team: **Bucs.**

Pittsburgh Windmill, The. Greb, Edward Henry.

Piute Pete. Kaufman, Morris.

Pladner, Emile (born 1906). Flyweight boxer: **Spider.**

Plains Empire City. Amarillo, Texas.

Planned Growing City. Garden Grove, California.

Plantation State. Rhode Island.

Plant Doctor. Carver, George Washington.

Plant Magician. Burbank, Luther.

Plant Wizard. Burbank, Luther.

Plastic Historian. Davidson, Jo.

Plattsburgh Idea. Program of military preparedness through training for civilians, 1915.

Playboy, The. Reynolds, Robert Rice.

Playboy of New York. Walker, James J[ohn].

Playboy of Pugilism. Baer, Max[imilian Adelbert].

Playboy of the Piano. Rubinstein, Arthur.

Player Who Is Never Caught from Behind. Bellino, Joseph.

Playground of the Americas. Miami, Florida; Miami Beach, Florida.

Playground of the Desert. Las Vegas, Nevada.

Playtown U.S.A. Las Vegas, Nevada.

Plinky. Topperwein, Elizabeth [Servanty].

Plow City. Moline, Illinois.

Plow 'Em Under Wallace. Wallace, Henry A[gard].

Plucky. Salinger, Pierre.

Plum. Wodehouse, Pelham Grenville.

Plumbers, The. Special Investigation Unit.

Plymouth, Massachusetts. U.S. town: **America's Home Town, Nation's Birthplace.**

Plymouth of the West. San Diego, California.

Poague, William Robert (born 1899). U.S. Representative from Texas: **The Professor.**

Pocket Rocket, The. Richard, Henri.

Poet of the People. Guest, Edgar A[lbert].

Poet of Violence. Chandler, Raymond.

Poindexter, Norwood (born 1926). Jazz saxophonist: **Pony.**

Poison Ivy. Andrews, Ivy Paul.

Poison Twins. Waner, Lloyd James and Waner, Paul Glee.

Poker Face. Garner, John Nance.

Polar Bears. Athletic teams of Ohio Northern University, Ada.

Polar Star State. Maine.

Policy King. Adams, Albert.

Polish City. Hamtramck, Michigan.

Polish Prince of American Pop Music. Vinton, Bobby.

Political Philosopher. Smith, Thomas Vernon.

Political Thor. Farley, James Aloysius.

Politician, The. Costello, Frank.

Polizzi, Al (born 1900). Gangster: **The Owl.**

Pollack, Ben[jamin] (1904–71). Jazz musician and drummer: **Father of Swing.**

Pollard, Jim (born 1922). Basketball forward: **Kangaroo Kid.**

Pollock, Jackson (1912–56). Abstract painter: **Jack the Dripper.**

Polo. Barnes, Paul D.

Polock Joe. Saltis, Joseph.

Pomeroy, John (1872–1950). Inventor: **Pop.**

Pony. Poindexter, Norwood.

Poodles. Hanneford, Edwin.

Po' Ol' Country Lawyer. Ervin, Sam[uel James, Jr.].

Poor Little Rich Boy. Hearst, William Randolph.

Poor Little Rich Girl. Vanderbilt, Gloria.

Poor Little Rich Girls. Duke, Doris and Hutton, Barbara.

Poor Man's Friend. Couzens, James.

Pop. Burns, Jerry; Idell, A. Provost; Ivy, Frank; Keeler, Oscar Bane; Lloyd, John Henry; Myers, Theodore E.; Pomeroy, John; Warner, Glenn Scobey; Zukor, Adolph.

Pop Anson's Colts. Chicago Cubs.

Pop Art. Art using familiar imagery derived from advertising, comic strips, etc.

Pope, The. Sinatra, Frank.

Pop-eye. Mehaffy, Leroy; Simon, William E.

Pop of Pop Art. Scull, Robert C.

Poppy Lady. Michael, Moina.

Pops. Armstrong, Daniel Louis; Foster, George Murphy; Snowden, Elmer Chester; Whiteman, Paul.

Populist and Imperialist. Papp, Joe.

Porkopolis. Chicago, Illinois; Cincinnati, Ohio.

Porkopolis of Iowa. Burlington, Iowa.

Porn Capital of America. San Francisco, California.

Port City. Beaumont, Texas; Mobile, Alabama.

Porter, Cole (1893–1964). Composer and lyricist: **Elegant Hoosier Tunesmith.**

Porter, The. Ricca, Paul.

Portland, Maine. U.S. city: **America's Sunrise Gateway, Beautiful City by the Sea, Forest City, Hill City, Vacation City on Casco Bay.**

Portland, Oregon. U.S. city: **City of Roses, Metropolis of Oregon, Rose City.**

Portly Master of the Involuntary Scream, The. Hitchcock, Alfred.

Port of Distinction. Green Bay, Wisconsin.

Port of the Pilgrims. Provincetown, Massachusetts.

Portsmouth, Virginia. U.S. city: **Navy's First City of the Sea.**

Posey. Jenkins, Freddy.

Possum. Whitted, George Bostic.

Post, Charles William (1854–1914). Breakfast food manufacturer: **Post Toasties King, Postum King.**

Post, Emily Price (1873–1960). Writer and columnist: **Final Authority on Etiquette.**

Post, Seraphim (active 1920s). Football player: **Dynamite.**

Post Toasties King. Post, Charles William.

Postum King. Post, Charles William.

Pot. Graves, Ernest.

Potash City. Saskatoon, Saskatchewan.

Potato. Gish, Lillian; Valdéz, Carlos.

Potatoes. Kaufman, Julian.

Potato Major. Shank, Samuel Lewis.

Potomac River City. Washington, D.C.

Potsy. Clark, George.

Pottawatomie Giant. Willard, Jess.

Pound, Ezra [Loomis] (1885–1972). Poet, critic, and propagandist: **Expatriate American Poet, Perpetual Adolescent of American Poetry.** Also known as William Atheling, Alfred Venison.

Pow Country. Region around Saskatoon, Sakatchewan, producing potash, oil, and wheat.

Powder Puff Derby. International Women's Air Race.

Powder River Division. Ninety-first Infantry Division.

Powell, Adam Clayton (1908–72). Clergyman and U.S. Representative from New York: **King**

Powell, Everard Stephen, Sr. (born 1907). Jazz clarinetist and saxophonist: **Rudy.** Also known as Musheed Karweem.

Powell, Gordon (born 1922). Jazz drummer: **Specs.**

Powell, Jody (born 1943). White House press secretary, with other members of President Jimmy Carter's administration: **Georgia Mafia.** Legal name: **Joseph Lester Powell.**

Powell, John Stephen (1857–1921). Judge: **Big Judge Powell.**

Powell, John Wesley (born 1941). Baseball first baseman: **Boog.**

Power City. Niagara Falls, New York; Rochester, New York.

Prado, Katie (1882–1957). Singer and brothel proprietor: **Belle of New York, Diamond Tooth Lil, Miss Lil, Queen of the Bowery, Toast of the Barbary Coast.** Also known as Evelyn Hildegard.

Prager, Emmuel (active 1925–40). Saxophonist and singer: **Colonel Manny.**

Pragmatic Humanist. Young, Whitney M[oore].

Pragmatist Philosopher. James, William.

Prairie City. Bloomington, Illinois.

Prairie Division. Thirty-third Infantry Division.

Prairie State. Illinois.

Pratt, Walter (born 1916). Hockey player: **Babe.**

Preacher. Roe, Elwin Charles.

Preacher, The. Short, Dewey Jackson.

Preppie. A student or alumnus of a preparatory school, esp. one of the elite boarding schools of the Northeast having a reputation for high scholastic achievement and social prestige.

Pres. Young, Lester Willis.

President. Young, Lester Willis.

President Nixon's Favorite Mayor. Lugar, Richard G[reen].

President of the United States. U.S. chief of state and head of government: **The Chief, Great White Father.**

Presidents. Athletic teams of Washington & Jefferson College, Washington, Pennsylvania.

President's Other Friend. Abplanalp, Robert H.

President's Rasputin. Haldeman, H[arry] R[obbins].

President's Worst Friend. Mitchell, John [Newton].

Presley, Elvis [Aron] (1935–77). Singer and actor: **Elvis the Pelvis, Hillbilly Cat, The Pelvis.**

Preston, Robert (born 1918). Actor: **Pied Piper of Broadway.** Born: Robert Preston Meservey.

Preston, Thomas Austin, Jr. (born 1929). Gambler and poker champion: **Amarillo Slim, Arizona Slim.**

Prettiest Carmen on Record. Swarthout, Gladys.

Prettiest Three-Million-Dollar Corporation with Freckles in America. Day, Doris.

Pretty Boy Floyd. Floyd, Charles.

Pretzel. Banks, David.

Pretzel City. Lancaster, Pennsylvania; Reading, Pennsylvania.

Prez. Young, Lester Willis.

Price, Clarence (1889–1968). Basketball and football coach: **Nibs.**

Pride of Pittsburgh. Martin, Anne.

Pride of Pragmatists. Haldeman, H[arry] R[obbins].

Pride of the Ghetto. Bernstein, Joseph.

Pride of the Pacific. Long Beach, California.

Pride of the Yankees. Gehrig, [Henry] Lou[is].

Prime Minister of the Underworld. Costello, Frank.

Primitive Baptist. Member of a Christian fundamentalist sect: **Hard-shell Baptist.**

Prince. Lasha, William B.

Prince Edward Island. Canadian province: **Garden of the Gulf, Garden Province, Million-Acre Farm, Princely Province, Confederation Province.**

Princely Province. Prince Edward Island.

Prince of Boodlers. De Pow, Johnny.

Prince of Broadway. Cohan, George M[ichael].

Prince of Darkness. Barend, John; Carson, Johnny.

Prince of Losers. Cook, Frederick Albert.

Prince of Peace. Carnegie, Andrew.

Prince of Restaurateurs. Rector, George.

Prince of Sophisticated Pornography. Hefner, Hugh.

Prince of the Air. Houdini, Harry.

Prince of the American Theater. Cohan, George M[ichael].

Prince of the Oyster Pirates. London, Jack.

Prince of Wails. Lombardo, Guy [Albert].

Prince of Wit and Wisdom. Rogers, Will.

Princess, The. Wills, Helen [Newington].

Princess Alice. Longworth, Alice Roosevelt.

Princess of Situation Comedy. Thomas, Marlo.

Princeton University. 1. Athletic teams of: **Tigers.** 2. Athletic teams of, with teams of Harvard and Yale: **Big Three.** 3. Athletic teams of, with seven other teams in college conference: **Ivy League.**

Pringle, Aileen (born 1895). Motion-picture actress: **Intellectual Aristocrat of the Screen.** Born: Aileen Bisbee.

Prisk, Laura B. [Caddell] (1875–1950). Public figure: **Mother of Flag Day.** Also known as Mrs. Enos L. Blue.

Prison Playwright. Brown, Rhozier Theopelius.

Private Secretary of God Almighty. Mencken, H[enry] L[ouis].

Procter, William Cooper (1862–1934). Businessman and head of Procter & Gamble: **Ivory Soap King.**

Prodigious Spender, The. Johnson, Lyndon Baines.

Production Line. Detroit Red Wings' hockey line of Gordie Howe, Ted Lindsay, and Sid Abel.

Prof. Weaver, Monte.

Professor, The. Poague, William Robert; Wilson, [Thomas] Woodrow; Scarne, John.

Professor Figgsbottle. Johnson, Don.

Professor Lamberti. Lambert, Basil Garwood.

Professor Seagull. Gould, Joe.

Professor Von Chopnick. Weil, Joseph R.

Profit Center of the Southwest. Phoenix, Arizona.

Progressive Party. Political party, early 20th century: **Bull Moose Party, Bull Moosers.**

Prohibition Portia. Willebrandt, Mabel Walker.

Project Bluebook. Twenty-one-year investigation (1948–69) of unidentified flying objects.

Promitis, Mary (active 1928). Marathon dancer: **Hercules Mary.**

Prophet, The. Klimek, Tillie.

Prophet of the Strenuous Life. London, Jack.

Prothro, James Thompson (1893–1971). Baseball third baseman and coach: **Doc.**

Provenzano, Tony (born 1934). Teamsters official: **Tony Pro.** Legal name: Anthony J. Provenzano.

Providence, Rhode Island. U.S. city: **Beehive of Industry, Roger Williams City, Southern Gateway of New England.**

Provincetown, Massachusetts. U.S. town: **Port of the Pilgrims.**

Provisional President of Africa. Garvey, Marcus Moziah.

Provision State. Connecticut.

Provo, Utah. U.S. city: **Pioneer Mormon City.**

Proxy Fighter by Proxy. Kirby, Allan Price.

Prussian Leprechaun. Leahy, Francis William.

Psychedelphia. Haight-Ashbury.

Psycho, The. Barend, John.

Psychopath, The. Oswald, Lee Harvey.

Ptarmigan. Native or resident of Alaska.

Public Enemy Number One. Dillinger, John [Herbert].

Public Relations Genius. Lee, Ivy Ledbetter.

Public Relations Pioneer. Bruno, Henry Augustine.

Puddinghead. Battle, Edgar W.

Puddler Jim. Davis, James John.

Pudge. Fisk, Carlton [Ernest]; Heffelfinger, William Walter; Munson, Thurman [Lee].

Pueblo, Colorado. U.S. city: **City of Homes and Industry, Fountain City, Steel City of the West.**

Pueblo Acoma, New Mexico. Native American community near Albuquerque: **Sky City.**

Puerto Rico. Commonwealth associated with the United States: **Garden of the Caribbean.**

Pug. Pearson, Walter Clyde.

Puget Sound, University of, athletic teams of: **Loggers.**

Pugilistic Poseur. Baer, Max[imilian Adelbert].

Pugnacious Pearson. Pearson, Drew.

Pulitzer, Joseph (1847–1911). Newspaper publisher: **Blind Publisher.**

Puller, Lewis B. (1898–1971). U.S. Marine Corps Lieutenant General: **Chesty.**

Pullman, Illinois. Former city, now part of Chicago: **City of Brick.**

Punch. Broadbent, Harry; Miller, Ernest; Sulzberger, Arthur Ochs.

Punch Line. Montreal Canadiens' hockey line of Maurice Richard, Joe Blake, and Elmer Lach.

Purdue University. 1. Athletic teams of: **Boilermakers.** 2. Athletic teams of, with other teams in regional conference: **Big Ten.**

Puritan City. Boston, Massachusetts.

Puritan State. Massachusetts.

Purnell, William (1915–1965). Jazz drummer: **Keg.**

Purple Aces. Athletic teams of the University of Evansville, Evansville, Indiana.

Purple Gang, The. Minnesota Vikings.

Pursuit. George, Harold H.

Push-'em-up Lazzeri. Lazzeri, Anthony Michael.

Pussyfoot. Johnson, William Eugene.

Q

Quad Cities. Rock Island, Moline, and East Moline, Illinois, and Davenport, Iowa.

Quail. Native or resident of California.

Quaker City. Philadelphia, Pennsylvania.

Quakers. Athletic teams of the University of Pennsylvania, Philadelphia.

Quaker State. Pennsylvania.

Quaker Town. Philadelphia.

Quality City. Rochester, New York.

Quarrier, Sidney (active 1927). Football player: **Red.**

Quebec. Canadian province: *La Belle Province.*

Queen Alice. Longworth, Alice Roosevelt.

Queen City. Cincinnati, Ohio; Davenport, Iowa.

Queen City of Canada. Toronto, Ontario.

Queen City of the East. Bangor, Maine.

Queen City of the Lakes. Buffalo, New York; Toronto, Ontario.

Queen City of the Lehigh Valley. Allentown, Pennsylvania.

Queen City of the Merrimack Valley. Manchester, New Hampshire.

Queen City of the Mississippi. St. Louis, Missouri.

Queen City of the Mountains. Knoxville, Tennessee.

Queen City of the Ohio. Cincinnati, Ohio.

Queen City of the Ozarks. Springfield, Missouri.

Queen City of the Pacific. San Francisco, California; Seattle, Washington.

Queen City of the Sea. Charleston, South Carolina.

Queen City of the South. Richmond, Virginia.

Queen City of the Trails. Independence, Missouri.

Queen City of Vermont. Burlington, Vermont.

Queen City on the Sound. Seattle, Washington.

Queen Helen. Wills, Helen [Newington].

Queen Marie of Hollywood. Dressler, Marie.

Queen of American Lakes. Lake George.

Queen of American Pop Music. Lee, Peggy.

Queen of Beaches. Long Beach, California.

Queen of Country Corn. Pearl, Minnie.

Queen of Jazz. Tucker, Sophie; Williams, Mary Lou.

Queen of Lake Michigan. Chicago, Illinois.

Queen of Summer Resorts. Newport, Rhode Island.

Queen of Technicolor. O'Hara, Maureen.

Queen of the American Stage. Marlowe, Julia.

Queen of the Bowery. Prado, Katie.

Queen of the Brazos. Waco, Texas.

Queen of the Comstock Lode. Virginia City, Nevada.

Queen of the Cowgirls. Evans, Dale.

Queen of the Cowtowns. Fort Dodge, Iowa; Dodge City, Kansas.

Queen of the Denver Red Lights. Silks, Mattie.

Queen of the Game Shows. Rose Marie, Baby.

Queen of the Gospel Song. Jackson, Mahalia.

Queen of the Gypsies. Adams, Rose.

Queen of the Hippies. Joplin, Janis.

Queen of the Lakes. Chicago, Illinois.

Queen of the Missions. Santa Barbara, California.

Queen of the Mississippi. St. Louis, Missouri.

Queen of the Mountains. Helena, Montana.

Queen of the Movies. Pickford, Mary.

Queen of the Neches. Beaumont, Texas.

Queen of the Nudists. Cubitt, Tanya.

Queen of the Ohio, Cincinnati, Ohio.

Queen of the Plains. Regina, Saskatchewan.

Queen of the Prairies. Saskatchewan.

Queen of the Prostitutes. Cowan, Sarah.

Queen of the Silent Serials. White, Pearl.

Queen of the South. New Orleans, Louisiana.

Queen of the Spas. Saratoga Springs, New York.

Queen of the Speakeasies. Guinan, Mary Louise Cecelia.

Queen of the Torch Singers. Morgan, Helen.

Queen of the Valley. Glendale, California.

Queen of the Vampires. Bara, Theda.

Queen of the West. 1. Evans, Dale. 2. Cincinnati, Ohio.

Queens. Borough of New York City: **Borough of Homes.**

Queen State. Maryland.

Quentin the Eagle. Roosevelt, Quentin.

Quesada, Elwood Richard (born 1904). U.S. Air Force Lieutenant General: **Pete.**

Quick, The. Werkman, Nick.

Quiet Corrupter. Remus, George B.

Quincy, Josiah (1859–1919). Politician: **Brahmin Democrat.**

Quincy, Massachusetts. U.S. city: **City of Presidents, Granite City, Shipbuilding City.**

Quinlan, Walter (active 1920–30). Gangster: **The Runt.**

Quinn, James (born 1890). Cowboy: **Chicago's Lone Cowhand.**

Quoddy. Passamaquoddy Bay.

R

Rabbi of Swat. Solomon, Moses.

Rabbit. Barnhill, John; Hodges, John Cornelius; Maranville, Walter James Vincent; McNair, Donald Erie; Molesworth, Keith F.; Noto, John J.

Rabbit, The. Patterson, Floyd.

Racine, Wisconsin. U.S. city: **Belle City, Belle City of the Lakes, City of Advantages, Czech Bethlehem, Danish Capital of the United States, Kringleville.**

Racing Legend. Horn, Ted.

Radcliff, Raymond A. (1906–62). Baseball outfielder: **Rip.**

Radcliffe College. Educational institution; with six other women's colleges: **Seven Sisters.**

Rader, Doug[las Lee] (born 1944). Baseball third baseman: **Red Rooster, Rooster.**

Raderman, Harry (active 1920s and 1930s). Jazz musician and trombonist: **Man Who Made the Trombone Laugh.**

Radical Prophet of American Youth. Dylan, Bob.

Radio Priest. Coughlin, Charles Edward.

Radio's Cheerful Little Earful. Little, John.

Radio's First Announcer. Cowan, Thomas H.

Radio's Greatest Commentator. Kaltenborn, H[ans] V[on].

Radio's Own Statue of Liberty. Smith, Kate.

Ragged Stranger, The. Ryan, Edward Joseph.

Ragged Stranger Murderer. Wanderer, Carl.

Ragin' Cajuns. Athletic teams of the University of Southwestern Louisiana, Lafayette.

Ragland, John Morgan Lee (1905–46). Boxer and burlesque and moving-picture comedian: **Rags.**

Raglin, Alvin [Redrick] (1917–55). Jazz bass player: **Junior.**

Rags. Matthews, Raymond; Ragland, John Morgan Lee.

Ragtime Jimmy. Durante, Jimmy.

Ragtown. Cincinnati, Ohio.

Railroad City. Altoona, Pennsylvania; Indianapolis, Indiana.

Railroad Gadfly. Young, Robert Ralph.

Railsplitters. Eighty-fourth Infantry Division.

Rainbow Division. Forty-second Division, American Expeditionary Forces; Forty-second Infantry Division.

Rainbow Warriors. Athletic teams of the University of Hawaii, Honolulu.

Rainey, Gertrude (1886–1939). Blues singer: **Ma.**

Raisin Center of the World. Fresno, California.

Rajah. Hornsby, Rogers.

Rajah of Swat. Hornsby, Rogers.

Raleigh, North Carolina. U.S. city: **City of Oaks, Oak City.**

Ralston Straight Shooter. Mix, Tom.

Ram. Ramirez, Roger.

Rambling Yodeler. Haley, William.

Ramirez, Roger (born 1913). Jazz musician: **Ram.**

Rams. Athletic teams of Colorado State University, Fort Collins; Fordham University, New York City; and the University of Rhode Island, Kingston.

Rand, Sally (1904–79). Fan dancer: **Fan-tastic Sally, Her Sexellency.** Born: Helen Gould Beck.

Randolph, A[sa] Philip (1889–1979). Labor leader: **The Chief, Father of the Civil Rights Movement, Mr. Black Labor.**

Randolph, Irving (born 1909). Jazz trumpeter: **Mouse.**

Randy. Matson, James Randel.

Rankin, John Elliott (1882–1960). Lawyer, politician, and U.S. Representative from Mississippi: **The Killer, T.V.A. Rankin.**

Rapid City. Cedar Rapids, Iowa.

Rapid City, South Dakota. U.S. city: **Denver of South Dakota, Eastern Gateway to the Black Hills, Gateway City of the Hills.**

Rapid Robert. Feller, Bob.

Raskin, Julius (born 1906). Basketball player and coach: **Little Tubby.**

Raskin, Morris (born 1906). Basketball player and coach: **Big Tubby.**

Rat. Rodgers, Ira E.; Thomas, Frank William; Westwick, Harry.

Ratoff, Gregory (1893–1960). Motion-picture director and actor: **Gregory the Great.**

Ratsy. Tourbillon, Robert Arthur.

Rattlers. Athletic teams of Florida A & M University, Tallahassee.

Rattlesnake Murderer. James, Robert.

Ravell, Carl (1910–68). Violinist, saxophonist, and singer: **Singing Maestro.** Born: Carl Ravazza.

Ray. Crawford, Holland R.; Nance, Willis.

Ray, Danny (born 1934). Jazz drummer: **Big Black.**

Ray, Hugh L. (1884–1956). Football official: **Shorty.**

Ray, James Earl (born 1928). Assassin of Dr. Martin Luther King, Jr.: **The Camouflaged Killer, Lovelorn Killer.** Also known as Paul Bridgman, Eric Starvo Gault, Harvey Lowmyer, Ramón George Sneyd, and John Willard.

Rayburn, Sam (1882–1961). U.S. Representative from Texas and Speaker of the House: **Mr. Sam, The Grand Old Man.**

Raymond, Maurice (active after 1950). Magician: **The Great Raymond, Master of Magic.**

Razorbacks. Athletic teams of the University of Arkansas, Fayetteville.

Reading, Pennsylvania. U.S. city: **Pretzel City, Penn's Town, Brewing City.**

Reagan, Ronald (born 1911). Actor and Governor of California: **Mr. Clean, The Most Happy Fellow, The Not-So-Favorite Son.**

Real Mayor of Chicago. Capone, Al[phonse].

Real McCoy. McCoy, Charles; McCoy, William.

Real Western Town, A. Pierre, South Dakota.

Rebel. Oliver, Thomas Noble.

Rebel Congress. First session of the Seventy-sixth Congress, January-August 1939, which opposed New Deal policies.

Rebel of Seventh Avenue. Cassini, Oleg [Loiewski.].

Rebels. Athletic teams of the University of Mississippi, University.

Rebozo, Charles Gregory (born 1912). Banker and real estate executive: **Bebe, The Nixon Family's Closest Friend.**

Recreational Slum. Lake Tahoe, California-Nevada.

Recreation Center. Anaheim, California.

Rector, George (1878–1947). Restaurateur and writer; **Prince of Restaurateurs.**

Red. Ames, Leon Kessling; Barker, George; Blaik, Earl H[enry]; Cagle, Christian K[eener]; Carlson, Henry C[liford]; Cochrane, Freddie; Conway, William; Coolidge, [John] Calvin; Dooin, Charles S[ebastian]; Dutton, Mervyn; Faber, Urban Charles; Flaherty, Ray; Godfrey, Arthur [Michael]; Grange, Harold E[dward]; Grooms, Charles Roger; Hayworth, Myron Claude; Herring, Arthur L.; Hickey, Howard; Jackson, Leonard; Kelly, Leonard Patrick; Kramer, Benjamin; Kress, Ralph; Latham, Dwight; Lewis, [Harry] Sinclair; McDaniel, Robert Hyatt; Matal, Tony; Murray, John Joseph; Owens, Thomas Llewellyn; Quarrier, Sidney; Rocha, Ephraim; Rolfe, Robert A[bial]; Ruffing, Chuck; Smith, James C[arlisle]; Salmon, Louis J.; Sanders, Henry Russell; Schoendienst, Albert Fred; Schlachter, Christopher; Sitko, Emil M.; Smith, Richard Paul; Strader, Norman; Sullivan, George James; Wolfe, George; Worthington, Al[an Fulton].

Red Arrow Division. Thirty-second Infantry Division.

Redbirds. Athletic teams of Illinois State University, Normal.

Red Bull Division. Thirty-fourth Infantry Division.

Red Chamber. The Senate of Canada.

Red Diamond Division. Fifth Infantry Division.

Red Head. Bow, Clara; Godfrey, Arthur [Michael].

Red-headed Kid from Wheeling. Reuther, Walter [Philip].

Red-headed Music-Maker. Hall, Wendell Woods.

Red Lady Mountain. Mount Emmons.

Redlegs. Cincinnati Reds.

Red Light Bandit. Chessman, Caryl.

Red Mike. Edson, Merritt Austin.

Red Necktie. Wearin, Otha Donner.

Red One. First Infantry Division.

Red Raiders. Athletic teams of Colgate University, Hamilton, New York, and Texas Tech University, Lubbock.

Red Rooster. Rader, Doug[las] Lee.

Reds. Klotz, Herman.

Redskins. Athletic teams of Miami University, Oxford, Ohio.

Red Star Division. Sixth Infantry Division.

Red Stockings. Cincinnati Reds.

Redwine, Wilbur (born 1926). Composer and pianist: **Skip.**

Reece, Al[phonso Son] (born 1931). Jazz trumpeter: **Dizzy.**

Reed, Nathaniel (1862–1950). Outlaw and evangelist: **Texas Jack.**

Reed, Thomas Brackett (1839–1902). U.S. Representative from Maine: **Czar Reed, Terrible Turk.**

Reed, Walter (1851–1902). Physician and U.S. Army surgeon: **Conqueror of Yellow Fever.**

Reese. Markewich, Maurice.

Reese, Harold Henry (born 1919). Baseball shortstop: **Pee Wee.**

Reese, Mason (born 1966). Child television actor: **Borgasmord Kid, Seven-Year-Old Huckster.**

Regan, Phil[ip] (born 1908). Singer and actor: **Singing Policeman.**

Regina, Saskatchewan. Canadian city: **Queen of the Plains.**

Reid, Joseph (born 1954). Poet and karate expert: **Karate Poet.**

Reilly, Edward J. (active 1930s). Criminal Lawyer: **Big Ed, Brother Reilly, Death House Reilly.**

Reincarnated Troubadour. Seeger, Pete[r].

Reindeer Bill. Killefer, William Lavier.

Reinhardt, S. Louis, Jr. (born 1899). Football player: **Spider.**

Reisor, Lawrence (active 1920s). Football player: **Smack.**

Reles, Abe (1908–41). Gangster, racketeer, and police informer: **Kid Twist, Singing Canary.** Born: Abraham Reles.

Rembrandt of the Comic Strip. Caniff, Milt[on Arthur].

Rembrandt of the Lens. Weston, Edward.

Rembrandt of the West. Remington, Frederic.

Remick, Lee (born 1935). Actress: **America's Answer to Brigitte Bardot.**

Remington, Frederic (1861–1909). Illustrator, painter, sculptor, and war correspondent: **Rembrandt of the West.**

Remus, George B. (1873–1952). Gangster and bootlegger: **King of the Bootleggers, Quiet Corrupter, Gentle Grafter.**

Rena, Henry (1898–1949). Jazz trumpeter: **Kid.**

Renaissance City of America. Pittsburgh, Pennsylvania.

Renegade Newspaper Heiress. Hearst, Patricia [Campbell].

Reno, Nevada. U.S. city: **Biggest Little City, Biggest Little City in the World, Center of Summer and Winter Sports, Glitter Gulch.**

Rentzel, [Thomas] Lance (active 1960s and 1970s). Football end: **Bambi.**

Resch, Glenn (born 1948). Hockey goalie: **Chico.**

Research Center of the Midwest. Ann Arbor, Michigan.

Restless Troubadour. Belafonte, Harry.

Retirement Center of the Nation. Tucson, Arizona.

Reuben. Award of the National Cartoonists Society.

Reulbach, Edward Marvin (1882–1961). Baseball pitcher: **Big Ed.**

Reuther, Walter [Philip] (1907–70). Labor leader: **Labor's Rugged Individualist, Red-headed Kid from Wheeling.**

Revlon Cosmetics King. Revson, Charles [Haskell].

Rev Moishe. Feinstein, Moshe.

Revson, Charles [Haskell] (1907–75). Cosmetics and fragrance manufacturer: **Revlon Cosmetics King.**

Revson, Peter (1939–74). Automobile racing driver: **Glamor Boy of the Race Drivers.**

Rey, Alvino (born 1909). Jazz musician: **King of the Electric Guitar.** Born: Albert McBurney.

Reynolds, Allie (born 1919). Baseball pitcher: **The Chief, Wahoo.** Legal name: Albert Pierce Reynolds.

Reynolds, Burt (born 1936). Actor: **Frog Prince.**

Reynolds, Robert Rice (1884–1963). U.S. Senator from North Carolina: **Our Bob, The Playboy.**

RFK. Kennedy, Robert F[rancis].

Rhem, Charles Flint (1901–69). Baseball pitcher: **Shad.**

Rhode Island. Thirteenth U.S. state: **American Venice, Land of Roger Williams, Little Rhody, Ocean State, Plantation State.**

Rhode Island, University of, athletic teams of: **Rams.**

Rhode Island Red. Native or resident of Rhode Island.

Rhodes, Eugene Manlove (1869–1934). Author: **Hired Man on Horseback, Novelist of the Cattle Kingdom.**

Rhodes, James Lamar (born 1927). Baseball outfielder: **Dusty.**

Rhodes, John Gordon (1907–60). Baseball pitcher: **Dusty.**

Ricca, Paul (1897–1972). Gangster: **The Porter, Mops, The Waiter.** Also known as Paul Barstow, Anthony Delucia, Paul Maglio, Paul Salvi, Paul Viela, Paul Villa.

Rice. Aiken, Gus.

Rice, [Henry] Grantland (1880–1954). Sports writer: **Granny.**

Rice Bowl. Football stadium of Rice University, Houston, Texas.

Rice State. South Carolina.

Rice University, athletic teams of: **Owls.**

Rich, Buddy (born 1917). Jazz drummer: **Baby Traps.** Legal name: Bernard Rich.

Rich, Robert Fleming (1883–1968). U.S. Representative from Pennsylvania: **Woolly Bob.**

Richard, Henri (born 1936). Canadian hockey player: **The Pocket Rocket.**

Richard, Maurice [Joseph Henri] (born 1921). Canadian hockey player: **The Rocket, Babe Ruth of Hockey.**

Richards, George (active 1928). Gambler: **Hump, Humpty.** Legal name: George McManus.

Richardson, Elliot Lee (born 1920). Lawyer and U.S. Attorney General: **Mr. Clean.**

Richard the Ruffian. Afflis, Richard.

Richest Hill on Earth. Butte, Montana.

Richest Man in Canada. Bronfman, Samuel.

Richest Man in the World. Bronfman, Edgar; Getty, J[ean] Paul, Sr.

Richfield Reporter, The. Hayes, Sam[uel].

Richman, Abraham Samuel (born 1921). Jazz musician: **Boomie.**

Richmond, University of, athletic teams of: **Spiders.**

Richmond, Virginia. U.S. city: **Capital of the Confederacy, Capital of the Old South, City of Monuments, City of Seven Hills, Cockade City, Queen City of the South.**

Rickard, Tex (1870–1929). Prize-fight promoter: **Dink, King of Sports Promoters, Magnificent Rube, Napoleon of Promoters.** Legal name: George Lewis Rickard.

Rickenbacker, Eddie (1890–1973). World War I flying ace, automobile racer, and airline executive: **Ace of Aces, Captain Eddie.** Legal name: Edward Vernon Rickenbacker.

Rickey, Branch [Wesley] (1881–1965). Baseball executive: **The Brain, The Mahatma.**

Rickles, Don (born 1926). Comedian: **Merchant of Venom, Mr. Warmth.**

Rickover, Hyman [George] (born 1900). U.S. Navy Admiral: **Father of the Atomic Submarine.**

Rico. Petrocelli, Americo Peter.

Riebel, Frederick, Jr. (1884–1948). Business executive: **Skip.**

Rifle. Waterfield, Robert S.

Rifle City. Springfield, Massachusetts.

Riggs, Bobby (born 1918). Tennis player: **Chicken Plucker, White Muhammad Ali.** Legal name: Robert Larimore Riggs.

Right Reverend New Dealer. Ryan, John A.

Riley, James Whitcomb (1849–1916). Poet: **Hoosier Poet.**

Ring Gorilla. Bloom, Phil.

Ringling, John (1866–1936). Circus owner: **Circus King.**

Ringmaster, The. Mencken, H[enry] L[ouis].

Rio Grande Valley. Valley on the U.S.-Mexican border: **Valley Between Two Worlds.**

Rip. Bassett, Arthur; Collins, Harry Warren; Collins, James Anthony; Connally, George Walter; Radcliff, Raymond A.

Ripper. Collins, James Anthony.

Ripper, The. Roberts, Jack.

Risberg, Charles August (1894–1975). Baseball shortstop: **Swede.**

Risko, Eddie (1911–57). Middleweight boxer: **Babe.** Born: Henry Pylkowski.

Risko, Johnny (1902–53). Heavyweight boxer: **Cleveland's Tireless Heavyweight, Cleveland Rubber Man, The Spoiler.**

River of Grass. Everglades, The.

River of the North. Yukon.

Riverside, California. U.S. city: **Home of the Orange, Mission City.**

Rivet. McClintic, James Vernon.

Riviera of America. Miami Beach, Florida.

Rixey, Eppa, Jr. (1891–1963). Baseball pitcher: **Jephtha.**

Rizzo, Frank (born 1920). Police chief and mayor of Philadelphia: **Supercop, Toughest Cop in America.**

Rizzuto, Phil[ip Francis] (born 1917). Baseball shortstop: **The Kid, Little Monkey, Scooter.**

Road Runner. Garr, Ralph Allen.

Roadrunner. Native or resident of New Mexico.

Roadrunner, The. Cournoyer, Yvan [Serge].

Roanoke, Virginia. U.S. city: **Star City of the South.**

Roberts, C. Luckeyth (born 1893). Musician: **Luckey.**

Roberts, Jack (active 1929–31). Football player: **Jack the Ripper, The Ripper.**

Roberts, Maurice (born 1905). Hockey player: **Moe.**

Roberts, Owen Josephus (1875–1955). Associate Justice of the U.S. Supreme Court: **Great Dissenter.**

Roberts, Theodore (1861–1928). Motion-picture actor: **Dad, Grand Old Man of the Screen.**

Roberts, Walter (active 1964–70). Football back and end: **Flea.**

Robertson, George Hepburn (1885–1955). Pioneer automobile racing driver, soldier, and business executive: **The First Great Racer.**

Robertson, James B. (born 1910). Country music singer: **Texas Jim.**

Robertson, Oscar [Palmer] (born 1938). Basketball player: **Big O, Oz.**

Robin. Hantz, Robert.

Robinson, Bill (1878–1949). Tap dancer: **Bojangles.**

Robinson, Brooks [Calbert, Jr.] (born 1937). Baseball third baseman: **Bobby the Robber, Mr. Impossible, Vacuum Cleaner.**

Robinson, Ikey L. (born 1904). Jazz musician: **Banjo.**

Robinson, Jackie (1919–72). Baseball player: **America's First Negro Big Leaguer.** Born: John Roosevelt Robinson.

Robinson, James D., III (born 1935). Businessman: **Jimmy Three Sticks.**

Robinson, Len (born 1951). Basketball player: **Truck.**

Robinson, Ray (born 1921). Middleweight boxer: **Sugar Ray.** Born: Walker Smith.

Rocha, Ephraim (born 1923). Basketball center and coach: **Red.**

Rochester, Minnesota. U.S. city, location of the Mayo Clinic: **Scientific Lourdes.**

Rochester, New York. U.S. city: **Aqueduct City, City Built by Hands, City of Homes, City of Varied Industries, Friendliest City, Flour City, Flower City, Kodak City, Power City, Photography Capital, Quality City, Snapshot City.**

Rochester, University of, athletic teams of: **Yellow Jackets.**

Rock. Rockne, Knute Kenneth.

Rock, The. 1. Alcatraz Federal Prison. 2. Graziano, Rocky.

Rockabye Rocky. Graziano, Rocky.

Rock Around the Clock Haley. Haley, William.

Rock City. Nashville, Tennessee.

Rockefeller, Barbara [Sears] (born 1917). First wife of Winthrop Rockefeller: **Bobo.**

Rockefeller, John D[avison] (1839–1937). Oil tycoon, industrialist, and philanthropist: **John D., Oil Baron, Standard Oil King.**

Rockefeller, Margaretta [Fitler] (born 1926). Wife of Nelson Rockefeller: **Happy.**

Rockefeller, Nelson [Aldrich] (1908–79). Governor of New York, U.S. Vice President, and art collector: **Dean of American Governors, Mr. Clean, Old Nels, Rocky, Spendthrift of Albany.**

Rocket, The. Richard, Maurice [Joseph Henri].

Rocket Capital of the Nation. Huntsville, Alabama.

Rocket City, U.S.A. Huntsville, Alabama.

Rockets. Athletic teams of the University of Toledo, Toledo, Ohio, and Slippery Rock State College, Slippery Rock, Pennsylvania.

Rocking Chair Lady. Bailey, Mildred.

Rockne, Knute Kenneth (1888–1931). Football coach: **Rock, Rock of Notre Dame, The Great Man.**

Rock of Notre Dame. Rockne, Knute Kenneth.

Rock of the Marne. 1. McAlexander, Ulysses Grant. 2. Third Division.

Rockwell, George E. (born 1926). Banker: **Banking's Technocrat.**

Rockwell, Norman (1894–1978). Artist: **Illustrator of Early Twentieth-century America.**

Rocky. Gilbert, Rod[rique]; Godfrey, Warren Edward; Millard, Edward R.; Nelson, Glenn Richard; Rockefeller, Nelson [Aldrich]; Stone, John Thomas.

Rocky Mountain Empire. Colorado.

Rocky Mountains. North American mountain chain: **Backbone of the Continent, Backbone of North America, Roof of the Continent.**

Roddey Burdine Memorial Stadium. Football stadium in Miami, Florida; site of annual Orange Bowl college football game: **Orange Bowl.**

Rodeheaver, Homer A[llen] (1880–1955). Evangelist, hymn writer, and publisher: **Rodey.**

Rodey. Rodeheaver, Homer A[llen].

Rodgers, Ira E. (1895–1963). Football player: **Rat.**

Rodomontade, The. Clarke, Norham Pfardt.

Rodriguez, Juan (born 1935). Golfer: **Chi Chi.**

Roe, Elwin Charles (born 1915). Baseball pitcher: **Preacher.**

Roebuck, Theodore (active 1925). Football player: **Tiny.**

Rogan, Wilbur (1893–1967). Baseball player and manager: **Bullet Joe.**

Rogers, Bruce (1870–1957). Book designer: **Master of the Typographical Art.**

Rogers, Buddy (born 1904). Motion-picture actor and bandleader: **America's Boyfriend.** Legal name: Charles Rogers.

Rogers, Roy (born 1912). Motion-picture singer and actor: **World's Top Boots-and-Saddle Star.** Born: Leonard Slye.

Rogers, Shorty (born 1924). Composer, jazz musician, and trumpeter: **The Elder Statesman, Modern King of Swing.** Legal name: Milton M. Rogers.

Rogers, Will (1879–1935). Humorist and actor: **Ambassador of Good Will, Cherokee Kid, Cowboy Philosopher, Man Who Can Say Anything and Make Everybody Like It, Prince of Wit and Wisdom.** Legal name: William Penn Adair Rogers.

Roger the Terrible. Touhy, Roger.

Roger Williams City. Providence, Rhode Island.

Rohatyn, Felix G. (born 1928). Investment banker: **Felix the Fixer.**

Rojas, Octavio [Rivas] (born 1939). Baseball infielder: **Cookie.**

Roland. Kirk, Ronald T.

Rolfe, Robert A[bial] (1908–69). Baseball third baseman and manager: **Red.**

Rolling W. Eighty-ninth Infantry Division.

Romney, George (born 1907). Business executive and Governor of Michigan: **Lonesome George.**

Roof of the Continent. Rocky Mountains.

Rooney, Pat, II (1880–1962). Dancer and entertainer: **Vaudeville's Ageless Song and Dance Man.**

Roosevelt, [Anna] Eleanor [Roosevelt] (1884–1962). Humanitarian and wife of President Franklin D. Roosevelt: **First Lady of the World, World's Most Admired Woman.**

Roosevelt, Franklin D[elano] (1882–1945). Thirty-second President of the United States: **FDR, The Boss, Houdini in the White House, Roosevelt II, Squire of Hyde Park, The Sphinx, That Man in the White House.** With Winston Churchill of Great Britain and Joseph Stalin of the U.S.S.R.: **Big Three.**

Roosevelt, James (born 1907). Son of and assistant to President Franklin D. Roosevelt: **Crown Prince of the New Deal, Modern Mercury, Son Jimmy.**

Roosevelt, Quentin (1897–1918). Aviator: **Quentin the Eagle.**

Roosevelt, Theodore (1858–1919). Twenty-sixth President of the United States: **Bull Moose, Driving Force, Dynamo of Power,**

Four Eyes, Great White Chief, Happy Warrior, Haroun-al-Roosevelt, Hero of San Juan Hill, Man on Horseback, The Meddler, Old Lion, Roosevelt I, Rough Rider, Teddy, Telescope Teddy, Theodore the Meddler, Trust-Buster, Trust-busting President, Typical American.

Roosevelt I. Roosevelt, Theodore.

Roosevelt II. Roosevelt, Franklin D[elano].

Rooster. Rader, Doug[las Lee].

Rope. O'Brien, James C.

Roper, Daniel Calhoun (1867–1943). Politician and lawyer: **Chief Executioner.**

Roper, Elmo (1901–71). Public opinion surveyor and analyst: **The Opinion Forecaster.**

Rory. Calhoun, Herman.

Rose, Billy (1899–1966). Theatrical producer, song writer, and shorthand expert: **Basement Barnum.** Born: William Samuel Rosenberg.

Rose, Mauri (born 1906). Automobile racing driver: **Man With The Mustache, Top Wheel at the Brickyard.**

Rose, Pete[r Edward] (born 1941). Baseball second and third baseman and outfielder: **Charlie Hustle.**

Rose, The. Rosenman, Samuel Irving.

Rose, William (born 1906). Banker: **The Generous Lender.**

Roseboro, John H. (born 1933). Baseball catcher: **Gabby.**

Rose Bowl. Pasadena Stadium.

Rose City. Portland, Oregon.

Rose Marie, Baby (born 1926). Child radio star and adult television performer: **Barney, Darling of the Air, Five-year-old Child Wonder, Queen of the Game Shows.** Born: Rose Marie Mazeppa.

Rosemary's Baby. List of secret donors who contributed illegal funds to the 1972 Nixon presidential reelection campaign.

Rosen, Al[bert Leonard] (born 1925). Baseball first and third baseman: **Flip.**

Rosenbaum, Louis Charles (1899–1954). Gambler: **Rosey.**

Rosenbloom, Maxie (1903–76). Light-heavyweight boxer and motion-picture actor: **Slapsie Maxie.** Born: Max Rosenbloom.

Rosenfeld, Sigmund (died 1922). Gambler: **Beansie, Honorable Rosenfeld.**

Rosenman, Samuel Irving (1896–1973). Judge and politician: **The Rose, Sammy the Rose.**

Rosenthal, Leonard (1872?–1955). Pearl dealer: **Pearl King of the World.**

Rose's Lobbygow. Schepps, Samuel.

Rosey. Grier, Roosevelt; Rosenbaum, Louis Charles; Rowswell, Albert K.

Rosie. Walker, Nancy.

Rosy. Caldwell, Herschel; McHargue, James Eugene; O'Donnell, Emmett, Jr.

Rotary Ann. Wife of a Rotarian.

Roth, Sam (1903?–51). Ticket broker: **Broadway Sam.**

Rothafel, Samuel Lionel (1881–1936). Theatrical producer and impresario: **Motion Picture Palace Potentate, Roxy.**

Rothstein, Arnold (1882–1928). Gambler: **The Big Bankroll, The Brain, Czar of the New York Underworld, The Dedicated Gambler, The Man to See, The Man Uptown, Master of Crime, Mr. A.A.R., Mr. Big, King of Gamblers.**

Rough Carrigan. Carrigan, William Francis.

Rough Rider. Roosevelt, Theodore.

Roundheels. Boyer, Mary Ann.

Round Man. Munson, Thurman [Lee].

Roundsman of the Lord. Comstock, Anthony.

Route 66. U.S. federal highway between Chicago and Los Angeles: **Main Street of America.**

Rowdy Dick. Bartell, Richard.

Rowdy Richard. Bartell, Richard.

Rowe, Lynwood Thomas (born 1912). Baseball pitcher: **Schoolboy.**

Rowell, Carvel William (born 1917). Baseball infielder and outfielder: **Bama.**

Rowland, Clarence H. (1879–1969). Baseball manager and umpire: **Pants.**

Rowswell, Albert K. (1883–1955). Sports announcer: **Rosey.**

Roxey. Crouch, Jack Albert.

Roxy. Rothafel, Samuel Lionel.

Roy, Leo (1906–55). Featherweight and lightweight boxer: **Kid.** Also known as Leo Paradis.

Royal City. Santa Fe, New Mexico.

Rubber Arm. Connally, George Walter.

Rubber Capital of the United States. Akron, Ohio.

Rubber City. Akron, Ohio.

Rubber King. Harter, Dow Watters.

Rubberlegs. Guttero, Lee.

Rube. Benton, John Cleveland; Bressler, Raymond Bloom; Caldwell, Raymond Benjamin; Marquardt, Richard William; Waddell, George Edward; Walberg, George Elvin.

Rubinstein, Arthur (born 1889). Pianist: **Playboy of the Piano.**

Ruby, Jack (1911–67). Nightclub owner and killer of Lee Harvey Oswald: **Assassin's Assassin.**

Rucker, George Napoleon (1884–1970). Baseball pitcher: **Nap.**

Rudd, W. L. (1845–1938). Soldier and Western ranger: **Colorado Chico, Little Red.**

Rudolph, Marvin (1938–79). Basketball referee: **Mendy.**

Rudolph, Richard (1887–1949). Baseball pitcher: **Baldy.**

Rudolph, Wilma [Glodean] (born 1940). Olympic runner: **Skeeter.**

Rudy. Powell, Everard Stephen, Sr.

Rudy the Omelet Man. Stanish, Rudolph.

Ruel, Herold D. (1896–1963). Baseball catcher and coach: **Muddy.**

Ruether, Walter Henry (1893–1970). Baseball pitcher and manager: **Dutch.**

Ruffing, Chuck (born 1904). Baseball pitcher: **Red.** Legal name: Charles Herbert Ruffing.

Rum Row. Line of hovering vessels carrying liquor for unlawful importation into the United States during Prohibition.

Running of the Roses, The. The Kentucky Derby.

Runt. Bishop, Cecil W.

Runt, The. Quinlan, Walter.

Runyon, [Alfred] Damon (1880–1946). Author and columnist: **Sentimental Cynic.**

Rupp, Adolph Frederick (1901–77). Basketball coach: **Baron of Bluegrass Country.**

Ruppert, Jacob, Sr. (1867–1939). Brewer and baseball club owner: **The Colonel, Four Straight Jake.**

Rushing, Jimmy (1903–72). Jazz singer: **Mr. Five by Five.** Legal name: James Andrew Rushing.

Rusie, Amos Wilson (1871–1942). Baseball pitcher: **Hoosier Thunderbolt.**

Rusin, Irving (born 1911). Jazz saxophonist: **Babe.**

Rusk, [David] Dean (born 1909). Educator and U.S. Secretary of State: **Old Dino.**

Russell, Bill (born 1934). Basketball player and coach: **Big Bill.**

Russell, Charles [Ellsworth] (1906–69). Jazz clarinetist: **Pee Wee.**

Russell, Charles Taze (1852–1916). Religious leader: **Pastor.**

Russell, Dillon (born 1920). Jazz bass player: **Curly.**

Russell, Frank M. (1895–1972). Television executive: **Scoop.**

Russell, John (1903–73). Basketball coach: **Honey.**

Rusty. Calley, William Laws; Gill, Ralph.

Russian Connection. Hammer, Armand.

Rutgers—The State University, Athletic teams of: **Scarlet Knights.**

Ruth, Babe (1895–1948). Baseball player, noted for hitting home runs: **Bambino, Idol of the American Boy, King of Swat, Sultan of Swat.** Legal name: George Herman Ruth.

Ruther, Wyatt (born 1923). Jazz bass player: **Bull.**

Rutkin, James (1900–56). Prohibition-era rumrunner: **Niggy.**

Rutland, Vermont. U.S. city: **Marble City.**

Ryan, Edward Joseph (died 1920). Murder victim: **The Ragged Stranger.**

Ryan, John A. (1860–1945). Priest, social reformer, and writer: **Right Reverend New Dealer.**

Ryan, John Collins (1906–59). Baseball shortstop: **Blondy.**

S

Sabath, Adolph Joachim (1866–1952). U.S. Representative from Illinois: **Dean of the House.**

Sabich, Vladimir (1946–1976). Professional skier: **Spider.**

Sabre. North American F-86A fighter plane, Korean War.

Sabreliner. North American T-39 jet training plane.

Sabrinas, The. Athletic teams of Amherst College, Amherst, Massachusetts.

Sac. Sacramento, California.

Sacco, Nicola (1891–1927). Anarchist executed (after widely publicized trial and appeal) for murder committed in South Braintree, Massachusetts in 1921. With Bartolomeo Vanzetti: **Braintree Martyrs.**

Sacramento, California. U.S. city: **Almond Capital of the World, Camellia Capital, City of the Plains, City of Trees, Heart of California, Sac, Sacto.**

Sacramento Solons. Baseball team in Sacramento, California (active after 1925).

Sacto. Sacramento, California.

Saddler, Joseph (born 1926). Featherweight boxer: **Sandy.**

Sad Sam. Jones, Samuel Pond.

Sadulpa Giant. Morris, Carl.

Sagebush State. Nevada; Wyoming.

Sagehen. Native or resident of Nevada.

Sagehen State. Nevada.

Sage of Baltimore. Mencken, H[enry] L[ouis].

Sage of Emporia. White, William Allen.

Sage of Happy Valley. Taylor, Alfred Alexander.

Sage of Hickory Hill. Watson, Thomas Edward.

Sage of McDuffie. Watson, Thomas Edward.

Sage of Potato Hill. Howe, Edgar Watson.

Sage of the Make-Believe World. Belasco, David.

Sage of Tishomingo. Murray, William Henry.

Sage of Uvalde. Garner, John Nance.

Sage State. Nevada.

Saginaw Kid. Lavigne, Kid.

Sailor. Kelly, Alvin Anthony.

Sailor City. San Diego, California.

Sailor Town. Norfolk, Virginia.

Saintly City. St. Paul Minnesota.

Saints. Athletic teams of St. Lawrence University, Canton, New York.

Saints' Rest. Oak Park, Illinois.

Sakall, S. Z. (1884–1955). Motion-picture actor: **Cuddles.** Born: Szoke Szakall.

Salad Bowl. Salinas Valley, California.

Salad Oil King. De Angelis, Anthony.

Salem, Massachusetts. U.S. city: **City of Peace, City of Witches, New England's Treasure House, Witch City.**

Salem, Oregon. U.S. city: **Cherry City.**

Salesman De Luxe. Hammer, Armand.

Salinas Valley, California. Fertile region in central California: **Lettuce Bowl, Salad Bowl.**

Salinger, Pierre (born 1925). Newsman, writer, presidential press secretary, and television commentator: **Plucky.**

Sallee, Harry Franklin (1885–1950). Baseball pitcher: **Slim.**

Sally Ann. Salvation Army.

Salmon, Louis J. (1880–1965). Football player: **Red.**

Salt. Walther, David.

Salt City. Syracuse, New York.

Saltis, Joseph (active 1920–30). Criminal: **Polock Joe.**

Salt Lake City, **U.S.S.** Cruiser, World War II: **One Ship Fleet.**

Salt Lake City, Utah. U.S. city: **City of the Saints, Mormon City, New Jerusalem, Utah Zion.**

Salt Lake State. Utah.

Salty. Parker, Francis James.

Salukis. Athletic teams of Southern Illinois University, Carbondale.

Salvation Army. Missionary organization: **Sally Ann.**

Sam. Mele, Sabath Anthony.

SAM. Surface-to-air missile.

Sammons, James (active 1920–30). Criminal: **Fur.**

Sammy Glick of the Cold War. Kissinger, Henry A[lfred].

Sammy the Rose. Rosenman, Samuel Irving.

Sam the Torch. Scarlow, Samuel.

Samuels, Howard J. (born 1919). Government official, industrialist, and president of New York Off-Track Betting Corporation: **Howie the Horse, OTB Czar.**

Samuels, Rae (active 1920s and 1930s). Entertainer: **Blue Streak of Vaudeville.**

Samuels, Samuel Earl (born 1876). Baseball third baseman: **Ike.**

Samurai in a Tam O'Shanter. Hayakawa, Samuel Ichiye.

San Antone. San Antonio, Texas.

San Antonio, Texas. U.S. city: **Alamo City, Citadel of History, City of Missions, Cradle of Texas Liberty, Home of the Alamo, Mission City, Old Garrison, St. Anthony's Town, San Antone, Santone.**

San Berdoo. San Bernardino, California.

San Bernardino, California. U.S. city: **City of Mineral Springs, Gate City, San Berdoo.**

Sand Cutter. Native or resident of Arizona.

Sande, Earl H. (1898–1968). Jockey and racehorse trainer: **Great Jockey of the Golden Age of Sports.**

Sanders, Farrell (born 1940). Jazz saxophonist: **Pharaoh.**

Sanders, Harland (born 1891). Restaurateur: **The Colonel, Colonel Sanders, Fried Chicken King.**

Sanders, Henry Russell (1905–58). Football coach: **Red.**

Sanders, Homer J., II (born 1967). Child motorcycle racer: **Dinger.**

Sanders, Joseph L. (1896–1965). Jazz musician: **Old Lefthander.**

Sanderson, Derek [Michael] (born 1946). Canadian hockey player: **Turk.**

Sand Hill State. Arizona.

San Diego, California. U.S. city: **Air Capital of the West, Bag Town, Birthplace of California, City by the Sea, City in Motion, City of the Silver Gate, Dago, Gateway to California, Jewel City of California, Sailor City, Sandy.**

San Diego State University, athletic teams of: **Aztecs.**

Sandy. Herring, Arthur L.; O'Brien, John T.; Saddler, Joseph; San Diego, California; Vance, Joseph Albert.

San Fran. San Francisco, California.

San Francisco, California. U.S. city: **Baghdad by the Bay, Bay City, City by the Golden Gate, Cisco, City of a Hundred Hills, City That Knows How, Cosmopolitan City, Cultural Center of the West, Frisco** (not used by natives), **Financial Center of the West, Golden Gate City, Last Lovely City, Paris of America, Porn Capital of America, Queen City of the Pacific, San Fran, Western Gate.**

Sanger, Margaret [Higgins] (1883–1966). Nurse, author, and reformer: **Founder of the Birth Control Movement.**

San Jac. San Jacinto, California.

San Jacinto, California. U.S. city: **San Jac.**

San Jose, California. U.S. city: **Garden City.**

San Jose State University, athletic teams of: **Spartans.**

San Leandro, California. U.S. city: **San Le.**

San Quentin Six. Six persons tried for murder during an escape attempt at San Quentin Penitentiary, 1971.

Sansan. Urbanized area between San Francisco and San Leandro, California.

Santa Ana, California. U.S. city: **City of Resources.**

Santa Barbara, California. U.S. city: **Channel City, City by the Sea, Newport of the Pacific, Queen of the Missions.**

Sante Fe, New Mexico. U.S. city: **Capital City Different, Royal City.**

Santa Fe Division. Thirty-fifth Infantry Division.

Santa Ship. Vessel of the Grace Line, routinely given the Spanish name of a female saint.

Santley, Joseph H. (1886–1962). Theatrical performer and songwriter: **Banjo.**

Santone. San Antonio, Texas.

Saperstein, Abraham (1901–66). Athlete and founder of the Harlem Globetrotters: **Barnum of Basketball.**

Sarasota, Florida. U.S. city: **City of Attractions.**

Saratoga Springs, New York. U.S. city: **City of Trees, Inevitable Spa City, Queen of the Spas.**

Sarge. Bagby, James Charles Jacob, Sr.; Connally, George Walter; Shriver, [Robert] Sargent.

Sarge, The. Moody, Orville.

Sarong Girl. Lamour, Dorothy.

Saskatchewan. Canadian province: **Breadbasket of Canada, Canada's Breadbasket, Central Prairie Province, Queen of the Prairies.**

Saskatoon, Saskatchewan. Canadian city: **Potash City.**

Sassafras. Welsh, Johnnie; Winter, George L.

Satchel. Paige, Leroy Robert.

Satchmo. Armstrong, Louis.

Saturday Fox. Meyer, Leo Robert.

Saturday Night Massacre, The. Dismissal, by President Richard M. Nixon on October 20, 1973, of special prosecutor Archibald Cox, who had demanded Watergate tapes, and resignations of Attorney General Elliot L. Richardson and Deputy Attorney General William D. Ruckelshaus, who had refused to fire Cox.

Sault Ste. Marie, Michigan. U.S. city: **Soo.**

Saunders, Clarence (1881–1953). Chain store operator: **Keydoozler, Piggly Wiggly Man.**

Savage, David (1947–73). Automobile racing driver: **Swede.**

Savannah, Georgia. U.S. city: **City of Historical Charm, City of Southern Charm, Cradle of Georgia, First City of the South, Forest City, Georgia's Oldest City, Garden City, Mother City of Georgia.**

Savior of Terre Haute. Martin, Anne.

Savior of the Constitution. Bloom, Sol.

Savoldi, Joseph (1909–74). Football back and wrestler: **Jumping Joe.**

Savransky, Morris (born 1929). Baseball pitcher: **Moe.**

Sawbuck. Sears, Roebuck and Company.

Sawdust City. Minneapolis, Minnesota.

Saxbe, William B[art] (born 1916). U.S. Senator from Ohio and U.S. Attorney General: **Old Blunderbuss.**

Saxie. Dowell, Horace Kirby.

Sayers, Gale (born 1943). Football back: **Magic.**

Say Hey Kid. Mays, Willie [Howard].

Scalise, Frank (1914–1957). Gangster: **Don Cheech.**

Scarface. Capone, Al[phonse].

Scarlet Knights. Athletic teams of Rutgers—The State University, New Brunswick, New Jersey.

Scarlow, Samuel (born 1888). Arsonist: **Sam the Torch.**

Scarne, John (born 1903). Author and expert on gambling: **The Professor, Virtuous Card Shark.**

Scat Man. Crothers, Sherman.

Scenic Center of the South. Chattanooga, Tennessee.

Scenic State. New Hampshire.

Schacht, Al[exander] (born 1892). Baseball pitcher and comedian: **Clown Prince of Baseball.** Also known as Murray Goodman.

Schaefer, Herman, Sr. (1855–1909). Billiards player: **Wizard.**

Schaefer, Herman A. (1877–1919). Baseball second baseman and outfielder: **Germany.**

Schaftel, Albert S. (born 1912). U.S. Army officer: **Brooklyn Rabbit, Foist Lieutenant.**

Schalk, Raymond William (1892–1970). Baseball catcher and manager: **Cracker.**

Scharein, Arthur Otto (1905–69). Baseball infielder: **Scoop.**

Scheer, Henry William (1900–76). Baseball second baseman: **Heinie.**

Schenck, Joseph M. (1882–1961). Motion-picture producer: **Uncle Joe.**

Schenectady, New York. U.S. city: **Electric City, Old Dorp.**

Schepps, Samuel (active 1912). Gambler: **Beau Brummel of Vagrants, Missing Witness, Murder Paymaster, Rose's Lobbygow.**

Schifrin, Boris (born 1932). Jazz pianist and composer: **Lalo.**

Schlachter, Christopher (active 1915). Football player: **Red.**

Schlock Rock's Godzilla. Cooper, Alice.

Schmaltz King. Lombardo, Guy [Albert].

Schmidt, Charles John (1886–1952). Baseball first baseman: **Butch, Butcher Boy.**

Schmidt, Maynard (born 1909). Criminal and procurer: **Short Pants Bully.**

Schmitt, Jack (born 1935). Geologist and astronaut: **Captain America, Dr. Rock, First Scientist in Space.** Legal name: Harrison Hagan Schmitt.

Schnabel, Martha (born 1926). Policewoman: **Officer Mama.**

Schneidman, Herman (born 1913), Football quarterback: **Biff.**

Schnozz, The. Durante, Jimmy.

Schnozzola. Durante, Jimmy.

Schoendienst, Albert Fred (born 1923). Baseball second baseman and manager: **Red.**

Schoenhaus, Isadore (active 1912). Criminal and taxi driver: **Itch.**

Schoolboy. Cohen, Alta Albert; Rowe, Lynwood Thomas.

Schoolmaster in Politics. Wilson, [Thomas] Woodrow.

Schuble, Henry George, Jr. (born 1906). Baseball shortstop and third baseman: **Heinie.**

Schulmerich, [Edward] Wes[ley] (born 1902). Baseball outfielder and football player: **Iron Horse.**

Schulte, Frank (1882–1949). Baseball outfielder: **Wildfire.**

Schultz, David (born 1950). Canadian hockey player: **The Hammer.**

Schultz, Dutch. Gangster: **Dutchman.** Born: Arthur Flegenheimer.

Schulz, Adolph George (1883–1951). Football center and coach: **Germany.**

Schulz, Charles M[onroe] (born 1922). Cartoonist: **Sparky.**

Schumann-Heink, Ernestine [Rössler] (1861–1936). Operatic contralto: **Grand Old Lady of Opera, Mother of All the Doughboys, Mother of the American Legion.**

Schuster, Arnold (1927?–52). Salesman and murder victim after identification of bank robber: **Good Citizen.**

Schwab, Frank John (1895–1965). Football player: **Dutch.**

Schwartz, Issy (born 1902). Flyweight boxer. **Corporal.**

Schwartz, Maurice (1890–1960). Actor: **Leading Figure of the Yiddish Theater.**

Scientific Lourdes. Rochester, Minnesota.

Scissors. Mayer, Erskine.

Scoop. Jackson, Henry [Martin]; Russell, Frank M.; Scharein, Arthur Otto.

Scoops. Carey, Max George; Carry, George [Dorman].

Scooter. Rizzuto, Phil[ip Francis].

Scopes, John Thomas (1900–70). Teacher and defendant in trial to test a Tennessee law against the teaching of the Darwinian theory of evolution, 1925: **Monkey Trial Defendant.**

Scots. Athletic teams of Alma College, Alma, Michigan.

Scotsman. Sutherland, John Bain.

Scott, Barbara Ann (born 1928). Canadian ice skater: **Tinker.**

Scott, Clyde (born 1924). Football back: **Smackover.**

Scott, [George] Ken[neth] (born 1918). Fabric and dress designer and restaurateur: **Falconetto.**

Scott, L. Everett (1892–1960). Baseball shortstop: **Deacon.**

Scott, Robert Walter (1861–1929). Politician and farmer: **Farmer Bob.**

Scott, Tom (born 1912). Composer and singer: **American Troubadour.** Legal name: Thomas Jefferson Scott.

Scott, Walter Edwin, Jr. (1872–1954). Gold prospector: **Death Valley Scotty.**

Scourge. Tropea, Arazio.

Scourge of the Bootleggers. Willebrandt, Mabel Walker.

Scourge of the District Police, The. Blanton, Thomas Lindsay.

Scrambler, The. Tarkenton, Francis.

Scranton, Pennsylvania. U.S. city: **Anthracite City, City of Black Diamonds.**

Scrap Iron. Courtney, Clint[on Dawson].

Scrapple City. Allentown, Pennsylvania.

Screaming Eagle Division. One Hundred and First Airborne Division.

Screeno. Bailey, Howard Henry.

Screen's Bad Girl. West, Mae.

Screwball. Beuling, George.

Screwey. Moore, John Edward.

Scripps, E[dward] W[yllis] (1854–1926). Journalist and newspaper publisher: **Father of Syndication, Old Hermit of Journalism.**

Scull, Robert C. (born 1917). Business executive and art collector: **Medici of the Minimals, Pop of Pop Art.**

Seabees. Naval construction battalions, World War II.

Sea Dart. Convair XF2Y-1 delta-wing seaplane, early 1950s.

Sea-girt Province. Nova Scotia.

Seagrave, Gordon Stifler (1897–1965). Missionary and doctor: **Burma Surgeon.**

Seagull. Native or resident of Utah.

Seaport of the West. Galveston, Texas.

Search-and-Rescue Patrol. Civil Air Patrol.

Sears, Eleonora R. (1881–1968). Athlete: **Universal Female Athlete.**

Sears, John W. (1894–1956). Baseball umpire: **Ziggy.**

Sears, Roebuck and Company. Business organization: **Sawbuck.**

Seat of Empire. New York.

Seattle, Washington. U.S. city: **Cannery City, City of Eternal Views, City of Seven Hills, Gateway to Alaska, Queen City of the Pacific, Queen City on the Sound, Skidrow on the Sound.**

Seattle's Sensational Son. Zioncheck, Marion A.

Seaver, Tom (born 1944). Baseball pitcher: **Tom Terrific.** Legal name: George Thomas Seaver.

Second Armored Division. U.S. Army division, World War II: **Hell on Wheels Division.**

Second City. Chicago, Illinois.

Second Infantry Division. U.S. Army division, World War II: **Indian Head Division.**

Second Man on the Moon. Aldrin, Edwin Eugene, Jr.

Second Nazareth. North Carolina.

Second William Jennings Bryan. Lee, Joshua Bryan.

Secret-Sharer, The. Dean, John, III.

Secret Six. Private anticrime group, Chicago, 1930s.

Sedate Capital of the Bible Belt. Oklahoma City, Oklahoma.

Sedric, Eugene Hall (1907–63). Jazz clarinetist and saxophonist: **Honey Bear.**

Seed. Goring, Robert Thomas.

Seeds, Robert Ira (born 1907). Baseball outfielder: **Suitcase Bob.**

Seeger, Pete[r] (born 1919). Folk singer and folklorist: **Reincarnated Troubadour, Thomas Jefferson of Folk Music.**

Seeker of Visions. Lame Deer.

Segura, Francisco (born 1921). Tennis player and coach: **Pancho.**

Selby, Norman (1873–1940). Welterweight boxer: **Kid McCoy.**

Selfridge, Harry Gordon (1864–1947). Merchant: **Mile-a-Minute Harry.**

Sellers, John B. (born 1924). Composer and singer: **Brother John Sellers.**

Seminoles. Athletic teams of Florida State University, Tallahassee.

Senator. Grimes, Burleigh Arland.

Senator Frankenstein Fishface. Vincent, Elmore.

Senator Sunday School. Church, Frank.

Sendak, Maurice (born 1928). Book illustrator: **Picasso of Children's Books.**

Senior Circuit. National League of Professional Baseball Clubs.

Sennett, Mack (1880–1960). Canadian director and producer of motion-picture comedies: **Father Goose, King of Comedy.** Born: Michael Sinnott.

Sentimental Cynic. Runyon, [Alfred] Damon.

Sentimental Gentleman of Swing, The. Dorsey, Tommy.

Sergeant Joe Friday. Webb, Jack.

Serious. Myers, Wilson Ernest.

Servant Jacob. Chenault, Marcus Wayne.

Servicemen's Readjustment Act. An act passed by Congress in 1944 providing funds for college education, home loans, and other benefits for veterans of the armed services: **GI Bill of Rights.**

Sevareid, Eric (born 1912). News commentator and author. With seven other broadcasters: **Murrow's Boys.**

Seven Blocks of Granite. Members of Fordham University football team, 1936: Al Babartsky, Johnny Druze, Ed Franco, Vince Lombardi, Leo Paquin, Nat Pierce, and Alex Wojciechowicz.

Seven Sisters. 1. Seven prestigious Eastern women's colleges: Barnard, Bryn Mawr, Mount Holyoke, Radcliffe, Smith, Vassar, and Wellesley. 2. The seven largest oil companies, originally Standard Oil of New Jersey, Standard Oil of California, Mobil Oil, Shell, British Petroleum, Texaco, and Gulf.

Seventeenth Airborn Division. U.S. Army division: **Golden Talon Division, Thunder from Heaven Division.**

Seventh Armored Division. U.S. Army division, World War II: **Lucky Seventh.**

Seventh Infantry Division. U.S. Army division, World War II: **Hourglass Division.**

Seventieth Infantry Division. U.S. Army division, World War II: **Trailblazer Division.**

Seventy-eighth Infantry Division. U.S. Army division, World War II: **Lightning Division.**

Seventy-ninth Division. U.S. Army division, World War I: **Liberty Division.**

Seventy-ninth Infantry Division. U.S. Army division, World War II: **Cross of Lorraine Division.**

Seventy-seventh Division, American Expeditionary Force. U.S. Army division, World War I: **Melting Pot Division, Metropolitan Division.**

Seventy-seventh Infantry Division. U.S. Army division, World War II: **New York's Own, Statue of Liberty Division.**

Seventy-sixth Division. U.S. Army division, World War I: **Liberty Bell Division.**

Seventy-sixth Infantry Division. U.S. Army division, World War II: **Onaway Division.**

Seven-Year-Old Huckster. Reese, Mason.

Severinsen, Doc (born 1927). Jazz musician and trumpet player: **Little Doc, World's Greatest Trumpet Player.** Born: Carl H. Severinsen.

Seward's Folly. Alaska.

Seward's Icebox. Alaska.

Sewell, James Luther (born 1901). Baseball manager: **Luke.**

Sewell, Truett Banks (born 1908). Baseball pitcher: **Rip.**

Seymour, Whitney North (born 1923). Lawyer: **Guardian of the Government.**

Shack, Eddie (born 1937). Hockey player: **The Entertainer.**

Shad. Barry, John C.; Collins, Lester [Rallingston]; Rhem, Charles Flint.

Shadow. Wilson, Rossiere.

Shag. Shaughnessy, Frank J.

Shahn, Ben[jamin] (1898–1969). Painter and graphic artist: **American Hogarth.**

Shake. Keane, Ellsworth McGranahan.

Shank, Clifford Everett, Jr. (born 1926). Jazz saxophonist, flutist, and composer: **Bud.**

Shank, Samuel Lewis (1872–1927). Politician: **Auctioneer Mayor, Indianapolis Potato Mayor, Potato Mayor.**

Shano. Collins, John Francis.

Shanty. Hogan, James Francis.

Shapiro, Jacob (1897–1947). Gangster: **Gurrah Jake.**

Shapoff, S. R. (born 1919). Horse trainer: **Skippy.**

Sharkey. Bonano, Joseph.

Sharkey, Jack (born 1902). Heavyweight boxer: **Bay Stater, Boston Gob, Boston Sailor, Gabby Lithuanian, The Lithuanian.** Born: Joseph Paul Zukauskas.

Sharpbacks State. New Jersey.

Shattuck, Claire Etrulia (1876–1954). Theatrical performer: **Truly.**

Shaughnessy, Clark Daniel (1892–1970). Football coach: **Soup.**

Shaughnessy, Frank J. (1883–1969). Baseball player, football coach, and business manager: **Shag.**

Shaute, Joseph Benjamin (1899–1970). Baseball pitcher: **Lefty.**

Shaw, Carolyn Hagner (born 1904). Special arbiter and hostess in Washington, D.C.: **Callie.**

Shaw, Frederick L. (1859–1938). Baseball pitcher: **Dupee.**

Shaw, Lawrence Timothy (1899–1977). Football coach: **Buck, Silver Fox.**

Shaw, [Warren] Wilbur (1902–54). Racing driver: **Mr. President.**

Shawn, Ted. (1891–1972). Dancer and choreographer: **Father of Modern Dance.** Born: Edwin Myers Shawn.

Shay. Minton, Sherman.

Shay, Dorothy (1921?–78). Singer and entertainer: **Park Avenue Hillbilly.** Born: Dorothy Sims.

Sheboygan, Wisconsin. U.S. city: **Bratwurst Capital; City of Cheese, Chairs, Children, and Churches; Wurst City in the World.**

Shell Oil Company. Business organization, with six other oil companies: **Seven Sisters.**

Shepard, Alan B[artlett], Jr. (born 1923). Astronaut: **First American in Space.**

Shepherd of the Loop. Thompson, John.

Sheppard, Morris (1875–1941). U.S. Representative and U.S. Senator from Texas: **Father of the Eighteenth Amendment.**

Sherdel, William H. (1896–1968). Baseball pitcher: **Wee Willie.**

Sheridan, Ann (1915–67). Motion-picture actress: **Oomph Girl.** Born: Clara Lou Sheridan.

Sheridan, Elmo R. (born 1907). U.S. Army officer, World War II. With Timothy J. O'Leary: **The Essobees, The Military Expedients.**

Sheriff. Blake, John Fred; Harris, David Stanley; Lee, Hal Burnham.

Sherman, Allie (born 1923). Football quarterback and coach: **Big Shrimp of Pro Football, Pedantic Professor.** Legal name: Alexander Sherman.

Sherman, Forrest Percival (1896–1951). U.S. Navy Admiral: **Flying Admiral.**

Shimmie Queen. Pennington, Ann.

Shipbuilding City. Chester, Pennsylvania; Quincy, Massachusetts.

Shipman, Samuel (1883–1937). Playwright: **Shippie.**

Shippie. Shipman, Samuel.

Shipwreck. Kelly, Alvin Anthony; Kelly, John Simms.

Shipyard Bunyan. Higgins, Andrew Jackson.

Shirer, William L[awrence] (born 1904). News commentator and author. With seven other broadcasters: **Murrow's Boys.**

Shishaldin. Alaskan volcano: **Smoking Moses.**

Shockers. Athletic teams of Wichita State University, Wichita, Kansas.

Shoe, The. Shoemaker, Willie.

Shoeless Joe. Jackson, Joseph Jefferson.

Shoemaker, Willie (born 1931). Jockey: **The Shoe.** Legal name: William Lee Shoemaker.

Shon. Klein, Alex.

Shooey. Malone, James H.

Shooting Star. Lockheed F-80C fighter plane, World War II and Korean War.

Shor, Bernard (1904–77). Restaurateur: **Toots.**

Short, Dewey Jackson (born 1898). U.S. Representative from Missouri: **Jenny, Laughing-Gas Man, The Preacher.**

Short, Elizabeth (1925–47). Murder victim: **Black Dahlia.**

Short Pants. Campagna, Louis.

Short Pants Bully. Schmidt, Maynard.

Shorty. Egan, William: Green, Wilfred Thomas; Long, Clair; Ray, Hugh L.; Shroeder, Rudolph W.

Shorty Sherock. Cherock, Clarence Francis.

Shotton, Burton Edwin (1884–1962). Baseball outfielder and manager: **Barney.**

Shoulders. Latman, Arnold Barry.

Shoun, Clyde Mitchell (1915–68). Baseball pitcher: **Hardrock.**

Showalter, Jackson Whipps (1860–1935). Chess player: **Kentucky Lion.**

Showdown Man. Norton, Homer Hill.

Show-Me State. Missouri.

Shrimp Bait. Miller, William Mosley.

Shriner, Herb[ert] (1918–70). Television personality: **Hoosier Hotshot.**

Shriners Bowl. Football stadium at San Francisco, California.

Shriver, [Robert] Sargent (born 1915). Lawyer and diplomat: **Sarge.**

Shroeder, Rudolph W. (died 1953). U.S. Army test pilot: **Shorty.**

Shu, Eddie. Shulman, Edward.

Shufflin' Phil. Douglas, Philip.

Shula, Don[ald Francis] (born 1930). Football coach: **Miami's Un-miraculous Miracle Worker.**

Shulman, Edward (born 1918). Jazz saxophonist and clarinetist: **Eddie Shu.**

Shulman, Max. (born 1919). Humorist: **Cultured Perelman, Master of Undergraduate Humor.**

Shultz, George [Pratt] (born 1920). Politician and U.S. Secretary of the Treasury: **Supercrat, Washington's Scholar-Athlete.**

Shupe, James (active 1920–30). Gangster: **Bozo.**

Sibbett, Morgan (born 1911). Business executive: **Monk.**

Sidewalk Statesman. Smith, Al[fred Emanuel].

Siegel, Benjamin (1906–47). Racketeer and gambler: **Bugsy, Nig.** Also known as Harry Rosen.

Sifford, Charles (born 1923). Golfer: **Jackie Robinson of Golf.**

Sightseeing Sixth. Sixth Division.

Sikes, J. V. (active 1927). Football player: **Siki.**

Siki. Sikes, J. V.

Sikorsky, Igor [Ivan] (1889–1972). Aeronautical engineer: **Father of the Helicopter, Uncle Igor.**

Silent Cal. Benge, Ray Adelphia; Coolidge, [John] Calvin.

Silent Charley. Murphy, Charles Francis.

Silent Jim. Tatum, James Moore.

Silent Majority. Conservative middle-class Americans as a group.

Silent Tom. Smith, Thomas.

Silicon Valley. Region near Santa Clara, California, home of computer companies like National Semiconductor Corporation.

Silk. Wilkes, Len.

Silk City. Paterson, New Jersey.

Silks, Mattie (1846–1929). Brothel proprietor: **Queen of the Denver Red Lights.** Born: Martha A. Thomson Ready.

Silo Charlie. Coughlin, Charles Edward.

Silver Dollar. West, James Marion, Jr.

Silver Fox. Shaw, Lawrence Timothy.

Silver Fox of the Northland. Bierman, Bernard William.

Silver Gate. Entrance of San Diego Bay, California.

Silver-haired Elderly Statesman of American Labor. Meany, George.

Silver Masked Tenor. White, Joseph M.

Silver Sage. Thomas, John William Elmer.

Silver State. Nevada; Colorado.

Silverstein, Joseph L. (1898–1950). Football player: **Bullet Joe.**

Silver-tongued Josh. Lee, Joshua Bryan.

Silver-tongued Orator. Bryan, William Jennings.

Silver Willy. Smith, William T.

Simmons, Al[oysius Harry] (1902–56). Baseball outfielder: **Bucket-foot.** Born: Alois Szymanski.

Simmons, Sarney (born 1929). Jazz pianist and composer: **Norman.**

Simon. Allgood, Miles Clayton.

Simon, William E. (born 1912). Investment banker, U.S. Secretary of the Treasury, and energy official: **Energy Czar, Pop-eye.**

Simpson, Harry Leon (born 1925). Baseball first baseman and outfielder: **Suitcase.**

Simpson, O[renthal] J[ames] (born 1947). Football back: **Orange Juice, The Juice, OJ.**

Sims, John Haley (born 1925). Jazz saxophonist and clarinetist: **Zoot.**

Sims, Phil[ip] (born 1933). Psychologist and consumer advocate: **Black Ralph Nader.**

Sinatra, Frank (born 1917). Singer and actor: **Chairman of the Board, The Dago, Frank Swoonatra, The General, King of Swoon, The Leader, The Man, Ol' Blue Eyes, Il Padrone, The Pope, The Voice.** Legal name: Francis Albert Sinatra.

Sinatra, Natalie (1895–1977). Mother of Frank Sinatra: **Dolly.**

Sin City. Las Vegas, Nevada.

Sinclair, Harry Ford (1876–1956). Oil tycoon and business executive: **Sinco.**

Sinclair, Upton [Beall] (1878–1968). Author: **All-American Mirror.**

Sinco. Sinclair, Harry Ford.

Singed Cat State. Montana.

Singing Canary. Reles, Abe.

Singing Lady. Wicker, Ireene Seaton.

Singing Maestro. Ravell, Carl.

Singing Policeman. Regan, Phil[ip].

Singing Story Lady. Wicker, Ireene Seaton.

Singleton, Arthur James (born 1898). Jazz drummer: **Zutty.**

Sing Sing. Ossining Correctional Facility, New York State penitentiary.

Sioux. Athletic teams of the University of North Dakota, Grand Forks.

Sioux City, Iowa. U.S. city: **City of Distinction, Industrial City of Iowa.**

Sioux Falls, South Dakota. U.S. city: **Gateway to the Dakotas.**

Sioux State. North Dakota.

Siple, Paul Allman (born 1908). Member of the first Byrd Antarctic expedition: **Boy Explorer.**

Siren of Sex. West, Mae.

Siren of the Screen. West, Mae.

Sirica, John [Joseph] (born 1904). Jurist and lawyer: **Maximum John.**

Sir Laurence Olivier of the White House. Haig, Alexander [Meigs, Jr.].

Sis. Kaplan, Harriet Jan; Smith, Mary Hopkins.

Sisk, John (born 1906). Football back: **Big Train.**

Sisk, Mildred (born 1900). Alleged radio propagandist for Nazi government and convicted traitor: **Axis Sally.** Born: Mildred Elizabeth Gillars.

Sissy. Farenthold, Frances [Tarlton].

Sister Aimee. McPherson, Aimee Semple.

Sister Amy. Archer-Gillian, Amy.

Sister Cities. San Diego, California, and Yokohama, Japan.

Sister Mahalia. Jackson, Mahalia.

Sit-down Striker. Hoffman, Clare E.

Sitko, Emil M. (1923–73). Football back: **Red, Six Yards.**

Sitting Bull. Summerall, Charles Pelot.

Siwash. Athletic teams of Knox College, Galesburg, Illinois.

Sixth Armored Division. U.S. Army division, World War II: **Super Sixth.**

Sixth Division. U.S. Army division, World War I: **Sightseeing Sixth.**

Sixth Infantry Division. U.S. Army division, World War II: **Red Star Division.**

Sixty-fifth Infantry Division. U.S. Army division, World War II: **Battle Axe Division.**

Sixty-ninth Regiment. New York National Guard regiment, World War I: **The Fighting Sixty-ninth.**

Sixty-sixth Infantry Division. U.S. Army division, World War II; **Black Panther Division.**

Sixty-third Infantry Division. U.S. Army division, World War II: **Blood and Fire Division.**

Six Yards. Sitko, Emil M.

Sizemore, Barbara (born 1928). Teacher and school superintendent: **Boat Rocker.**

Skeeter. Bigbee, Carson Lee; Rudolph, Wilma Glodean.

Skeets. Gallagher, Richard S.; Morris, Leonard Carter; Nehemiah, Renaldo.

Skelton, Red (born 1913). Comedian: **Marcel Marceau of Television.** Legal name: Richard Bernard Skelton.

Ski. Melillo, Oscar Donald.

Ski Capital U.S.A. Aspen, Colorado.

Skid Row. Urban street or neighborhood inhabited by derelicts.

Skidrow on the Sound. Seattle, Washington.

Skid Row Slasher. Murderer, Los Angeles, 1974–75.

Skinnay. Ennis, Edgar Clyde, Jr.

Skinner, Otis (1858–1942). Actor: **Dean of the American Stage, Dean of the American Theater.**

Skinny. Johnson, William; Wainwright, Jonathan Mayhew.

Ski-nose. Hope, Bob.

Skip. James, Nehemiah; Martin, Lloyd; Redwine, Wilbur; Riebel, Frederick, Jr.

Skippy. Shapoff, S. R.

Skitch. Henderson, Lyle Cedric.

Skull, The. Canham, Charles Draper William.

Sky City. Pueblo Acoma, New Mexico.

Sky High Irvin. Irvin, Leslie Leroy.

Skylab's Mr. Fix-it. Conrad, Charles, Jr.

Skymaster. Douglas C-54 cargo plane, World War II.

Skyscraper Man. The typical, modern, urban man.

Sky-storming Yankee. Curtiss, Glenn Hammond.

Slam. Stewart, Leroy.

Slamming Sammy. Snead, Sam[uel Jackson].

Slapsie Maxie. Rosenbloom, Maxie.

Slasher. Atkinson, Ted.

Slater, Fred[erick E.] (1898–1966). Football tackle: **Duke.**

Slats. Baxter, Raymond H.; Gill, Amory Tingle.

Slaughter, Enos Bradsher (born 1916). Baseball outfielder: **Country.**

Slayton, Donald Kent (born 1924). Astronaut: **Deke.**

Sleeping Clairvoyant. Cayce, Edgar.

Sleeping Giant. Cayce, Edgar.

Sleeping Prophet. Cayce, Edgar.

Sleepy. Matsumoto, Hidehiko.

Sleepy Jim. Crowley, James.

Sleepy Phil. Knox, Philander Chase.

Slick. Jones, Wilmore.

Slick Willie. Sutton, William Francis.

Slide. Hampton, Locksley Wellington.

Sliding Billy. Watson, Billy.

Slim. Caldwell, Raymond Benjamin; Exterminator; Karpis, Alvin; Sallee, Harry Franklin; Thomas, Alvin Clarence.

Slinging Sammy. Baugh, Samuel Adrian.

Slingshot. O'Brien, David.

Slippery Rock State College, athletic teams of: **Rockets.**

Sloan, Harry (born 1923). Publisher of paperback joke books: **King of the Nonbooks.**

Slogan Man. Smythe, J[ohn] Henry, [Jr.].

Slogan Smythe. Smythe, J[ohn] Henry, [Jr.].

Sloppy. Thurston, Hollis John.

Slosson, George F. (1854–1949). Billiard player: **The Student.**

Slot, The. Mission Street.

Slow Drag. Pavageau, Alcide.

Slow Motion Shorty Park. Park, Arthur.

Slugger. Burns, John Irving.

Slumbering Giant of Capital Hill. Library of Congress.

Smack. Henderson, James Fletcher; Reisor, Lawrence.

Smackover. Scott, Clyde.

Smallest Capital in America. Carson City, Nevada.

Small Paul Revere. Ashbrook, John Milan.

Smeed. Taylor, [Joseph] Deems.

Smelly Pelley. Pelley, William Dudley.

Smiley. Burnette, Lester Alvin; Johnson, Howard W.

Smilin' Ed. McConnell, James Ed.

Smiling Jim. Farley, James Aloysius.

Smith, Alexander Benjamin (1071–1919). Baseball infielder: **Broadway.**

Smith, Al[fred Emanuel] (1873–1944). Governor of New York: **Assemblyman from the Bowery, Happy Warrior, Hero of the Cities, Sidewalk Statesman.**

Smith, Andrew Latham (1883–1926). Football coach: **Wonder Maker.**

Smith, Bessie (1894–1937). Jazz singer: **Empress of the Blues.**

Smith, C. Arnholt (born 1901). Business executive and fund raiser: **Mr. San Diego.**

Smith, Charles Aaron (born 1945). Football tackle and end: **Bubba.**

Smith, Cladys (born 1908). Jazz trumpeter, trombonist, singer, and bandleader: **Jabbo.**

Smith, Clarence (1904–29). Jazz pianist and singer: **Pinetop.**

331

Smith, Ellison DuRant (1866–1944). U.S. Senator from South Carolina: **Cotton Ed.**

Smith, Francis Marion (1846–1931). Manufacturer: **Borax King.**

Smith, Harry (active 1930). Football player: **Germany.**

Smith, Hezekiah Leroy Gordon (1909–67). Jazz violinist, singer, songwriter, and bandleader: **Stuff.**

Smith, Holland M[cTyeire] (1882–1967). U.S. Marine General: **Father of Modern Amphibious Warfare, Pacific Cyclone, Howlin' Mad** (to distinguish him from U.S. Army General Holland R. Smith).

Smith, Howard K[ingsbury] (born 1914). News commentator. With seven other broadcasters: **Murrow's Boys.**

Smith, Jack (1898–1950). Radio singer: **Whispering Jack Smith, Whispering Baritone.**

Smith, James (born 1932). Football back: **Jetstream.**

Smith, James C[arlisle] (1890–1966). Baseball third baseman: **Red.**

Smith, James Monroe (1888–1946). Embezzler: **Jingle Money Smith.**

Smith, John Philip (1904–73). Football coach and athletic director: **Little Clipper.**

Smith, John Robert (born 1933). Jazz organist and pianist: **Johnny Hammond.**

Smith, Joseph (born c. 1883). Actor: **Sunshine Boy.**

Smith, J. R. (active 1934). Football player: **Jackrabbit.**

Smith, Kate (born 1909). Singer and actress: **First Lady of Radio, Moon over the Mountain Girl, Radio's Own Statue of Liberty, Songbird of the South.** Legal name: Kathryn Elizabeth Smith.

Smith, Mary Hopkins (active 1900–40). Missionary: **Sis.**

Smith, Richard Paul (1904–78). Baseball catcher, football back and coach, and industrial executive: **Red, Toledo's Red Smith.**

Smith, Robert (born c. 1938). Disc jockey: **Wolfman Jack.**

Smith, Thomas (1878–1957). Racehorse trainer: **Silent Tom.**

Smith, Thomas Vernon (1890–1964). U.S. Representative from Illinois: **Philosophy Smith, Political Philosopher.**

Smith, Tony (born 1912). Sculptor: **Master of the Monumentalists.**

Smith, Vernon (active 1929–31). Football player: **Catfish.**

Smith, Wallace (1929–73). Lightweight boxer: **Bud.**

Smith, Walter Bedell (1895–1961). U.S. Army General and government official: **Beetle, Beedle, Bulldog, General Manager of the War.**

Smith, William Joseph (born 1899). Featherweight boxer: **Midget.**

Smith, William T. (active 1907). Politician: **Silver Willy.**

Smith, Willie (1897–1973). Jazz pianist and composer: **Willie the Lion.** Born: William Henry Joseph Berthol Bonaparte, Bertholoff Smith.

Smith College. Educational institution; with six other women's colleges: **Seven Sisters.**

Smithwick, A. P. (1927–73). Steeplechase jockey: **Paddy.**

Smog City. Los Angeles, California.

Smoke Bowl. Football stadium in Richmond, Virginia.

Smokey. Alston, Walt[er Emmons]

Smokies. Great Smoky Mountains.

Smoking Moses. Shishaldin.

Smokin' Joe. Frazier, Joe.

Smoky City. Pittsburgh, Pennsylvania.

Smoky Joe. Wood, Joe.

Smoky Mountain Boy. Acuff, Roy [Claxton].

Smoot, Reed (1862–1941). Mormon Church leader and U.S. Senator from Utah: **Harding Enthusiast.**

Smothers, Dick (born 1939). Singer and entertainer. With Tom Smothers (Smothers Brothers): **Naughtiest Boys on Television.** Legal name: Richard Smothers.

Smothers, Tom (born 1937). Singer and entertainer. With Dick Smothers (Smothers Brothers): **Naughtiest Boys on Television.** Legal name: Thomas Bolyn Smothers 3d.

Smyth, Edward J. (1887–1974). Heavyweight boxer: **Gunboat Smith, The Gunner.**

Smythe, J[ohn] Henry, [Jr.] (1883–1956). Writer of patriotic slogans and civic leader: **Slogan Man, Slogan Smythe.**

Snake. Ames, Knowlton L.

Snake Man. Ditmars, Raymond Lee.

Snapping Turtle. Glass, Carter.

333

Snapshot City. Rochester, New York.

Snavely, Carl Grey (born 1894). Football coach: **Football Scholar.**

Snead, Sam[uel Jackson] (born 1912). Golfer: **Slamming Sammy.**

Snick. Student Nonviolent Coordinating Committee (Student National Coordinating Committee).

Snider, Duke (born 1926). Baseball centerfielder: **Duke of Brooklyn.** Born: Edwin Donald Snider.

Snipe. Hansen, Roy Emil.

Snooky, Lanson, Roy; Young, Eugene.

Snorky. Capone, Al[phonse].

Snorter. Connally, George Walter.

Snowden, Elmer Chester (1900–73). Jazz banjo player and guitarist: **Pops.**

Snowden, Fred (born 1936). Basketball coach: **Desert Fox.**

Snozz. Lombardi, Ernest Natali.

Snub. Mosley, Lawrence Leo.

Snuffy. Stirnweiss, George Henry.

Snyder, Frank J. (1893–1962). Baseball catcher: **Pancho.**

Snyder, Martin (active 1920s). Racketeer and manager and husband of Ruth Etting: **Colonel, The Gimp, Moe.**

Snyder, Ruth (died 1928). Murderer of her husband, Albert Snyder: **Granite Woman, Momsie.**

Soap Box Derby Center. Akron, Ohio.

Social Historian of Cafe Society. Beebe, Lucius.

Society Detective. Schindler, Raymond C.

Socker. Coe, Charles Francis.

Sodak. Native or resident of South Dakota.

Soggy. Lyon, David Gordon.

SoHo. Area just south of Houston Street, New York City.

Solar Energy Capital. Los Angeles, California.

Solar Energy State. Arizona.

Solario, Isadore (active 1963). Basketball coach: **Spin.**

Soldier's Inspiration. Grable, Betty.

Solid South. Southern states formerly certain to vote heavily for Democratic candidates.

Solly Moore. Moretti, Salvatore.

Solomon, Moses (1900–66). Baseball outfielder: **Hickory, Rabbi of Swat.**

Solters, Julius Joseph (1906–75). Baseball outfielder: **Lemons, Moose.** Born: Julius Joseph Soltesz.

Soltysik, Patricia (1950?–74). Revolutionary and member of the Symbionese Liberation Army: **Female Brain of the S.L.A., Mizmoon.**

Somniferous Malloy. Malloy, Michael.

Son. House, Eddie James, Jr.

Songbird of the South. Smith, Kate.

Son Jimmy. Roosevelt, James.

Sonny. Capone, Albert Francis; Gluck, Edward; Moyse, Alphonse; Whitney, Cornelius Vanderbilt; Workman, Ray[mond].

Sonny Red. Kyner, Sylvester.

Son of Sam. Berkowitz, David Richard.

Sonoratown. The Mexican district of a city.

Soo. Saulte Ste. Marie, Michigan.

Soo Line. Minneapolis, St. Paul, and Saulte Ste. Marie Railroad.

Soonerland. Oklahoma.

Sooners. Athletic teams of the University of Oklahoma, Norman.

Sooner State. Oklahoma.

Soreback. Native or resident of Virginia.

Sorrell, Vic[tor Garland] (1901–72). Baseball pitcher: **Ace, Baby Doll, Lawyer, The Philosopher.**

Soss, Wilma [Porter] (born c. 1907). Organization official and financial broadcaster: **Corporate Gadfly.** Also known as Mrs. J. Albert Soss.

Soubier, Cliff (active 1920s and 1930s). Radio performer: **Barnacle Bill the Sailor.**

Soul City. Harlem.

Sound, The. Getz, Stan[ley].

Sound Money Glass. Glass, Carter.

Soup. Shaughnessy, Clark Daniel.

Sour-Faced Clown, The. Griebling, Otto.

Sousa, John Philip (1856–1932). Composer and bandmaster: **March King.**

South, Eddie (1904–62). Jazz violinist: **Dark Angel of the Violin.** Legal name: Edward Otha South.

South Carolina. Eighth U.S. state: **Iodine State, Palmetto State, Rice State, Swamp State.** With North Carolina: **Carolinas.**

South Carolina, University of, athletic teams of: **Fighting Gamecocks.**

South Dakota. Fortieth U.S. state: **Artesian State, Blizzard State, Coyote State, Land of Grass Roots, Land of Plenty, Sunshine State.** With North Dakota: **Dakotas, Nosodak, Twin Sisters.** With North Dakota and Wyoming: **Dakoming.**

South Dakota, University of, athletic teams of: **Coyotes.**

South Dakota State University, athletic teams of: **Jackrabbits.**

Southern California, University of. 1. Athletic teams of: **Trojans.** 2. Athletic teams of, with other teams in regional conference: **Pacific Ten.**

Southern Crossroads City. Atlanta, Georgia.

Southern Gateway of New England. Providence, Rhode Island.

Southern Illinois University, athletic teams of: **Salukis.**

Southern Methodist University, athletic teams of: **Mustangs.**

Southern Mississippi, University of, athletic teams of: **Golden Eagles.**

Southern Sam. Ervin, Sam[uel James, Jr.].

Southern University, athletic teams of: **Jaguars.**

Southwestern Louisiana, University of, athletic teams of: **Ragin' Cajuns.**

Southworth, William H. (1893–1969). Baseball outfielder and manager: **Billy the Kid.**

Sox. Griffis, Silas Seth.

Spaatz, Carl (1891–1974). U.S. Air Force General: **Tooey.**

Space Capital of the Nation. Huntsville, Alabama.

Space Capital of the World. Huntsville, Alabama.

Space Center. Houston, Texas.

Space City. Houston, Texas.

336

Space Hub. Cape Canaveral, Florida.

Spaceport, U.S.A. Cape Canaveral, Florida.

Space Port, U.S.A. Galveston, Texas.

Spade. Cooley, Donald.

Spaeth, Sigmund [Gottfried] (1885–1965). Musicologist: **Tune Detective.**

Spahn, Warren [Edward] (born 1921). Baseball pitcher: **Spahnie.**

Spahnie. Spahn, Warren Edward.

Spalding, Albert (1888–1953). Violinist: **America's Own Violinist.**

Spanglish. Spanish-English dialect spoken near the Mexican border.

Spanier, Francis Joseph (1906–67). Jazz cornetist and bandleader: **Muggsy.**

Spanish State. New Mexico.

Spanish Town. Tampa, Florida

Spanky. McFarland, George Emmett.

SPAR. Female member of the U.S. Coast Guard.

Sparkling City by the Sea. Corpus Christi, Texas.

Sparky. Anderson, George Lee; Lyle, Albert Walter; Schulz, Charles Monroe; Wade, Malcolm.

Spartans. Athletic teams of Michigan State University, East Lansing, and San Jose State University, San Jose, California.

Spaulding, E. Jack (1888–1953). U.S. Navy officer: **Father of the Seabees.**

Spaulding, William Henry (1880–1966). Football coach: **Beloved Bruin.**

Speaker, Tris[tram E.] (1888–1958). Baseball outfielder and manager: **Gray Eagle, Spoke.**

Spearhead Division. Third Armored Division.

Spears, Clarence Wiley (1894–1964). Football coach and physician: **Doc, Cupid, Fats.**

Special Investigation Unit. Secret group established by President Richard M. Nixon in 1971 to stop unofficial or improper disclosure of government or political secrets: **The Plumbers.**

Specs. O'Keefe, Joseph J.; Powell, Gordon; Wright, Charles.

Spectacular Rogue. Means, Gaston Bullock.

Spector, Isadore (active 1939–41). Football player: **Spook.**

Speculator King. Livermore, Jesse Lauriston.

Speed King of the Air. Turner, Roscoe.

Speedy. Jones, Rufus.

Spelling, Aaron (born 1926). Television producer: **Big Four.**

Spendthrift of Albany. Rockefeller, Nelson [Aldrich].

Sperm. Thurmond, [James] Strom.

Sphinx, The. Roosevelt, Franklin D[elano].

Sphinx of the Rock Island. Moore, William Henry.

Spider. Jackson, Phil; Nelson, Roger Eugene; Pladner, Emile; Reinhardt, S. Louis, Jr.; Sabich, Vladimir.

Spiders. Athletic teams of the University of Richmond, Richmond, Virginia.

Spike. Briggs, Walter O., Jr.; Dubs, Adolph; Gray, Glen; Hamilton, George; Hunt, Frazier; Wallace, J. K.

Spin. Solario, Isadore.

Spindle City. Fall River, Massachusetts; Lowell, Massachusetts.

Spinelli, Ethel Leta Juanita. Criminal: **The Duchess.**

Spiro T. Eggplant. Agnew, Spiro [Theodore].

Spitball Pitcher. Perry, Gaylord Jackson.

Spitelara, Joe (born 1937). Jazz clarinetist and saxophonist: **Pee Wee.** Legal name: Joseph T. Spitelara.

Spitz, Mark Andrew (born 1950). Olympic swimmer: **King of Amateur Swimming.**

Splendid Splinter. Williams, Ted.

Spoiler, The. Risko, Johnny.

Spokane, Washington. U.S. city: **Heart of the Inland Empire, Home of the Mining Barons.**

Spoke. Speaker, Tris[tram E.]

Spokesman for the Lost Generation. Hemingway, Ernest.

Spokesman for the Negro. Washington, Booker T[aliaferro].

Sponge. Storie, Howard Edward.

Spook. Spector, Isadore.

Spooks. Gerber, Walter.

Spoon River Poet. Masters, Edgar Lee.

Sport. Bucher, George.

Sprafka, Joseph (active 1916). Football player: **Galloping Sprafka.**

Springfield, Illinois. U.S. city: **Home of Abraham Lincoln.**

Springfield, Massachusetts. U.S. city: **Rifle City.**

Springfield, Missouri. U.S. city: **Queen City of the Ozarks.**

Spruce Goose. Eight-engine wooden flying boat designed and built by Howard Hughes in the 1940s.

Spud. Davis, Virgil Lawrence; Chandler, Spurgeon Ferdinand; Murphy, Lyle.

Spud State. Idaho.

Square Deal. Aid to labor and industry pledged by President Theodore Roosevelt, 1902.

Square Scourge of Washington. Anderson, Jack[son Northman].

Squatter State. Kansas.

Squatty. Munson, Thurman [Lee].

Squeaky. Bluege, Otto Adam; Fromme, Lynette Alice.

Squire of Hyde Park. Roosevelt, Franklin D[elano].

Stabile, Jack (active 1920–30). Gangster: **Stickum.**

Stagecoach Town. Fort Worth, Texas.

Stagg, Amos Alonzo (1862–1965). Football coach: **Football's Old Man River, Grand Old Man of Football, Lonnie, Unreconstructed Amateur.**

Stahl, John Meloy (1860–1944). Expert on agriculture and economics: **Father of Rural Free Delivery.**

Stamford, Connecticut. U.S. city: **Lock City.**

Standard Oil Company. Business organization: **Mother of Trusts.**

Standard Oil Company (New Jersey). Business organization (later, Exxon Corporation); with six other oil companies: **Seven Sisters.**

Standard Oil Company of California. Business organization; with six other oil companies: **Seven Sisters.**

Standard Oil King. Rockefeller, John D[avison].

Stanford University. 1. Athletic teams of: **Cardinals.** 2. Athletic teams of, with other teams in regional conference: **Pacific Ten.**

Stanish, Rudolph (born 1913). Chef and banquet manager: **Maestro of tha Omelet, Rudy the Omelet Man.**

Stanley, Augustus Owsley, III (born 1935). Drug manufacturer and peddler: **Hippieland's Court Chemist, King of Acid, LSD King, LSD Tycoon, Mr. LSD.**

Stan the Man. Musial, Stan.

St. Anthony's Town. San Antonio, Texas.

Star City of the South. Roanoke, Virginia.

Starfighter. Lockheed F-104 fighter-interceptor.

Starkweather, Charles (1940–59). Robber and mass murderer: **Little Red.**

Starlifter. Lockheed C-141 cargo-troop transport plane.

Star of the South. Alabama

Star of the Southland. Long Beach, California.

Starr, Ray[mond Francis] (1906–63). Baseball pitcher: **Iron Man.**

Stars and Stripes. The flag of the United States.

Star-Spangled Banner. The flag of the United States.

Star-Spangled Banner State. Maryland.

State City. Harrisburg, Pennsylvania.

State of Contrasts. Alaska.

State of Surprises. Indiana.

State of the Confederacy. Texas.

States, The. United States of America.

Statue of Liberty. Statue in New York Harbor: **The Lady, Lady with the Lamp, Mother of Exiles, New Colossus.**

Statue of Liberty Division. Seventy-seventh Infantry Division.

St. Augustine, Florida. U.S. town: **America's Oldest City, Fountain of Youth City.**

St. Bonaventure College, basketball teams of. With teams of Canisius College and Niagara University; **Little Three.**

Steadman, Vera (born 1900). Motion-picture actress: **Original Bathing Girl.**

Stearns, Harold Edmund (1891–1943). Writer: **America's Foremost Expatriate.**

Steel Baron. Carnegie, Andrew.

Steel Butterfly, The. Young, Loretta.

Steel City. Bethlehem, Pennsylvania; Gary, Indiana; Pittsburgh, Pennsylvania.

Steel City of the West. Pueblo, Colorado.

Steele, John Washington (1843–1920). Oil operator: **Coal-Oil Johnny.**

Steelers. Team of the Pittsburgh Pirates Football Club.

Steel King. Carnegie, Andrew.

Steel-Master Philanthropist. Carnegie, Andrew.

Steel State. Pennsylvania.

Steffens, [Joseph] Lincoln (1866–1936). Journalist and reformer: **Golden Rule Fellow, King of the Muckrakers, Municipal Muckraker.**

Steichen, Edward (1880–1973). Photographer: **Master Photographer, World War Photographer.**

Steinberg, Paul (born 1880). Basketball player and football coach: **Twister.**

Steinmetz, Charles Proteus (1865–1923). Electrical engineer and inventor: **Electrical Wizard, Steiny.** Born: Karl August Rudolf Steinmetz.

Steiny. Steinmetz, Charles Proteus.

Stephens, Vern[on Decatur, Jr.] (1920–68). Baseball shortstop: **Junior, Little Slug of the Boston Red Sox.**

Stephens, William P. (1855–1946). Journalist: **Father of American Yacht Reporting.**

Stern, Marie Simchow (born 1909). Illustrator: **Masha.**

Sternaman, Ed[ward] (active 1916). Football player: **Dutch.**

Steuer, Max D. (1871–1940). Criminal lawyer: **Greatest Criminal Lawyer of His Time.**

Steverino. Allen, Steve.

Stewart, Humphrey John (1854–1932). Composer and musician: **Walter Damrosch of the Pacific Coast.**

Stewart, James [Maitland] (born 1908). Actor, aviator, and U.S. Air Force General: **Grand Old Man of the Aw Shucks School.**

Stewart, Leroy (born 1914). Jazz bass player: **Slam.**

Stewart, Nels (1901–57). Hockey player: **Old Poison.**

St. George. McGovern, George [Stanley].

Sticks. Hooper, Nesbert

Stickum. Stabile, Jack.

Stieglitz, Alfred (1864–1946). Photographer and art patron: **Documentary Photographer.**

Stilwell, Joseph Warren (1883–1946). U.S. Army General: **Old Tu'key Neck, Uncle Joe, Vinegar Joe.**

Stimson, Henry L[ewis] (1867–1950). U.S. Cabinet member: **Stimy.**

Stimy. Stimson, Henry Lewis.

Stinky. Davis, Harry Albert.

Stirnweiss, George Henry (1919–58). Baseball second baseman and athletic coach: **Snuffy.**

Stix. Hooper, Nesbert.

St. John. Wooden, John [Robert].

St. Joseph's College, basketball team of, with other Philadelphia area teams: **Big Five.**

St. Lawrence University, athletic teams of: **Saints.**

St. Louis, Missouri. U.S. city: **Arch City, Child of the River, Gateway Arch City, Gateway to the West, Great River City, Mound City, Parking Lot City, Queen City of the Mississippi, Queen of the Mississippi.**

St. Louis Cardinals. National League baseball team: **The Birds, Gas House Gang.**

St. Louis University, athletic teams of: **Billikens.**

St. Norbert College, athletic teams of: **Green Knights.**

Stockton, California. U.S. city: **California's Inland Harbor, Home of Diamond Walnuts.**

St. Olaf College, athletic teams of: **Oles.**

Stone, John Vernon (born 1918). Baseball pitcher: **Rocky.**

Stone Mason of Tor House. Jeffers, [John] Robinson.

Stoney. McLinn, George E.

Storie, Howard Edward (1911–68). Baseball catcher: **Sponge.**

Storm, The. Van Lier, Norman, III.

Stormin' Norman. Van Lier, Norman, III.

Stormy. Weatherly, [Cyril] Roy.

Stormy Petrel. Chandler, William Eaton.

Storyville. Area of New Orleans where prostitution was tolerated, 1896–1917, and where early jazz developed.

Stout, Allyn McClelland (1904–74). Baseball pitcher: **Fish Hook.**

St. Paul, Minnesota. U.S. city: **Boston of the West, Gateway to the Famed Northwoods, North Star City, Saintly City.** With Minneapolis, Minnesota: **Twin Cities, Twin City.**

St. Paul Cyclone. O'Dowd, Mike.

St. Paul Phantom, The. Gibbons, Mike.

St. Pete. St. Petersburg, Florida.

St. Petersburg, Florida. U.S. city: **City of Homes, Geriatric City, St. Pete, Sun City, Sunshine City.**

Strader, Norman (1902–56). Football back and coach: **Red.**

Strangler, The. Lewis, Ed.

Stratford Streak. Morenz, Howie.

Stratofortress. Boeing B-52 bomber.

Stratojet. B-47 bomber.

Stratotanker. Boeing KC-135 tanker-transport plane.

Strauss, Harry (died 1941). Gangster: **Pittsburgh Phil.**

Strawberry. Townsend, John Gillis, Jr.

Strawberry Blonde. Minton, Yvonne.

Straw Hat Circuit. Circuit of summer theaters in the Middle Atlantic and New England States.

Strayhorn, Billy (1915–67). Jazz composer and pianist: **Swee' Pea.** Legal name: William Thomas Strayhorn.

Streamline. Ewing, John.

Street, Charles Evard (1882–1951). Baseball catcher and manager: **Gabby.**

Street, The. Fifty-second Street; Wall Street.

Street of Sorrows. Wall Street.

Street of Swing. Fifty-second Street.

Street Singer. Tracy, Arthur.

Stretch. Gregory, Francis Arnold.

Stringbean. Akeman, David.

String Town. Bremerton, Washington.

Strip, The. Main street of Las Vegas, Nevada.

Stripp, Joseph Valentine (born 1903). Baseball first and third baseman: **Jersey Joe.**

Stroll. Barney, Lemuel J.

Strong Boy of Boston. Sullivan, John Lawrence.

Strong Man of Wall Street. Whitney, Richard.

Strong-willed Mayor. Daley, Richard Joseph.

Stroud, Robert Franklin (1890–1963). Murderer, convict, and ornithologist: **Bird Man of Alcatraz.**

Struttin' Jim. Bottomley, James Leroy.

Stryfe, Paul (1907–66). Lawyer, mathematician, economist, and writer: **Einstein's Editor.** Legal name: James Roy Newman.

Stryker, Lloyd Paul (1885–1955). Criminal lawyer and writer: **Knight with the Rueful Countenance, Nation's Most Redoubtable Criminal Lawyer.**

Stuart, Lyle (born 1922). Publisher: **Bad Boy of Publishing.**

Stuart, Richard Lee (born 1932). Baseball first baseman: **Irrepressible Egoist, Old Stonefingers.**

Stub. Allison, Leonard B.

Stubby. Kruger, Harold; McGovern, Hugh; Pearson, Charles M.

Stub Toe State. Montana.

Student, The. Slosson, George F.

Student Nonviolent Coordinating Committee (later called **Student National Coordinating Committee).** Organization advocating Black Power (originally an interracial civil rights group), 1960s: **Snick.**

Studioland. Hollywood, California.

Studs. Terkel, Louis.

Stuff. Smith, Hezekiah Leroy Gordon.

Stuff and Guff. Statue of two bellringers below statue of Minerva, Herald Square, New York City.

Stuffy. McInnis, John Phelan.

Stuhldreher, Harry [Augustus] (1901–65). Football quarterback, coach, and steel company executive. With other members of Notre Dame backfield: **Four Horsemen.**

Stumpy. Brady, Floyd Maurice; Goodrich, Gail.

Sturhahn, Herbert (active 1926). Football player: **Cobbles.**

Stutz, Charles E. (1883?–1959). Pioneer automobile manufacturer. With Harry C. Stutz: **Fathers of the Bearcat.**

Stutz, Harry C. (1876–1930). Pioneer automobile manufacturer. With Charles E. Stutz: **Fathers of the Bearcat.**

Sucker State. Illinois.

Suds City. Milwaukee, Wisconsin.

Sugar. Cain, John; Cain, Merritt Patrick.

Sugar Bowl. Football stadium of Tulane University, New Orleans, Louisiana.

Sugar Daddy of Big Bankers. Burns, Arthur [Frank].

Sugar Hill. Area of expensive dwellings within Harlem district of New York City, extending fron West 138th Street to West 155th Street and from Eighth Avenue to Convent Avenue.

Sugar Ray. Robinson, Ray.

Sugar State. Louisiana.

Suitcase. Simpson, Harry Leon.

Suitcase Bob. Seeds, Robert Ira.

Sullivan, Ed[ward Vincent] (1902–74). Newspaper columnist and television personality: **Great Stone Face, Unsmiling Irishman.**

Sullivan, George James (born 1929). Canadian hockey center and coach: **Red.**

Sullivan, Jack (1878–1947). Welterweight and middleweight boxer: **Twin.**

Sullivan, John L[awrence] (1858–1918). Heavyweight boxer: **Boston Strong Boy, Great John L., John L., Strong Boy of Boston.**

Sullivan, Louis Henri (1856–1924). Architect. **Founder of Functionalism.**

Sullivan, Mark (1874–1952). Journalist, columnist, and commentator: **Dean of Washington Correspondents, Friend of Presidents.**

Sullivan, Michael (1878–1937). Welterweight and middleweight boxer: **Twin.**

Sullivan, Steve (born 1897). Lightweight boxer: **Kid.** Born: Stephen J. Tricamo.

Sullivan, Timothy Daniel (1862–1913). Politician and U.S. Representative from New York: **Big Feller, Big Tim, Last of the Big Time Grafters.**

Sullivan, William J., Sr. (1875–1965). Baseball catcher and manager: **Father of the Catcher's Chest Protector.**

Sultan of Swat. Ruth, Babe.

Sulzberger, Arthur Ochs (born 1926). Newspaper publisher: **Punch.**

Sulzberger, Iphigene Ochs (born 1892). Newspaper publisher: **Grey Lady of the** *Times.*

Summerall, Charles Pelot (1867–1955). U.S. Army General: **Sitting Bull.**

Summer City. Duluth, Minnesota.

Summit City. Akron, Ohio.

Sun Belt. Southern United States, esp. the region stretching from the Gulf Coast states to southern California.

Sun Bowl. Football stadium of the Texas College of Mines and Metallurgy, El Paso; site of annual Sun Bowl college football game.

Sunburst Division. Fortieth Infantry Division.

Sun City. Corpus Christi, Texas; St. Petersburg, Florida; Yuma, Arizona.

Sundance Kid, The. Brown, Henry.

Sunday, Billy (1862–1935). Baseball outfielder and evangelist: **Huckster of the Tabernacle, Parson.** Legal name: William Ashley Sunday.

Sunday Lady of Possum Trot. Berry, Martha McChesney.

Sun Devils. Athletic teams of Arizona State University, Tempe.

Sunflower State. Kansas.

Sunny. Clapp, Charles; Murray, James [Arthur].

Sunny Jim. Bottomley, James Leroy; Coffroth, James W.; Cosmano, Vincenzo; Fitzsimmons, James Edward.

Sunset Division. Forty-first Division.

Sunset Land. Arizona.

Sunset State. Arizona; Oregon.

Sunset Strip. Mile-long entertainment section of Sunset Boulevard, Los Angeles.

Sunshine Boy. Smith, Joseph.

Sunshine Capital of the United States. Yuma, Arizona.

Sunshine City. St. Petersburg, Florida; Tucson, Arizona; Yuma, Arizona.

Sunshine Coast. Coast of British Columbia near Vancouver.

Sunshine Division. Fortieth Division.

Sunshine Empire. California.

Sunshine Province. Alberta.

Sunshine State. Florida; New Mexico; South Dakota.

Super Bowl. Annual football game between the American Football League champions and the National Football League champions, usually held in various stadiums in Miami, Los Angeles, New Orleans, and Houston.

Super Circus Girl. Hartline, Mary.

Supercop. Rizzo, Frank.

Supercrat. Shultz, George [Pratt].

Superfortress. Boeing B-29 bomber, World War II.

Superhenry. Kissinger, Henry A[lfred].

Superior, Wisconsin. U.S. city: **City of the Northland, Four Season City, Hub of North America.** With Duluth, Minnesota: **Twin Ports.**

Super John. Williamson, John.

Super Jolly. Sikorsky CH/HH-53B/C helicopter.

Superman of the Prize Ring. Louis, Joe.

Supermex. Trevino, Lee [Buck].

Super Sabre. North American F-100 fighter plane.

Super Sixth. Sixth Armored Division.

Super Soda Pop Peddler. Kendall, Donald McIntosh.

Superstar of Pornography. Chambers, Marilyn.

Surfburgia. California beach communities, collectively.

Suther, John (active 1930). Football player: **Flash.**

Sutherland, John Bain (1889–1948). Football coach: **Dour Scot, Jock, Overland Man, Scotsman.**

Sutphin, William Halstead (born 1887). U.S. Representative from New Jersey: **Barnacle Bill.**

Sutton, William Francis (born 1901). Reformed bank robber: **Slick Willie, The Actor, Willie the Actor.** Also known as George Gordan.

Swain, Frederick Dwight (born 1909). Jazz musician: **Teeny.**

Swamp State. South Carolina.

Swanson, Claude Augustus (1862–1939). U.S. Secretary of the Navy: **Big Navy Claude.**

Swarthmore College, athletic teams of: **Little Quakers.**

Swarthout, Gladys (1904–69). Singer: **Prettiest Carmen on Record.**

Sweater Girl. Turner, Lana.

Sweatshirt Kid. Fischer, Bobby.

Swede. Hagberg, Rudolf; Johnson, Walter Perry; Larson, Emery Ellsworth; Oberlander, Andrew J.; Risberg, Charles August; Savage, David; Umbach, Arnold William.

Swee' Pea. Strayhorn, Billy.

Sweet D. Davis, Walt[er].

Sweet Emma the Bell Gal. Barrett, Emma.

Sweetest Swinger in Minnie. Carew, Rodney Cline.

Sweetheart of Columbia Records. Etting, Ruth.

Sweetheart of Second Avenue. Picon, Molly.

Sweetheart of the A.E.F. Janis, Elsie.

Sweetheart of the Foxholes. Lamour, Dorothy.

Sweethearts of the Air. De Rose, Peter and Breen, May Singhi.

Sweet Mama Stringbean, Waters, Ethel.

Sweet-Potato Man. Carver, George Washington.

Sweets. Edison, Harry.

Sweet Wine Center of the World. Fresno, California.

Swimming Pool City. Palm Springs, California.

Swindler of the Century. Koretz, Leo; Means, Gaston Bullock

Swing, Joseph May (born 1894). U.S. General: **Uncle Joe.**

Swing Alley. Fifty-second Street.

Swinger from Binger. Bench, Johnny.

Swing Street. Fifty-second Street.

Swirbul, Leon A. (1898–1960). Industrialist: **Jake.**

Swope, Herbert Bayard (1882–1958). Journalist: **Natural Force.**

Sy. Oliver, Melvin James.

Sycamore City. Terre Haute, Indiana.

Sycamores. Athletic teams of Indiana State University, Terre Haute.

Sydenstricker, Absalom (1852–1931). Missionary in China and father of Pearl Buck: **Fighting Angel.**

Sykowski, Abram (born 1892). International swindler and confidence man: **Dean of the Con Men, Frog Man, Human Frog, Kid Tiger, Modern Cagliostro.** Also known as Maxim Amedez, Alexander Dannot, Count Alexander Novarro Fernández, Max Frimen, Carlos Ladenis, Max Landeau, Carlos Nunn, Prince Alexander Romanoff, Alfred Roschildt.

Syllable-accenting American. Houdini, Harry.

Symons, Thomas William (1849–1920). Military engineer: **Father of the Barge Canal.**

Syndicate, The. Mafia.

Syracuse, New York. U.S. city: **City of Isms, City of Salt, Salt City.**

Syracuse University, athletic teams of: **Orangemen.**

T

Tacoma, Washington. U.S. city: **City of Destiny, Commencement City, Gateway to Mount Rainier, Lumber Capital.**

Tad. Jones, Thomas Albert Dwight.

Tadpole State. Mississippi.

Taffy. Wright, Taft Shedron.

Taft, Robert A[lphonso] (1889–1953). U.S. Senator from Ohio: **Mr. Republican.**

Taft, William Howard (1857–1930). Lawyer, twenty-seventh President of the United States, and Chief Justice of the United States: **The Big Chief.**

Tail Gunner Joe. McCarthy, Joseph R[aymond].

Talkative Tom. Blanton, Thomas Lindsay.

Tall Corn State. Nebraska.

Tall Pine of the Pottawatomie. Willard, Jess.·

Tall State. Illinois.

Tall Texan. Kilpatrick, Benjamin.

Tallu. Bankhead, Tallulah [Brockman].

Tallulah's Papa. Bankhead, William Brockman.

Tally. Gilliam, John [Rally].

Talmadge, Eugene (1884–1946). Governor of Georgia: **Old Gene.**

Talmadge, Herman Eugene (born 1913). U.S. Senator from Georgia: **Ol' Hummon.**

Talon. Northrop T-38 training plane.

Tamiami Trail. Florida road: **Alligator Alley.**

Tammany Tiger. Walker, James J[ohn].

Tampa, Florida. U.S. city: **Cigar Capital of America, Cigar City, Pirate City, Spanish Town.**

Tampa Bay Buccaneers. Football team: **Bucks.**

Tanana River City. Fairbanks, Alaska.

Tangerine Bowl. Football stadium in Orlando, Florida; site of annual Tangerine Bowl college football game.

Tania. Hearst, Patricia [Campbell].

Tank. McLaren, George W.

Tanner, Richard J. (1870–1943). Wild West showman: **Diamond Dick.**

Taps. Gallagher, John.

Tar Baby. Langford, Sam.

Tarbell, Ida Minerva (1857–1944). Editor and author: **Dean of Women Authors of America, Miss Tarbarrel, Mother of Muckrakers.**

Target Island. Kahoolawe, Hawaii.

Tarheeler. Native or resident of North Carolina.

Tarheels. Athletic teams of the University of North Carolina, Chapel Hill.

Tarheel State. North Carolina.

Tarkenton, Francis (born 1940). Football quarterback: **The Scrambler.**

Tarkington, [Newton] Booth (1869–1946). Novelist and playwright: **Gentleman from Indianapolis.**

Tarnished President. Nixon, Richard M[ilhous].

Tarzan. Cooper, Charles.

Tarzan Burroughs. Burroughs, Edgar Rice.

Tashrak. Zevin, Israel Joseph.

Tatum, James Moore (born 1913). Football coach: **Silent Jim.**

Tatum, Reese (1919–67). Basketball player: **Goose.**

Taxpayer's Haven. Hialeah, Florida.

Taylor, Alfred Alexander (1848–1931). U.S. Representative from Tennessee and Governor of Tennessee: **Knight of the Red Rose, Sage of Happy Valley, Uncle Alf.**

Taylor, [Charles] Bud (1903–62). Boxer, manager, and fight promoter: **Blond Terror from Terre Haute, Terre Haute Terror.**

Taylor, Chuck (1901–69). Basketball player and editor: **Ambassador of Basketball.** Legal name: Charles H. Taylor.

Taylor, James Wren (1898–1974). Baseball catcher and manager: **Zack.**

Taylor, [Joseph] Deems (1885–1966). Composer and music critic: **Smeed.**

Taylor, Maxwell D[avenport] (born 1901). U.S. Army General and diplomat: **Mr. Attack.**

Taylor, Robert (1911–69). Motion-picture actor: **Beautiful Bob.** Born: Spangler Arlington Brugh.

Taylor, Robert Dale (born 1939). Baseball catcher: **Hawk.**

Taylor, Robert Love (1850–1912). Governor of Tennessee and U.S. Senator from Tennessee: **Apostle of Sunshine, Fiddling Bob, Knight of the White Rose, Our Bob.**

Taylor, Theodore (1916–75). Blues guitarist: **Hound Dog.**

T-bird. Thunderbird.

T-bone. Walker, Aaron.

Teacher of Millions. Laubach, Frank Charles.

Teagarden, Clois Lee (born 1915). Jazz drummer: **Cub.**

Teagarden, Jack (1905–64). Jazz musician: **Big T.** Legal name: Weldon John Teagarden.

Teapot Dome. Scandal involving naval oil reserves at Teapot Dome, Wyoming, and at Elk Hills, California, leased without competitive bidding by Albert B. Fall, U.S. Secretary of the Interior, to private oil operators; Senate investigation of Fall led to his conviction and imprisonment for accepting bribes, 1921–30.

Tebbetts, George Robert (born 1912). Baseball catcher and manager: **Birdie.**

Tebeau, Oliver W. (1864–1918). Baseball first baseman and manager: **Patsy.**

Tech Hawks. Athletic teams of Armour Institute of Technology, Chicago, Illinois.

Teddy. Roosevelt, Theodore.

352

Teddy Ballgame. Turner, Ted; Williams, Ted.

Teeny. Swain, Frederick Dwight.

Teenyboppers' Super-Puppy. Cassidy, David.

Telescope Teddy. Roosevelt, Theodore.

Television City. Hollywood, California.

Television's Tiny Terror. Efron, Marshall.

Temple, Shirley (born 1928). Child motion-picture actress and government official: **Eighth Wonder of the World, Goldilocks.** Also known as Shirley Temple Black (Mrs. Charles A. Black).

Temple, The. Actors Studio.

Templeton, John Marks (born 1912). Businessman and investor: **Master Money Manager.**

Templeton, Robert L. (1897–1962). Football player and track coach: **Dink.**

Temple University. 1. Athletic teams of: **Owls.** 2. Basketball team of, with other Philadelphia area teams: **Big Five.**

Tenacious Muckraker. Pearson, Drew.

Tennessee. Sixteenth U.S. state: **Big Bend State, Hog and Hominy State, Interstate State, Lion's Den State, Volunteer State.**

Tennessee, University of, athletic teams of: **Volunteers.**

Tennessee, University of (at Chattanooga), athletic teams of: **Moccasins.**

Tennessee Ernie. Ford, Ernest Jennings.

Tennessee Plowboy, The. Arnold, Eddie.

Tennessee State University, athletic teams of: **Tigers.**

Tennessee-Tombigbee Waterway. Barge canal under construction between the Tennessee River and the Gulf of Mexico, along the Tombigbee River: **Tenn-Tom.**

Tennis Tycoon. King, Billie Jean [Moffitt].

Tenn-Tom. Tennessee-Tombigbee Waterway.

Ten Provinces. The Dominion of Canada.

Tenth Armored Division. U.S. Army division, World War II: **Tiger Division.**

Tenth Mountain Division. U.S. Army division, World War II: **Mountaineer Division.**

Terkel, Louis (born 1912). Writer: **Studs.**

Terps. Athletic teams of the University of Maryland, College Park.

Terrace City. Yonkers, New York.

Terrapin State. Maryland.

Terre Haute, Indiana. U.S. city: **Sycamore City.**

Terre Haute Terror. Taylor, [Charles] Bud.

Terrible John. Torrio, John.

Terrible Terry. McGovern, John Terrence.

Terrible Touhy. Touhy, Roger.

Terrible Turk. Reed, Thomas Brackett.

Terrible Turner. Turner, Richmond Kelly.

Terriers. Athletic teams of Boston University, Boston, Massachusetts.

Terris, Sid (born 1904). Bantamweight boxer: **Ghost of the Ghetto.**

Terry, Bill (born 1898). Baseball first baseman and manager: **Memphis Bill.** Legal name: William Harold Terry.

Terry, William H. (1864–1914). Baseball pitcher: **Adonis.**

Tesla, Nikola (1857–1943). Physicist, electrician, and inventor: **Eccentric Genius, Father of the Tesla Turbine.**

Tesreau, Charles Monroe (1889–1946). Baseball pitcher: **Jeff.**

Tewibble, The. Clarke, Norham Pfardt.

Tex. Carleton, James O.; Clevenger, Truman Eugene; Coulter, DeWitt; Garms, Debs G.; Thornton, Charles Bates.

Texaco. Business organization; with six other oil companies: **Seven Sisters.**

Texarkana, Arkansas. U.S. city. With Texarkana, Texas: **Twin Cities.**

Texarkana, Texas. U.S. city. With Texarkana, Arkansas: **Twin Cities.**

Texas. Guinan, Mary Louise Cecelia.

Texas. Twenty-eighth U.S. state: **Alligator State, Banner State, Beef State, Blizzard State, Jumbo State, Lone Star State, Orange State, State of the Confederacy.** With New Mexico: **Texico.** With Oklahoma: **Texhoma, Texola.**

Texas, University of, athletic teams of: **Longhorns.**

Texas, University of (at Arlington), athletic teams of: **Mavericks.**

Texas, University of (at El Paso), athletic teams of: **Miners.**

Texas A & M, athletic teams of: **Aggies.**

Texas Christian University, athletic teams of: **Horned Frogs.**

Texas Computer Millionaire. Perot, H. Ross.

Texas Division. Thirty-sixth Infantry Division.

Texas Gulf Sulphur Company. Business organization: **Tough Guy.**

Texas Jack. Reed, Nathaniel.

Texas Jim. Robertson, James B.

Texas Southern University, athletic teams of: **Tigers.**

Texas Tech University, athletic teams of: **Red Raiders.**

Texas Titan. Ling, James Joseph.

Texas Tom. Connally, Tom.

Texas Tornado, The. DeBakey, Michael Ellis.

Texhoma. Texas and Oklahoma.

Texico. Texas and New Mexico.

Texola. Texas and Oklahoma.

Thalberg, Irving Grant (1899–1936). Motion-picture producer: **Boy Producer.**

That Bad Eartha. Kitt, Eartha [Mae].

That Girl. Thomas, Marlo.

That Man in the White House. Roosevelt, Franklin D[elano].

Thaw, Harry Kendall (1871–1947). Playboy and murderer of Stanford White: **The Mad Pittsburgh Playboy.**

Theodore the Meddler. Roosevelt, Theodore.

Thersites of American Drama Critics. Nathan, George Jean.

Thiel College, athletic teams of: **Tomcats.**

Thielemans, Jean (born 1922). Jazz guitarist, harmonica player, and whistler: **Toots.**

Third Armored Division. U.S. Army division, World War II: **Spearhead Division.**

Third Division. U.S. Army division, World War I: **Marne Division, Rock of the Marne.**

Third Infantry Division. U.S. Army division, World War II: **Marne Division.**

Thirteenth Armored Division. U.S. Army division, World War II: **Black Cat Division.**

Thirtieth Division, American Expeditionary Force. U.S. Army division, World War I: **Old Hickory Division.**

Thirty-eighth Infantry Division. U.S. Army division, World War II: **Cyclone Division.**

Thirty-fifth Infantry Division. U.S. Army division, World War II: **Santa Fe Division.**

Thirty-first Infantry Division. U.S. Army division, World War II: **Dixie Division.**

Thirty-fourth Infantry Division. U.S. Army division, World War II: **Red Bull Division.**

Thirty-one Knot Burke. Burke, Arleigh Albert.

Thirty Rock. The National Broadcasting Company.

Thirty-second Infantry Division. U.S. Army division, World War II: **Red Arrow Division.**

Thirty-seventh Infantry Division. U.S. Army division, World War II: **Buckeye Division.**

Thirty-sixth Division. U.S. Army division, World War I: **Lone Star Division, Panther Division.**

Thirty-sixth Infantry Division. U.S. Army division, World War II: **Texas Division.**

Thirty-third Infantry Division. U.S. Army division, World War II: **Illinois Division, Prairie Division.**

Thomas, Alvin Clarence (born 1892). Gambler: **The Derby Kid, Slim, Titanic Thompson.**

Thomas, Frank William (1898–1959). Football coach: **Rat.**

Thomas, J[ohn] Parnell (1895–1970). U.S. Representative from New Jersey: **Impeachment Thomas.**

Thomas, [John William] Elmer (1876–1965). U.S. Representative and Senator from Oklahoma: **Silver Sage.**

Thomas, Marlo (born 1937). Television actress: **Miss Independent, Princess of Situation Comedy, That Girl, The Velvet Steamroller.**

Thomas, Walter Purl (born 1907). Jazz musician; **Foots.**

Thomas Jefferson of Folk Music. Seeger, Pete[r].

Thompson, David (born 1954). Basketball forward: **The Franchise.**

Thompson, Dorothy (1894–1961). Journalist: **Cassandra of the Columnists, Contemporary Cassandra.**

Thompson, Eli (born 1924). Jazz saxophonist: **Lucky.**

Thompson, James R[obert] (born 1936). Governor of Illinois: **Big Jim.**

Thompson, John (1862–1944). Chicago clergyman: **Shepherd of the Loop.**

Thompson, John (1876–1951). Middleweight boxer: **Cyclone.**

Thompson, John Taliaferro (1860–1940). Army engineering officer and inventor of firearms: **Father of the Tommy Gun.**

Thompson, [Marion] Lee (born 1928). Automobile racing driver: **Mickey.**

Thompson, Russell (died 1953). Bible salesman and alleged machine-gun merchant: **Machine-Gun Frank.**

Thompson, William Hale (1869–1944). Mayor of Chicago: **Big Bill.**

Thompson submachine gun. Portable, .45-caliber weapon, designed to be fired from the shoulder or hip; named after John Taliaferro Thompson, who, aided by John N. Blish, invented it: **Tommy Gun.**

Thomson, Elihu (1853–1937). Electrical engineer and inventor: **The Beloved Scientist.**

Thornhill, Claude E. (1893–1956). Football tackle and coach: **Tiny.**

Thornton, Charles Bates (born 1913). Industrialist: **Tex.**

Thor of the Ring. Dempsey, Jack.

Three-Finger Brown. Luchese, Thomas.

Three-Fingered Brown. Brown, Mordecai Peter Centennial.

Three-Fingers Brown. Castellito, Anthony.

Three-Minute Brumm. Brumm, George Franlin.

Three-Twelve. Luciano, Charles.

Thud. Republic F-105 fighter-bomber, Vietnam War.

Thunderbird. Type of Ford automobile: **T-bird.**

Thunderbird Division. Forty-fifth Infantry Division.

Thunderbolt. Republic P-47 fighter-bomber, World War II.

Thunderbolt, The. Papke, Billy.

Thunderbolt Division. Eighty-third Infantry Division; Eleventh Armored Division.

Thunderchief. Republic F-105 fighter-bomber, Vietnam War.

Thunder from Heaven Division. Seventeenth Airborne Division.

Thundering Herd. 1. Athletic teams of Marshall University, Huntington, West Virginia. 2. Merrill Lynch, Pierce, Fenner & Smith.

Thunderjet. Republic F-84E fighter plane, Korean War.

Thunder Maker. Jones, Howard [Harding].

Thunderstreak. Republic F-84 fighter plane, Korean War.

Thurmond, [James] Strom (born 1902). U.S. Senator from South Carolina: **Sperm.**

Thursday's Child. Kitt, Eartha [Mae].

Thurston, Hollis John (1899–1973). Baseball pitcher: **Sloppy.**

Tic. Forrester, Elijah Lewis.

Tickner, Charlie (born 1953). Figure skater: **Mr. Perseverance.** Legal name: Charles Tickner.

Tico. Harris, William.

Tidal Basin Bombshell. Foxe, Fanne.

Tierney, James Arthur (1894–1953). Baseball second and third baseman: **Cotton.**

Tiffany, Louis Comfort (1848–1933). Designer and manufacturer: **Perfecter of Opalescent Glass.**

Tiger. Flowers, Theodore; Hoak, Donald Albert; Northrup F-5 fighter plane; Williams, Dave.

Tiger Division. Tenth Armored Division.

Tiger Jack. Fox, John Linwood.

Tigers. Athletic teams of Auburn University, Auburn, Alabama; Clemson University, Clemson, South Carolina; Grambling University, Grambling, Louisiana; Jackson State University, Jackson, Mississippi; Memphis State University, Memphis, Tennessee; University of Missouri, Columbia; University of the Pacific, Stockton, California; Princeton University, Princeton, New Jersey; Tennessee State University, Nashville; and Texas Southern University, Houston.

Tilden, Bill (1893–1953). Tennis player: **Big Bill, Court Jouster.** Legal name: William Tatem Tilden II.

Tillman, Benjamin Ryan (1847–1918). Governor of South Carolina and U.S. Representative from South Carolina: **Agricultural Moses, Father of the Shell Manifesto, Pitchfork Ben.**

Tilly. Bishop, Max Frederick; Walker, Clarence William.

Tilmon, James (born 1934). Aviator: **Jet Age Renaissance Man.**

Timberwolf Division. One Hundred and Fourth Infantry Division.

Tim-Tom. Conway, Thomas.

Tin Goose. Ford Tri-motor airliner, 1920s.

Tink. Tinkham. George Holden.

Tinker. Scott, Barbara Ann.

Tinkham, George Holden (1870–1956). U.S. Representative from Massachusetts: **Big Game Hunter, Lion Hunter, Tink, Wiskers.**

Tin Lizzie. Model-T Ford.

Tino. DeAngelis, Anthony.

Tin Pan Alley. Area of Manhattan frequented by song writers and publishers; originally the theatrical district of Broadway.

Tinsel City. Hollywood, California.

Tiny. Archibald, Nate; Bonham, Ernest Edward; Bradshaw, Myron; Grimes, Lloyd; Kahn, Norman; Roebuck, Theodore; Thornhill, Claude E.

Tiny Tim. Khaury, Herbert Buckingham.

Tioga. Burns, George Henry.

Tip. O'Neill, Thomas P., Jr.; Tobin, John.

Tipton Slasher. Yanger, Benny.

Tire City of the United States. Akron, Ohio.

Titanic Thompson. Thomas, Alvin Clarence.

Titans. Athletic teams of California State University, Fullerton.

Titletown, U.S.A. Green Bay, Wisconsin.

Tittle, Y[elberton] A[braham] (born 1926). Football quarterback: **Bald Eagle, Colonel Slick, Y.A.**

T-Man. Agent of the United States Treasury Department.

Toast of the Barbary Coast. Prado, Katie.

Toat. Todd, Michael.

Tobacco Bill. Crosby, William R.

Tobacco State. Kentucky.

Tobacco Trust. American Tobacco Company, 1911.

Tobey, David (born 1898). Basketball player and official: **Pep.**

Tobin, Daniel J[oseph] (1875–1955). Labor leader: **Big Dan, Uncle Dan.**

Tobin, John (active 1929–32). Football player: **Tip.**

Toby. Hardwicke, Otto.

Todd, Michael (1909–58). Promoter and theatrical producer: **America's Greatest Showman, Cut-Rate Showman, Nazim of Necromantic Nudity, New Ziegfeld, Toat.** Born: Avrom Hirsch Goldbogen.

Todman, William [Selden] (1916–79). Television producer. With Mark Goodson: **Maharajahs of Paneldom.**

Toe. Blake, Hector.

Toe, The. Groza, Lou[is].

Togie. Pittinger, Charles R.

Tokle, Torger D. (1920–45). Ski jumper: **Flying Norseman.**

Tokyo Rose. D'Aquino, Iva Ikuko Toguri.

Tolan, Edward (1909–67). Track star: **Midnight Express.**

Toledo, Ohio. U.S. city: **Corn City, Glass Capital of Ohio, Glass City, Mud Hen City.**

Toledo, University of, athletic teams of: **Rockets.**

Toledo's Red Smith. Smith, Richard Paul.

Tomahawk. Curtiss P-40 fighter plane, World War II; U.S. Navy cruise missile, 1970s.

Tomato State. Ohio.

Tomboy with the Voice. Day, Doris.

Tombstone, Arizona. U.S. town: **Town Too Tough to Die.**

Tomcats. Athletic teams of Thiel College, Greenville, Pennsylvania.

Tomlin, Truman (born 1908). Jazz musician: **Pinky.**

Tommy Gun. Thompson submachine gun.

Tommy the Cork. Corcoran, Thomas Gardiner.

Tom Terrific. Seaver, Tom.

Tom-tom-beater. Early automobile publicity man.

Tonguepoint Mott. Mott, James Wheaton.

Tony. Antoinette Perry Award.

Tony Pro. Provenzano, Tony.

Tony Scarface. Capone, Al[phonse].

Tony the Silent. Piet, Tony.

Tooey. Spaatz, Carl.

Too Tall Jones. Jones, Ed[ward].

Toothpick. 1. Jones, Samuel Pond. 2. Native or resident of Arkansas.

Toothpick State. Arkansas.

Tootie. Heath, Albert.

Toots. Mondello, Nuncia; Shor, Bernard; Thielemans, Jean.

Topeka, Kansas. U.S. city: **Center of the Nation.**

Top Football Coach in America. Parker, Buddy.

Top of the Nation. Colorado.

Topperwein, Elizabeth [Servanty] (died 1945). Champion trap-shooter: **Plinky.**

Topsy. Duncan, Rosetta.

Top Wheel at the Brickyard. Rose, Mauri.

Tormé, Mel[vin Howard] (born 1925). Singer: **Velvet Fog.**

Tornado Jake. Weimer, Jake.

Toronto, Ontario. Canadian city: **Queen City of Canada, Queen City of the Lakes.**

Torrio, John (1885–1957). Chicago gangster: **Father of Modern American Gangsterdom, The Fox, The Immune, Little John, Terrible John.** Also known as Frank Langley, J.T. McCarthy.

Torture Murderess. Baniszewski, Gertrude Wright.

Toscanini, Arturo (1867–1957). Orchestra conductor: **The Maestro.**

Totah, Nabil Marshall (born 1930). Jazz bass player: **Knobby.**

Toughest Cop in America. Rizzo, Frank.

Tough Guy. Texas Gulf Sulphur Company.

Tough Ombres. Ninetieth Infantry Division.

Tough Tony. Anastasio, Anthony.

Touhy, Roger (1898–1959). Gangster: **Black Roger, Roger the Terrible, Terrible Touhy.**

Tourbillon, Robert Arthur (born 1885). Robber and swindler: **Ratsy, Cromwell, Harry Hussey, Dapper.** Also known as Con Collins.

Towers, John Henry (1885–1955). U.S. Navy Admiral: **Father of Naval Aviation.**

Town Crier. Woollcott, Alexander [Humphreys].

Towne, Stuart (born 1906). Magician, editor, and author: **The Great Merlini.** Legal name: Clayton Rawson.

Townsend, Francis Everett (1867–1960). Physician and social reformer: **Father of the Townsend Plan, Hammer of Thor.**

Townsend, John Gillis, Jr. (1871–1964). U.S. Senator from Delaware: **Strawberry.**

Town That Roses Built. Pasadena, California.

Town Too Tough to Die. Tombstone, Arizona.

Toy Bulldog. Walker, Mickey.

Toy Cannon, The. Wynn, Jim.

Tracy, Arthur (active 1925–35). Radio singer and accordionist: **Street Singer.**

Tracy, Spencer (1900–67). Motion-picture actor. **Old Bucko.**

Trader Vic. Bergeron, Victor Jules.

Tradewind. Convair P5Y or R3Y turboprop seaplane, late 1940s.

Trailblazer Division. Seventieth Infantry Division.

Tram. Trumbauer, Frank.

Tramp Champ. Nicholson, Alexandra.

Tramp Poet. Kemp, Harry Hibbard.

Trane. Coltrane, John.

Trappier, Arthur Benjamin (born 1910). Jazz drummer: **Traps.**

Traps. Trappier, Arthur Benjamin.

Traynor, Harold Joseph (1899–1972). Baseball shortstop and manager: **Pie.**

Treasure State. Montana.

Tree. Adams, John W.

Tree Planters' State. Nebraska.

Trevino, Lee [Buck] (born 1939). Golfer: **Supermex.**

Triad. Curtiss biplane, 1911.

Tribe. Cleveland Indians.

Tricky. Lofton, Lawrence.

Tricky Dick. Hyland, Richard; Nixon, Richard M[ilhous].

Tricky Sam. Nanton, Joseph.

Trietsch, Paul (active 1920s and 1930s). Singer and novelty musician: **Hezzie.**

Trigger. Alpert, Herman S.

Trigger Mike. Coppola, Michael.

Trimountain City. Boston, Massachusetts.

Triple Crown. The winning of the Kentucky Derby, the Preakness, and the Belmont Stakes.

Triple-Threat Girl. Garland, Judy.

Tripsville. Haight-Ashbury.

Tris. Speaker, Tristram.

Tri-State Capital. Memphis, Tennessee.

Tri-State Terror. Underhill, Wilbur.

Trojan, The. Evers, John Joseph.

Trojans. Athletic teams of the University of Southern California (USC), Los Angeles.

Tropea, Arazio (died 1925). Gangster; **Scourge.**

Tropic Lightning Division. Twenty-fifth Infantry Division.

Tropic Metropolis. Miami, Florida.

Troubled Pied Piper of Los Alamos. Oppenheimer, J[ulius] Robert.

Trout, Paul Howard (1915–72). Baseball pitcher: **Dizzy.**

Troy, New York. U.S. city: **Collar City.**

Truck. Parham, Charles Valdez; Robinson, Len.

Trudeau, Edward Livingston (1848–1915). Physician and pioneer in tuberculosis research: **Doctor Who Would Not Die.**

True Athenian. Mehre, Harry J.

Truly. Shattuck, Claire Etrulia.

Truman, Harry S (1884–1972). Thirty-third President of the United States: **Give 'Em Hell Harry, Haberdasher Harry, HST, High Tax Harry, Man from Missouri, Man of Independence.**

Trumbauer, Frank (1901–56). Jazz saxophonist: **Tram.**

Trummy. Young, James Osborne.

Trumpeting Behemoth. Hirt, Al[ois Maxwell].

Trust Buster. Roosevelt, Theodore.

Trust-busting President. Roosevelt, Theodore.

Tschirky, Oscar (1866–1950). Maître d'hotel: **Oscar of the Waldorf.**

Tubby. Hall, Alfred; Hayes, Edward Brian.

Tuckahoe. Native or resident of Virginia.

Tucker, Preston [Thomas] (1903–56). Automobile industrial executive: **Father of the Tucker Torpedo.**

Tucker, Richard (1913–75). Operatic tenor: **Met's Second Caruso.** Born: Reuben Ticker.

Tucker, Sophie (1884–1966). Entertainer: **Last of the Red-Hot Mamas, Mary Garden of Ragtime, Queen of Jazz.** Born: Sophie Abuza.

Tuckerman, Earle (active 1920s and 1930s). Radio singer: **Dusty.** With Harvey Hindermyer: **The Gold Dust Twins.**

Tucson, Arizona. U.S. city: **Ancient and Honorable Pueblo, Center of the Copper Circle, Heart of the Old Southwest, Old Pueblo, Retirement Center of the Nation, Sunshine City, Western Gateway to Mexico.**

Tuffy. Leemans, Alphonse.

Tufts University, athletic teams of: **Jumbos.**

Tug. McGraw, Frank Edwin; Wilson, Kenneth L.

Tugwell, Rexford Guy (1891–1979). Economist and U.S. Undersecretary of Agriculture: **Barrymore of the Brain Trust, Mr. American.**

Tulane University, athletic teams of: **Green Wave.**

Tully. Kossack, N.E.

Tulsa, Oklahoma. U.S. city: **Fair Little City, Most Northern Southern City, Oil Capital of the World, Ozarks' Western Gateway.**

Tulsa, University of, athletic teams of: **Golden Hurricane.**

Tune Detective. Spaeth, Sigmund [Gottfried].

Tunney, Gene (1898–1978). Heavyweight boxer: **Fighting Marine.** Legal name: James Joseph Tunney.

Turk. Broda, Walter; Edwards, Albert Glen; Murphy, Mel[vin E.]; Sanderson, Derek [Michael].

Turner, Alfred L. (born 1911). Football player: **Warhorse.**

Turner, Clyde Douglas (born 1919). Football center and coach: **Bulldog, The Dog, Kid from Sweetwater.**

Turner, Frederick Jackson (1861–1935). Historian: **America's Foremost Historian.**

Turner, John C. (1896–1949). Composer and musician: **Happy.**

Turner, Joseph (born 1911). Blues singer: **Big Joe.**

Turner, Lana (born 1920). Motion-picture actress: **Sweater Girl.** Born: Jean Mildred Frances Turner. Also known as Jud Turner.

Turner, R[ichmond] Kelly (1885–1961). U.S. Admiral, World War II: **Terrible Turner.**

Turner, Roscoe (1895–1970). Aviation pioneer: **Speed King of the Air.**

Turner, Ted (born 1938). Business executive and sportsman: **The Mouth of the South, Teddy Ballgame.** Legal name: Robert Edward Turner 3d.

Turpentine State. North Carolina.

Turpin, Ben[jamin] (1874–1940). Motion-picture comedian: **Cross-eyed Comedian.**

Turpin, Charles Murray (1878–1946). U.S. Representative from Pennsylvania: **Ben.**

Tuscaloosa, Alabama. U.S. city: **Athens of Alabama.**

Tuss. McLaughry, De Ormond.

T.V.A. Rankin. Rankin, John Elliott.

Twelfth Armored Division. U.S. Army division, World War II: **Hellcat Division.**

Twentieth Amendment. Amendment of the United States Constitution eliminating a post-election congressional session and advancing the presidential inaugural: **Lame Duck Amendment.**

Twentieth-Century Borgia. Archer-Gillian, Amy.

Twentieth Century Gabriel. Hawkins, Erskine.

Twentieth-Century Moses. Chaplin, Charlie.

Twenty-eighth Infantry Division. U.S. Army division, World War II: **Keystone Division.**

Twenty-fifth Infantry Division. U.S. Army division, World War II: **Tropic Lightning Division, Pineapple Division.**

Twenty-fourth Infantry Division. U.S. Army division, World War II: **Victory Division.**

Twenty-ninth Infantry Division. U.S. Army division, World War II: **Blue and Gray division.**

Twenty-seventh Division. U.S. Army division, World War I: **New York Division.**

Twenty-sixth Infantry Division. U.S. Army division, World War II: **Yankee Division.**

Twin. Sullivan, Jack; Sullivan, Michael.

Twin Citian. Native or resident of St. Paul or Minneapolis.

Twin Cities. Champaign and Urbana, Illinois; Minneapolis and St. Paul, Minnesota; Texarkana, Arkansas, and Texarkana, Texas; Miami and Miami Beach, Florida; Winston-Salem, North Carolina.

Twin City. Minneapolis and St. Paul, Minnesota; Winston-Salem, North Carolina.

Twin Ports. Duluth, Minnesota, and Superior, Wisconsin.

Twin Sisters. North Dakota and South Dakota.

Twin States: Vermont and New Hampshire.

Twister. Steinberg, Paul.

Twist King. Checker, Chubby.

Two-edged Knife, The. Bilbo, Theodore Gilmore.

Twofer. Two theater tickets for the price of one.

Two-Gun Alterie. Alterie, Louis.

Two Gun Crowley. Crowley, Francis.

Two-Gun Girl. Guinan, Mary Louise Cecelia.

Two-Gun Hart. Capone, Vincenzo.

Two-Ton Baker. Baker, Richard E.

Two-Ton Tony. Galento, Tony.

Two-Way Corrigan. Corrigan, Mark.

Tyler, George Albert (1889–1953). Baseball pitcher: **Lefty.**

Typhoid Mary. Mallon, Mary.

Typical American. Roosevelt, Theodore.

U

Uatoab Clarke. Clarke, Norham Pfardt.
Ubiquitous Financier of the Universe. Mellon, Andrew William.
Udall, Morris K. (born 1922). U.S. Representative from Arizona: **Mo.**
Uhle, George Ernest (born 1898). Baseball pitcher: **Bull.**
Ukelele. Union Carbide.
Ukelele Ace. Marvin, Johnny.
Ukelele Ike. Edwards, Cliff.
Umbach, Arnold William (born 1903). Wrestling coach: **Swede.**
Umbrella Mike. Doyle, Michael J.
Uncle Alf. Taylor, Alfred Alexander.
Uncle Charlie. Adams, Charles Francis; Moran, Charles B.
Uncle Cornpone. Johnson, Lyndon Baines.
Uncle Dan. Beard, Daniel Carter; Tobin, Daniel Joseph.
Uncle Dud. Leblanc, Dudley J.
Uncle Fudd. McComb, Robert.
Uncle Gene. Ormandy, Eugene.
Uncle George. Cohan, George M[ichael].
Uncle Igor. Sikorsky, Igor [Ivan].
Uncle Jim. Wilson, James Walter.
Uncle Joe. Cannon, Joseph Gurney; Schenck, Joseph M.; Stilwell, Joseph Warren; Swing, Joseph May.
Uncle John. Crockett, John C.

Uncle Milty. Berle, Milton.

Uncle Pike. Noble, Clem.

Uncle Sam. 1. Ervin, Sam[uel James, Jr.]. 2. United States of America (or its government).

Uncle Sam's Crib. Treasury of the United States.

Uncle Sam's Favorite Niece. Lamour, Dorothy.

Uncle Sam's Icebox. Alaska.

Uncle Sam's Pocket Handkerchief. Delaware.

Uncle Sap. Uncle Sam as a gullible figure in world politics.

Uncle Tim. Leary, Timothy [Francis].

Uncle Toby. Cross, Wilbur [Lucius].

Uncle Tom. 1. Corwine, Thomas R. 2. Black who is abjectly servile or deferential to whites.

Uncle Walter. Cronkite, Walter [Leland, Jr.].

Uncle Whit. Chambers, [Jay David] Whittaker.

Uncrowned Champion. Basilio, Carmen.

Underhill, Wilbur (1897–1934). Bank robber: **Tri-State Terror.**

Undisputed King of Handcuffs. Houdini, Harry.

Undisputed Master of Light Verse. Nash, [Frederic] Ogden.

Undisputed Queen of the Movies. Grable, Betty.

Union Carbide. Business organization: **Ukelele.**

United Nations Capital. New York City.

United States, **S.S.** American luxury ocean liner, 1952–69: **Big U.**

United States Air Force Academy, athletic teams of: **Falcons.**

United States Coast Guard Academy, athletic teams of: **Cadets.**

United States Department of State: Foggy Bottom.

United States Marine Corps. Military force: **Devil Dogs, Leathernecks.**

United States Military Academy (also called West Point), athletic teams of: **Black Knights, Cadets.**

United States Naval Academy (also called Annapolis), athletic teams of: **Middies, Midshipmen.**

United States of America (the country or its government): **God's Country, Land of the Free, Nation of Cities, The States, Uncle Sam, U.S., U.S.A., U.S. of A.**

Universal Female Athlete. Sears, Eleonora R.

University City. Cambridge, Massachusetts; Gainesville, Florida.

Unknown Soldier. Moody, Orville.

Unlikely Villain. Calley, William Laws.

Unreconstructed Amateur. Stagg, Amos Alonzo.

Unreconstructed Rebel. Glass, Carter.

Unsinkable Molly Brown. Brown, Margaret Tobin.

Unsmiling Irishman. Sullivan, Ed[ward Vincent].

Unspoiled Empire. New Mexico.

Unterberg, David (born c. 1912). Lawyer and consumer advocate: **Condominium Gadfly, Don Quixote.**

Upsala College, athletic teams of: **Vikings.**

Upton, Thomas Herbert (born 1926). Baseball shortstop: **Muscles.**

Urbana, Illinois. U.S. city. With Champaign, Illinois: **Twin Cities.**

U.S. The United States of America.

U.S.A. The United States of America.

U.S. of A. The United States of America.

Utah. Forty-fifth U.S. state: **Beehive State, Mormon State, Land of the Mormons, Deseret State, Honey State, Land of Honey Bees, Land of the Saints, Salt Lake State.**

Utah, University of, athletic teams of: **Utes.**

Utah State University, athletic teams of: **Aggies.**

Utah Zion. Salt Lake City, Utah.

Utes. Athletic teams of the University of Utah, Salt Lake City.

Uvalde Jack. Garner, John Nance.

V

Vacation City on Casco Bay. Portland, Maine.

Vacationland. Maine.

Vacationland of Opportunity. Alaska.

Vacation State. Nevada.

Vacuum Cleaner. Robinson, Brooks [Calbert, Jr.].

Vagabond Lover. Vallee, Rudy.

Valdéz, Carlos (born 1913). Jazz guitarist and bongo drummer: **Potato.**

Valentine State. Arizona.

Valiant, James (born c. 1940). Wrestler: **Irascible Easterner.**

Valkyrie. B-70 delta-winged bomber, 1960s.

Vallee, Rudy (born 1901). Musician and actor: **The Crooner, Vagabond Lover.** Born: Hubert Prior Vallee.

Valley Between Two Worlds. Rio Grande Valley.

Valley Gang. Group of transporters of illicit beer, Chicago, 1920s.

Valley Isle. Maui, Hawaii.

Valley of God's Pleasure. Shaker Heights and adjoining suburbs of Cleveland, Ohio.

Valley of Opportunity. Region adjacent to Binghamton, New York.

Valley of Wonders. Yellowstone National Park.

Valli, Virginia (born 1899). Motion-picture actress: **Outdoor Girl of the Films.**

Vance, Clarence Arthur (1891–1961). Baseball pitcher: **Dazzy.**

Vance, Joseph Albert (born 1905). Baseball pitcher: **Sandy.**

Vancoo. Vancouver, British Columbia.

Vancouver, British Columbia. Canadian city: **City by the Lion's Gate, Vancoo.**

Vandals. Athletic teams of the University of Idaho, Moscow.

Vandegrift, Alexander Archer (1887–1973). Commandant of the U.S. Marine Corps: **Guadalcanal General.**

Vanderbilt, Gloria (born 1924). Heiress and clothing designer: **Poor Little Rich Girl.**

Vanderbilt University, athletic teams of: **Commodores.**

Vander Meer, John [Samuel] (born 1914). Baseball pitcher: **Double No-Hit Kid.**

Van Dine, Harvey (active 1910–20). Gangster: **Little Songbird from Italy.**

Van Duren, Kathleen Rockwell Waner Matson (1880?–1957). Alaska gold rush character: **Klondike Kate.**

Vanished Judge. Crater, Joseph Force.

Van Lier, Norman, III (born 1947). Basketball player: **Stormin' Norman, The Storm.**

Van Zandt, James Edward (born 1898). U.S. Representative from Pennsylvania: **Father of the Bonus.**

Vanzetti, Bartolomeo (1888–1927). Anarchist executed (after widely publicized trial and appeal) for murder committed in South Braintree, Massachusetts in 1921. With Nicola Sacco: **Braintree Martyrs.**

Vapor City. Hot Springs, Arkansas.

Varco, Joseph Vincent Di (born 1911). Gangster: **Little Caesar.**

Vassar College. Educational institution; with six other women's colleges: **Seven Sisters.**

Vast Wasteland. Television.

Vaudeville's Ageless Song and Dance Man. Rooney, Pat, II.

Vaudeville's Youngest Headliner. West, Mae.

Vaugh, James Leslie (1888–1966). Baseball pitcher: **Hippo.**

Vaughan, Joseph Floyd (1912–52). Baseball shortstop and third baseman: **Arky.**

Vaughan, Sarah (born 1924). Singer: **The Divine One.**

Vaughn, Miles W. (1894–1949). Press service executive: **Peg.**

Vecchio, Mary (active 1970s). Prostitute: **Hapless Hooker.**

Veep, The. Barkley, Alben William.

Vega. Any of various passenger/cargo land planes and floatplanes built by the Lockheed Aircraft Company, 1927–35.

Vegas. Las Vegas, Nevada.

Vegetable Sisters of the Stage. Cherry Sisters.

Vehicle City. Flint, Michigan.

Velvet Fog. Tormé, Melvin Howard.

Velvet Steamroller. Thomas, Marlo.

Venice of America. Annapolis, Maryland; Fort Lauderdale, Florida.

Vermont. Fourteenth U.S. state: **Beckoning Country, Green Mountain State.** With New Hampshire: **Twin States.**

Vermont, University of, athletic teams of: **Catamounts.**

Vesco, Robert L[ee] (born 1935). Fugitive financier, accused of mutual fund swindle and corporate misconduct: **Bootstrap Kid.**

V for 5th and Victory. Fifth Armored Division.

Víbora Seca. Floyd, Jacob J.

Vibrato, The. Eckstine, Billy.

Vicious Circle. Algonquin Round Table.

Vickers. Kaufman, Wallace.

Vicksburg, Mississippi. U.S. city: **Gibraltar of the Confederacy.**

Victory and OK Division. Ninety-fifth Infantry Division.

Victory Division. Twenty-fourth Infantry Division.

Vidal, Gore (born 1925). Author: **Masked Marvel of Modern Letters.**

Vikings. Athletic teams of Lawrence University, Appleton, Wisconsin, and Upsala College, East Orange, New Jersey.

Village, The. Greenwich Village.

Village of Museums. Cooperstown, New York.

Villanova University. 1. Athletic teams of: **Wildcats.** 2. Basketball team of, with other Philadelphia area teams: **Big Five.**

Vincent, Clinton D[ermott] (1914–55). U.S. Army Air Forces General and aviator, World War II: **Casey.**

Vincent, Elmore (active 1920s and 1930s). Radio comedian: **Senator Frankenstein Fishface.**

Vinegar Bill. Essick, William Earl.

Vinegar Joe. Stilwell, Joseph Warren.

Vinton, Bobby (born 1935). Musician and singer: **Polish Prince of American Pop Music.** Legal name: Stanley Robert Vinton, Jr.

Virginia. Tenth U.S. state: **Ancient Dominion, Beckoning Land, Cavalier State, Land of Romance, Mother of Presidents, Mother of States, Old Dominion.** With Delaware and Maryland: **Del-Mar-Va, Delmarva.**

Virginia, University of, athletic teams of: **Cavaliers.**

Virginia City, Nevada. U.S. town: **City That Saved the Union, Queen of the Comstock Lode, World's Liveliest Ghost Town.**

Virginia Military Institute, athletic teams of: **Keydets.**

Virginia Polytechnic Institute & State University, athletic teams of: **Gobblers.**

Virgin Islands. U.S. territory: **Land of the Trade Winds.**

Virtuous Card Shark. Scarne, John.

Voice, The. Sinatra, Frank.

Voice of Broadway. Kilgallen, Dorothy.

Voice of New England. Frost, Robert Lee.

Voice of R.C.A. Monroe, Vaughn [Wilton].

Voice of Silver. Pittman, Key.

Voice of the Century. Anderson, Marian.

Voice of the Hangover Generation. O'Hara, John [Henry].

Voice of the Voiceless. Anderson, Jack[son Northman].

Volpe, Anthony (active 1920–30). Gangster: **Mops.**

Volstead, Andrew J. (1860–1947). Lawyer, prohibitionist, and U.S. Representative from Minnesota: **Father of the Volstead Act, Goat of the Wets, The Obscure Mr. Volstead.**

Volunteer. Native or resident of Tennessee.

Volunteers. Athletic teams of the University of Tennessee, Knoxville.

Volunteer State. Tennessee.

Von Karman, Theodore (1881–1963). Physicist and aeronautical engineer: **Father of Supersonic Flight.**

Von Stade, Frederica (born 1945). Operatic mezzo-soprano: **Flicka.**

Von Stroheim, Erich [Oswald Hans Carl Maria von Nordenwall] (1885–1957). Motion-picture actor and director: **Man You Love to Hate.**

Von Zell, Harry (born 1906). Radio announcer: **Giggles.**

Vukie. Vukovich, William.

Vukovich, William (1918–54). Racing driver: **Mad Russian, Vukie.**

W

WAC. Women's Army Corps.

Waco, Texas. U.S. city: **Athens of Texas, Palace of King Cotton, Queen of the Brazos.**

Waddell, Doc (1863–1952). Circus chaplain and publicity agent: **Bishop of the Big Top.** Born: William Shackleford Andres.

Waddell, George Edward (1876–1914). Baseball pitcher: **Rube.**

Waddles, Charleszetta (born 1912). Humanitarian: **Black Angel of the Poor, Mother Waddles.**

Wade, Malcolm (born 1914). Basketball player: **Sparky.**

WAF. Women in the Air Force.

Wagner, Boyd (1916–43). World War II flying hero: **Buzz.**

Wagner, George Raymond (1915?–63). Wrestler: **Gorgeous George, Gorgeous Georgeous.**

Wagner, John Peter (1874–1955). Baseball shortstop: **Flying Dutchman, Hans, Honus.**

Wagner, Leon Lamar (born 1934). Baseball outfielder: **Cheeks, Daddy Wags.**

Wags. Army corps of dogs during World War II; K-9 Corps.

Wahl, Stephen Peters (born 1919). Football coach: **Brick.**

Wahoo. Reynolds, Allie.

Wahoo Sam. Crawford, Samuel Earl.

Wah Wah. Jones, Wallace.

Waikiki, Hawaii. U.S. town: **Birthplace of Surfing.**

Wainwright, Jonathan Mayhew. (1883–1953). U.S. Army General: **Skinny.**

Waiter, The. Ricca, Paul.

Wajcieckowski, Earl (1898–1926). Bootlegger and racketeer: **Father of the One-Way Ride, Hymie the Polack.** Also known as Earl Weiss, Hymie Weiss.

Wake Forest University, athletic teams of: **Demon Deacons.**

Walberg, George Elvin (born 1896). Baseball pitcher; **Rube.**

Walcott, Joe (born 1914). Heavyweight boxer: **Jersey Joe.** Born: Arnold Raymond Cream.

Waldorf, Lynn O. (born 1902). Football coach: **Pappy.**

Walker, Aaron (born 1913). Blues singer and guitarist: **T-Bone.**

Walker, Albert Bailey (1910–54). Murder suspect: **Ab.**

Walker, Chet (born 1940). Basketball player: **The Jet.**

Walker, Clarence William (1889–1959). Baseball outfielder: **Tilly.**

Walker, Douglas C. (1899–1970). Baseball player and football coach: **Peahead.**

Walker, [Ewell] Doak, [Jr.] (born 1927). Football back: **All-American Mustang, The Doaker, Little Man in Pro Football.**

Walker, Fred[erick E.] (born 1910). Baseball outfielder and coach: **Dixie.**

Walker, Harry William (born 1918). Baseball outfielder and manager: **The Hat.**

Walker, James J[ohn] (1881–1946). Mayor of New York City: **Beau James, Father of the New York State Boxing Bill, Gentleman Jimmy, Mayor Jimmy, Playboy of New York, Tammany Tiger, The Wisecracker.**

Walker, Mickey (born 1901). Welterweight and middleweight boxer: **Toy Bulldog.**

Walker, Nancy (born 1922). Actress and comedienne: **Rosie.** Born: Anna Myrtle Swoyer.

Walker, Sidney (born 1921). Lightweight boxer: **Beau Jack.**

Walk of Fame. Forecourt of Grauman's Chinese Theater, Hollywood, California, whose cement bears the footprints of motion-picture stars.

Wallace, George [Corley] (born 1919). Politician and Governor of Alabama: **Headless Horseman, Lonesome George.**

Wallace, Henry A[gard] (1888–1965). Agricultural editor, cabinet officer, and Vice President of the United States: **Plow 'Em Under Wallace.**

Wallace, Henry [Cantwell] (1866–1924). Agricultural editor, publisher, and U.S. Secretary of Agriculture: **Farmer's Farmer.**

Wallace, J. K. (1891–1950). Trombonist: **Spike.**

Wallace, Roderick John (1873–1960). Baseball shortstop: **Bobby.**

Wallard, Lee (1910–63). Racing driver: **First Indy Four-Hour Winner.**

Waller, Thomas Wright (1904–43). Jazz musician: **Black Horowitz, Fats.**

Wall Street. Street in New York City and surrounding financial district: **The Street, Street of Sorrows.**

Wall Street's Favorite Bureaucrat. Casey, William Joseph.

Walsh, Ed[ward Augustin] (1881–1959). Baseball pitcher: **Big Ed, Big Moose.**

Walt Disney Productions. Business organization: **Mickey Mouse.**

Walter Damrosch of the Pacific Coast. Stewart, Humphrey John.

Walters, Barbara (born 1931). Journalist, interviewer, and television anchor woman: **First Lady of Talk.**

Walters, William Henry (born 1909). Baseball pitcher and manager: **Bucky.**

Walter Whiz. Johnson, Curtis Lee.

Walther, David (born 1948). Racing driver; **Salt.**

Walton, J. C. (1881–1949). Governor of Oklahoma: **Iron Jack.**

Waltz King. King, Wayne Harold.

Wanamaker, John (1839–1922). Merchant: **Pious John.**

Wanderer, Carl (died 1921). Murderer: **Butcher Boy, Hero Husband, Ragged Stranger Murderer.**

Wanderone, Rudolf Walter, Jr. (born 1903). Professional pool player: **Minnesota Fats, New York Fats.**

Waner, Lloyd James (born 1906). Baseball outfielder: **Little Poison, Muscles.** With Paul Glee Waner: **Poison Twins.**

Waner, Paul Glee (1903–65). Baseball outfielder: **Big Poison.** With Lloyd James Waner: **Poison Twins.**

War Admiral (active 1937). Racehorse: **Bay Dancer.**

Warburg, Paul Moritz (1868–1952). Banker: **Father of the Federal Reserve System.**

Warburton, Irvine E. (born 1911). Football quarterback: **Cotton.**

Warcog. Women's Reserve in the Coast Guard.

Ward, Willie (born 1898). Boxer: **Kid Norfolk.**

Wares, Clyde Ellsworth (1886). Baseball shortstop: **Buzzy.**

Warhawk. P-40 fighter plane, World War II.

Warhop, John Milton (1884–1960). Baseball pitcher: **Chief, Crab.**

Warhorse. Turner, Alfred L.

Warm Springs, Georgia. U.S. city: **Little White House City.**

Warnecke, Lonnie (1909–76). Baseball pitcher and umpire: **Arkansas Hummingbird, Country, Dixie, Ol' Arkansas.**

Warner, Glenn Scobey (1871–1954). Football coach: **Pop.**

Warren, Harry (born 1893). Composer: **The Forgotten Man of American Music.** Born: Harry Guarana.

Warren, Lindsay Carter (born 1889). U.S. Representative from North Carolina: **Accounts.**

Warwick, Grant David (born 1921). Hockey player: **Knobby.**

Washburne, Joseph (born 1904). Jazz musician, singer, and composer; **Country.**

Washington. U.S. state: **Chinook State, Clam State, Evergreen State.**

Washington, Booker T[aliaferro] (1856–1915). Educator, lecturer, and author: **Black Messiah, Spokesman for the Negro.**

Washington, D.C. Federal district of the U.S.: **Capital City, Federal City, Nation's State.**

Washington, Ford Lee (1903–55). Jazz musician and entertainer: **Buck.**

Washington, University of. 1. Athletic teams of: **Huskies.** 2. Athletic teams of, with other teams in regional conference: **Pacific Ten.**

Washington & Jefferson College, athletic teams of: **Presidents.**

Washington & Lee University, athletic teams of: **Generals.**

Washington's Cinderella Woman. McLean, Evalyn Walsh.

Washington Senators. American League baseball team; earlier name, Washington Nationals: **The Nats.**

Washington's Profumo. Baker, Bobby.

Washington's Resident Humorist. Buchwald, Art[hur].

Washington's Scholar-Athlete. Shultz, George [Pratt].

Washington State University. 1. Athletic teams of: **Cougars.** 2. Athletic teams of, with other teams in regional conference: **Pacific Ten.**

Wasps. Athletic teams of Emory & Henry College, Emory, Virginia.

Watchdog of Central Park. Ochs, Adolph Simon.

Watchdog of the Treasury. Blanton, Thomas Lindsay; Byrd, Harry Flood; Cannon, Joseph Gurney.

Waterbury, Connecticut. U.S. city: **Brass City, Crossroads of Connecticut.**

Waterfield, Robert S. (born 1920). Football quarterback: **Rifle.**

Watergate. Scandal ensuing from burglary of Democratic National Committee headquarters at Watergate office and hotel complex, Washington, D.C., June 17, 1972; revelations of White House involvement and attempted cover-up; and related events leading to resignation of President Richard M. Nixon, August 9, 1974.

Watergate Defendant, The. Dean, John, III.

Watergate Guard. Wills, Frank.

Watergate Seven, The. Bernard L. Barker, Virgilio R. Gonzalez, E. Howard Hunt, Jr., G. Gordon Liddy, James W. McCord, Eugenio Martinez, and Frank A. Sturgis, who were convicted of breaking into and "bugging" Democratic National Committee headquarters and of engaging in other political espionage. Also known as the Watergate Burglars.

Watergate's Warbler. Mitchell, Martha.

Waterloo of the Revolution. Yorktown, Virginia.

Waters, Ethel (1900–77). Jazz singer: **Baby Star, Sweet Mama Stringbean.**

Watson, Billy (1867–1945). Comedian of burlesque days: **The Original** (to distinguish him from "Sliding Billy" Watson).

379

Watson, Billy (active early 1900s). Musician: **Sliding Billy.**

Watson, Edwin Martin (1883–1945). U.S. Army General: **Pa.**

Watson, John Broadus (1878–1958). Psychologist: **Founder of Behaviorism.**

Watson, Milton W. (born 1893). Baseball pitcher: **Mule.**

Watson, Thomas Edward (1856–1922). U.S. Representative and U.S. Senator from Georgia: **Sage of Hickory Hill, Sage of McDuffie.**

Watterson, Henry (1840–1921). Editor, politician, and U.S. Representative from Kentucky: **Marse Henry.**

WAVES. Women Appointed for Voluntary Emergency Service, U.S. Navy.

Waxey Gordon. Wexler, Irving.

Wayne, John (1907–79). Motion-picture actor: **Duke, The Duke, Big John.** Born: Marion Michael Morrison.

Wearin, Otha Donner (born 1903). U.S. Representative from Iowa: **Red Necktie.**

Weary Willlie. Kelly, Emmett.

Weatherly, [Cyril] Roy (born 1915). Baseball outfielder: **Stormy.**

Weaver, Monte (born 1906). Baseball pitcher: **Prof.** Legal name: Montgomery Morton Weaver.

Weaver, Zebulon (1872–1948). U.S. Representative from North Carolina: **Old Zeb.**

Webb, Jack (born 1920). Author, actor, and producer: **Sergeant Joe Friday.** Also known as John Farr, Tex Grady.

Webber (or Weber), Louis (active 1912). Gambler: **Bridgey.** Also known as Henry Williams.

Webby. Webster, Harold Tucker.

Webfoot. Native or resident of Oregon. Plural: **Webfeet.**

Webfoot State. Oregon.

Webster, H[arold] T[ucker] (1885–1952). Cartoonist: **Mark Twain of Cartoonists, Webby.**

Weeb. Ewbank, Wilbur Charles.

Weed. Groza, Alex.

Weegee. Fellig, Arthur.

Wee Tommy. Leach, Thomas William.

Wee Willie. Keller, William Henry; Messino, William; Sherdel, William H.; Wilkin, Wilbur.

Weicker, Lowell [Palmer, Jr.] (born 1931). Watergate investigator and U.S. Senator from Connecticut: **White Knight.**

Weil, Joseph R. (1877–1976). Swindler and confidence man: **Chicago's Minister of Human Cupidity, Genius of Racing, Professor Von Chopnick, Yellow Kid.** Also known as H. Huntington Black, Dr. Richard T. Dorrance, V. Timkin Farnsworth, Colonel Rutherford B. Lehigh, T. Raymond Manningham, Daniel O'Connell, H. Jefferson Warrington, Walter H. Weed, Dr. James R. Wilson.

Weiland, Ralph (born 1904). Hockey player: **Cooney.**

Weimer, Jake (1883–1944). Baseball pitcher: **Tornado Jake.** Legal name: John William Weimer.

Weinberg, Stephen Jacob (1890–1960). Imposter: **Amiable Swindler, Little Big Man from Brooklyn, Great Imposter, Imposter's Imposter.** Also known as Stanley Clifford Weyman.

Weiss, Paul (born 1901). Philosopher: **America's Foremost Speculative Philosopher.**

Weissmuller, Johnny (born 1904). Swimmer and motion-picture actor: **Best of the Tarzans.**

Welk, Lawrence [LeRoy] (born 1903). Television personality, musician, and accordionist: **King of Musical Corn, Liberace of the Accordion, Mr. Music Maker.**

Welles, [George] Orson (born 1915). Actor, playwright, director, and producer: **Boy Wonder, Your Obedient Servant.**

Wellesley College. Educational institution; with six other women's colleges; **Seven Sisters.**

Wells, Amos, Jr. (born 1934). Blues singer: **Junior.**

Welsh, Johnnie (active 1920s and 1930s). Radio comedian: **Sassafras.**

Welsh Parson. Davis, James John.

Wene, Elmer H. (1892–1957). Poultryman and U.S. Representative from New Jersey: **Day-old Chick.**

Werkman, Nick (born 1942). Basketball player: **The Quick.**

Wesleyan University. 1. Athletic teams of: **Cardinals.** 2. Athletic teams of, with teams of Amherst College and Williams College: **Little Three.**

West, James Marion, Jr. (1903–57). Texas multimillionaire: **Silver Dollar.**

West, Mae (born 1892). Stage and screen actress, playwright, and sex symbol: **Baby Vamp, Diamond Lil, Screen's Bad Girl, Siren of Sex, Siren of the Screen, Vaudeville's Youngest Headliner.** Also known as Jane Mast.

West, Nathanael (1903–40). Author: **Ironic Prophet.** Born: Nathan Weinstein.

Western Carolina University, athletic teams of: **Catamounts.**

Western City of Ships. Oakland, California.

Western Gate. San Francisco, California.

Western Gateway to Mexico. Tucson, Arizona.

Western Illinois University, athletic teams of: **Leathernecks.**

Western Kentucky University, athletic teams of: **Hilltoppers.**

Western Maryland Railway. U.S. railroad: **Wet Mary.**

Western Michigan University, athletic teams of: **Broncos.**

Western Prairie Province. Alberta.

Westmore, George H[amilton] (1918–73). Motion-picture makeup man: **Buddy.**

Westmoreland, William Childs (born 1914). U.S. Army General and Chief of Staff: **Inevitable General, Westy.**

Weston, Edward (1887–1958). Photographer: **Rembrandt of the Lens, Picasso of the Camera.**

West Texas State University, athletic teams of: **Buffaloes.**

West Virginia. Thirty-fifth U.S. state: **Appalachian State, Free State, Fuel State, Little Mountain State, Mountain State, Panhandle State.**

West Virginia University, athletic teams of: **Mountaineers.**

Westwick, Harry (1876–1957). Hockey player: **Rat.**

Westy. Westmoreland, William Childs.

Wetback. Mexican who enters the United States illegally, as by swimming the Rio Grande River.

Wet Mary. Western Maryland Railway.

Wet Tortugas. Florida Keys.

Wetzel, Damon (active 1935–36). Football back: **Iron Man.**

Wexler, Irving (1889–1952). Bootlegger and gangster: **Waxey Gordon.**

Weyerhaeuser, Frederick (1834–1914). Industrialist: **Lumber King.**

Weyhing, Gus (1866–1955). Baseball pitcher: **Cannonball.** Legal name: August Weyhing.

Whalen, Grover [Aloysius] (1886–1962). Businessman, city official, and promoter: **Apostle of the Grand Manner, The Billion Dollar Barker, Doorman of the Western Hemisphere, Gardenia Grover, The Gorgeous Greeter.**

Whaling City. New Bedford, Massachusetts.

Wharf of North America. Nova Scotia.

Wheatley, Bill (born 1909). Basketball player: **Galloping Ghost.**

Wheaton Iceman. Grange, Harold E[dward].

Wheat Provinces. Alberta, Manitoba, and Saskatchewan.

Wheat State. Kansas; Minnesota.

Wheeler, Burton K[endall] (1882–1975). Lawyer and U.S. Senator from Montana: **Great Liberal.**

Wheeler, Helen Rippier (born 1926). Educator, librarian, author, and feminist: **Dragon Lady.**

Wheeler, Wayne Bidwell (1869–1927). Lawyer, legislator, and prohibitionist: **Author of the Volstead Act, Hireling of the Anti-Saloon League, New David.**

Wheeling, West Virginia. U.S. city: **Nail City.**

Whigham, Haydn (born 1943). Jazz trombonist: **Jiggs.**

Whip, The. Blackwell, Ewell.

Whiskers. Special agents of the Department of Justice, especially of the Federal Bureau of Investigation.

Whiskey Town. Peoria, Illinois.

Whispering Baritone. Smith, Jack.

Whispering Jack Smith. Smith, Jack.

Whispering Tenor, The. Austin, Gene.

Whit. Wyatt, John Whitlow.

White, Byron Raymond (born 1917). Football halfback and Associate Justice of the U.S. Supreme Court: **Whizzer.**

White, Edward Douglass (1845–1921). U.S. Senator from Louisiana and Chief Justice of the United States: **Mentor of the Rule of Reason.**

White, Joseph M. (1891–1959). Singer: **Silver Masked Tenor.**

White, Josh[ua Daniel] (1908–69). Folk singer: **Most Famous Folk Singer of His Race.**

White, Joyner Clifford (born 1909). Baseball outfielder: **Jo-Jo.**

White, Pearl (1889–1939). Motion-picture actress: **Queen of the Silent Serials.**

White, Stanford (1853–1906). Architect: **America's Foremost Architect, The Builder.**

White, Theodore H[arold] (born 1915). Reporter and author: **Dean of American Reporters.**

White, William Allen (1868–1944). Newspaper editor: **Sage of Emporia.**

White, [William] Jack (active 1910–20). Gangster: **Three-Fingered White.**

White Chief of the Pawnees. Lillie, Gordon W.

White-Fingered White. White, [William] Jack.

White Hope. White heavyweight boxer who would end the reign (1908–15) of black champion Jack Johnson.

White Hope Champion. McCarty, Luther.

White House Hatchet Man. Colson, Charles W[endell].

White House Pet. O'Day, Caroline Goodwin.

White House Tommy. Corcoran, Thomas Gardiner.

White Knight. Agnew, Spiro [Theodore]; Whitney, Richard; Weicker, Lowell [Palmer, Jr.].

Whiteman, Paul (1891–1967). Bandleader: **Dean of American Popular Music, King of Jazz, Pops.**

White Man's Negro. Fetchit, Stepin.

White Mountains. Mountain range in New Hampshire: **Crystal Hills.**

White Mountain State. New Hampshire.

White Muhammad Ali. Riggs, Bobby.

White Slave Act. Mann Act, 1910, prohibiting transportation of women from one state to another for immoral purposes.

White Stockings. Chicago White Sox.

Whitey. Bimstein, Morris; Fields, W[illiam] C[laude]; Ford, Edward Charles; Kaufman, Martin Ellis; Mitchell, Gordon B.; Phillips, Barton; Piet, Tony; Young, Lemuel Floyd.

Whitney, Arthur Carter (born 1906). Baseball third baseman: **Pinkey.**

Whitney, Bartholomew Reynolds (born 1908). U.S. Army General: **Old Blood and Butts.**

Whitney, Cornelius Vanderbilt (born 1899). Businessman, government official, and playboy: **Sonny.**

Whitney, Gwladys [Crosby Hopkins] (active 1930s). Horsewoman and wife of Cornelius Vanderbilt Whitney: **Gee.**

Whitney, John Hay (born 1904). Financier, publisher, and ambassador: **Jock.**

Whitney, Richard (1888–1974). Financier, President of the New York Stock Exchange, and embezzler: **Hero of Wall Street, Strong Man of Wall Street, White Knight.**

Whitted, George Bostic (1890–1942). Baseball infielder and outfielder: **Possum.**

Whittemore, Arthur (born 1916). Concert pianist: **Buck.**

Whizzer. White, Byron Raymond.

Wichita, Kansas. U.S. city: **Air Capital, Cow Capital.**

Wichita State University, athletic teams of: **Shockers.**

Wicker, Ireene Seaton (born 1905). Singer, actress, and radio script writer: **Singing Lady, Singing Story Lady.**

Wid. Conroy, William Edward.

Widmark, Richard (born 1914). Actor: **Young Man with a Sneer.**

Wiener, Norbert (1894–1964). Mathematician and author: **Father of Automation.**

Wilcox, Ella Wheeler (1850–1919). Journalist and verse writer: **People's Poet.**

Wild Bill. Davis, William Strethen; Davison, William; Donovan, William Joseph; Elliott, Gordon [William]; Haywood, William Dudley; Kunstler, William [Moses]; Lovett, William.

Wildcat. Grumman F4F fighter plane, World War II.

Wildcat Division. Eighty-first Infantry Division.

Wildcats. Athletic teams of the University of Arizona, Tucson; the University of New Hampshire, Durham; Kansas State University, Manhattan; the University of Kentucky, Lexington; Northwestern University, Evanston, Illinois; and Villanova University, Villanova, Pennsylvania.

Wilder, Thornton [Niven] (1897–1975). Author and playwright: **Grand Old Novelist.**

Wildfire. Schulte, Frank.

Wild Hickory Nut, The. Gibbons, Euell.

Wild Horse Annie. Johnston, Velma.

Wild Hoss of the Osage. Martin, John Leonard.

Wild Man of Hoboken. Kennedy, Matthew Patrick.

Wild Shaman of the Beat Generation. Ginsberg, Allen.

Wild West Division. Ninety-first Division.

Wilhelm, Irving Key (1878–1936). Baseball pitcher and manager: **Kaiser.**

Wilkes, Len (born 1937). Baseball player: **Silk.**

Wilkes-Barre, Pennsylvania. U.S. city: **Black Diamond City.**

Wilkes College, athletic teams of: **Colonels.**

Wilkin, Wilbur (1915?–1973). Football tackle: **Wee Willie.**

Willard, Jess (1883–1968). Heavyweight boxer: **Big Jess, Cowboy Jess, Kansas Giant, Pottawatomie Giant, Tall Pine of the Pottawatomie.**

Willebrandt, Mabel Walker (1889–1963). Lawyer, politician, and Assistant U.S. Attorney General: **Prohibition Portia, Scourge of the Bootleggers.**

William & Mary, College of, athletic teams of: **Indians.**

Williams, Albert (born 1917). Reformed jewel thief and writer: **Matinee Burglar, World's Foremost Jewel Thief.** Also known as Albie Baker, Albert Cooper.

Williams, Barney (1891–1949). Boxer: **Battling Levinsky, King Levinsky.** Born: Barney Lebrowitz.

Williams, Charles Melvin (born 1908). Jazz trumpeter: **Cootie.**

Williams, Claude Preston (1893–1959). Baseball pitcher: **Lefty.**

Williams, Dave (born c. 1953). Hockey player: **Tiger.**

Williams, George Dale (born 1917). Jazz arranger; **Fox.**

Williams, Gurney (1906-65). Cartoonist: **Human Gagometer.**

Williams, Hank (1923–53). Country music singer, guitarist, and composer: **King of Country Music.** Legal name: Henry Williams.

Williams, James Thomas (1876–1965). Baseball second baseman: **Buttons.**

Williams, Mary Lou (born 1910). Jazz pianist and singer: **Queen of Jazz.** Born: Mary Elfrieda Scruggs.

Williams, Ted (born 1918). Baseball outfielder: **Big Guy, The Kid, Splendid Splinter, Teddy Ballgame.** Legal name: Theodore Samuel Williams.

Williams, Walt[er Allen] (born 1943). Baseball outfielder: **No Neck.**

Williamsburg, Virginia. U.S. town: **City That Turned Back Time.**

Williamsburg of the North. Bennington, Vermont.

Williams College. 1. Athletic teams of: **Ephmen.** 2. Athletic teams of, with teams of Amherst College and Wesleyan University: **Little Three.**

Williamson, John (born 1952). Basketball player: **Super John.**

Williamson Gang. Gang of swindlers started by Robert Logan Williamson, 1890s.

Willie Bobo. Correa, William.

Willie Fudd. Grumman WF-2 military plane, Vietnam War.

Willie the Actor. Sutton, William Francis.

Willie the Lion. Smith, Willie.

Willie the Wallop. Mays, Willie Howard.

Willig, George H. (born 1950). Toy designer and climber of Manhattan's World Trade Center's south tower: **The Human Fly.**

Willing Willie. Moretti, Willie.

Willkie, Wendell [Lewis] (1892–1944). Lawyer, politician, and business executive: **Barefoot Boy of Wall Street.**

Will-o'-the-Wisp. Pep, Willie.

Wills, Frank (born c. 1948). Security guard and discoverer of the Watergate break-in: **Watergate Guard.**

Wills, Helen Newington (born 1906). Tennis player and author: **Little Miss Poker Face, Queen Helen, The Princess.** Also known as Helen Wills Moody and Helen Wills Roark.

Wilmington, Delaware. U.S. city: **Dupontonia, Dupont Town, First City of the First State.**

Wilson, Charles Edward (1886–1972). Industrialist and government official: **Electric Charlie.**

Wilson, Charles Erwin (1890–1961), business executive and U.S. Secretary of Defense: **Engine Charlie.**

Wilson, Charles Kemmons (born 1912). Hotel owner: **Host with the Most.**

Wilson, Edith Bolling Galt (1872–1961). Wife of President Woodrow Wilson: **First Lady of the World.**

Wilson, Edmund (1895–1972). Literary critic, editor, and novelist: **Bunny.**

Wilson, Harry E. (born 1902). Football back: **Lighthorse Harry.**

Wilson, Imogene (1906–48). Dancer and show girl: **Bubbles.** Born: Mary Imogene Robertson. Also known as Mary Nolan.

Wilson, James Walter (1825–1945). Former slave and oldest U.S. citizen (1940s): **Uncle Jim.**

Wilson, Jimmie (1900–47). Baseball catcher, outfielder, and manager: **Ace.** Legal name: James Wilson.

Wilson, John Owen (1883–1954). Baseball outfielder: **Chief.**

Wilson, Kenneth L. (active 1930s). Athletic director and Big Ten Football Conference Commissioner: **Tug.**

Wilson, Lewis Robert (1900–48). Baseball outfielder: **Hack.**

Wilson, Robert C. (born 1916). Politician and U.S. Representative from California: **Mr. Inside.**

Wilson, Roger (1897–1928). Mass murderer: **Dark Strangler, Gorilla Murderer.** Born: Earle Leonard Nelson.

Wilson, Rossiere (born 1919). Jazz drummer: **Shadow.**

Wilson, [Thomas] Woodrow (1856–1924). Educator and twenty-eighth President of the United States: **Coiner of Weasel Words, The Phrasemaker, Phrasemaker of Versailles, The Professor, Schoolmaster in Politics.** With David Lloyd George of Great Britain and Georges Clemenceau of France: **Big Three.**

Wiltse, George L. (1880–1959). Baseball pitcher: **Hooks.**

Wilt the Stilt. Chamberlain, Wilt[on Norman].

Winchell, Walter (1897–1972). Journalist: **America's One-Man Newspaper.** Born: Walter Winchel.

Windy City. Chicago, Illinois.

Winfield, Ed[ward] (born 1901). Automobile racing driver: **Father of Hot Rodding.**

Wingate's Raiders. Force of jungle fighters under U.S. General Orde Wingate, World War II.

Winged Victory Division. Forty-third Infantry Division.

Wing Foot, The. Goodyear Tire and Rubber Company balloon, which crashed in Chicago in 1919.

Wingie. Carpenter, Theodore.

Wingy. Manone, Joseph Mathews.

Wink. Midgett, Elwin W.

Winkles, Bobby [Brooks] (born 1932). Baseball manager: **Winks.**

Winks. Winkles, Bobby [Brooks].

Winner, Charles (1885–1956). Cartoonist: **Doc.**

Winnie. 1. Coty American Fashion Critics Award. 2. Harding, Warren G[amaliel].

Winnie Mae. Plane in which Wiley Post and Harold Gatty flew around the world, 1932.

Winston-Salem, North Carolina. U.S. city: **Camel City, Golden Hyphen, Twin Cities, Twin City.**

Winter, George L. (1878–1951). Baseball pitcher; **Sassafras.**

Winter Garden of the East. Southern Florida.

Winter Garden of the Gulf. The lower Rio Grande Valley.

Winter Garden of the West. Imperial Valley, California.

Wire King of America. Gates, John Warne.

Wisconsin. Thirtieth U.S. state: **America's Dairyland, Badger State, Copper State, Land o'Lakes.**

Wisconsin, University of. 1. Athletic teams of: **Badgers.** 2. Athletic teams of, with other teams in regional conference: **Big Ten.**

Wise Charley. McNary, Charles Linza.

Wisecracker, The. Walker, James J[ohn].

Wiskers. Tinkham, George Holden.

Wisniewski, Henry (active 1929–32). Football player: **Pistol Pete.**

Witch City. Salem, Massachusetts.

Witch of Wall Street. Green, Hetty.

Witz. Dingell, John David.

Wizard. Schaefer, Herman, Sr.

Wizard, The. Gibbons, Mike.

Wizard of American Drama. Belasco, David.

Wizard of Baseball. McPhail, Leland Stanford.

Wizard of Menlo Park. Edison, Thomas Alva.

Wizard of Ooze. Dirksen, Everett McKinley.

Wizard of the Wires. Edison, Thomas Alva.

Wizard of Tuskegee. Carver, George Washington.

Wizard of Wacky Inventions. Goldberg, Rube.

Wobblies. Industrial Workers of the World.

WOC. Business executives in temporary government service without compensation.

Wodehouse, P[elham] G[renville] (1881–1975). Author: **Plum.**

Wojciechowicz, Alex[ander] (born 1915). Football player. **Wojie.** With other members of Fordham team: **Seven Blocks of Granite.**

Wojie. Wojciechowicz, Alex[ander].

Wolfe, George (born 1908). Basketball player: **Red.**

Wolfe, Thomas [Clayton] (1900–38). Novelist: **Hungry Gulliver.**

Wolfe, William (1951–74). Leader of the Symbionese Liberation Army: **Cujo.**

Wolfman Jack. Smith, Robert.

Wolfpack. Athletic teams of North Carolina State University, Raleigh.

Wolgast, Ad[olph] (1888–1955). Lightweight boxer; **Michigan Wildcat.**

Wolverine. Native or resident of Michigan.

Wolverines. Athletic teams of the University of Michigan, Ann Arbor.

Wolverine State. Michigan.

Woman in Red. Cumpanas, Ana.

Woman Who Always Speaks Her Mind. Oliver, Edna May.

Women's Reserve in the Coast Guard. Reserve corps, World War II: **Warcog.**

Wonder Boy. Kramer, Stanley E.

Wonder Boy of the Financial District. Koretz, Leo.

Wonder City of the World. New York City.

Wonderland of America. Boulder, Colorado.

Wonder Maker. Smith, Andrew Latham.

Wonder State. Arkansas.

Wong, Pearl (active 1970s). Restaurateur in New York City: **Dragon Lady of Broadway.**

Wood, Joe (born 1889). Baseball pitcher; **Smokey Joe.** Legal name: Joseph Wood.

Wooden, John [Robert] (born 1910). Basketball player and coach: **India Rubber Man, St. John.**

Wooden Joe. Nicholas, Joe.

Woodrum, Clifton Alexander (1887–1950). U.S. Representative from Virginia: **Choirmaster of the House.**

Woods, Frank (active 1910–20). Motion-picture executive: **Daddy.**

Woods, The. Boise City, Idaho.

Woodstein. Woodward, Bob and Bernstein, Carl.

Woodward, Bob (born 1943). Journalist and investigator of Watergate scandal. With Carl Bernstein: **Woodstein.** Legal name: Robert Upshur Woodward.

Woody. Hayes, Wayne Woodrow; Jensen, Forrest Ducenus.

Woollcott, Alexander [Humphreys] (1887–1943). Writer, critic, and actor: **Louisa May Woollcott, Town Crier.**

Woolly Bob. Rich, Robert Fleming.

Woolworth, Frank Winfield (1852–1919). Retail merchant: **Father of the Dime Store, Father of the Five and Ten.**

Wooster, College of, athletic teams of: **Fighting Scots.**

Wop with the Mop. Capone, Al[phonse].

Workman, Raymond (1909–66). Jockey: **Sonny.**

Workshop of the World. Pennsylvania.

World Citizen Number One. Davis, Garry.

World's Biggest Bookend. Secretariat building of the United Nations, New York.

World's Champion Cowboy. Mix, Tom.

World's Fastest Human. Paddock, Charles W.

World's First Black Combat Aviator. Bullard, Eugene.

World's Foremost Jewel Thief. Williams, Albert.

World's Funniest Woman. Davis, Joan.

World's Greatest Eccentric Juggler. Fields, W[illiam] C[laude].

World's Greatest Harbor. Hampton Roads, Virginia.

World's Greatest Trumpet Player. Severinsen, Doc.

World's Liveliest Ghost Town. Virginia City, Nevada.

World's Longest Parking Lot. Long Island Expressway.

World's Most Admired Woman. Roosevelt, [Anna] Eleanor [Roosevelt].

World's Most Pulchritudinous Evangelist. McPherson, Aimee Semple.

World's No. 1 Industrial Architect. Kahn, Albert.

World's No. 1 Party-Giver. Mesta, Perle.

World's Playground. Atlantic City, New Jersey.

World's Premier Winter Resort. Palm Beach, Florida.

World's Second Richest Man. Mellon, Andrew William.

World's Sweetheart. Pickford, Mary.

World's Tallest Economist. Galbraith, John Kenneth.

World's Top Boots-and-Saddle Star. Rogers, Roy.

World's Workshop. Pittsburgh, Pennsylvania.

World War Croesus. McAdoo, William Gibbs.

World War Photographer. Steichen, Edward.

Worsley, Lorne John (born 1929). Canadian hockey goalie: **Gump.**

Worthington, Al[lan Fulton] (born 1930). Baseball pitcher: **Red.**

Wortman, Frank (1903–70). Gangster and racketeer: **Buster.**

Wounded Hero. Mantle, Mickey [Charles].

Wounded Wonder. Criqui, Eugene.

Wrecker, The. Morse, Wayne [Lyman].

Wright, Albert (1912–57). Featherweight boxer: **Chalky.**

Wright, Charles (born 1927). Jazz drummer: **Specs.**

Wright, Forrest Glenn (born 1902). Baseball shortstop: **Buckshot.**

Wright, Frank Lloyd (1869–1959). Architect: **America's Greatest Architect.**

Wright, Taft Shedron (born 1913). Baseball outfielder: **Taffy.**

Wrigley, William, Jr. (1861–1932). Industrialist and manufacturer of chewing gum: **Chewing Gum King, Chicle King, Monarch of Mastication.**

Wrong-Way. Corrigan, Douglas Gorce.

Wurst City in the World. Sheboygan, Wisconsin.

Wyatt, John Whitlow (born 1908). Baseball pitcher: **Whit.**

Wynn, Early (born 1920). Baseball pitcher; **Gus, Old Indian.**

Wynn, Ed (1886–1966). Comedian: **Perfect Fool.** Born: Isaiah Edwin Leopold.

Wynn, Jim (born 1942). Baseball outfielder: **The Toy Cannon.** Legal name: James Sherman Wynn.

Wyoming. Forty-fourth U.S. state: **Cowboy State, Equality State, Land of the Purple Sage, Sagebrush State.** With North Dakota and South Dakota: **Dakoming.**

Wyoming, University of, athletic teams of: **Cowboys.**

Y

Y.A. Tittle, Y[elberton] A[braham].

Yablonski, Joseph A. (1911–70). United Mine Workers president and murder victim: **Jock.**

Yachting Capital of the World. Newport, Rhode Island.

Yakima, Washington. U.S. city: **Fruit Bowl of the Nation.**

Yale, Frankie (1885–1927). Gangster: **Beau Brummel of the Brooklyn Underworld.** Born: Francesco Uale.

Yale University. 1. Athletic teams of: **Bulldogs.** 2. Athletic teams, athletes, students, or alumni(ae) of: **Elis.** 3. Athletic teams of, with seven other teams in college conference: **Ivy League.**

Yanger, Benny (1882–1958). Boxer: **Tipton Slasher.** Born: Frank Angone.

Yank. Durham, Yancey; Lawsin, John R.

Yankee. 1. Citizen of the United States. 2. Person from the northern United States. 3. Person from New England.

Yankee Athens. New Haven, Connecticut.

Yankee City. Newburyport, Massachusetts.

Yankee Clipper. DiMaggio, Joe.

Yankee Clipper of the Accordion. Contino, Dick.

Yankee Division. Twenty-sixth Infantry Division.

Yankee Doodle Dandy. Cohan, George M[ichael].

Yankee Stadium. Baseball stadium, New York City: **House That Ruth Built.**

Yanks. New York Yankees.

Yanqui Matador. Fulton, John.

Yardbird. Parker, Charlie.

Yastrzemski, Carl Michael (born 1939). Baseball outfielder: **The Hawk, Yaz.**

Yaz. Yastrzemski, Carl Michael.

Yellow. Nuñez, Alcide.

Yellowhammer. Native or resident of Alabama.

Yellowhammer State. Alabama.

Yellowhorse, Moses J. (1900–64). Baseball pitcher: **Chief.**

Yellow Jackets. Athletic teams of Georgia Institute of Technology (Georgia Tech), Atlanta, and the University of Rochester, Rochester, New York.

Yellow Kid. Weil, Joseph R.

Yellowstone National Park. U.S. national park: **Valley of Wonders.**

Yiddish Curver. Pelty, Barney.

Yiddisher Vild-Kat, Der. Loeb, Albert Lorch.

Yiddish Mark Twain. Aleichem, Shalom; Zevin, Israel Joseph.

Yip. Harburg, E.Y.

Yippie. Member of the Youth International Party.

Yolanda. Harris, Emily.

Yonkers, New York. U.S. city: **Terrace City.**

Yorktown, Virginia. U.S. town: **Waterloo of the Revolution.**

Yost, Fielding Harris (1871–1946). Football coach: **Hurry Up Yost.**

"You-Name-It-We-Make-It" State. Ohio.

Young, Claude H. (born 1926). Football back: **Buddy.**

Young, Denton True (1867–1955). Baseball pitcher: **Cy.**

Young, Eleanor (died 1941). Society glamour girl: **Cookie.**

Young, Eugene (born 1919). Jazz trumpeter: **Snooky.**

Young, James Arthur (born 1926). U.S. Army General: **Man Who Would Not Die.**

Young, James Osborne (born 1912). Jazz trombonist and singer: **Trummy.**

Young, Lemuel Floyd (born 1907). Baseball shortstop and second baseman: **Pep, Whitey.**

Young, Lester Willis (1909–59). Jazz saxophonist: **Pres, President, Prez.**

Young, Loretta (born 1913). Motion-picture and television actress: **The Iron Butterfly, The Steel Butterfly.** Born: Gretchen Young.

Young, Robert R[alph] (1897–1958). Railroad executive: **Daring Young Man of Wall Street, Railroad Gadfly.**

Young, Whitney M[oore] (1921–71). Civil rights leader, educator, and organization official: **Pragmatic Humanist.**

Youngest Big City in the United States. Phoenix, Arizona.

Youngest State. Hawaii.

Young Guard. Group of younger congressmen supporting the policies of President Franklin D. Roosevelt.

Young Man with a Sneer. Widmark, Richard.

Young Montreal. Billingkoff, Morris.

Young Thunderbolt. Lea, Luke.

Young Torquemada. Mitchel, John Purroy.

Your Obedient Servant. Welles, [George] Orson.

Yucca Country. The Southwestern United States.

Yukon. U.S. river: **River of the North.**

Yukon, The. Area of Alaska and Canada: **Husky Territory.**

Yukon Territory. Canadian territory: **Land of Legend.**

Yuma, Arizona. U.S. city: **Sun City, Sunshine Capital of the United States, Sunshine City.**

Yussel the Muscle. Jacobs, Joe.

Z

Zabel, George W. (1891–1970). Baseball player: **Zip.**

Zachary, Rubin (born 1915). Jazz trumpeter: **Zeke.**

Zack. Taylor, James Wren.

Zaharias, Babe [Didrikson] (1914–56). Athlete: **Athletic Phenomenon of All Time—Man or Woman.** Born: Mildred Ella Didrikson.

Zale, Tony (born 1913). Middleweight boxer: **Man of Steel.** Born: Anthony Florian Zaleski.

Zanuck, Darryl F[rancis] (born 1902). Motion-picture producer: **The Chief.**

Zarilla, Allen Lee (born 1919). Baseball outfielder: **Zeke.**

Zavada, Joseph (1916?–65). Bank robber: **King of the Bank Robbers.**

Zawoluk, Robert (born 1930). Basketball player: **Zeke.**

Zebra Killings. Murders in San Francisco, 1974.

Zeider, Rollie [Hubert] (1883–1967). Baseball infielder: **Bunions.**

Zeitlin, Dennis (born c. 1937). Pianist and psychiatrist: **Dr. Jazz.**

Zeke. Barnes, Virgil J.; Japanese fighter plane, World War II; Zachary, Rubin; Zarilla, Allen Lee; Zawoluck, Robert.

Zenith City of the Unsalted Sea. Duluth, Minnesota.

Zernial, Gus [Edward] (born 1923). Baseball outfielder: **Ozark Ike.**

Zero. Japanese Mitsubishi fighter plane, World War II.

Zevin, Israel Joseph (1872–1926). Journalist and short story writer: **Tashrak, Yiddish Mark Twain.**

Zez. Confrey, Ed[ward E.].

Ziegfeld, Flo[renz, Jr.] (1867–1932). Theatrical producer: **Lorenzo the Magnificent of the Stage, Ziggy.**

Ziegler, Ronald (born 1939). Presidential press secretary: **Ziggy.**

Ziggy. Sears, John W.; Ziegfeld, Flo[renz, Jr.]; Ziegler, Ronald.

Zimmerman, Henry (1887–1969). Baseball second and third baseman: **Heinie.**

Zioncheck, Marion A. (1901–36). Playboy and U.S. Representative from Washington: **Congressional Playboy, Seattle's Sensational Son.**

Zip. Zabel, George W.

Zips. Athletic teams of the University of Akron, Akron, Ohio.

Zit. Zittel, Carl F.

Zittel, Carl F. (1877–1943). Theatrical critic and publisher: **Zit.**

Zivic, Ferdinand Henry John (born 1913). Welterweight boxer: **Fritzie, Old Fritz.**

Zoeller, Frank Urban (born 1951). Golfer: **Fuzzy.**

Zographos, Nicholas (1885–1953). Gambler: **Nick the Greek.**

Zonk. Csonka, Larry.

Zoot. Sims, John Haley.

Zucca, Rita Louise (born 1912). Alleged radio propagandist for the Nazi government: **Axis Sally.**

Zukor, Adolph (1873–1976). Motion-picture producer: **Henry Ford of the Movies, Pop.**

Zurke, Robert (1910–44). Jazz pianist: **Old Tomcat of the Keys.**

Zutty. Singleton, Arthur James.

Zwillman, Abner (1904–59). Politician and racketeer: **Longy.**